MW00377522

Reviving Japan's Economy

Reviving Japan's Economy

edited by

Takatoshi Ito
Hugh Patrick
David E. Weinstein

The MIT Press
Cambridge, Massachusetts
London, England

MIT Press books may be purchased at special quantity discounts for business or sales promotional use. For information, please email special_sales@mitpress.mit.edu or write to Special Sales Department, The MIT Press, 55 Hayward Street, Cambridge, MA 02142.

This book was set in Palatino by Sztrecska Publishing and was printed and bound in the United States of America.

Library of Congress Cataloging-in-Publication Data

Reviving Japan's economy : problems and prescriptions / edited by Takatoshi Ito, Hugh Patrick, David E. Weinstein.
p. cm
Papers from a research project administered through the Center on Japanese Economy and Business, Columbia University, and the Research Center for Advanced Science and Technology, University of Tokyo, and with revisions made after a closed March 2004 academic conference held in Tokyo.
Includes bibliographic references and index.
ISBN 0-262-09040-6 (alk. paper)
1. Japan—Economic conditions—1989—Congresses. 2. Japan—Economic policy—1989—Congresses. 3. Japan—Commerce—Congresses. I. Ito, Takatoshi, 1950– . II. Patrick, Hugh T. III. Weinstein, David E.
HC462.95.R48 2005
338.952′009′051—dc22 2005051096

10 9 8 7 6 5 4 3 2 1

Contents

Contributors

Editors

Takatoshi Ito is Professor at the Graduate School Faculty of Economics and Research Center for Advanced Science and Technology, University of Tokyo and a research associate of National Bureau of Economic Research. His research interests include macroeconomics, the Japanese economy and East Asian economic cooperation. On leave from Hitotsubashi University, he served between 1999–2001 as Deputy Vice Minister for International Affairs in the Ministry of Finance and between 1994–1997 as Senior Advisor at the Research Department of the International Monetary Fund. He served as Assistant and Associate Professor of Economics at the University of Minnesota between 1979–1988, and a visiting professor at Harvard University from 1992 to 1994. He was President of Japanese Economic Association in 2004–2005. Professor Ito received a B.A. and a M.A. in Economics from Hitotsubashi University in 1973 and 1975, and a M.A. and Ph.D. in Economics from Harvard University in 1977 and 1979.

Hugh Patrick is Director of the Center on Japanese Economy and Business at Columbia Business School, Co-Director of Columbia's APEC Study Center, and R.D. Calkins Professor of International Business Emeritus. His research interests include Japanese economic performance, macroeconomic policy, institutional change, corporate governance, and Asia-Pacific economic relations. He joined the Columbia faculty in 1984 after some years as Professor of Economics and Director of the Economic Growth Center at Yale University. In November 1994 the Government of Japan awarded him the Order of the Sacred Treasure, Gold and Silver Star (Kunnitō Zuihōshō). Professor Patrick received his B.A. at Yale University in 1951, earned M.A. degrees in Japanese Studies (1955) and Economics (1957) and his Ph.D. in Economics at the University of Michigan in 1960.

David E. Weinstein is Carl S. Shoup Professor of the Japanese Economy and Vice-Chairman in the Department of Economics at Columbia University, Associate Director of Research at the Center on Japanese Economy and Business, and Co-Director of the Japan Project at the National Bureau of Economic Research. In addition he is a consultant for the Federal Reserve Bank of New York and a member of the Council on Foreign Relations. Previously, he held faculty appointments as Sanford R. Robertson Associate Professor of Business Administration at the School of Business Administration at the University of Michigan, and Associate Professor of Economics at Harvard University. Professor Weinstein received his B.A. at Yale University in 1985 and his Ph.D. in Economics from the University of Michigan in 1991.

Authors

Christian Broda is Assistant Professor of Economics at the University of Chicago, Graduate School of Business. His research interests include international finance, open economy macroeconomics, exchange rate regimes and trade with emerging markets. He has worked in the International Research Department of the Federal Reserve Bank of New York, and has been a visiting professor at Columbia University and Universidad Di Tella. Dr. Broda received his B.A. in Economics from the Universidad de San Andres, Argentina in 1997 and his M.A. and Ph.D. in Economics from Massachusetts Institute of Technology in 1999 and 2001.

Takero Doi is Associate Professor of Economics at Keio University. His research areas include public finance, especially Japanese governmental financial institutions and local government finances. Between 2002–2004, he was a senior economist at the Ministry of Finance Research Institute, and a visiting scholar at the Graduate School of International Relations and Pacific Studies at University of California, San Diego in 2001–2002. Professor Doi received his B.A. in Economics from Osaka University in 1993 and his M.A. and Ph.D. in Economics from the University of Tokyo in 1995 and 1999.

Mariko Fujii is Professor at the Research Center for Advanced Science and Technology at the University of Tokyo. Her research interests include asset pricing, the term structure of interest rates, and financing of the public sector. Prior to joining the University of Tokyo, she was a career official of the Ministry of Finance, where she held a number of positions, including most recently Director of the International Research Division of the Customs and Tariff Bureau, 1997–1999. Dr. Fujii received her B.A. degree in Economics from the University of Tokyo in 1977 and Ph.D. from the University of Tokyo as well in 2001.

Mitsuhiro Fukao is Professor of Economics in the Faculty of Business and Commerce of Keio University. His research interests include macroeconomics, the Japanese banking and life insurance industries, and corporate governance. Previously, he was Head of the Strategic Research Division in the Bank of Japan Department of Research and Statistics, having entered the Bank in 1974. He spent two one-year terms at the OECD doing research on monetary and fiscal policy. He is Research Director on finance at Japan Center for Economic Research. Professor Fukao earned his B.A. in Engineering from Kyoto University in 1974 and his Ph.D. in Economics from the University of Michigan in 1981.

James Harrigan is Senior Economist and Research Officer in the International Research Department of the Federal Reserve Bank of New York and is a member of the National Bureau of Economic Research. His research interests include international trade, economic geography, and the Japanese economy. Before joining the Bank, he was Assistant Professor in the Economics Department at the University of Pittsburgh. Dr. Harrigan received his Ph.D. in Economics from UCLA in 1991.

Masanori Hashimoto is Professor of Economics and Chairman of the Department of Economics at The Ohio State University, and a member of its Institute for Japanese Studies. His research interests include human capital analysis, economics of training, employment relations, economic demography, and Japanese labor markets. He is a Research Fellow of Institute for the Study of Labor (IZA) in Bonn, Germany; and previously was a National Fellow at the Hoover Institution at Stanford University (1983–1984). He currently serves as co-editor of *Japan Economic Review* and associate editor of *Journal of the Japanese and*

International Economies. Professor Hashimoto received his B.A. and Ph.D. in Economics from Columbia University in 1965 and 1971.

Yoshio Higuchi is Professor of Labor Economics at Keio University. His research interests include the employment policy and employment practices in Japanese firms from the viewpoint of human capital theory. Professor Higuchi is a member of the Minimum Wage Council and Labor Policy Council. Professor Higuchi currently serves as Chairman of the Tokyo Center for Economic Research, and Executive Director of National Life Finance Corporation. Professor Higuchi received his B.A., M.A. and Ph.D. in Business and Commerce from Keio University in 1976, 1977, and 1991.

Takeo Hoshi is Pacific Economic Cooperation Professor of International Economic Relations at the Graduate School of International Relations and Pacific Studies (IR/PS) at University of California, San Diego and Research Associate at National Bureau of Economic Research. His research interests include the Japanese financial system, the banking system and macroeconomic policy. He has been Editor-in-chief of the *Journal of the Japanese and International Economies* since 1999. He is a founding member of Japan's Shadow Financial Regulatory Committee, a group of non-partisan economists who continue to make recommendations related to the Japanese financial system. Professor Hoshi received his B.A. in Social Sciences from the University of Tokyo in 1983, and a Ph.D. in Economics from the Massachusetts Institute of Technology in 1988.

Tokuo Iwaisako is Associate Professor at the Institute of Economic Research, Hitotsubashi University. His research interests include financial economics and macroeconomics. He was an Assistant Professor at University of Tsukuba (1997–2001) and Hitotsubashi University (2001–2002), and visiting researcher, Economic Planning Agency (1997–1999). Professor Iwaisako received his B.A. and M.A. degrees in Economics from Hitotsubashi University in 1990 and 1992 and his Ph.D. in Economics from Harvard University in 1997.

Anil Kashyap is the Edward Eagle Brown Professor of Economics and Finance at the University of Chicago's Graduate School of Business and Co-Director of the Japan Project at the National Bureau of Economic Research. His principal research interests include Japan (particularly the financial system), monetary policy, and the sources of business cycles. He is a consultant to the Federal Reserve Bank of Chicago. Professor Kashyap is one of editors of the Journal of the Political Economy and is on the editorial board of the Journal of the Japanese and International Economies, the Journal of Financial Intermediation, and the Journal of Risk Finance. He earned his B.A. degree in 1982 in Economics and Statistics from the University of California at Davis and his Ph.D. in Economics in 1989 from the Massachusetts Institute of Technology.

Kenneth N. Kuttner is the Danforth-Lewis Professor of Economics at Oberlin College, and a faculty research fellow of the National Bureau of Economic Research. His research interests include macro and monetary economics. Prior to joining Oberlin College, he was as an Assistant Vice President in the research departments of the Federal Reserve Banks of New York and Chicago. He currently serves as an associate editor of the *Journal of Money, Credit and Banking,* and as the macroeconomics co-editor for *Economics Letters*. Professor Kuttner earned a Ph.D. from Harvard University in 1989, and an A.B. degree from the University of California at Berkeley in 1982.

Frederic S. Mishkin is Alfred Lerner Professor of Banking and Financial Institutions at Columbia Business School and a research associate of the National Bureau of Economic Research. His areas of research include monetary policy and the impact on financial markets and the aggregate economy. He is a president of the Eastern Economics Association, senior fellow of the FDIC Center for Banking Research, a consultant to and member of the Academic Advisory Panel of the Federal Reserve Bank of New York, and from 1994 to 1997, served as its Executive Vice President and Director of Research as well as was an associate economist of the Federal Open Market Committee of the Federal Reserve System. He has been a visiting scholar or consultant to the Board of Governors of the Federal Reserve System, the World Bank, the Inter-American Development Bank, the International Monetary Fund and Japan's Ministry of Finance, as well as to numerous central banks throughout the world. Professor Mishkin received his B.S. in Economics from the Massachusetts Institute of Technology in 1973 and his Ph.D. in Economics from MIT in 1976.

Shujiro Urata is Professor of Economics at Waseda University. His research interests include international trade, foreign direct investment, corporate small and medium enterprises, and APEC and regional integration. Previously he was a research associate at the Brookings Institution (from 1978–1981), an economist at the World Bank (from 1981–1986) and a visiting fellow at the East-West Center and OECD. Professor Urata received his B.A. in Economics from Keio University in 1973 and his M.A. and Ph.D. in Economics at Stanford University in 1976 and 1978.

Preface

Prompted by our deep concerns over Japan's persistent, debilitating economic malaise since 1991, in 2002 we met one summer evening in Tokyo, together with Professor Tokuo Iwaisako of Hitosubashi University, and conceived a comprehensive policy-oriented research project to recommend economically optimal solutions to major problems thwarting Japan's return to a self-sustaining, full employment growth path. We invited Professor Mariko Fujii of the University of Tokyo to join us in establishing an organizing committee for our project. Following committee discussions, we then invited a number of distinguished Japanese and American scholars to participate in this joint endeavor, and to our delight all accepted. The project has been administered through the Center on Japanese Economy and Business, Columbia University and the Research Center for Advanced Science and Technology, University of Tokyo.

Our group held a preliminary paper draft and brainstorming workshop at Columbia University in August 2003. Complete chapter drafts were received at the end of March 2004, and we three editors commented extensively and intensively on each. In June 2004, the project held a two-day closed academic conference in Tokyo with a few invited commentators to discuss the issues once again and to review the revised chapter drafts. Final papers were completed at the end of August 2004, with final revision and copy-editing proceeding through March 2005 before an expedited publication schedule.

While the Japanese economy recovered from its early 2002 trough until the first quarter of 2004, to our dismay its performance suddenly became flat for the rest of the year. Now, as of late March 2005 the economy is in a recovery mode once again, but it is far from certain that even this time good, self-sustained growth will be achieved. Given this uncertain economic climate, this volume is even more timely in offering a range of thoughtful, well-considered and implementable policy solutions to restore Japan's long-run economic health. We sincerely hope that this book will be a significant contribution to finally achieving this long-elusive goal.

A project of this scope and range depends upon many different sources of support. Our deepest thanks go to our fellow authors, each of whom committed very seriously and responsibly to this task. Special thanks are due to our co-organizers Mariko Fujii and Tokuo Iwaisako. We are also indebted to Gerald Curtis, Merit Janow and Adam Posen who contributed substantially to our brainstorming session and in other matters.

Inevitably this project was costly because it required each of us to travel at least once to the other's country, and because various kinds of research and administrative support were essential. We are particular indebted to the Itoh Foundation USA, which made possible the initial brainstorming workshop; the Toshiba International Foundation with timely grants for both phases of the project; the Japan Foundation Center for Global Partnership; the Zengin Foundation for Studies on Economics and Finance; the Center for International Research on the Japanese Economy at University of Tokyo; and the Weatherhead East Asian Institute at Columbia University. Roppongi Academy Hills provided us with a wonderful conference facility in the Roppongi Mori Building.

Scholars do our thing, but we cannot succeed in comprehensive projects of this sort without immense support from others. We thank especially Larry Meissner, who assiduously, carefully, and creatively copy-edited the chapters, in the process posing many constructive questions for the authors. Yvonne Thurman was the highly effective program officer responsible at the Center on Japanese Economy and Business for overseeing the project; after her promotion to Center Associate Director, she turned the final stages of project management to Jennifer Olayon, who took over admirably and Jeff Lagomarsino, who assisted her. Satoshi Koibuchi, Takeshi Kudo and Makoto Takaoka together with Chieko Ishizaka, Miki Nakauchi and Naoko Tamiya helped in various ways to make sure that the conference in Tokyo would run as smoothly as possible. We are indebted to Sally and Steve Sztrecska for preparing the chapters into camera-ready form. And we are especially indebted to Elizabeth Murry who not only shepherded the book through

The MIT Press but did an important and effective final copy-editing of the chapters.

Takatoshi Ito, University of Tokyo
Hugh Patrick, Columbia University
David E. Weinstein, Columbia University
March 2005

1 Problems and Prescriptions for the Japanese Economy: An Overview

Takatoshi Ito

and

Hugh Patrick

With the bursting of its asset and real estate market bubble in 1990 and 1991, Japan's economy entered into a long period of mediocre performance that by 2002 and early 2003 was accompanied by growing pessimism about Japan's future among scholars, policymakers, and economic commentators, both inside and outside Japan. This pessimism was shared by the Japanese public. The growth rate had become negative again, banks were failing, and stock prices were plummeting to the level of a decade earlier. Deflation seemed to be worsening, while the unemployment rate was increasing to an unprecedented level. Monetary policy seemed impotent after the benchmark interest rate became zero. Fiscal policy seemed to be powerless as large government spending and tax cut packages failed to lift the economy long enough to generate a self-sustaining recovery.

Moreover, Japan is in the midst of a profound transformation process—economic, demographic, social, and political—that will take several decades to complete. These fundamental forces are deeply intertwined with the cyclical and structural roots of Japan's fourteen-year malaise.

By mid-2004 there was growing optimism that the economy was finally emerging from its 13 years of poor performance to return to sustained growth, but also nagging doubts persisted that this recovery was no more than a cyclical upturn. Earlier recovery attempts in 1996 and 2000 had been followed by disappointing recessions. This proved to be true once again, as a strong first quarter in 2004 was followed by three quarters of essentially flat growth. While the economy will probably recover once again in 2005, it seems unlikely that the recovery will be sufficiently strong or durable to get back onto the path of sustained growth to achieve the economy's full potential. Our deep concern is that fundamental economic and institutional problems will remain inadequately address, possibly inducing another crisis (see Patrick, 2004).

Japan does have feasible, optimal economic policy solutions to the major economic problems and issues that have undermined its fundamental economic strengths since the early 1990s. Even if Japan has entered a period of improving economic conditions, and that is not to be taken for granted, it has not yet adopted the kinds of policies that would maximize its growth potential, improve its people's quality of life, and contribute to strengthening the global economy. The basic purpose of this book, and the two-year research project on which it is based, is to develop and recommend policy solutions to return Japan to long-run sustainable economic growth. The following chapters, written by outstanding Japanese and American economists are forward-looking, but founded on a careful analysis of Japan's recent economic history.

As general context for the following chapters, in this introduction we outline the long-term economic transformation now underway and relate the major economic problems in Japan's 14 years of malaise to that extended process. Subsequent chapters in the book cover the costs of the economic malaise, aggregate demand and macroeconomic policy, monetary policy, financial system difficulties, corporate restructuring and financing, and Japan's new trade policy. Some of the analyses found in subsequent chapters are incorporated into this overarching discussion, which ends by summarizing a few of the major conclusions reached by the authors.

This collaborative project has involved deep and sustained interactions among the 15 well-known Japanese and American economists who authored these 11 chapters. We share a high degree of agreement but certainly not complete consensus on all the proposed policy solutions to Japan's economic problems, and there has been no effort to force consensus. The authors are responsible for their own studies, and we bear sole responsibility for this chapter.

1 Japan's Ongoing Fundamental Transformation

While a great deal of analytical emphasis has appropriately focused on the cyclical and structural difficulties of Japan's malaise since 1990, it is important to recognize the more fundamental long-term forces at work. Three major economic transformations have been underway: the completion of the catch-up process of fast growth as Japan changed from a low income country to a mature economy with a high per capita GDP and standard of living; the ongoing demographic transition to long life expectancy, low fertility, and an aging population; and the evolution from a system of relational capitalism to market-based capitalism. (For an even longer-term history of the evolution of Japan's economic system, see Teranishi 2005.)

Japan's extraordinarily successful postwar economic growth was based significantly on its ability to close the huge gap between the Japanese level of productivity and technology and the world's productivity frontier. This was achieved through the effective utilization of an initially cheap, abundant and skilled labor force; entrepreneurial business investment that applied newly available technologies; a rapidly increasing (and ultimately) very high saving rate that provided domestic financing for the burgeoning rate of business investment, the development of synergistic postwar economic institutions and supportive government economic policies. By the mid-1970s, Japan had caught up with the West, becoming the world's second largest economy with European levels of per capita GDP and a high standard of living. From 1980 on, Japan became an increasingly large foreign investor, both direct and portfolio, and by the 1990s by a wide margin had become the world's largest creditor nation. Japanese banks were the largest in the world and had very high credit ratings, and Japanese institutions were buying prime properties worldwide. Now, after more than a decade of stagnation, there is a widespread sense in Japan that it has failed to make a transition from a super-effective manufacturing economy (exemplified by firms such as Toyota, Sony, and Nippon Steel) to a high-tech service-oriented economy (characterized by companies like Microsoft, Goldman Sachs and CNN).

In the high growth, catch-up era, from the early 1950s to the mid 1970s, Japan's postwar economic system developed and flourished. It was founded, especially for big business, on the permanent employment system of industrial relations, the bank-based system of corporate finance, and the separation of shareholder ownership and management control. Large firms then and still now are controlled by entrenched professional managers, trained and promoted from within to serve as chief executive officers and board members. Any weak firms and banks were merged with healthy ones through backroom discussions and the encouragement of regulators. Declining industries, such as coal, changed through a very gradual process; a few industries that were obviously uncompetitive, such as aluminum, shrank much more rapidly.

The economic system was opaque and cozy, with power centered on business leaders, central government officials, and Liberal Democratic Party (LDP) leaders. The LDP was the sole governing party from its 1955 inception until 1993, and since 1996 has continued to be the dominant leader in a series of coalition governments.

In some respects, by the late 1980s Japan had become a victim of its own economic success. The economy grew too large to be managed effectively based on personal relationships. Japan was gradually moving toward a more market-based, open economic system. For good domestic and foreign policy reasons, the government initially reduced its early postwar controls over prices, then foreign exchange rates, foreign capital flows, and trade in manufactured goods. Piecemeal financial deregulation, a twenty-year process, began in the mid-1970s. Many government enterprises were partially or totally privatized in the 1980s. Airlines are now 100% privately owned; railway companies are partially private; and the formerly monopolistic domestic and international telephone companies are substantially privatized and compete against private communication companies. Other deregulation has taken place, though many regulations persist.

In Japan, as in other countries, development and growth brought major changes in the economic structure. Agriculture declined to minor economic significance (but remains politically potent); the share of the manufacturing sector rose sharply and then gradually declined; and the portion of the economy centered on business and personal services naturally rose. With wages increasing continually and the yen appreciating, by the 1980s Japan no longer was a cheap-labor economy; labor-intensive industries, facing the onslaught of cheap imports, increasingly invested abroad while declining at home. One of Japan's major anomalies is that the productivity gap between manufacturing, especially of exports, and services, mostly non-tradables, has remained very wide, and still is the most extreme of any major OECD economy. This wide gap suggests both a potential for better growth through more effective resource reallocation and the real difficulties of major structural adjustment for low-productivity service industries, especially retail and wholesale trade, and construction.

It is our view that Japan successfully overcame several economic challenges in the past, but since the 1990s Japan has really stumbled. We should not forget how Japan overcame difficulties in the 1970s and 1980s (for a comprehensive review of the Japanese economy before the bubbles burst in 1990 and 1991, see Ito 1992). The economic turmoil of the 1970s brought on the first set of challenges, and the mid-1970s was the first inflection point for the Japanese economy. The yen had just been floated for the first time since World War II. Inflation reached 30% in 1973, due partly to monetary easing the year before but particularly due to the quadrupling of oil prices. Strong tightening to halt inflation caused negative growth in 1974 for the first time in the postwar period. Following the first oil crisis, business optimism and investment slowed more than the gradual reduction in household saving rates. The energy resource constraint and increasingly obvious pollution problems put a brake on the overwhelmingly growth-oriented focus of corporate management and government policy.

Deficit-financing government bonds were issued in increasingly large amounts for the rest of the 1970s to help the economy regain its growth path. Private sector aggregate demand was no longer excessive relative to supply, and weakened sufficiently to require government macroeconomic stimulus. Credit rationing was no longer necessary, and credit became easy; the Keynesian paradox of excess saving, initially perceived to be cyclical, became long-term and structural. Japan, as the world's second largest economy, has from the 1980s been unable to export all of its excess domestic savings because the requisite concomitant huge trade (and current account) surpluses were and are unacceptable to the United States and Europe.

The second big challenge the Japanese economy faced was in the mid-1980s, when yen appreciation brought about another big shock to the Japanese economy. The first half of the 1980s were marked by dollar appreciation vis-à-vis all other currencies. Japanese exports soared and the economy enjoyed rapid growth. By 1984 Japan's current account in its balance of payments had turned to substantial surpluses, while that of the United States had turned to large deficits. The Plaza Accord of September 1985 was supposed to correct exchange rate misalignments and restore equilibrium exchange rates for the major OECD countries. The yen appreciated from 260 per dollar in February 1985 to 240 just before the Plaza Accord in September, and to 200 in December 1985. It then kept appreciating, in part because of the collapse of oil prices, and reached a then record high of 150 yen per dollar by the fourth quarter of 1986.

Given the severe appreciation in the yen's value, fears arose about the collapse of Japanese exports and the economy in general, but the economy was more resilient than expected. Monetary policy was greatly eased from 1985, and the economy embarked on rapid growth based on private demand. Accordingly, the government was able to pursue fiscal consolidation throughout the 1980s, and achieved a balanced, even surplus, budget by the end of the decade. Japan recovered from the yen appreciation of 1985–86, and from spillover effects from the American stock-price declines of late 1987 (Black Monday, October 19, and its aftermath). At the end of 1989, the Japanese economy was at the peak of its asset-price and real estate bubbles. Land and stock prices had risen four-fold in 6 years. No one would dare to forecast those gains would be erased in the following 13 years.

The bursting of the bubble and the ensuing stagnation of the 1990s through 2004 has been the third and biggest challenge faced by postwar Japan, and it has been much more protracted than necessary. Asset price declines resulted in huge amounts of non-performing loans, giving rise to the banking crisis of 1997–98. After the basic interest rate became zero, monetary policy was a much less effective tool since 1995. Fiscal deficits and government debt have become so large that further fiscal stimulus has not seemed feasible to policymakers.

Japan's decades of success led to some fundamental assumptions that attained the status of myth before being seen as mistaken. The two myths of the late 1980s were that land prices would never decline, since they never really had for the entire 40-year postwar period; and that rapid GDP growth would continue indefinitely. The 1990–91 bursting of the twin bubbles shattered the land price myth, and raised doubts about maintaining an annual growth rate greater than 4%. Nonetheless, faith in naturally renewed growth led to mythical expectations during the 1990s that growth would be restored fairly soon and the economy would recover; thus it was felt that painful business and government structural adjustments could be postponed until conditions improved, and that was how decision makers behaved through much of the 1990s. We are concerned that excessively optimistic perceptions are widely voiced once again in early 2005.

1.1 Demography

Japan's long-term demographic transformation is as profound as its economic one. Over the course of its modern economic development, Japan has transited from relatively high birth and death rates, low life expectancy, a young population, and moderate population growth to a nation of very low death rates, even lower birth rates, and the longest life expectancy in the world. As a result, Japan has a rapidly aging population. Since 1995 there has been an absolute decline in the working-age group (15–64), and by 2007 population size will peak. Population stability occurs when the completed fertility rate is about 2.1; currently it is only 1.29. The Japanese level is comparable to Italy's very low fertility rate, both of which are among the lowest of OECD countries.

In this volume Broda and Weinstein cogently point out how unrealistic is the common assumption that Japan's low birth rates will persist indefinitely; that means that the Japanese eventually will disappear. Changes in demographic behavior are typically long run, but it is reasonable to assume that some decades hence, the ever-richer Japanese will desire to have more children and the population will stabilize. Or perhaps Japan will decide to give up ethnic homogeneity and accept large numbers of permanent immigrants, as Hashimoto and Higuchi suggest in their chapter. Demographic assumptions are important in analyzing long-run issues of fiscal sustainability, namely how much government revenues will have to be raised as a share of GDP to meet social security commitments to the elderly.

High or low dependency rates—the number of children and elderly as a percentage of the working-age population—provide information on growth prospects and the needs for government expenditures (including income transfers), but depending on the characteristics of the social security system these dependency rates do not necessarily imply fiscal and economic problems. However, the current Japanese social security system, designed as a pay-as-you-go program, is already in deep trouble. Too many of the young are not paying in premiums, and corporations are exiting the corporate part of the social security system when possible. Clearly the institutional arrangements and the implementation of policies have to be improved, an issue we stress even though it transcends the topics of this book.

1.2 Transformation Policy Choices

One key issue for Japan's long-term economic performance is the degree and nature of the factors determining potential growth: changes in labor supply, capital investment per worker, and technological change (total factor productivity increase). Another key issue is what portion of GDP society decides to have the government spend on its people—elderly, young, and those of working age. The ratio can be high as in Scandinavia, quite high as in many European countries, or more modest as in Japan and the United States. A third issue is how to pursue policies that assure labor, capital, and other resources are fully and efficiently utilized.

What proportion of GDP will the Japanese be willing to transfer to their elderly in the form of public pensions and health care? Should Japan maintain high ethnic homogeneity, or should it encourage substantial permanent immigration? Should it provide incentives to increase fertility, including more adequate support structures for working mothers and their children? How much should politically-important but economically-inefficient sectors and activities be subsidized, and how can such programs be made more efficient given appropriate transfer programs? As economists, we are good at making recommendations on efficiency issues, but are hesitant to make recommendations about these important social choices.

While beyond the scope of this study, social and political changes are a major component of the transformation process. We note several important trends. Today's young Japanese grew up in relative comfort, in contrast to their grandparents' experiences in a war-ravaged 1940s Japan and their parents' experience in the 1950s and 1960s. In contemporary Japan young adults are considerably better educated, have more international awareness and experience, and aspire to realize their own career goals. Today's young adults have a wide range of interests and lifestyle opportunities, although they have been constrained by their poor employment situation. We do not know what figures most importantly in their life-cycle decisions, but the fact is that they are postponing marriage: half the Japanese women and men aged 30 are not married.

Given that the current young adult generation is affluent and behaves quite differently than previous generations, Japan's economic structure, as well as its social structure, may well change in the future. The saving rate may drop in addition to a natural decline due to an aging society, and employment practices may change as more young people, voluntarily and involuntarily, find only temporary, part-time jobs as their first professional positions. Hashimoto and Higuchi find this trend very unsatisfactory for effective career development, as discussed in chapter 10.

The postwar Japanese family model—analogous to the American model of the 1950s—of the husband working permanently for a large organization and the wife at home raising their two or three children was always an inaccurate stereotype. Most Japanese men have always worked for small- or medium-sized enterprises and changed jobs from time to time; some two-fifths of married women re-enter the work force, usually part-time, once their children start school. However, Japan is the only advanced country that has had a significant drop in the female labor force participation rate for the child-bearing and child-caring age group. It is debatable whether this is a voluntary choice or involuntary.

1.3 Political Change

In the 1990s there was a significant change in the political environment. The Liberal Democratic Party (LDP), always a collection of factions, began to split. In the July 1993 elections, the LDP lost its majority in the Lower House. LDP splinter groups formed coalitions with other parties to obtain a majority in the Diet, and in August Morihiro Hosokawa became the first non-LDP prime minister since 1955. However, that coalition collapsed after 20 months. The LDP first managed to form a coalition with the Socialist Party (now the Social Democrat Party of Japan) yielding the prime ministership to its leader, Tomiichi Murayama. Since January 1996 the LDP has formed coalitions with several smaller parties, including now the New Komei Party, and regained the prime ministership.

The major opposition party in the 1950s through 1970s, the Socialist Party [later renamed the Social Democrat Party (SDP)] participated in the coalition government in the early 1990s, but later essentially disappeared. By 2003, the Democratic Party of Japan (DPJ) had emerged as a rival to the LDP. The DPJ is an amalgam of members of most pre-1993 opposition parties (other than the SDP and Communists), newly elected members, and those LDP splinter groups that did not rejoin the LDP.

In the November 2003 House of Representative election and the July 2004 House of Councilors election, the DPJ actually gained more votes in total than the LDP, but these victories did not convert to control of either house. For both houses, most members are elected by districts, the rest proportionally. For the lower house since 1994 the districts are single-seat (replacing multi-member districts); for the upper, they are prefectual.

While many commentators observe that Japan is approaching a "two-party system" like the United States, one conspicuous difference is that currently the small, but well organized New Komei Party holds balancing power in the Diet. Prime Minister Junichiro Koizumi's term as LDP president and hence as prime minister ends in September 2006.

His successor is far from certain. The possibility of further party member realignments based more on common policy positions than on history is real.

1.4 International Context

Japan's demographic and political transformation is not unique, and not isolated. The world has changed dramatically as well. The cold war confrontation between the United States and the former Soviet Union ended in the late 1980s, and the United States has emerged as the sole military hegemon. The September 11, 2001 terrorist attacks on New York and Washington fundamentally altered American foreign policy, with repercussions for all countries.

The world trading system has been strengthened by the creation in 1995 of the World Trade Organization (WTO) out of its forerunner, the General Agreement on Trade and Tariffs (GATT), despite its remaining limitations. Global financial markets have become increasingly important: huge short-term and long-term capital flows, exchange rate movements, and expectations about interest rates, now strongly affect the economic policies of all major nations. The creation of the system of arbitration panels under the WTO has significantly decreased the chance of unilateral actions in bilateral trade disputes. Some prominent trade disputes between Japan and the United States, such as the Fuji versus Kodak film case, were settled under the WTO panel in favor of Japan.

In addition to these global multinational approaches, regional approaches to trade have proliferated. One of the most important of these is the North American Free Trade Agreement among the United States, Canada, and Mexico. Moreover the Free Trade Agreement of the Americas (FTAA) is being negotiated. The FTAA will cover the entire western hemisphere from Canada to Argentina. An even more important regional trading group is the European Union; with its 2004 expansion from 15 to 25 members, most of Europe and much of its periphery are now one market.

In East Asia, while Japan remains the largest and by far the most technologically sophisticated economy, the big change is the economic rise of China. The Chinese economy has grown at almost 10 percent annually over the past two decades, just like Japan in the 1950s and 1960s. China has joined the WTO, and has become a major factor in regional and global trade. Given its still low level of income and its still huge numbers of rural workers, China has the potential to continue to grow rapidly for another two decades. China provides Japanese companies with both great economic challenges and opportunities. As the Japanese experience over the past two decades well demonstrates, a rapidly growing large economy is better for the world economy than a slowly growing one.

The prospects of North Korean nuclear capability have added a new security dimension to regional cooperation. If anything, the North Korean issue has strengthened the security alliance between Japan and the United States. At the same time, the six-party talks under Chinese leadership are a new approach to regional security cooperation. However, each country—North Korea, China, the United States, Japan, South Korea, and Russia—has its own interests and anxieties. With a strong economy, many South Koreans now have little sense of military threat from North Korea and are increasingly sympathetic to their North Korean brethren, as reflected in the last presidential election. We live in an uncertain world and, as various pundits have articulated, the future of East Asia is more uncertain than its past.

2 Economic Malaise Since 1990

The Japanese economy has performed poorly over the 14 years since 1991. It has suffered the malaise of inadequate growth, a soaring unemployment rate and deepening under-employment, bank failures, slow and inadequate corporate restructuring, sub-optimal resource allocation, and slow, protracted institutional and structural reforms. Despite immense macroeconomic stimulus, policies of forbearance, relationship-based inertia and policy mistakes have contributed to the lengthy persistence of this poor performance. Termed by many as stagnation, though certainly not collapse, the "lost decade" became a popular nickname for this stalled period of economic growth. We prefer to term the 1990s as a decade of underperformance and malaise, since in fact many institutional and other changes took place. (There are many studies of the Japanese economy in the 1990s; see for example, Blomstrom et al, 2003; Cargill et al 1997, 2001; Katz 1998, 2003; Lincoln 1999; OECD, 2004; Porter et al, 2000; Posen 1998; and Saxonhouse and Stern, 2003.) Indeed, the succession of recoveries and recessions in the first five years of the 21st century undermine predominant focus on the 1990s; we now have to think of Japan's underperformance extending at least 15 years rather than 10.

While certainly influenced by the specifics of Japan's long-run transformation process, all the problems recounted above have been made substantially worse by poor economic performance since 1991. A variety of forces have been at work to undermine Japan's economy. The bursting of the huge real estate and stock market bubbles in 1990–91 resulted in severe balance sheet and non-performing loan problems for banks, other financial institutions, and corporations. Given the excess of borrowing and irrational exuberance over real estate and stocks in the 1980s, the collapse of asset markets was inevitable, but major policy mistakes were made in handling the bursting of the bubbles. An increasingly huge non-performing loan problem was hidden for too long, and has been addressed in wrong ways; a new financial regime, based on an arm's length relationship between the regulator and the regulated, has been very slow to emerge. In 1995 the Ministry of Finance declared that none of Japan's 20 major banks would fail, but Hokkaido Takushoku Bank suddenly failed in November 1997. Subsequently, the Ministry of Finance's regulatory functions were separated out into the new, cabinet-level Financial Supervisory Agency (FSA). Several more big banks failed, and others merged. Japan will soon have three major banking groups representing most banking sector assets, in addition to the still huge postal savings system.

Japan has been caught in the combination of these inadequacies and of the long-run fundamental transformation discussed above. While the economy cyclically rebounded between the early 2002 trough and the first quarter of 2004, the subsequent abruptly stalled economic performance for the rest of 2004 is indicative of the reality that major economic problems persist. As discussed below, aggregate demand remains inadequate; deflation has yet to end; land prices continue to decline; corporate, financial institution, and public sector restructuring is far from completed; and unemployment, under-employment, and misallocated labor and capital are particularly serious.

It is clear that solid aggregate demand and good, sustained growth will contribute significantly to the solution of Japan's economic problems. Growth reduces adjustment costs, undergirds financial restructuring, and enhances the effectiveness and efficiency of markets for goods, services, labor, land, and capital. However, growth alone is not enough. Supply-side improvements—efficiency-enhancing deregulation and restructuring—must go hand in hand with development and maintenance of inadequate aggregate demand, in both the near-term and the longer-run. Corporate restructuring destroys jobs in the short-run while creating them in the long-run. This means social safety nets need to be better designed and deployed.

Japan's macroeconomic difficulties have been deeply intertwined with the weakening of the Japanese financial system. In 1990 Japan's banks and life insurance companies were considered to be not only the largest but the strongest in the world. Today, these financial institutions are still huge, but recognized as the weakest of any advanced industrial nation. Bank lending to business has declined steadily. Banks hold a large amount of government bonds and equities, but have failed to develop fee businesses sufficiently. Their balance sheets are still greatly at risk from securities market fluctuations. Japan's government is an exceptionally large financial intermediary, crowding out private-sector institutions, rather than complementing them by serving areas characterized by market failures. Government financial institutions, with a huge share of household deposits and life insurance policies held in the postal savings system, account for some 40% of all loans, and are especially important mortgage lenders to households and to smaller business enterprises. As Japan's private sector financial system has been fundamentally deregulated and liberalized, many government financial institutions have been rendered weak and redundant as their economic rationale has evaporated.

While moving ahead slowly and cautiously on domestic structural reform, the Japanese government has embarked on a bold new foreign trade policy, initiating negotiations for bilateral (and perhaps eventually regional) free trade areas (FTAs) or more comprehensive, regional trading agreements. These new policies and the issues they raise are discussed by Urata in chapter 11. Whether this new approach is an appropriate trade strategy, and whether it will be complementary to, or competitive with, Japan's global commitments and objectives under the WTO remains to be seen; certainly it is parallel to the earlier North American and European Union regional trade policy commitments. The major stumbling block for Japanese trade policy continues to be the still-high degree of protection provided small and very inefficient, but politically powerful, agricultural, forestry, and fishery interests.

2.1 The Costs of Japan's Long Malaise

The costs of Japan's poor economic performance and slowness to adjust since 1991 are not hidden but are not necessarily obvious. Despite widespread fears and even dire predictions, the economy did not collapse. While there certainly have been crises for individual companies and even some government institutions, no systemic crisis has occurred. The closest call was in the banking and financial systems between September 1997 and March 1998, but a full-fledged crisis, such as a widespread bank run, was averted. Nonetheless, we can conceive of possible adverse scenarios in which large unexpected shocks could create conditions that might precipitate a collapse, such as another major Tokyo earthquake, hyperinflation, or war.

Probably the greatest cost of the economic malaise has been the GDP foregone due to below-potential growth for so many years. Japan's GDP could be on the order of 25% higher today if the economy had achieved its growth potential. Its high standard of living could be significantly higher.

In human terms, Japan's most serious problem is a combination of unemployment, under-employment, and misallocated labor. The recent reduction in the reported unemployment rate from the 5.5% peak in 2002 to 4.5% in January 2005 is an improvement, but it masks major declines in the quality of jobs and in the withdrawal of persons of working age (15–64) from the labor force. As Hashimoto and Higuchi emphasize in chapter 10, between 1997 and 2003 the labor force participation rate dropped to its lowest level ever. During this period, employment declined by 2.4 million persons: 1.2 million withdrew or never entered the labor force, and 1.2 million became unemployed. Worse, from 1997 full-time regular employment until the beginning of 2005 continually decreased, while part-time and temporary employment has risen steadily and now comprises more than a quarter of total employment. Compared to full-time male employees, the hourly wages of part-time male workers are only 51%, full-time female workers only 66%, and part-time female workers only 44%. Large department stores now rely predominantly on part-time workers. More broadly, firms with more than 1000 employees are replacing retiring full-time workers with part-timers; whereas part-time employees comprised 3.9% of their workers 1995, this ratio increased to 8.6% in 2002, and is even higher today. The Japanese economy has been experiencing de facto wage reduction, reflecting weak labor demand and slow productivity growth. This wage reduction is good in the sense that the unemployment rate is less high than otherwise, but bad in the sense that the full potential of the work force is not being realized because of inadequate demand for labor.

In longer-term perspective, the weak labor market has harmed the young—those aged 15 to 24 years—disproportionately. The unemployment rate for 20–24 year olds not in school in 2002 was 9.3%, but in 1990 this rate was only 3.8%; for those aged 15–19 years, the corresponding figures are 12.8% in 2002 versus 6.6% in 1990. The "idle labor" rate, measuring those neither in school nor in the labor force, for those aged 20–24 years was 17.0% in 2002, up from 11.3% in 1990; for those aged 15–19 years, 24.3% in 2002, up from 14.6% in 1990. Equally serious has been the increase in young part-time workers. In 2003, male part-timers aged 20–24 comprised 28.3% of their employed age group, up from 14.9% in 1990 and even lower levels from earlier periods. Some 35.2% of female workers aged 20–24 were part-timers in 2003, up from 18.4% in 1990 and lower ratios earlier. 54.5% of these young part-time workers are female.

Some of these young people have voluntarily chosen alternative lifestyles made possible by high wages in an affluent society. The estimates of the non-accelerating inflation rate of unemployment (NAIRU) has risen from its exceptionally low earlier levels, but at about 3.5% it remains significantly below the actual unemployment rate. Survey data indicate most young people would prefer full-time regular jobs. The significant rise in the proportion of part-time workers, a category especially comprised of young people, reflects the still weak demand for labor. In the longer run, this underemployment means that young workers are not obtaining the benefits of skill development through on-the-job training. This is a major hidden cost of Japan's mediocre economic performance since 1991 (in addition to the Hashimoto and Higuchi chapter, see Sato and Sato, 1997).

3 Aggregate Demand and Macroeconomic Policy

All the studies contained in this book make it clear that Japan's most important economic policy objective is to achieve good, sustained, full employment growth. This theme runs throughout this chapter as well. Certainly, while some of Japan's slower growth has been due to changes on the supply side, a main thesis of this book is that Japan's poor macroeconomic performance has been largely due to inadequate aggregate demand necessary to maintain full utilization of labor and other resources (see, for example, Amyx, 2004; Ihori and Sato, 2002; Mikitani and Posen, 2000; Posen, 1998).

Japan's macroeconomic policy since 1991 has been one of extraordinary stimulus, but even this has been insufficient in what have become even more extraordinary circumstances. The government has run budget deficits of close to 6–8% annually since 1997. Gross government debt now exceeds 161% of GDP though importantly, as Broda and Weinstein stress in chapter 2, the net debt actually is much lower because the government both owns substantial financial assets and on a consolidated basis owns a significant proportion of its own debt. Nonetheless, both gross and net debt levels will continue to rise for some time. The Bank of Japan has reduced interest rates as much as possible, with the benchmark overnight bank call rate, analogous to the American federal funds rate, at zero. Yet these macroeconomic policies have not been sufficient to prevent deflation, albeit mild, since the mid-1990s. Even more importantly, between 1992 and 2003 Japan's GDP averaged only 1.2% annual growth, substantially below its potential. During that time there were three recessions followed by inadequate recoveries, including slightly negative growth (technical recession) for the middle two quarters of 2004, and only a slightly positive fourth quarter (though Japan's quarterly GDP data are weak, and subsequent adjustments so substantial, that they are only rough indicators).

While it is true macroeconomic stimulus prevented a full-fledged financial crisis and collapse into a 1930s-style depression, that is no great achievement. Other rich, advanced nations have gone through difficult economic times in the last half-century, but relative to its potential none has done so poorly for so long as Japan. The lack of a successful macroeconomic policy has harmed all parts of the economy, and continues to do so.

The Japanese economy was particularly hurt by two major macroeconomic policy mistakes involving premature tightening. The first, in early 1997, raised the consumption tax and other taxes while cutting government expenditures, a fiscal tightening swing of some 2% of GDP. The second misstep occurred in August 2000 when the Bank of Japan raised interest rates in the midst of deflation, ending monetary ease; while the size of the rate increase was small, that action had a huge adverse effect on expectations.

Expanding aggregate demand continues to be essential. Only this will narrow the supply-demand gap, restore true full employment, and foster more positive expectations about Japan's economic future, the key to ending deflation. Growth, as must be repeatedly stressed, is necessary both to affect the short-term contractionary effects of industrial restructuring and to provide the foundation for restructuring still weak banks, life insurance companies, and other financial institutions.

Although some policy analysts have continued to propose an even more aggressive short-term cyclical fiscal stimulus in order to revitalize the economy and ensure sustained recovery and growth, many observers consider increased government spending economically very inefficient, with too many wasteful pork-barrel public works projects. Building bridges, tunnels, dams, and reclaimed land in sparsely populated areas with little future demand for these services is worse than tax cuts, because the infrastructure investment not only results in construction debt but requires maintenance costs and labor misallocation for years to come. Overspending on public works, partly due to collusion in bidding, is widespread in Japan; most voters, even in areas where the proposed infrastructure is located, have become skeptical of the value of public works. There has been little domestic call for fiscal stimulus through public works and, indeed, the share of GDP devoted to public infrastructure investment has declined steadily since the mid-1990s.

Fiscal stimulus proposals through tax cuts have gone nowhere because of deep Japanese anxiety about the persistent huge government budget deficits and the high gross government debt-to-GDP ratio. The specter of a fiscal crisis sooner or later looms large in the media and the public consciousness, but apparently not in the presumably more sophisticated financial markets, where long-term interest rates on 20 year government bonds remain very low, around 2% or less.

A key policy dilemma is how to increase aggregate demand while curbing government budget deficits and the high government debt-to-GDP ratio. Essentially this task is a matter of timing between the near-term versus the long-term. Over the longer term Japanese saving rates will continue to decline and private business investment and personal consumption demand will rise sufficiently to end the output gap, restoring normal aggregate demand and full employment growth without requiring huge budget deficits. Eventually as well, further near-term increases in the government debt ratio will end and then decrease. These problems are manageable, both in the near- and long-term. A key fiscal issue is whether in the long run the Japanese government will be able to achieve fiscal sustainability, namely to finance increasing expenditures as a proportion of GDP for the rising elderly share of the population while providing government services to the rest of its citizens as well. The economic issue is how much government tax revenues will have to increase as a share of GDP to meet societal commitments; or how much these existing commitments will have to be cut in order to maintain incentives for firms and workers to stay in Japan; or how to alter income distribution.

In one of the most important and controversial studies in this volume, Broda and Weinstein in chapter 2 present a careful empirical analysis that argues Japan does not face a future fiscal crisis. They found that the potential tax burden of long-term fiscal sustainability is much less dire than the Japanese government currently projects. Broda and Weinstein estimate that, in due course, government revenues as a share of GDP will have to increase only modestly unless Japan decides to increase welfare levels to the equivalent of current European levels.

Broda and Weinstein base their analysis on several key points. First, net government debt, not gross, is the correct measure of the government's financial position. It is necessary to subtract the Japanese government's financial assets from its liabilities, and Japanese government institutions hold more than half the outstanding gross government debt. For example, the government holds some $840 billion in foreign exchange reserves, which represents about 18% of GDP; these reserves are financed by government borrowing; and are basically a wash on the balance sheet of the government special accounts. Broda and Weinstein estimate that the government's net debt as of March 2002 was 64% of GDP. They then use a more comprehensive public sector definition of the net debt, consolidating the central bank's assets and liabilities (which reduces the net debt ratio to 46%) and the government's unstated liabilities (based on the estimates of Doi and Hoshi, 2003) to arrive at a net public sector debt of 62%, which they use as their baseline estimate for long-term sustainability. They argue there is no need to reduce this level; net debt can rise as rapidly as nominal GDP without causing problems.

In order to have government expenditures for all Japanese, old and young, increase at the same rate as GDP growth, Broda and Weinstein estimate that in the long run government revenues will have to be only 34.6% of GDP, almost the same ratio as in 1990 before tax cuts were enacted. The OECD estimates that the average ratio of Japanese government revenues to GDP for 1980–2000 was 30.9%, and forecasts the ratio for 2004 to be 29.8%.

The Broda and Weinstein estimate of fiscal sustainability is based on reasonable assumptions. These include the population projections made in an IMF study that fertility rates will eventually rise, that population decline will level off by 2060 and that the share of elderly will then remain constant. The fiscal costs of paying benefits to the elderly during the period of demographic transition will be spread over 100 years, meaning that several Japanese generations will share these costs. This assumption implies that the ratio of net (and gross) government debt will continue rising for some years before beginning to decline, but this increase is manageable. Broda and Weinstein note that while the share of expenditures on the elderly will increase as they become a larger part of the population, total government expenditures on children will decrease as their numbers decline. They also estimate sustainable tax rates under alternative, more stringent assumptions.

These relatively optimistic projections are indeed good news. A fiscal crisis will not occur so long as people and institutions continue to believe that Japan can restore fiscal balance in the long run. Tax revenues will have to rise, but only moderately, as a share of GDP. Normal growth will help to increase tax revenues from their current cyclical downturn, but tax rates will have to increase somewhat, though not a great deal unless Japan moves to a European-style welfare state or decides to finance the transition process for the elderly in a much shorter time frame.

Broda and Weinstein also make the important point that inflation has only a temporary effect upon reducing government debt, everything else remaining equal. Inflation does not solve the long-run government debt problem since it only reduces the value of accumulated past government debt, not the government's future liabilities embedded in its commitments to all Japanese, but especially to the elderly. Moreover, although an inflationary doubling of the price level would halve the government's gross debt, because so much debt is held by the government itself, the net reduction would be relatively small.

While fiscal stimulus may be desirable in the short-run, it is difficult to cut taxes now while planning to raise them later. The political reality is that the LDP coalition government, which seems likely to remain in power until 2007, has rejected any additional fiscal stimulus measures. Instead it has consistently attempted to keep the annual budget deficit to GDP level more or less constant, and has announced a medium-term goal of achieving a primary budget balance by 2012. Broda and Weinstein assert that this goal is too extreme a tightening path, especially if the economy grows below potential. As with all long-term policy pronouncements, this may well be altered by changing events or new analyses.

4 Monetary Policy

This volume includes two important complementary chapters on monetary policy. Inadequate monetary policy is one of the most important factors in understanding the Japanese economy's malaise in the 1990s and early 2000s. The Bank of Japan was consistently behind the curve from 1993 to 2000, and made a key policy error in August 2000 by tightening money while deflation persisted. Harrigan and Kuttner in chapter 3 convincingly argue that the Bank of Japan could have done better, if only it had known what the United States Federal Reserve would have done in a similar situation, as did indeed begin to occur in America in the early 2000s. Ito and Mishkin in chapter 4 provide a comprehensive set of policies for ending Japan's sustained deflation (see also Cargill et al, 1997 and 2000; OECD, 2004; and Mikitani and Posen, 2000).

As the Japanese economy fell into mild deflation in the mid-1990s, the need for more effective monetary policy increased. Most mainstream economists believe that inflation and deflation are monetary phenomena in the long-run, and that a central bank can influence the course of the inflation rate, not by fine-tuning, but by achieving a medium-run average. From this general viewpoint, the Bank of Japan's failures to prevent deflation from setting in and then allowing it to remain for a prolonged period represent mismanaged monetary policy. Specifically, the timing of adopting the zero interest rate policy (ZIRP) was late; additional actions while ZIRP was in place were taken too late, only sending tentative and at times inconsistent messages; and premature tightening in the midst of ongoing deflation was a major mistake. Even with a zero interest rate, a central bank should influence expectations by promising a credible course of monetary policy and target inflation rates.

Harrigan and Kuttner compare the macroeconomic situations and monetary policy responses to the ending of asset price bubbles in Japan in 1991 and in the United States in 2000. Growth acceleration and stock price increases prior to the burst bubbles were similar in both countries. Japanese fiscal balances improved during the boom years, but deteriorated in the down years, and the United States showed a similar pattern with even less favorable fiscal consequences. One substantial difference is that Japan has been running current account surpluses in its balance of payments while the United States has been running increasingly large current account deficits in the years following the peak of its bubble.

Harrigan and Kuttner argue that monetary easing by the Bank of Japan after the bubble's peak was slower than in the United States when measured by the respective actual interest rates adjusted for the inflation. Japan's delay in cutting the interest rate in the early post-bubble stages very likely contributed to the start of the long stagnation. One mitigating factor is that in 1991 and 1992 actual disinflation exceeded expectations, so that failing to cut the interest rate more aggressively may be somewhat excused. However, this excuse does not hold after 1993. In particular, the Bank of Japan's decision to keep the call rate unchanged at 2.25% in 1994 and in the first quarter of 1995 actually contributed to a further decline in economic activity by slightly tightening monetary policy in real terms. If in 1991–94 the Bank of Japan had acted like the Federal Reserve in 2001–04, disinflation may not have set in as rapidly as it did, and more aggressive interest rate cuts in 1994 and 1995 might have even prevented the eventual deflation that occurred and still persists.

Harrigan and Kuttner apply an econometric model of a central bank setting the interest rate in reaction to the gap GDP and the expected inflation rate, the so-called Taylor equation. Then they fit the Japanese data with the estimated American coefficients to determine what would have happened if the Bank of Japan had acted like the Federal Reserve. They find that the interest rate would have been reduced to zero by mid-1993, and remained there at least through 1995. They also critically review the Bank of Japan's monetary policy from 1995 to 2003 and find its response to deflation has been misguided, notably the rate hike in August 2000, or long overdue, as evinced by the quantitative easing beginning only in March 2001.

There is no question the Bank of Japan's very easy monetary policy currently in place should continue until sustained growth is restored and deflation ends. Once sustained good economic performance is achieved, the appropriate monetary policy—when and how to exit the current policy of quantitative easing and zero overnight call market interest rates—is addressed in the chapter 4. Ito and Mishkin argue for price-level targeting to catch up with the hypothetical trend line of 1% core CPI increases extending from the 1997 level. (Given the upward bias of the CPI, a 1% rise in fact maintains price stability.) This policy is history-dependent: the longer deflation continues, the higher the average inflation rate will need to be during the catch-up period. By committing to such a strategy, inflationary expectations will become higher as deflation persists (since the requisite "catch-up" will become greater). This aspect of price-level targeting is particularly attractive in a period of deflation. Once the price level catches up with the targeted trend line, Ito and Mishkin propose that the Bank of Japan shift to regular inflation-rate targeting, for the sake of simpler communication to the public.

The effective coordination of fiscal policy and monetary policy is a key for success in maximizing policy efforts. In the early years following the Bank of Japan's independence in 1998, especially under Governor Masaru Hayami, relations between the Bank of Japan and its former master, the Ministry of Finance, were not smooth (see Ito, 2004). Bank of Japan executives resisted suggestions from the Ministry of Finance to ease monetary policy more aggressively as a threat to its independence, arguing instead that the Ministry's fiscal policies should be more expansive. However, the Ministry of Finance's monetary policy suggestions turned out to be correct, and resisting them was a costly mistake. Since April 2003, under Governor Toshihiko Fukui, the relationship has improved. When the same message is sent both from the government and the Bank of Japan, and when fiscal policy and monetary policy actions are presented as a coordinated package, the effects on the economy will be maximized.

5 Financial System Difficulties

Japan's macroeconomic difficulties have exacerbated the prolonged and profound weakening of it's financial system, and this problem is analyzed in three related chapters: Hoshi and Kashyap consider the banking system, Fukao examines the life insurance industry, and Doi focuses on the government financial institutions. What once was considered to be an extraordinarily large, strong and effective financial system has become one of the weakest among advanced industrial nations. Virtually every Japanese financial institution has been overwhelmed by the major declines in stock and real estate prices, non-performing loans, very low interest rate spreads for banks, negative carry for life insurance companies, persistent if mild deflation, and the consequences of management mistakes.

In chapter 5 Hoshi and Kashyap stress that, despite huge write-offs of non-performing loans and improvements in the last few years, the capital position of almost all Japanese banks remains extraordinarily weak. Through mergers and failures the reduction from 20 big banks in 1990 to 8 in 2004 has created even larger but not stronger banks. Mergers have not yet resulted in substantial cost cutting or in the development of new, more effective business models. Moreover, bank lending policies have worsened asset quality. While total bank loans have decreased significantly, loans to very weak, large borrowers (called "zombie firms") have been maintained and in some cases even increased. Hoshi and Kashyap emphasize that under Minister Heizo Takenaka supervisory and regulatory reforms by the Financial Services Agency (FSA) to restructure bank balance sheets and identify and deal with non-performing loans have been a substantial improvement over the past, but should be further strengthened and pursued even more vigorously. Nonetheless, these are only the first steps to restoring competitiveness and strength to Japanese banks. Hoshi and Kashyap stress the reality that many banks remain undercapitalized and need to be recapitalized. Several ways to capitalize banks have been proposed and implemented. The government can inject capital into weak but solvent banks that are essential to the financial system's stability or in regional banks to support the local economy, as has been done in the past. If injected as shares, the government can sell these in the market, rather than having the bank pay the capital back to the government, in order to maintain capital.

Japan's banking system continues to be plagued by overbanking, resulting in very thin lending spreads and low profitability. As Hoshi and Kashyap make clear in their policy recommendations, even ending deflation and restoring good economic growth will not be sufficient to create a competitive banking system within a reasonable time period. Moreover, once the economy returns to normal and interest rates rise, Japanese banks will suffer losses on their immense government bond portfolios; it is not certain that gains in their stock holdings will be sufficient to cover these losses. The major Japanese banks need both to improve their information technology infrastructure and to develop new, fee-based sources of income, still extraordinarily low by international comparison. The traditional bank model of accepting deposits and lending these funds is no longer profitable since large, sound firms can raise funds and borrow through the capital market. Japan's banks are slow to adapt to a new deregulated environment by changing their business model, and this needs to change (see Hoshi and Kashyap, 2001; Hoshi and Patrick, 2000; and Ishigaki and Hiro, 1998).

Bank restructuring has progressed more slowly for regional and local banking institutions, especially second-tier banks and credit associations, many of which continue to have severe non-performing loan problems. The June 2004 legislation providing 2 trillion yen (about $18 billion) of government funds to facilitate bank rescues and mergers by injecting needed capital without declaring them insolvent signals that the Financial Services Agency is finally prepared to tackle regional bank balance sheet problems. How strongly and effectively this agency will move, and how the politically powerful local banking institutions will respond, remains a serious concern.

In Japan the government is an exceptionally large financial intermediary. The post office system, through postal savings accounts, holds some 30% of total household deposits and 37% of the life insurance industry's gross assets, both far larger amounts than held by any private financial institution. Some of these funds are invested in government bonds, but a significant portion, together with government-controlled monies, are transferred to a host of government financial institutions and special public corporations through the Ministry of Finance's Fiscal Investment and Loan Program (FILP) and other channels which have recently been put in place by FILP reforms introduced in April 2001. Nonetheless, these financial flows, and government financial institutions and special public corporation activities, have been very opaque.

In chapter 6 Doi provides the first careful, detailed English-language analysis of government financial institutions and special public corporations, each of which is a major source both of the burgeoning government debt and increases in government financial claims on the private sector. However, these entities have huge non-performing loans (on the order of 36 trillion yen) which are yet to be addressed. Doi focuses on 10 major government financial institutions and special public corporation, which together make about 20% of total loans to the private sector and an even larger share for small business and for household mortgages.

As the economy has matured and the financial system has been fundamentally deregulated and liberalized, Doi stresses that many government financial institutions have become weak and redundant, and their economic rationales have evaporated. Government financial institutions distort markets by competing unfairly with the private sector. They are inefficient because their activities are explicitly or implicitly guaranteed by the government; this soft budget constraint means that deficits are inevitably covered by government subsidies. The potential liabilities of the government are open-ended, as there are no clear bankruptcy statutes for the government financial institutions or the special public corporations.

Doi identifies the specific set of problems for each major government financial institution or special public corporation and proposes appropriate solutions. More broadly, he recommends that these government institutions be required to raise funds by selling their bonds in the market, as has only just begun, in order to impose market discipline. However, so far the spreads show the market views these bonds as having at least an implicit government guarantee. Doi also recommends that some institutions be closed and that the others be transformed into state-owned companies with limited liability and a hard budget constraint.

Reforming the postal system through privatization has long been a major priority for Prime Minister Junichiro Koizumi, despite opposition from many of his fellow LDP politicians who benefit from the local power of the special postmasters in some 24,000 post offices. The Koizumi government now has underway proposals for major privatization of the postal system over a long-term (17-year) period (see Cargill and Yashiro, 2003). How this will play out politically and economically is not at all clear. Assuming some bill will be passed, what will be the specific details of privatization embodied in the legislation? How effective will they be? How will the post-Koizumi government actually implement or alter any policies enacted by the Koizumi administration. In our view, this will continue to be a contentious yet important issue for several more years. Nonetheless the major economic issues are clear.

Japan's postal system has three business lines: mail delivery service, postal savings accounts, and postal life insurance. Each function is a giant in its respective industry, so simple privatization will create huge institutions with strong market power, in conflict with a good solution in terms of competition policy. Moreover, as Doi points out, cross-subsidies are a source of unfair competition. However, separating each business line into regional divisions could reduce the value of the services provided to households.

The incumbent provider of postal delivery services, the Ministry of Public Management, Home Affairs, Posts and Telecommunications, argues that mail service should be universal, and that private-sector entrants should be required to provide universal service. This stance would make new-entry prohibitively expensive. Package deliveries are competitive markets, as several private-sector delivery services and the postal system compete with each other. Private companies argue that the postal system has an unfair advantage because it does not pay taxes on their real estate holding or profits.

The postal savings and postal life insurance systems compete directly and powerfully with private financial institutions. In an effort to deregulate and privatize postal financial services, there are several absolutely necessary requirements, and others that are more controversial. The first requirement in reforming the postal saving system is that it should have to pay the same deposit insurance premium as banks. This change would achieve a level playing field and eliminate the government's current free guarantee of deposits. The postal savings system may be effective in collecting deposits, but it has little expertise in the portfolio management of these funds; it has no capability to make efficient, informed loan decisions. However, the Ministry of Finance wants the postal system to expand into lending operations. Doi proposes that the system be transformed into a narrow bank, that accepts savings deposits but only holds government bonds as assets. This would obviate any increases in banking services in an already over-crowded financial system, and eliminate the need to develop expertise in providing lending services. It also eliminates the threat of market power, while providing depositors with safe assets and the government with continued ready access to household savings.

In his chapter on the life insurance industry, Fukao incorporates an analysis of the government postal life insurance system (*Kampo*), which controls more assets than the five largest private companies combined. Kampo receives substantial government subsidies, explicit and implicit, including tax exemption, government guarantees, and cross-selling with deposits. These subsidies should be addressed first. How to privatize postal life insurance while ending its excessive market power is one of the key challenges of any privatization program.

Fukao paints a stark picture of the life insurance industry from the 1990s to the present. The private-sector now comprises some 40 companies of which many are new entrants, both Japanese and foreign firms, following reduced entry restrictions in the 1990s. Seven traditional companies failed in the 1990s due to weak management of interest rate risks, excessive exposure to stock market declines, perverse incentives, and lax regulatory supervision; in fact, though not reported at the time, these firms were deeply insolvent when they went bankrupt and were sold off.

Fukao focuses on the 10 major companies that together now have a dominant market share of the life insurance industry. The fundamental problem for all these firms is negative carry, the fact that the guaranteed rates of return on policies sold prior to the mid-1990s are substantially above the current rates of return on company assets in Japan's low interest-rate environment. As a consequence, these life insurance companies are suffering losses and depletion of their capital. Fukao shows that the adjusted solvency ratios are substantially weaker than reported, and several companies are in considerable difficulty. If negative carry persists, more firms may go bankrupt or be forced to reduce the guaranteed rates to policyholders, the latter of which is now allowed but will have adversely affect their reputations in increasingly competitive markets.

Fukao also analyzes the problems of this industry's poor asset-liability management, weak corporate governance, weak regulatory supervision, double-gearing between life insurance companies and banks, and the market distortions generated by Kampo. He proposes a range of policies to restore the industry's strength, including more effective supervision and regulation, ending the inclusion of deferred tax assets in the measurement of their capital, and the prohibition of double gearing.

Chapters 5–7 make clear how significant the remaining problems of financial system reform are, and propose what should be done. Structural reform of Japan's banks, life insurance companies, and especially its government financial institutions is essential to overcome distortions in resource allocation and economic activities.

6 Corporate Restructuring and Financing

All sectors, companies, and households have suffered through Japan's long period of economic malaise. Credit is the life blood of all businesses, and the banking system's profound weaknesses have had great adverse spill-over effects on all economic activity, as Iwaisako discusses in his chapter analyzing business investment and restructuring. Well functioning, competitive banking and financial systems are essential to allocate resources more efficiently so as to increase GDP.

Although corporate restructuring has made some progress, much remains to be done before Japan can become a normal, efficient economy based on competitive markets unimpeded by large amounts of nonperforming assets. The average return on equity remains low in international comparison, and the gap between strong and weak firms in all size categories has widened. In addition to the highly publicized cases of very large, inefficient, heavily indebted zombie firms subsisting on credit rollover and new injections from main banks, many small- and medium-sized enterprises remain weak due to a combination of still-huge debt burdens and lost competitiveness in a changing domestic and global business environment. The government made progress on this front by creating the Industrial Revitalization Corporation Japan in April 2003, a semi-public arm of corporate restructuring. Together with the main banks, it takes stakes in and restructures the overly-indebted companies. Firms with good cash flow have focused primarily on paying down debt to restore balance sheets. However, too many firms have yet to develop, much less implement, more effective business models. Restructuring inefficient government special corporations and agencies so far has been quite slow. These problems will endure even after the private-sector economy returns to a stable equilibrium growth path.

Iwaisako notes that business investment has slowed to about 15% of GDP, but is still higher than in the United States and certainly high relative to the GDP growth rate. The slowdown in business investment was due primarily to lack of business demand and the need to restore balance sheet equilibrium by paying down debt, despite a brief credit crunch in late 1997 and early 1998. Iwaisako identifies as a major problem the slowdown in productivity growth, due in part to the slowdown in the reallocation of capital and labor across industries. He identifies the misallocation of bank credit as a serious problem. Because banks are weak and insiders in the non-performing loan problems, they have continued lending to weak borrowers, termed evergreening. Banks have not been able to engage in their earlier monitoring and restructuring roles as outside, objective arbiters.

New private financial institutions engaged in business restructuring have developed only since the late 1990s. Not surprisingly, restructuring brings to the fore conflicts between conventional business practices based on management control and the painful requirements of restructuring and of new corporate governance modes. Most restructuring has been taking place through normal private-market mechanisms and this is desirable. Government policies have been supportive, especially in legal and institutional changes to make management decision choices, corporate governance, and capital markets more effective.

Yet government policies to deal with the asset management difficulties of large, virtually insolvent Japanese companies have been ad hoc and partial. This is in stark contrast to countries such as Korea, in which a government asset management company was established and required to purchase bad bank loans, with the government temporarily taking over majority ownership of the banks. The Japanese government established the Reconstruction and Collection Corporation in the mid-1990s, but it has served mainly to take over non-performing loans of financial institutions in difficulty, and has not concentrated much on the restructuring of the corporate borrowers. The Industrial Revitalization Corporation Japan is more active in restructuring large companies but inevitably will have a relatively limited direct role since it has only a five year charter.

Iwaisako considers two important cases of government intervention in restructuring corporate debt. One is the nationalization of the Long-Term Credit Bank, the terms of its eventual sale to Ripplewood, and its re-establishment as Shinsei Bank. He notes that the government and business community were implicitly expecting Shinsei to play according to the existing game, in effect to keep lending to existing borrowers regardless of quality, not to exercise the put option on non-performing loans they had taken on, and in general not to rock the boat. Instead Shinsei behaved as a rational economic actor. This incurred the wrath of traditionalists, but was ultimately a successful strategy. The second case was the placing of the excessively diversified, heavily indebted Kanebo into the Industrial Revitalization Corporation Japan process in mid-2004. Management was changed, equity was written off as were a considerable portion of the bank loans, the successful cosmetics division is being sold, and the non-profitable divisions are being restructured, sold or closed.

Iwaisako draws several conclusions. Restructuring often needs a third, outside, party that is not involved in embedded and tangled long-term relationships among the company, its main banks, and other interested players. Government intervention should be limited in order not to crowd out private market restructuring efforts; it is desirable only when there are obvious market failures, as generous government bail-outs come at the expense of taxpayers and healthy competitors. He judges the Industrial Revitalization Corporation Japan to have been successful. However, Iwaisako is more skeptical of the increasingly extensive restructuring activities of the Development Bank of Japan, which is more vulnerable to political pressure and because its objective to ensure its own survival may be more important than efficient resource allocation.

Efficient corporate restructuring usually involves downsizing, including reducing the numbers of employees. In Japan, job cuts have been mostly through natural attrition and, in extreme cases, early retirement buy-outs. As Hashimoto and Higuchi discuss in chapter 10, labor market adjustments inevitably are specific, depending on age, skill, gender, and geographical location. They propose programs to enhance labor mobility, including training programs to ensure the smooth transition of workers to new employers rather than trying to protect existing jobs. They also emphasize the importance of good GDP growth to reduce unemployment, increase labor force participation rates through new employment, and make the reallocation of labor easier.

Most Japanese corporate finance has continued to be provided by banks and, especially for small- and medium-sized enterprises, government financial institutions. The government's Big Bang policies of the late 1990s have accelerated the development of capital markets. Nonetheless, the Tokyo capital market is still relatively costly, and the legal framework does not adhere to international best practices. Its rules and regulations are not foreigner-friendly; prospectuses and balance sheets have to be written in Japanese. Stock transactions and registrations are now electronically based, registration of ownership can be done with the stock depository, and changes in ownership are much easier than before. Further development of the Tokyo capital market is necessary.

In chapter 9 Fujii analyzes the development of Japan's corporate bond market since the late 1990s, which is important because bond issuance will become a significant source of business finance, as it is in other advanced countries. She uses her own survey of participants in the Tokyo capital market, and analyzes market effectiveness through bond pricing models. Respondents identified taxation issues and lack of human capital (professional expertise) as major problems.

Prior to deregulation culminating in the Big Bang financial reforms, regulations restricted corporate bond issues to only a few top-class companies. Now government restrictions on corporate bond issuance are minimal, and previously high issuance costs have been reduced substantially. However, a market has not yet developed for high yield, below investment-grade, bonds. Nor has an appropriately priced middle-market evolved for more risky bank loans. Fujii concludes that corporate bond market pricing is working reasonably well because prices and their credit-default swaps are consistent based on monthly data. Estimates of changes in the implied ratings by credit rating agencies and their actual bond ratings move together quite closely. Nonetheless, liquidity remains low.

Fujii recommends that Japan's government encourage the private market by leaving it alone, while making appropriate changes in the tax code to ensure that tax treatment is equal and neutral. Market participants, Japanese and foreign, have to develop and apply increasingly sophisticated financial technology, rather than relying on government policy prescriptions. She recommends that the government stay away from attempting to regulate high-risk markets, such as venture capital, distressed assets, and high-yield bonds. Of course there are areas where the government regulators should take useful initiatives, such as providing a more efficient settlement system and specific measures to reduce barriers that raise administrative costs.

7 Japan's New Trade Policy

Japan's foreign economic policy has long been founded on its comprehensive security, political, and economic alliance with the United States; its commitment to an open, globally multilateral trading system under the first General Agreement on Trade and Tariffs and how its successor the World Trade Organization; and the market-based system of global financial and direct investment flows (see Lincoln, 1999). Japan and the United States have provided learning experiences and models for each other, as exemplified in this volume by the Harrigan and Kuttner chapter on lessons for American macroeconomic policies taken from Japan's experience with deflation. These approaches and commitments have not changed. However, a new strategic dimension has emerged in response to the increasing reliance on regional trading arrangements by the United States and the European Union, and due to China's rise as an economic power. Japan also has embarked on a new trade policy, one of bilateral cooperation under free trade agreements or, more comprehensively, economic partnership agreements.

Traditionally, Asian countries have not formed significant preferential trading arrangements. The ASEAN Free Trade Area is a regional trade agreement, but the lowering of tariffs among its 10 Southeast Asian members has been slow. Japan, Korea, and China were the only three outliers, as they had not joined any regional preferential agreements. Japan's first free trade agreement, with Singapore, became effective in 2002. Korea concluded its first negotiated free trade agreement, with Chile, in 2004. Now there are frenzied free trade negotiations among all the Asian nations. China has just signed a free trade agreement with ASEAN. Thailand is negotiating more than a dozen free trade agreements. The United States has negotiated a free trade agreement with Singapore and Australia. Japan signed one with Mexico in 2004, and is negotiating separately with the Philippines, Thailand, Malaysia, and

Korea, as well as with ASEAN as a group. How these will shape trading arrangements in Asia remains to be seen.

In chapter 11 Urata explains Japan's trade policy motivations and strategy, and strongly recommends that Japan pursue free trade agreements in a manner complementary to the World Trade Organization. One reason is defensive. In the worst case scenario, Japan may become isolated from a world characterized by three dominant free trade zones—the greatly expanded European Union; the North American Free Trade Agreement (NAFTA) governing Canada, Mexico and the United States, the proposed Free Trade Area of the Americas and ongoing American bilateral free trade negotiations; and an expanded ASEAN Free Trade Area with an increasingly powerful China. Another motivation arises from Japan's increasing policy focus on East Asia, the world's most rapidly growing economic region. The 1997–98 currency, financial, and economic crisis greatly increased East Asian interest in greater regional economic cooperation. Urata argues that free trade agreements will both expand Japan's market access in trade and investment and contribute to Asian economic growth. Japan's policy approach is more comprehensive than liberalizing trade barriers; it focuses on investment, movements of skilled workers, and facilitation and cooperation in a range of areas. In this respect, Japan aims to support the global system by addressing and testing solutions to a range of international economic issues not currently covered by the World Trade Organization. At its best, in Urata's view, an effective policy of free trade agreements can be a catalyst for Japan's economic revitalization.

Urata recognizes that the strongest Japanese opponents to this new free trade policy are the powerful domestic protectionist forces and lobbies, particularly in agriculture, fisheries, and other labor-intensive sectors which are Japan's most economically inefficient industries. The conflicts between these sectors and other business and industrial interests have become increasingly open and pronounced, in part due to the negotiation realities of free trade agreements. For some, the free trade approach reflects foreign pressure (gaiatsu) to force changes that are overdue on these domestic issues. Japan needs a fundamental reform in its approach to these inefficient sectors, perhaps by shifting to a system of guaranteed income subsidies for existing farmers combined with free imports and acceptance of world prices that will benefit consumer welfare. Even without dramatic policy solutions, these sectors will gradually weaken due to a lack of interest among young people in working in them, and domestic policies will have to move toward a more efficient resource allocation. The question is how soon and how efficiently these changes will occur. Until Japanese policymakers can overcome the domestic protectionist forces, it will be very difficult to pursue and implement a comprehensive free trade strategy because Japan's trading partners will insist on access to these protected markets.

8 Major Policy Recommendations

Comprehensive and detailed policy recommendations are made by the chapters' authors, founded on their careful analysis. We do not attempt to summarize their recommendations here, but offer a few broad near-term and medium to long-term policy recommendations based on the analyses provided in this volume.

Japan's highest priority in the near-term is to end deflation and put its economy back on a good, sustainable growth track, still far from being achieved as of the beginning of 2005. Since a substantial output gap still exists, growing above its long term potential for a few years will not cause substantial inflation. Growth should be supported by monetary and fiscal policy to ensure adequate aggregate demand. Until the price-level target described by Ito and Mishkin is achieved, continuing the zero interest rate policy and quantitative easing is appropriate. The Bank of Japan should learn from the United States Federal Reserve Board in carefully avoiding deflation as well as inflation, as suggested by Harrigan and Kuttner. Once sustained growth is achieved, the fiscal situation can be dealt with in the medium- and longer-run, as Broda and Weinstein show.

Restoring health to banks and insurance companies is another key task to getting the economy back on track. Hoshi and Kashyap, and Fukao, in their respective studies, emphasize the importance of rigorous supervision and regulation, together with rigorous implementation by the Financial Services Agency to restore financial institution balance sheets and to create the right incentives. Regional and local banking institutions in particular need to reduce their still-high non-performing loans, which entail substantial restructuring, merger and consolidation. Solvency margin regulations and rules for life insurance companies have to be tightened, as Fukao strongly asserts.

We do not endorse the "cleansing view" that recessions effectively and naturally improve resource allocations and bring about adequate structural reform, and indeed Japan's past 14 years of malaise indicate that is not the result. As the economy recovers, reforming and restructuring policies and efforts should be strengthened for all financial institutions and businesses, private and governmental. The full and effective utilization of labor in appropriate jobs, as detailed by Hashimoto and Higuchi, and the effective reallocation of capital as emphasized by Iwaisako, is the way to enhance productivity improvements and achieve better growth in both the near and medium terms. In particular the creation of better job opportunities for younger Japanese workers is essential to maintaining a highly skilled labor force. In addition, existing market and social norms have meant that in Japan female labor is not allocated well. Institutional support for child-bearing and child-caring women is essential to take advantage of their potential productivities, and appropriate policies could increase the incentives to have children, thereby raising the fertility rate. Better-functioning capital markets, especially the further development of the corporate bond market, will contribute to the more effective allocation of resources, as Fujii argues.

In the medium to longer-term, once deflation is over and sustained growth is achieved, the Bank of Japan should adopt some form of inflation targeting, preferably explicit, as is proposed by Ito and Mishkin. Then it will be possible to reduce, even eliminate, government budget deficits, and stabilize the government gross and net debt ratios relative to gross domestic product. As Broda and Weinstein show, fiscal sustainability can be achieved without huge increases in taxes so long as the transition costs are financed over a sufficiently long time period. Structural reforms of the government financial institutions and special public corporations, and of local government institutions, as Doi forcefully argues, are essential in order to allocate resources more efficiently and to reduce the government's contingent liabilities inherent in the existing soft budget system. For social and political reasons, reforming government institutions cannot be accomplished quickly, but the process has to begin and be strengthened now. The Japanese government's fiscal difficulties provide policymakers an incentive to make the difficult decisions the governmental reforms necessarily entail.

Two aspects of Japan's relations with other countries, particularly those in Asia, are especially significant in the medium to longer term. One is the development of free trade agreements and, more precisely, economic partnership agreements to liberalize trade and investment flows, as Urata argues. The deepening of Japan's economic integration with its neighbors has significant political and security implications that probably exceed these economic benefits. The other aspect is for

Japanese to decide what is the appropriate role of foreign workers in their economy. In an immediate context, in free trade agreement discussions with Japan, the demands of Thailand and the Philippines for liberalized worker visas are stimulating Japanese debate over these issues, with a generally positive view. But in the longer-run with Japan's aging and declining population looming, the issue of how and to what degree to allow and even encourage foreign-worker immigration must be squarely faced.

We are confident that in due course the Japanese economy can and will rise again. The nation's economic and social fundamentals are still strong. As the government and private sectors accept and implement the policy recommendations contained in this volume, the economy will do better on both the demand and supply sides. While Japan's near-term growth potential is quite high because of under-utilized labor and other resources, even in the longer-run it is not only quite likely but probable that the Japanese will achieve per capita GDP growth rates at least as good as is the average for the other G7 countries. Japan will continue to be a major global economic player and technology leader, far ahead of the rest of Asia and second only to the United States. And the standard of living and economic well-being of Japan will continue to improve, a fundamental objective of this and indeed all economic analysis.

References

There is an extensive professional literature in Japanese and English on various aspects of Japan's economy over the past 15 years. Most is in the form of journal articles. Since the authors of the other chapters refer to the literature in their respective fields, we limit our references primarily to relevant books in English as general background.

Amyx, Jennifer. 2004. *Japan's Financial Crisis: Institutional Rigidity and Reluctant Change.* Princeton, NJ: Princeton University Press.

Blomstrom, Magnus, Jenny Corbett, Fumio Hayashi, and Anil Kashyap, editors. 2003. *Structural Impediments to Growth in Japan.* Chicago: University of Chicago Press.

Cargill, Thomas and Naoyuki Yoshino. 2003. *Postal Savings and Fiscal Investment in Japan.* New York: Oxford University Press.

Cargill, Thomas, Michael M. Hutchison, and Takatoshi Ito. 1997. *The Political Economy of Japanese Monetary Policy.* Cambridge, MA: MIT Press.

Cargill, Thomas F., Michael M. Hutchison, and Takatoshi Ito. 2001. *Financial Policy and Central Banking in Japan.* Cambridge, MA: MIT Press.

Doi, Takero and Takeo Hoshi. 2003. Paying for the FILP. In *Structural Impediments to Growth in Japan.* (Chicago: University of Chicago Press). Originally published as NBER Working Paper 9385 (December 2002).

Hoshi, Takeo and Anil Kashyap. 2001. *Corporate Financing and Governance in Japan: The Road to the Future.* Cambridge, MA: MIT Press.

Hoshi, Takeo and Hugh Patrick, editors. 2000. *Crisis and Change in the Japanese Financial System.* Innovations in Financial Markets and Institutions, vol. 12. Boston: Kluwer Academic Publishers.

Ihori, Toshihiro and Masakazu Sato, editors. 2002. *Government Deficit and Fiscal Reform in Japan.* Innovations in Financial Markets and Institutions, vol. 7. Boston: Kluwer Academic Publishers.

Ishigaki, Kenichi and Hiroyuki Hino, editors. 1998. *Toward the Restoration of Sound Banking Systems in Japan – The Global Implications.* Kobe: Kobe University Press and International Monetary Fund.

Ito, Takatoshi. 1992. *The Japanese Economy.* Cambridge, MA: MIT Press.

______. 2004. Inflation Targeting and Japan: Why has the Bank of Japan not adopted Inflation Targeting? In *The Future of Inflation Targeting,* 220–267, editors C. Kent and S. Guttmann. Canberra: Reserve Bank of Australia.

Katz, Richard. 1998. Japan: *The System That Soured: The Rise and Fall of the Japanese Economic Miracle.* Armonk, NY: M.E. Sharpe.

______. 2002. *Japanese Phoenix: The Long Road to Economic Revival.* Armonk, NY: M.E. Sharpe.

Lincoln, Edward J. 1999. *Troubled Times: U.S.-Japan Trade Relations in the 1990s.* Washington, D.C.: Brookings Institute Press.

Mikitani, Ryoichi and Adam Posen. 2000. *Japan's Financial Crisis and its Parallels to U.S. Experience.* Washington, D.C.: Institution for International Economics.

Organization for Economic Cooperation and Development. 2004. *OECD Economic Surveys – Japan.* Paris: OECD.

Patrick, Hugh. 2004. The Japanese Economy: Sustained Recovery and Growth Not Yet Assured. *Center on Japanese Economy and Business, Annual Report 2003–2004.* New York: Columbia University Publications.

Porter, Michael, Hirotaka Takeuchi, and Mariko Sakakibara. 2000. *Can Japan Compete?* Cambridge, MA: Perseus.

Posen, Adam. 1998. *Restoring Japan's Economic Growth.* Washington, D.C.: Institute for International Economics.

Saxonhouse, Gary R. and Robert M. Stern, editors. 2003. The Bubble and the Lost Decade. *The World Economy* 26: (March) 267–381.

Sato, Mari and Hiroko Sato, editors. 1997. *Japanese Labour and Management in Transition: Diversity, Flexibility and Participation.* London: Routledge.

Teranishi, Juro. 2005. *Evolution of the Economic System in Japan.* Northampton, MA: Edward Elgar.

Part I

Macroeconomic Policy

2

Happy News from the Dismal Science: Reassessing Japanese Fiscal Policy and Sustainability

Christian Broda

and

David E. Weinstein

The idea that Japan is on the verge of a government fiscal crisis is such an accepted commonplace that it seems pointless to venture back into well-trodden terrain.[1] The news media is rife with reports of government debt to GDP ratios approaching 200 percent, budget deficits amounting to 10 percent of GDP, lower future growth due to a shrinking labor force, and an aging population that will result in a doubling of the ratio of public pension and medical benefit recipients to the employed. Add to this the announcement in May 2002 by Moody's that it downgraded Japanese government debt to a level equal to that of Mauritius and several other developing countries, and it is no wonder that so many people have predicted a meltdown of government finances.

And yet, there are valid reasons for questioning these dire predictions. To understand why, remember that a fiscal crisis that could not be resolved through higher taxes or lower expenditures would result in one of two outcomes: either the government would default on its debt or, more likely, it would be forced to print money and inflate in order to cover its obligations. In either case, expectation of a fiscal crisis would imply that holders of long-term government debt face considerable risk. If this risk is high, then the yield on long-term government bonds should be higher today in order to compensate bond holders for future expected losses due to default or inflation. In other words, the long-term bond market is designed to price inflation and default risk. However, in 2003, the yield on newly-issued 20-year Japanese government bonds (JGBs) fluctuated between 0.8% and 1.9% while the yield for 10-year bonds moved between 0.5% and 1.5% (MOF website). Given that the amount of long-term JGBs outstanding was 172 trillion yen in 2001 or 34 percent of GDP, this suggests that there is a vast amount of money betting that Japan will pay off its debt through conventional fiscal policy.[2]

One possible explanation for the calmness of the bond market is that bond holders are confused or that there is some market imperfection underlying the low rates.[3] While this might be true, the vast amount of money betting against a fiscal crisis suggests that it might be fruitful to consider an alternative explanation—namely that bond holders actually know what they are doing and that the stories of a future fiscal meltdown are ultimately not that convincing. In order to explore this alternate scenario, we will question the data, the theory, and the forecasts underlying the predictions of a fiscal crisis. Our findings suggest that by using the correct data, better theory, and more sensible forecasts, our understanding of the history and potential future of Japan's fiscal policy is radically altered.

1 Theory: What Do We Mean by Fiscal Sustainability?

The key policy question is whether Japan may be forced into a fiscal crisis at some future point in time. To answer this, it is necessary to determine just what is a sustainable fiscal policy. Only then is it possible to clearly identify a set of policies that are consistent with fiscal sustainability and that can guide policymakers to achieve this goal.

Following Blanchard (1990), we define a fiscal policy as sustainable if the current policy can be continued indefinitely with a stable government debt-to-GDP ratio. If the deficits are too high, the stock of government debt expands until the private sector ceases being willing or able to supply the government with credit, forcing a crisis in the form of monetizing or repudiating the debt. Similarly, if surpluses are too high, the government is forced to purchase private assets and gradually nationalize the economy. Of course, many short run factors—macroeconomic shocks, fiscal stimulus packages, wars, etc—can cause a country's tax rate to deviate from this level in the short run. As such, the concept is most useful when thinking about long-run average tax rates.

Although we deal with certain "irrational" limits on government debt, we are more interested in the inevitability of a fiscal crisis than in whether one can construct scenarios in which a solvent government can be forced into crisis. Also, remember that irrationality, multiple equilibria, and political factors can make fiscal policy *more* likely to be sustainable. For example, a major question in public economics is why governments do not default even when the country would be better off doing so.[4]

Critical to determining whether a fiscal policy is sustainable is understanding the past and predicting the future. Reviewing past fiscal policy is a critical component of understanding the level of current liabilities of the Japanese government, as well as understanding what long-run average baseline tax and expenditure levels one should use in assessing sustainability. Unfortunately, the policy debate over the level of Japanese debt reflects confusion among some academics, market analysts, and government officials who often use gross debt levels as their starting point to assess Japan's fiscal sustainability, a focus which is equivalent to treating Japan's financial assets as worthless. This confusion can lead to an extremely misleading understanding of the current fiscal situation. Moreover, as Posen (1998) has pointed out, there also is deep confusion over what is meant by fiscal policy in Japan.

Forecasts of the future are, of course, problematic. Therefore, we provide a wide range of forecasts and demonstrate robustness over many "reasonable" views of the future. These forecasts require us to make projections about population and income dynamics, as well as what implicit and explicit obligations current and future generations have. We present the results from over 60 different scenarios about the future covering a wide range of possibilities of GDP and population growth rates, pension benefits, social welfare policies, monetary policies, and time horizons.

As this discussion suggests, there is more than a little art in constructing sustainability numbers. That, however, does not mean that these estimates are useless. In particular, sustainability calculations can give us guidance about how much adjustment is needed to achieve a particular policy and, moreover, what policy is likely to be implemented. For example, the Japanese may believe that its government should dramatically raise its per capita public pension benefits, and improve medical benefits for the elderly, dramatically expand per capita expenditures on younger people in the form of education and other social expenditures, while also expanding public investment as a share of GDP. That vision is not feasible without a significant rise in taxes. However, if one adopts a view that shifts in demographic categories imply proportional shifts in government transfers to that category—fewer children imply fewer schools rather than empty classrooms, for example—then our calculations suggest that sustainability may well be feasible with little adjustment.

Indeed, the main contribution of this chapter is to argue that the current debt and deficit levels in Japan have almost no impact on long-run sustainability calculations and that the "right" long-run tax level simply depends on the forecast of the "right" long-run expenditure level. As a result, the monetization or reduction of today's debt level does not have much impact on the sustainable tax rate. Put simply, if one forecasts that Japan will need to raise per capita government expenditures and transfers significantly in order to pay better pensions and elderly health costs, Japan's tax rates will have to rise to the levels that we see in a typical European country today. If Japan maintains a generous, but not too generous, growth in benefits, future outlays and taxes will look more like the current ones in the United States. Neither of these scenarios strikes us as reasons to worry about fiscal sustainability.

2 Computing Sustainability: Theory

It is useful to begin the description of the methodology used in this paper by reviewing some basic fiscal arithmetic that underlies any discussion of sustainability (c.f. Blanchard 1990). The government's intertemporal budget constraint is the natural starting point.

For our purposes, government expenditures (including transfers) are divided into one of three categories: public pension payments and medical benefits for the elderly, H_t; all other expenditures, except interest, G_t; and interest on the debt, where B_t is the level of government net debt and i_t is the interest rate on that debt. The elderly are defined, conventionally, as those 65 or older.

In period t it can be stated as follows:

$$(G_t + H_t + i_t B_{t-1}) - T_t = (B_t - B_{t-1}) + (M_t - M_{t-1}) \tag{1}$$

where T_t stands for fiscal revenues (e.g. taxes), H_t is transfers to the old, and G_t is other government non-interest expenditures. B_t and i_t are the level of government net debt and the interest rate on that debt in period t, respectively, and M_t is the money supply (i.e. base money) in period t. Equation (1) simply states that fiscal deficits (the left-hand side of (1)) can be financed by issuing new debt, $(B_t - B_{t-1})$, or through changes in money supply, $(M_t - M_{t-1})$.

It is useful to rewrite the government budget constraint in terms of ratios to GDP (in nominal terms), indicated by lowercase letters. Then, rearranging the government's budget constraint enables us to obtain the following expression of the government debt-to-GDP ratio, b_t:

$$b_t = g_t + h_t - \tau_t + \frac{1 + i_t}{1 + \eta_t} b_{t-1} - \lambda_t m_t \tag{2}$$

Here τ_t is T_t/GDP_t, η_t is the growth rate of nominal GDP, and λ_t is the growth rate of the nominal money supply. For reasons that will become clear below, we assume that $(i_t - \eta_t) \geq 0$, that is, the interest rate is greater than the growth rate of GDP.

Expressed in this way, the budget constraint implies that the evolution of the debt-to-GDP position, b_t, is a function of three components. The first component reflects the impact of current fiscal policy on b_t. A positive primary fiscal deficit, $g_t + h_t - \tau_t > 0$, raises b_t. The second component reflects the burden of the past debt level on the current level of b_t. With a nominal interest rate on government debt that exceeds the nominal growth rate of GDP, interest rate payments grow at a faster rate than GDP which implies that, *ceteris paribus*, the debt-to-GDP ratio, b_t, will increase relative to b_{t-1}. Third, conditional on the level of initial debt and primary deficit, a positive growth rate of the money supply implies a lower level of b_t because expansions in the money supply reduce the amount of debt (bonds) held by the private sector.

Equation (2) can be easily expanded to examine the relationship between debt-to-GDP ratios n years into the future with today's debt-to-GDP ratios. For notational simplicity, it is assumed that i_t and η_t are constant over time, and that today's level of debt-to-GDP is given by b_0. We can then express the level of debt-to-GDP in period n as:

$$b_n = \sum_{t=1}^{n} \left(\frac{1+i}{1+\eta}\right)^{n-t} (g_t + h_t - \tau_t - \lambda_t m_t) + \left(\frac{1+i}{1+\eta}\right)^{n} b_0 \tag{3}$$

This equation is central for the definition of fiscal sustainability that we adopt below. It states that the level of debt-to-GDP n periods into the future is the sum of the accumulated primary deficits that grow at the rate $(1 + i/1 + \eta)$, and the value of the initial level of debt raised by the same rate.

2.1 *Fiscal Sustainability Defined*

We can now proceed to define the concept of fiscal sustainability and derive an indicator that renders this definition operational. While there are several ways to define fiscal sustainability, we will follow closely the method suggested by Blanchard et al (1990). They define a fiscal policy as sustainable if the path of taxes and expenditures $\{g_t, h_t, \tau_t\}|_{t=1,\ldots,n}$ is such that the ratio of debt-to-GDP eventually converges back to its initial level over the finite horizon under consideration.[5]

Formally, by rearranging and pre-multiplying both sides of (3) by $(1 + \eta/1 + i)^n$ we obtain the crucial equation for sustainability:

$$\sum_{t=1}^{n}\left(\frac{1+\eta}{1+i}\right)^{t}(\tau_t - g_t - h_t + \lambda_t m_t) \geq b_0 - b_n\left(\frac{1+\eta}{1+i}\right)^{n} \quad (4)$$

The condition for fiscal sustainability n years into the future is that $b_n = b_0$. In other words, a fiscal policy is sustainable in n-years time if the present discounted value of the ratio of primary surpluses to GDP plus of monetary financing is greater than or equal to the difference between the current level of the debt-to-GDP ratio and the desired discounted debt-to-GDP ratio n periods ahead.[6] Simply put, this implies that a government with outstanding debt that faces interest rates in excess of growth rates ($i_t > \eta_t$) must eventually run a primary surplus or increase base money in order to achieve fiscal sustainability.

Several characteristics of a sustainable fiscal policy are noteworthy. First, there are a number of conceptually equivalent ways of deriving an indicator that assesses sustainability from equation (4). We will use an indicator of sustainability that relies on government revenues.[7] This enables us to answer the question of how costly will it be for Japan to stabilize its government debt and pay for a particular set of policies. As in Blanchard et al. we opt for an index of fiscal sustainability given by $(\tau^* - \tau)$, where τ^* is the constant tax rate ($\tau_t = \tau^* \forall t$) that solves (4) with equality for a given path of $\{\lambda_t, g_t, h_t, b_0\} \mid_{t=1,\ldots,n}$, and τ is the *actual* tax revenues-to-GDP ratio.[8] Formally,

$$\tau^* = \frac{i-\eta}{1+\eta}\left[b_0 + \left(1 - \left(\frac{1+\eta}{1+i}\right)^{n}\right)^{-1} \sum_{t=1}^{n}\left(\frac{1+\eta}{1+i}\right)^{t}(g_t + h_t - \lambda_t m_t)\right]. \quad (5)$$

This indicator has several desirable properties. First, τ^* has a simple interpretation. It is the constant tax rate that achieves an unchanged debt-to-GDP ratio over the relevant horizon, given forecasts of government spending. In addition, the difference between τ^* and τ, the tax "gap", is a measure of the size of the adjustment needed to attain sustainability were the adjustment to take place today. In general, what a positive tax gap implies for different countries depends on the initial level of τ. If τ is high, a positive gap is probably more worrisome than if τ is low, as the chance of having to resort to monetization or repudiation increases if existing tax pressures are already high.

Another important characteristic of sustainable fiscal policy is related to the role played by the discount factor $(1 + \eta/1 + i)$. Consider the case where the average nominal interest rate on government bonds is lower than the nominal growth rate, $i_t - \eta_t < 0$, which is known as the "dynamic inefficiency" case. In such a case, or when capital accumulation has exceeded the optimal level,[9] equation (3) implies that an economy can run a constant deficit forever without ever having to monetize or worry that it's debt-to-GDP ratio will explode. Here, concerns on explosive debt-to-GDP paths are unwarranted because the economy can grow out of any debt problem. Interestingly, we have observed long periods in Japan's history where $i_t - \eta_t < 0$ (i.e. the average nominal interest rate on government bonds was lower than the nominal growth rate).[10] Nevertheless, we will follow convention and assume that $i_t - \eta_t$ is positive.[11] In the next section, we calculate the sustainable tax rate for different values of $i_t - \eta_t$ and we discuss the most relevant case for Japan in the future.

A requirement that is not completely justified from this definition of sustainability is that the ratio of debt-to-GDP has to return to its initial level rather than any other finite level of debt. For instance, a policy aimed to stabilize the debt-to-GDP ratio at 40 percent rather than 20 percent should not be characterized as an unsustainable policy. While this is certainly true, changing the level of finite desired debt n periods ahead has a relatively small effect on the sustainable tax rates when n is large enough. This is because of discounting, which implies that two different levels of debt-to-GDP far in the future, say 100 years from now, can arise from nearly exactly the same sustainable tax rate today; in the limit, as n grows to infinity, they make no difference.[12] Finally, note that the fiscal policy that is sustainable for n periods ahead many not be sustainable over a shorter period. For example, we will show that it is much harder for Japan to keep the debt level stabilized over a 35 year period than over a 100 year period.

3 Computing Sustainability

The previous section made clear that in order to perform a sustainability calculation one must know what the current level of debt is, what the evolution of government expenditures is likely to be, what economic growth is likely to look like, and what is likely to happen with monetary policy. We will make estimates of each variable in turn.

3.1 *Government Debt*

Conceptually, government debt in a sustainability calculation corresponds to the current amount of net liabilities held by the government.[13] In practice, this is government assets less liabilities or net government debt. One wants to focus on net debt because government borrowing used to finance government lending does not need to be paid off with taxes. Revenue generated by the repayment of government loans can be used to cover borrowed funds in much the same way that a bank's lending portfolio offsets the liabilities created by the deposit accounts. (We will make adjustments for bad loans later.) Given that the Bank of Japan (2004) reports that 40 percent of all lending in Japan is made by public financial institutions, focusing only on the liability side of the balance sheet without adjusting for the substantial assets on the other side, can easily lead to an overly pessimistic view of the government's financial health. Similarly, Japan's foreign exchange reserves (financed by bond issues), which total to 18 percent of GDP [see the Ito and Patrick chapter in this volume], constitute an important reason why net and gross debt diverge.

The accounting method used in Japan for transfers of funds within the government can create misunderstanding regarding debt levels. Certain accounts run surpluses because tax revenue exceeds expenditures (e.g. public pensions until 1994 in the case of Japan) while other accounts run deficits. In a consolidated or "unified budget" accounting system, all tax revenue is pooled together and bonds are issued to cover any aggregate difference between expenditures and revenues. In the Japanese system, by contrast, accounts are kept separate, and so surpluses in one account are lent to another. For example, surplus funds in the social security system may be used to make deposits in other government accounts, e.g. the Fiscal Investment and Loan Program. When these transfers occur, the social security account receives an asset in the form of a deposit and the other branch of the government records a liability of the same magnitude.

This system is useful for understanding the history of past intra-governmental transfers and expectations of future transfers, but it can be very confusing when thinking about the net worth of the public sector. For example, in a consolidated accounting system, if the social security tax raises one hundred yen of revenue and rest of the government spends one hundred yen, the debt of the government would equal zero. In the Japanese system, however, this transfer of say, one hundred yen, often involves the purchase of a bond or the creation of a government deposit account. Hence, the same transfer would involve the general account borrowing from the social security system, which creates a liability for the general account of one hundred yen, and the social security system obtaining an asset (i.e a deposit in the government) worth 100 yen. In both accounting systems, the financial implications to the aggregate public sector are identical, but the accounting practices would make the balance sheets look quite different—the consolidated government debt would be zero, but the unconsolidated accounts would show a *gross* Japanese government debt of one hundred yen. Of course, in the unconsolidated accounts the Japanese government would have a one hundred yen asset to offset the one hundred yen liability so net debt in the two systems would be identical, but the point remains that the gross debt would look quite different. This underscores the importance of looking at public assets less liabilities or net government debt.

Unfortunately, the most commonly used number in popular and some academic discussion of Japanese debt is what is called "gross debt" in official government statistics. It corresponds to total liabilities of the central and local governments including the social security system. In FY2002, this number stood at 161 percent of GDP, which was higher than any other country in the OECD [BOJ and OECD website]. However, just as it would have been wrong to have assumed that Japan was in worse financial health in the previous example because the government owed one hundred yen to itself, one should be deeply skeptical that gross debt numbers contain much—*if any*—information about fiscal health. Indeed, they can be highly misleading. To make this point concrete, the value of the net debt of the Japanese public sector was only 64 percent of GDP in FY2002.[14] In other words, the gross debt number overstates the fiscal problem by a factor of 2.5! To put this into perspective, Japan's level of net debt in 2002 was not that much above the Maastricht Treaty's upper bound of 60 percent for membership in the EU and well below the level of high debt countries like Italy and Belgium.

The standard net debt number, however, also overstates Japanese government debt levels because it does not take into account bonds held by the Bank of Japan.[15] How to treat holdings by the BOJ depends on what one's forecast of monetary policy predicts. If one assumes that the money base will not change as a share of GDP, then debt held by the central bank never needs to be repaid and one does not need to count the bonds held by the central bank as a liability of the consolidated government. This will constitute our baseline scenario. However we will also consider the implications of a substantial increases and decreases in the monetary base. The reason why this matters is that the BOJ owns a large amount of the outstanding JGBs. Although bonds held by the BOJ are not counted as part of the government net debt, the 80 trillion yen worth of government securities held by the BOJ and 10 trillion yen in BOJ financial surplus in 2002 means that if one assumes that the money base will not change, the net debt of the consolidated Japanese public sector was only 46 percent—only 29 percent of the number that is typically used.[16]

Pessimists will be quick to point out that this number does not make allowances for future obligations of the Japanese government. These allowances will enter into our sustainability calculation, but they should not be counted as a part of current net liabilities. Doing so is worse than wrong; it can lead to misleading predictions about the efficacy of monetary policy in reducing the debt.

Suppose, for example, that it is true that Japan faces major future deficits due to the aging of the population. Now consider the impact of a one time unanticipated 100 percent rise in the Japanese price level that cuts the value of nominal government debt in half. Since the level of net debt is 46 percent of GDP, then this large inflation would only reduce the real government debt by a relatively modest 23 percent of GDP and do nothing about the *future* liabilities (assuming they are all indexed to inflation). By contrast, if one mistakenly counted future liabilities as current liabilities by working with the gross debt figure of 161 percent, one would erroneously calculate that a doubling in the price level would reduce the real debt burden of the Japanese public sector by 81 percent of GDP! The difference between the numbers arises from the fact that the gross debt number double counts (or really quadruple counts) current liabilities and undercounts future liabilities. As this simple example makes clear, using the right data can make a big difference for policy analysis. If one erroneously uses gross debt instead of net debt, one would be tempted to see inflation as a solution to Japan's debt problem, when in fact it is not because, as we will soon see, the problem is not the current level of liabilities but the future level.[17]

3.2 *Government Bad Loans*

One aspect with government debt levels that is more difficult to estimate are bad loans made by the government to the private sector or bad loans made to public enterprises. These amounts could mean that the official debt statistics understate the true level of debt because some of the assets (e.g. loans) may have a market value below book value. Constructing estimates of the magnitude of these bad loans is a serious undertaking in its own right and beyond the scope of this paper. We therefore opted to use Doi and Hoshi's (2002) estimates of bad loans to local governments and public enterprises as an estimate.

Doi and Hoshi, however, overstate the consolidated government bad loan problem for two reasons. First, Doi and Hoshi were interested in defaults by local governments to the central government. Yet failures to repay loans made between branches of the government do not change net debt since a loss to the central government arising by a default on a loan payment by a local government would be offset by the gain accruing to the local government from writing off the loan. This suggests that we should reduce the Doi and Hoshi estimate by the 35–40 trillion yen that constitute losses from government loans to local governments. Second, the Doi and Hoshi paper performs a present discounted calculation of future losses by public enterprises and so using their numbers overstates the level of current liabilities.

On the other hand, Doi and Hoshi had no information about hidden bad loans that have not appeared on any balance sheet, so it is possible that their estimates are not such overestimates of hidden government liabilities as one might expect from the above. Moreover, the Hoshi and Kashyap chapter in this volume estimates that the banking sector would require as much as another 35 trillion yen to be adequately capitalized. If some portion of this money must come from the government, then this figure should be added to the level of government liabilities.

We therefore decided to take Doi and Hoshi's 79 trillion yen estimate of bad loans to local government and public enterprises as our proxy for hidden liabilities on public corporation and bank balance sheets that will need to be covered by the government. This raises the net debt ratio up to 62 percent of GDP in fiscal year 2002 and serves as the basis for the net debt ratio that we use in the remainder of the paper.

3.3 *Current Government Outlays*

Although it is commonly argued that Japan's large deficits arose from large fiscal stimulus packages, there is ample reason to be skeptical about this claim. Once again data definitions matter, and there is much to be gained by carefully using the right numbers. The starting point for understanding Japanese government expenditures and revenues is Figure 2.1, which plots the evolution of revenues and expenditures as a share of GDP over the last two decades. The plot makes plain two points. First, there was a substantial rise in government expenditures after 1991, and secondly, tax revenues fell by about 3 percentage points of GDP (which the underlying data reveal was largely due to a decline in personal income tax revenue).

Adam Posen and Kenneth Kuttner have explored the reasons for movements in expenditures and tax revenues. One important result in Kuttner and Posen (2002) is that in all likelihood almost the entire precipitous decline in tax revenues that we see in Figure 2.1 is due to the recession. They show that if we assume a tax elasticity of 1.25, then the increase in the output gap implies that had economic growth in Japan not slumped, Japan's government budget deficit would have been substantially smaller. In other words, if Japanese economic performance improves, we should expect to see a substantial increase in Japanese government revenues as a share of GDP. This underscores the impor-

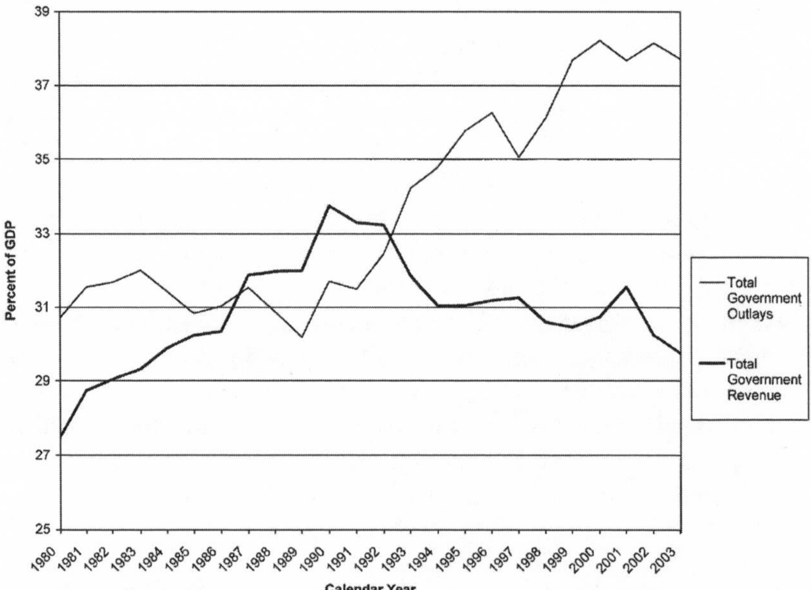

Source: *OECD Economic Outlook* #75 (2004). Total Government Outlays corresponds to Total Government Disbursements Government as a percent of GDP in the source; and Total Government Revenue is Total Government Receipts.

Figure 2.1
Evolution of Japanese Government Revenues and Outlays

tance of using long-run tax-to-GDP ratios as a baseline in our calculations rather than their current values.

To understand the source of the increase in the ratio of government expenditures to GDP, we need to delve deeper into the data. A common misconception is that this increase is the result of a massive fiscal stimulus. First, it is important to remember that an increase in this ratio can occur without a fiscal stimulus: holding fixed the growth rate of government expenditures, declines in economic growth will imply relatively higher expenditure-to-GDP ratios. Posen (1998) sharpens this point by showing that the reputed fiscal stimulus is completely absent from the national accounts data after 1996.

Figure 2.2 presents both the government outlay data and the national accounts public demand data (public demand being the sum total of all government expenditures on goods and services in the system of national accounts). As the figure makes clear, although government outlays rose dramatically in the 1990s, public demand was fairly flat

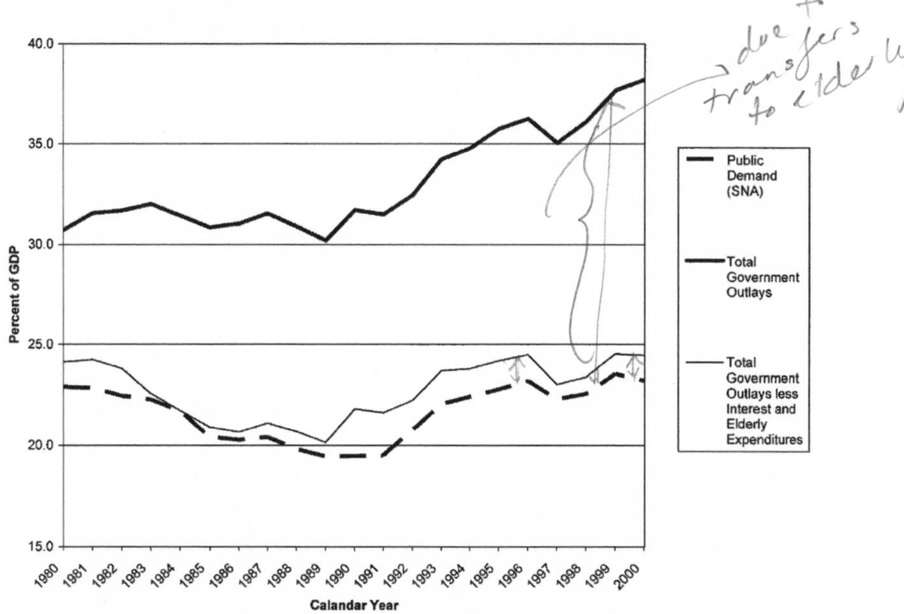

Source: Public Demand data is taken from the Economic Planning Agency SNA data. Total government outlays (Total Government Disbursements in the source) and interest expenditures (which are net) are from the OECD's Economic Outlook #75 (2004). Elderly Expenditures are taken from Faruqee and Muhleisen (2001).

Figure 2.2
Public Demand vs. Government Outlays

after 1996. This gives rise to what might be called "the mystery of the missing stimulus"—why is it that government outlays are rising in the government outlay data but public demand is flat in national accounts data?

The answer once again goes back to data definitions. Public demand in the national accounts covers all public expenditures for goods and services. As the name suggests, movements in this variable directly shift Japanese aggregate demand and provide a major basis for government stimulus policies. Looking more closely at the graph, we see that between 1991 and 1996 public demand rose by 4 percentage points of GDP while government outlays rose by 5 percentage points: this indicates that 80 percent of the increase in government outlays was due to a conventional fiscal stimulus policy. After 1996 public demand has been flat.

Moreover, the level of fiscal stimulus has not been at a particularly high level relative to historical patterns. It is worth pausing for a moment to consider this fact. Despite all the discussion in Japan about fiscal policies that built "bridges to nowhere", the data clearly state that the dramatic expansion in government outlays in recent years did not arise from public works projects [see Economic and Social Research Institute data cited in references]. In other words, the rise in government expenditures in recent years must be due to something other than the purchase of goods and services. This is even true if we slice the data more finely and focus on public works projects. The ratio of public investment to GDP averaged 0.077 in the 1980s and 0.078 in 1990s.

Government outlay data includes two important categories of expenditures that are not included in the national account's definition of public demand: interest and transfer payments. The reason for this is that interest and transfer payments do not entail the purchase of goods and services and therefore do not directly increase in aggregate demand. Interest payments by government institutions probably do not even indirectly affect aggregate demand since it is hard to imagine that it matters to households whether their interest bearing securities are JGBs or bank deposits. Transfer payments, on the other hand, can indirectly affect aggregate demand by raising private consumption. This will happen if these payments are not anticipated or if households that receive them are credit constrained. When the Japanese government handed out 20,000 yen coupons to families with children as part of a fiscal stimulus plan, it was a transfer payment that was not fully anticipated and may have gone to households that could not borrow to spend more [c.f.

Hsieh and Shimizutani (2001)]. As a result, the coupon plan may have stimulated some expenditure. However, when a worker retires with positive net wealth and collects social security pension payments, this probably does not affect aggregate demand because workers typically adjust their lifetime consumption and savings decisions to take these expected payments into account.

This result suggests that we should check whether the difference in total expenditures arises from new transfers or simply interest payments and anticipated transfers. In order to make this calculation, we need data on transfers. There are two large transfers made by Japan's government to Japanese over the age of 64: public pension payments and medical benefits.[18] Fortunately, Faruqee and Muhleisen (2001) built a dataset using Japanese SNA data that carefully breaks out transfers to those over 64 from total government outlays. If we subtract transfers to the elderly and interest payments on debt from total expenditures, we obtain the thin line in Figure 2.2. The striking feature of this plot is that total expenditures less those for interest and elderly tracks the SNA public demand expenditures data very closely. The only difference between the two lines is due to transfer payments to those younger than 65, amounts which are small and stable relative to GDP. Moreover given that gross interest payments on Japanese debt have remained between 3 and 4 percent of GDP for every year between 1981 and 2000, it is clear that the increase in government expenditures since 1996 is due overwhelmingly to transfers to the elderly.

The dramatic rise in elderly expenditures might be stimulative if it arose from an unexpected increase in benefits to the elderly. One reasonable assumption as to how people expect benefits to the elderly to rise is that these will rise roughly in proportion to GDP. As one can see in Figure 2.3, after an initial run up in the early 1980s, real per capita transfers to the elderly (i.e. those over age 64) has tracked real GDP relatively well for the last fifteen years.[19] This suggests that the recent increase in expenditures on the elderly is explained not by an expansion of per capita benefits for them but rather by the fact that the number of elderly eligible to receive these payments rose sharply. A similar story seems to apply for real expenditures on people other than the elderly. Figure 2.3 shows expenditures on a per-non-elderly person basis roughly tracking real GDP between 1980 and 2000.

Alternatively, it is also reasonable to suggest that people might expect government transfers to each elderly person will track the real per capita income of the working age population. This would be the case if

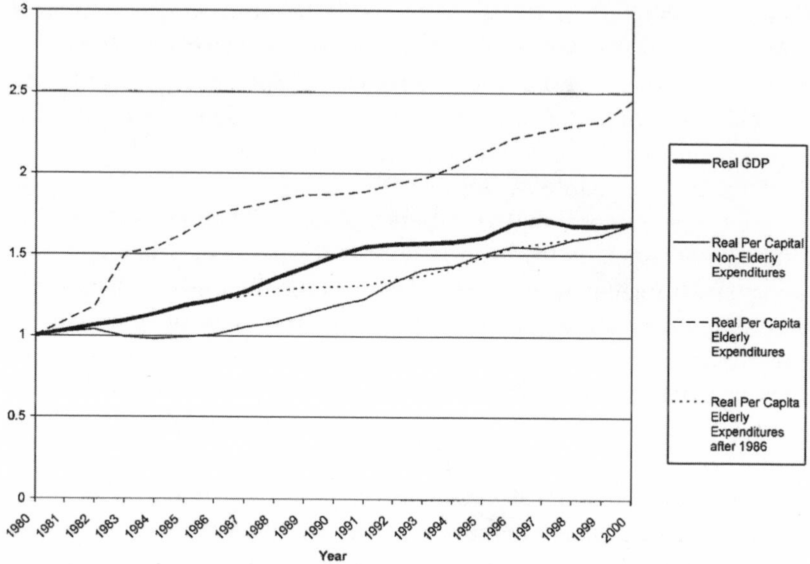

Note: Expenditures on the elderly are public pension and medical benefits for those over age 64. Expenditures per non-elderly person equal total government expenditures less those on the elderly and interest, divided by the non-elderly population. Data from Faruqee and Muhleisen (2001)

Figure 2.3
Evolution of Per Capita Government Expenditures on Elderly and Non-Elderly in Japan (1980 = 1)

government expenditure on the elderly maintained their income relative to the income of wage earners. One obtains a similar picture if one looks at real per capita benefits relative to real per capita GDP. Between 1980 and 2000 real per capita benefits for those under age 65 rose on average 0.4 percent faster than real per capita income. Similarly between 1986 and 2000, real per capita elderly benefits rose 0.3 percent faster than real per capita GDP. All of this increase was due to the decline in per capita income after 1997. If real per capita GDP had grown after 1997 at the same rate as it had from 1990 to 1997, per capita expenditures and real per capita GDP would have moved at the same rate.

This discussion of government expenditures reveals a number of key points that we will use in our sustainability calculation. The substantial increase in Japan's government deficit was due to three factors. First, poor economic performance coupled with some tax cuts lowered tax revenues by approximately 3 percentage points of GDP; second, poor economic performance coupled with a fiscal stimulus in the early nineties raised expenditures by 4 percentage points of GDP; and third, an aging population required greater transfers. It is also important to bear in mind that there has been no dramatic increase in real per capita elderly benefits relative to GDP or GDP per worker. Since the mid-1980's per capita transfers to the elderly have risen roughly in proportion to GDP per worker or GDP. In other words, the growth in government expenditures is due principally to the rising number of people receiving benefits, not to dramatic increases in benefits per recipient.

To return to the sustainability calculation, we make use of several stylized facts. Government outlays have demonstrated some volatility in response to business cycles but the ratio of pension and medical outlays per elderly person relative to GDP or GDP per capita has been essentially flat. The same can be said for all other outlays (except interest payments) on a per non-elderly person basis. We therefore use the average of these variables over 1980 to 2000 as our estimate of the baseline level of outlays per capita. This avoids the problem of having our results affected by fluctuations in expenditure levels that are driven by business cycles but does allow the outlays to fluctuate with population shares.[20]

One way to check the reasonableness of our assumptions is to use them to estimate Japan's structural deficit—i.e. a deficit when cyclical factors are removed—and then compare our forecast with that of the OECD. It would be disturbing if our approach could not explain a large share of the deterioration in Japanese government accounts. This is potentially a difficult hurdle since our model of government expenditures is quite simple—the deficit as a share of GDP is the average ratio per capita expenditure to GDP between 1980 and 2000 times the number of people in each category plus interest expenses less the historical average tax to GDP ratio. Hence our forecast of the deficit is primarily affected by the number of elderly and non-elderly in the populace.

Using this methodology, we forecast Japan's structural deficit for 2005 to be 6.3 percent of GDP. By contrast, the OECD (2003) forecast for the structural deficit in 2005 is 6.6 percent of GDP. The closeness of these two numbers is striking given that the OECD obtains its estimate through sophisticated econometric techniques whereas ours is simply obtained by holding fixed historical per capita expenditure levels. Moreover, if we use our methodology to "forecast" the deficit in 1990, we find that Japan's structural deficit was only 3.1 percent of GDP in that year. Hence, our methodology can explain the very sharp deterioration in government finances that we observed in the 1990's and yields estimates of the 2005 deficit that are close to those of the OECD. This gives us confidence that our methodology is a sensible way of thinking about the evolution of Japan's government finances.

3.4 Population

Changes in birth rates take a long time to affect changes in pension levels; hence one needs to use a sufficiently long time horizon cut to make sure that the budgetary implications of a shift in fertility are fully captured.[21]

Japanese forecasts of fertility tend to be far more pessimistic than forecasts based on economic theory, demography, or actual data. The Japanese National Institute of Population and Social Security Research (NIPSSR), which underlies many government and academic analyses of pension burdens, builds its population forecast by assuming that the existing fertility rate will not change in the future.[22] To get some sense of what this assumption implies, if the current situation continues—that is there is no change in immigration policy and the typical child is born to a 29 year-old woman, and the fertility rate is 1.3, then this methodology implies that that there will be fewer than 20,000 people under the age of 20 in around 500 years and that the last Japanese baby will be born in about 1000 years!

The implausibility of this notion underscores the problem of building a sustainability forecast based on NIPSSR data. Any social pension scheme that is financed out of current worker wages will be ultimately unsustainable if one predicts workers will disappear before the elderly do. Unfortunately, Japanese sustainability forecasts built using this data therefore basically *assume* unsustainability rather than being able to answer *whether* the Japanese fiscal situation is unsustainable. [See, for example, Dekle (2003) and Takayama, Kitamura and Yoshida (1999a and 1999b); a notable exception is Faruqee and Muhleisen (2001)]

An alternative approach is to make use of economic demography. Economic demographers typically assume that two forces are likely to be important in determining fertility rates-the first is the substitution effect and the second is the income effect. As wages rise, the opportunity cost of having children rises and fertility falls. In other words, higher wages cause people to substitute emphasizing their careers and earning more money for having (more) children. However, if wages rise enough, the marginal utility of income starts to fall and families become more likely to decide to have children. Put simply, while having both spouses work matters a lot for the typical household, it probably does not matter so much for wealthy households. The question, of course, is how much money is enough to cause the income effect to dominate. Figure 2.4 plots international fertility rates against per capita GDP.[23] As one can see in the figure (and in regression analysis), the trough in fertility occurs at a PPP GDP per capita of 25,000 dollars—precisely the level that Japan is at now.[24]

Theoretical and empirical economic analyses, therefore, indicate that Japanese fertility rates will not remain low forever, but rather will rise at some point in the future. This prediction suggests that Japan's long-run population will be lower than the current level, but not zero, a result which has important implications for sustainability calculations. Managing a demographic transition from a high population to a lower one is much easier than managing a transition towards zero: the key difference

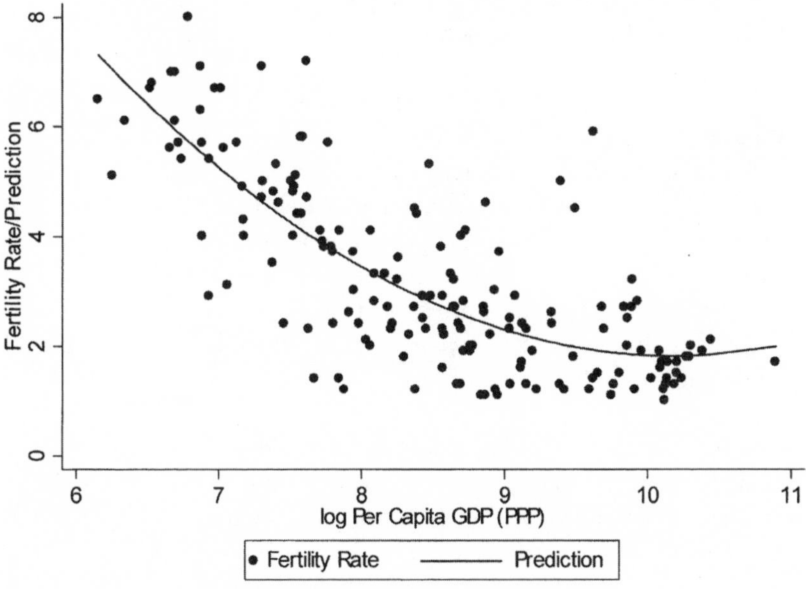

Note: These are natural logarithms

Figure 2.4
International Fertility Rates vs. PPP GDP Per Capita

is the temporary nature of the budget shortfall necessary to cover the *temporarily* high share of the elderly in this long-run perspective.

3.5 Effects on Policy Options

Using forecasts based on the premise that the Japanese will continue to exist, policy alternatives abound. An important option arises from the fact that although the social pension scheme is often billed as a pay-as-you-go system, in reality it is nothing of the sort. Until 1994, Japan's relatively young population meant that social security payroll taxes exceeded pension expenditures, while future social security outlays are likely to entail deficits for many years. This is a natural outcome of a process in which the costs of the social pension scheme are smoothed across generations. The alternative would be to have had even lower taxes in the 1980s and 1990s and extremely high taxes in the future. However, once one realizes that the Japanese government does smooth the costs of the demographic transition (i.e. making current generations pay for future retirements), the next question is whether this smoothing can be used to alleviate some of strain associated with the aging society.

To answer this we need to be clear about the time period of the demographic transition. We will use annual forecasts of the Japanese population constructed by Faruqee and Muhleisen (2001) who project that the population of Japanese aged 15–64 will stabilize in 2060. Despite this ultimate stabilization in population, Faruqee and Muhleisen's forecasts indicate that in 2060 there will be 29 percent fewer Japanese in this age bracket than there are now. This figure suggests that even if one believes that ultimately Japan's fertility rates will recover, it will still take more than half a century for the size of the Japanese labor force to stabilize.

One implication of this lag is that it can make a very big difference to a sustainability calculation whether one expects the demographic transition to be paid for within 40 years, as is often assumed, or in 100 years. The intuition is as follows: if the Japanese population is moving towards a new stable lower level, then the aging of the population is a temporary phenomenon that will ultimately disappear after the generations with the low fertility rates die. Because the cost of the transition is temporary, one can reduce the per capita cost of this transition by spreading it out over current and future generations. In other words, spreading out this temporary cost over a century among all working people may result in significantly lower taxes for the current generation of workers relative to spreading the cost only over 40 years.

3.6 *Interest and Growth Rates*

An interesting feature of the mathematics underlying fiscal sustainability is that one does not need to take a strong stand on the actual level of interest rates and growth rates but simply their relative level.[25] Obviously, forecasts of the gap between interest rates and growth 100 years in the future are little more than educated guesswork. We therefore opted to put forward a number of scenarios that should capture most people's assumptions about what the future is likely to look like. The assumption one makes regarding whether Japan still needs to raise its capital to GDP ratio gives rise to the basic intuition about this gap. Higher interest rates *ceteris paribus* yield more savings and more rapid capital accumulation. Theory suggests that if the Japanese capital to output ratio is to remain stable, it should be the case that interest rates should equal the growth rate, i.e. there will be no gap. On the other hand, if one believes that Japan is still converging to an even higher capital to GDP ratio than it has now, then one should use a positive gap between interest and growth rates, as this positive gap is associated with more rapid increases in capital accumulation.

The correct gap, however, is clearly a judgment call. As Blanchard et al (1990) note, increasing this gap affects the calculation in two opposing ways. First, a higher interest rate gap tends to raise the sustainable tax rate because it increases the cost of servicing any existing level of debt. On the other hand, a higher gap lowers the cost of an aging society because future costs are discounted at a higher rate. Blanchard et al. (1990) recommend using a gap between interest and growth rates of two percentage points, even though in many countries the gap has been much smaller in recent decades.

Japan is an illustrative case in point. In the 1960s and the 1970s the average difference between the average yield on Japanese government bonds and nominal GDP growth was *negative* [Source: IMF, *International Financial Statistics Yearbook*]. In the 1980s the gap was 0.4, and in the 1990s it was still only 1.4 percent. Hence, our baseline specification, which is based on a gap of 2, is relatively high in light of Japan's experience in the last four decades.

3.7 *Future Government Expenditures*

Unlike the factors that contribute to economic growth, there is far less agreement on the determinants of political economy. In general, government expenditures are forecast using assumptions about the rates of growth of expenditures on different population groups. It is useful to write the total expenditure per capita in period *t* as follows:

Total Expenditure per capita$_t$ =

$$\frac{(1+\gamma)^t H_0}{n_{\text{old},t}} \times \frac{n_{\text{old},t}}{n_t} + \frac{(1+\mu)^t G_0}{n_{\text{young},t}} \times \frac{n_{\text{young},t}}{n_t} \qquad (6)$$

where "young" is defined as the population of 64 years of age and below, n_t is the total population in time *t* (i.e., $n_t = n_{\text{old},t} + n_{\text{young},t}$), and γ and μ are the rates of growth of the expenditure per old and young, respectively.

We consider three possible versions of future government expenditures.

Case 1, the most common in the literature, assumes that i) *per person* government transfers to the elderly, H/n_{old}, rise at the same rate as real GDP (i.e., $\gamma = g$); and ii) per person government expenditures unrelated to elderly benefits and interest payments, G/n_{young}, grow at the rate of GDP minus the rate of growth of the young population (i.e., $\mu = g - \pi_{\text{young}}$, where π_{young} is the rate of population growth of the young). The first assumption implies that per recipient transfers *to the elderly* as a share of GDP remain constant over time. The second implies that per recipient expenditures on the young as a share of GDP grow at the rate that the young population is declining. In other words, if the share of the young in the total population falls over time, this implies that non-elderly related government expenditures per young person are an ever increasing share of GDP.[26]

This asymmetry in government expenditures assumed in Case 1 is unlikely to be true in practice because if per recipient expenditures on a demographic category are constant, then aggregate expenditures should depend on the number of people within that category. Put differently, if an aging population means an increase in government transfers to the elderly, then by the same logic, a drop in fertility rates should mean a decrease in expenditures on younger Japanese. Fewer young people should mean fewer schools, fewer police, and less unemployment insurance. This suggests that in the case of a population that is contracting at the same time it is aging, as is the case in Japan, there is an important cost offset associated with reductions in expenditures on the young. Unless one builds this relationship into the calculation, one will significantly overestimate future expenditures. This problem raises the question of what the right future path of expenditures is likely to be. It seems improbable that the Japanese would easily accept a decline in per capita government services, but how rapidly must these rise?

Case 2 is a little less generous to the young than Case 1: all per capita transfers rise in proportion to GDP. In terms of equation (6), this implies that, $\gamma = \mu = g$. That is, non-interest expenditures for different population groups are treated symmetrically and grow at the rate of GDP.

Case 3 is a more generous expansion of public goods and transfers in that the growth of all per capita transfers rises proportionally with per worker GDP growth. This implies that $\gamma = \mu = g - \pi_{wp}$, where π_{wp} is the rate of growth of the working population.

For Japan, Case 3 implies a higher growth rate of per capita expenditures than Case 2, as the working population is falling over the entire forecasting horizon. It is important to remember, however, that both forecasts imply very substantial increases in the amount of government services and transfers provided to the typical Japanese citizen over the next century. In other words, assuming a 1.5 percent real per capita income growth rate (which is slower than the growth rate of real per capita GDP between 1989 and 2002), the real value of per capita government outlays rises by 3.25 or 4.4 times in Cases 2 and 3, respectively, over the next 100 years—in either case a significant improvement over current levels.

Figures 2.5 through 2.7 show the evolution of total transfers to each population group as a share of GDP under the three different cases. These figures use the population projections from Faruqee and Muhleisen (2001) previously described.[27] Figure 2.5 highlights the path of expenditures under the assumptions of Case 1. It shows the rising transfers to the elderly as a share of GDP until 2050, and the constant share of GDP that corresponds to the young (assumption ii)). In this scenario, total government expenses as a share of GDP peak in 2050 at a level of 38.3 percent of GDP. Figure 2.6 shows the offsetting cost of expenditures on the young under the assumption that expenditures for different population groups are treated symmetrically and grow at the rate of GDP (Case 2). As opposed to Case 1, this scenario predicts that aggregate government outlays will rise over the next 20 years and peak

Japan 2005–2100: Projections of Government Expenses as a Percent of GDP by Population Group under Different Scenarios

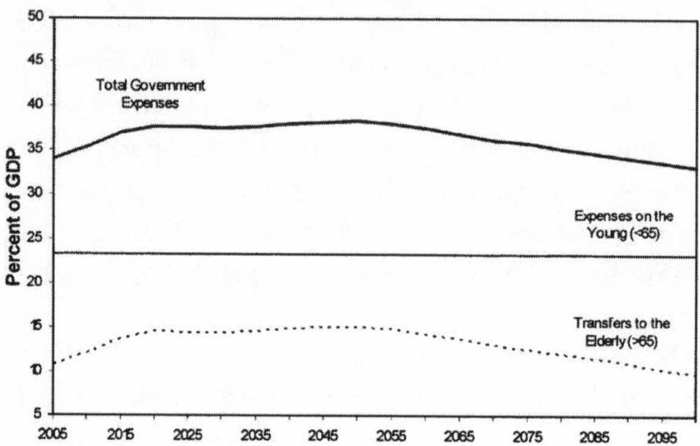

Figure 2.5
Case 1 (Asymmetric: $\gamma = g$; $\mu = g - \pi$(young))

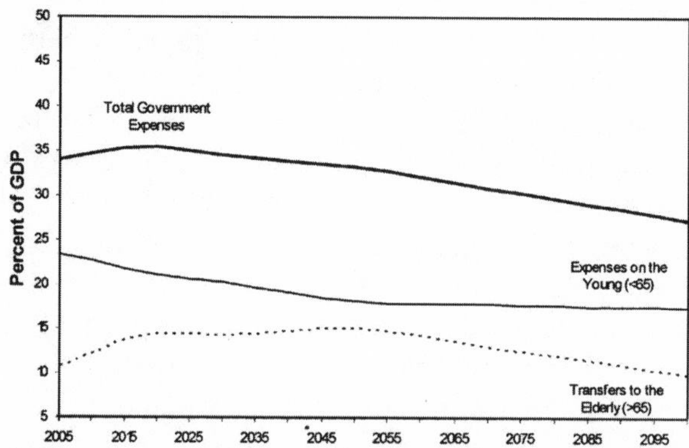

Figure 2.6
Case 2 (Symmetric: $\gamma = \mu = g$)

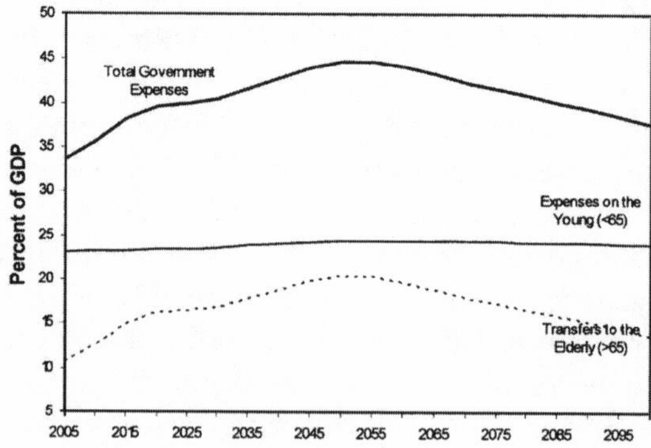

Figure 2.7
Case 3 (Symmetric: $\gamma = \mu = g - \pi$(working pop))

at 35.5 percent of GDP, and then total expenses will gradually fall by the end of the twenty-first century to levels last seen in the 1980's. Finally, the last figure shows the much more generous welfare program suggested by Case 3, where per-capita expenditures are assumed to grow at the rate of GDP per worker.

4 Sustainability

The mathematics underlying sustainability suggest that unless monetary policy, taxes, and expenditures are precisely aligned, there will be a tendency for the debt-to-GDP ratio to rise or fall. We are less interested in the knife-edge result of whether taxes and expenditures are perfectly aligned; rather, the real issue is how much taxes need to move in order to achieve sustainability.[28] If only a small movement is needed then one should have little concern about sustainability. On the other hand, an implied large movement might be grounds for worry.

This concern, of course, begs the question of how big is a large movement in tax rates? We can think of three sensible policy answers and policy responses. The first is anything bigger than zero. The second is raising taxes back to the levels they were before the tax cuts of the 1990s. The third is an increase that would raise Japan's tax rates above the level of the typical OECD or European economy. To make these numbers concrete, consider that in Japan the average rate of government revenue to GDP between 1990 and 2000 was 32.2 percent.[29] This number serves as our baseline estimate for the long run overall Japanese tax rate. Government revenue as a share of GDP peaked in 1990 at 34.3 percent, just prior to a series of tax cuts designed to offset the bursting of the bubble. This implies that a Ministry of Finance policy that took Japanese tax rates back to their 1990 level would increase revenues by approximately 2 percentage points of GDP.

The third policy entails an increase that would raise Japan's taxes above a typical OECD economy. We need comparable international tax data in order to understand the last option. The OECD provides data on current government receipts relative to GDP, which is a comprehensive statement of taxes and other transfers to the government.[30] Figure 2.8 presents this data for OECD countries in 1997, the last year for which comparable data were available for the United States. The striking feature this graph is that Japan's taxes are the second lowest in the OECD—almost 3 percentage points of GDP below government revenues in the US! Raising Japan's tax rates to the average level for

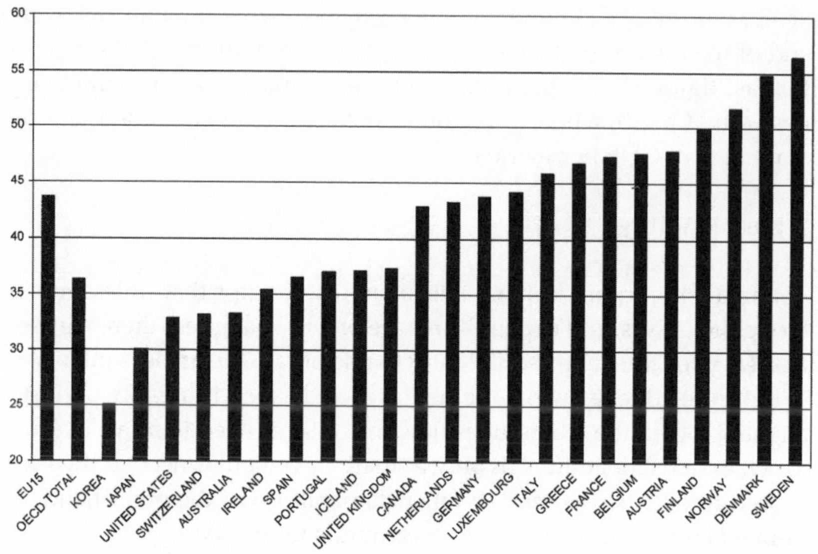

Note Data are from the OECD

Figure 2.8
Current Government Receipts as a Percent of GDP in 1997

the OECD would entail a Japanese tax increase of 6.3 percentage points of GDP, and raising them to EU levels would entail a whopping 13.6 percentage points of GDP increase in tax rates or a 50 percent rise in Japanese government revenue.

4.1 Our Estimates

With these benchmark figures, we can turn to our estimates. A lot of assumptions are behind any sustainability forecast. Reasonable people can (and do) disagree about the future level of economic variables, including interest rates, GDP growth rates, government expenditure growth, monetary policy, and fertility rates. While we believe that certain assumptions are more reasonable than others, we think that providing a range of estimates to cover all plausible outcomes is a more sensible way of handling the inherent uncertainty about what the future is likely to be. In this section we assume that changes in the money supply are not used to finance government expenditures (i.e., $\lambda = 0$ in equation (3)). We will assess the impact of monetary expansions on the sustainability calculation in the next section.

Tables 2.1 and 2.2 present the results from all of our simulations of the future. We will discuss the results starting with the most pessimistic view from the sustainability standpoint and move towards more optimistic views of the future. In all of these cases we assume a real GDP growth rate of 2 percent.[31] Sustainability is calculated either to 2040 (that is, the debt-to-GDP ratio in 2040 must equal that of today) or to 2100. (For convenience, calculations to 2100 are referred to as being over a 100-year period, and to 2040 over a 40-year period.) Columns 1 and 2 present results using NIPSSR population estimates, and Columns 3–5 use Faruqee and Muhleisen (2001). The difference between the variables in each column is the difference between sustainable tax rate under different interest rate and the growth rate assumptions. Changes in the money supply are not used to finance government expenditures (that is, $\lambda = 0$ in equation (3)) except in the last row, as discussed later.

Table 2.1
Sustainable Tax Rates with Elderly Benefits Growing Proportional to GDP per Worker, Cases 1 and 3

	Sustainable Tax Rates, Cases 1 and 3				
	Case 3				Case 1
Population Forecast	NIPSSR		IMF		IMF
Sustainability Horizon	2100	2040	2100	2040	2100
Rate Gap[1]					
0	44.9	40.2	40.7	39.0	39.7
1	44.4	40.4	41.0	39.3	40.1
2	43.9	40.6	41.1	39.6	40.4
3	43.3	40.8	41.1	39.8	40.5
4	42.9	41.0	41.2	40.1	40.6
Monetary Policy[2]	43.2	39.6	40.5	38.5	39.7

Entries are percentages of GDP. As explained in the text, Case 3 is growth in per capita expenditures equal to per worker GDP growth, with no monetary-policy effects. Case 1 is growth in per capita elderly expenditures equal to that of per worker GDP and the share of other government expenditures to GDP remaining constant. NIPSSR means that organization's population forecasts are used; IMF means the Faruqee and Muhleisen (2001) forecasts are used.

[1]The rate gap is the interest rate minus the nominal GDP growth rate.

[2]This row shows the results of monetizing 50% of government debt. Specifically, monetary policy is used to increase M/GDP by 30% during the first 5 years. The interest rate minus the growth rate is 2.

Table 2.2
Sustainable Tax Rates with Elderly Benefits Growing Proportional to GDP, Cases 1 and 2

	Sustainable Tax Rates, Cases 1 and 2				
	Case 2				Case 1
Population Forecast	NIPSSR		IMF		IMF
Sustainability Horizon	2100	2040	2100	2040	2100
Rate Gap[1]					
0	32.3	35.3	32.2	34.6	36.4
1	33.7	35.9	33.4	35.2	37.1
2	34.9	36.5	34.6	35.8	37.8
3	36.0	37.0	35.6	36.4	38.3
4	36.9	37.6	36.4	37.0	38.8
Monetary Policy[2]	34.3	35.4	33.9	34.8	37.1

Entries are percentages of GDP. As explained in the text, case 2 is growth in per capita expenditures proportional to GDP, with no monetary-policy effects. Case 1 is growth in per capita elderly expenditures equal to that of GDP and the share of other government expenditures to GDP remaining constant. NIPSSR means that organization's population forecasts are used; IMF means the Faruqee and Muhleisen (2001) forecasts are used.
[1]The rate gap is the interest rate minus the nominal GDP growth rate.
[2]This row shows the results of monetizing 50% of government debt. Specifically, monetary policy is used to increase M/GDP by 30% during the first 5 years. The interest rate minus the growth rate is 2.

In column 1 of the first panel, we assume that Japan is on the road to developing an extremely generous welfare state in which all public expenditures will rise proportionally to GDP per worker (i.e., Case 3 in the previous section). In the scenario where the interest rate gap is 2 percentage points, we find that the sustainable tax rate is 43.9 percent. The assumptions underlying this scenario are so pessimistic that we obtain some perverse results. Because we assume that the per capita expenditures upon the elderly will rise with per capita income, future costs matter much more than past debt levels. As a result, the sustainable tax rate is lower when growth is low relative to interest rates because high interest rates enable the government to run surpluses today and use the interest on the surpluses to pay for the future retirees. This also explains why moving to a 40 year horizon causes the sustainable tax rate to fall. The combination of an ever shrinking labor force and ever higher retirement benefits means that it becomes increasingly hard to pay for the retirees. As a result one needs lower taxes to pay for retirees over a 40-year period than over a 100-year period.

One argument against believing this scenario is that perhaps we have stacked the data too much against sustainability and therefore employed odd assumptions that yield odd results. However, pessimists might truly worry about a collapsing Japanese population in the face of a government unable to rein in expenditures. Indeed, given that the tax rates in this bleak scenario exceed the 32.2 percent average tax rate for the 1990s, the scenario implies that Japan must raise its taxes substantially, i.e. the approximate equivalent of 10 percent of GDP.[32] It is important to bear in mind, however, that the implied tax rates are still lower than those currently being paid in the typical EU country or even in Canada.

In other words, if the Japanese want per capita government expenditures to rise at the same rate as per worker income, they are going to have to pay for it. Put differently, in order to justify defaulting on its promises as an option in this most generous social welfare case and most pessimistic population growth case, one has to assume that defaulting is a better option for the Japanese government than raising taxes to the average level of the typical EU country. It seems hard to imagine the Japanese government making this choice, and this improbability likely explains why the bond market is not anticipating a default.

Other scenarios are better from a taxpayer's standpoint. Suppose that instead of using the NIPSSR population estimates we switch to the IMF [i.e. Faruqee and Muhleisen (2001)] estimates which allow the population to stabilize at a new lower level. In these forecasts, the proportion of Japanese under age 15 relative to those aged 15 to 64 does not stabilize until 2045, but this eventuality makes a big difference in the sustainability calculations. Using this more optimistic forecast of the Japanese population but the same assumptions underlying Case 3, reduces the required tax rate increase by 2.8 percentage points of GDP.[33] While this forecast still requires a tax increase of 9 percent of GDP, the implied sustainable tax level is now at the level of the average tax rate in the typical OECD country.[34] In other words, if one accepts that the Japanese population is likely to stabilize, then the sustainable tax rate for Japan looks like the typical tax burden in an OECD country. While this clearly implies some painful adjustment, it hardly seems grounds for deep worry about a future fiscal crisis.

Up until this point, we have been assuming that the Japanese will want to pay for very generous growth in real benefits (Case 3). It is also possible that the Japanese may want to slow down the benefits growth somewhat during this demographic transition. In particular, it makes sense to consider the case in which per capita benefits grow at the same rate as GDP, rather than GDP per capita (i.e., Case 2). Note that this still implies that there is enormous growth in real benefits, with the only restriction being that there is a little more fiscal discipline in the expansion of these benefits.

In column 3 of the second panel, we consider Case 2 for the 100-year horizon using the IMF [Faruqee and Muhleisen (2001)] population projections. The magnitude of the sustainable tax rate is dramatically lower. In order to afford this growth rate of expenditures and assuming an interest rate gap of 2 percentage points, Japanese tax rates only need to rise to 34.6 percent of GDP: about the same level as in 1990! In other words, if benefits rise a little less rapidly than per capita income, then Japanese debt is sustainable with a tax burden that is on the order of the level in the United States or the level in Japan before the bubble burst. An important reason for the relatively optimistic forecast we obtained is that we treat young and old symmetrically—i.e. for a given per capita expenditure level, the aggregate expenditure level is determined by the number of people in each category. This is contrast to other forecasting frameworks (e.g. Dekle (2002), Dang et al (2000), Faruqee and Muhleison (2001)) which effectively assume that the remaining non-interest expenses do not decline as the number of people under the age of 65 declines. Implicitly this approach can imply very large per capita gains for the young as expenditures stay constant relative to GDP but the number of young declines. This difference can be seen in the path of expenses to the young in Case 2 and 3 (see Figures 2.7 and 2.8). To demonstrate the impact of this assumption, we assumed that elderly benefits grew with GDP but that the remaining non-interest related government expenditures always stayed proportional to GDP regardless of the number of young. This is reported in the last column of Table 2.2. As one can see, the assumption that benefits to the young depend on the number of young does not alter the conclusion that Japanese tax rates need not rise above typical levels in the OECD, though it does have a fairly substantial impact on the calculations if one assumes that per capita expenditures for the elderly (but not young) will increase as much as GDP. In this case, the cost savings arising from having fewer young people in the future imply that the Japanese government can spend on average 3 percentage points of GDP less than would be needed if expenditures on the young did not depend on the number of young.

The fact that allowing per capita public benefit levels to grow at the rate of real GDP means that only a small increase in taxes is necessary to restore Japan to fiscal soundness is a point that seems to have been missed in policy circles. Essentially the choice for Japan is having lower growth rates in per capita benefits and tax rates comparable to the US or having more generous growth rates in benefits and tax rates comparable to those in Europe. Which option is more attractive is something that Japanese voters will need to decide, but neither future alternative seems bleak.

4.2 Limiting the Debt-to-GDP Ratio

The type of sustainability calculations used in this paper does not restrict the levels of debt-to-GDP ratios over the forecasting horizon. This implies that under certain scenarios debt-to-GDP ratios may rise to levels higher than financial markets are willing to accept at particular points in time. An example of this behavior is shown in Figure 2.9. The solid line represents the path of debt-to-GDP for column 3 in Table 2.2,

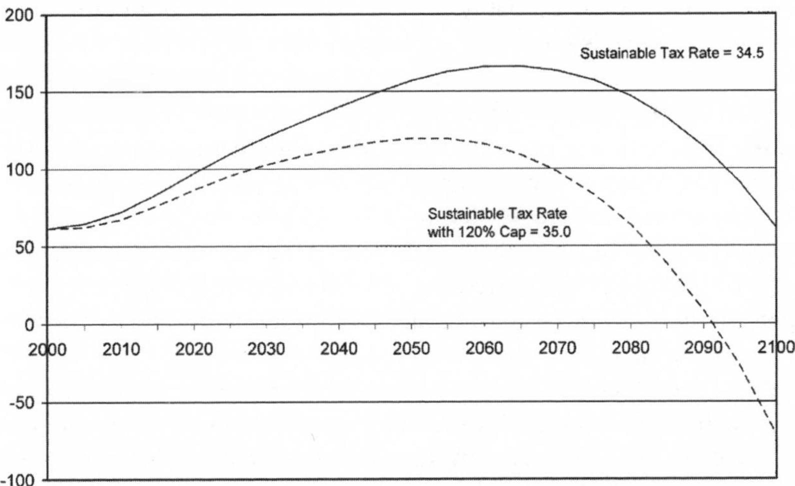

The solid line represents the path of the debt-to-GDP ratio for Table 2.2 column 3 with an interest rate gap of 2, so the sustainable tax rate is 34.6%. The dotted line is a tax rate of 35%, and it stays below a 120% net debt-to-GDP level. Because tax rates are assumed to be constant over the entire horizon, a higher tax rate than the sustainable tax rate implies that debt to GDP ratios are smaller at the end of the sustainability period than at the beginning. In the case depicted in Figure 2.9, the Japanese government moves from a net debtor position to a net creditor position around 2090.

Figure 2.9
Japan's Net Debt/GDP Dynamics, 2005–2100

where the sustainable tax rate is 34.6 percent (with an interest rate gap of 2). It shows that the debt-to-GDP ratio surpasses 160 percent around 2070. While these levels of debt are unprecedented even for advanced economies, we show that a small increase in the tax rate would render a path of debt that never rises above 120 percent of GDP in the next 100 years. (The 120 percent level has been observed in developed financial markets in recent years) This path is shown by the dotted line, and it represents a tax rate of just 35%, an increase of only 0.4 percentage points. As we can see from the figure, a small increase in the tax rate suffices to maintain debt-to-GDP ratios at levels that have been observed in developed financial markets in the last few decades and that are consistent with the interest gaps used in Tables 2.1 and 2.2.[35]

4.3 Effect of Phasing in the Tax Increase

Another assumption underlying this type of sustainability exercise is that taxes are increased immediately to their long-run sustainable level (in our exercise this would happen in 2005). While we see large changes in tax rates in short periods of time around the world, a more feasible tax path would probably have taxes increasing only gradually to their sustainable level over a prolonged period of time. For this reason we redid the estimates in Tables 2.1 and 2.2 with the additional restriction that taxes would only slowly converge to their long-run level. The changes in sustainable tax rates with these additional restrictions are very small. For instance, when taxes are assumed to increase linearly from the average tax rate of 32.2 percent to the sustainable tax rate in the next 10 years, the sustainable tax rate changes from 34.6 percent (IMF population projections, interest rate gap of 2, Case 2) to 35.0 percent. In the same case using the NIPSSR population projections, the sustainable tax rates increased from 34.9 to 35.5 percent.

Obviously, there are myriad ways in which the taxes might be phased in to achieve sustainable levels, and it is not possible to go through all of the cases here. How certain can we be then that waiting a few years will not dramatically alter the calculations? The answer is that a rough rule of thumb about the cost of waiting to implement the sustainable tax rate is that every fifty percentage point of GDP increase in the debt level will raise the sustainable tax rate by slightly more than 1 percentage point using a 100 year horizon.

The intuition for this result stems from the interest burden of debt. If Japanese policymakers discovered that their debt to GDP ratio was

50 percentage points of GDP higher, then given an interest rate to GDP growth gap of 2 percent would imply that tax revenues would have to be permanently raised by an additional 1 percent of GDP just to stabilize the debt. Paying off the additional debt over a 100 year horizon would require an additional 0.16 percent of GDP payment. Hence, even if we thought that delays in paying off the debt would result in a substantially higher debt to GDP ratio in the short term, this would not change the long-run sustainable tax rate by much.

4.4 Monetary Policy

Thus far, we have been assuming that the only means available for the government to finance expenditures is through taxes (i.e., $\lambda = 0$ in equation (3)). However, governments can also benefit through unanticipated inflation that lowers the real value of net debt. As shown in equation (3), a positive rate of money growth, λ, implies that for given paths of government expenses and taxes the accumulation of debt over time is smaller. Indeed, many analysts have been concerned that Japan's debt levels might induce the Bank of Japan to monetize the debt.

It is relatively easy within our framework to consider the impact of monetizing approximately 50 percent of the Japanese net debt (i.e. $\lambda_t m_t = 0.3$).[36] We implement this by considering an open market operation in which the Bank of Japan monetizes half of the outstanding government debt (i.e. increases base money by 30 percent of GDP). In the case when the gap between nominal interest rates and nominal GDP growth is 2 percentage points, this lowers the sustainable tax rate by only 0.6 percentage points. This is very small in comparison to the difference in the tax rates that arise as a result of the higher or lower growth rates in per capita benefits discussed above.

Again, the main reason for the small impact is that most of the pressure on the government budget constraint is not current liabilities, which can be affected by inflation, but future liabilities, which cannot. As a result, monetizing a significant portion of the outstanding Japanese government debt will not really change the sustainable tax rate.

The insensitivity of these calculations to major swings in monetary policy also suggests that even if the Bank of Japan needs to ultimately reduce the money supply to mop up liquidity, this will not have a large impact on Japanese fiscal sustainability. Between March 2001 and March 2004, the Japanese monetary base grew by 8 percent of GDP. As the previous example indicates, even if the BOJ intervened in the market by selling off all of the bonds that it accumulated-thereby increasing our net debt number by this amount-the impact on the sustainable tax rate would only be a few tenths of a percent of GDP.

Thinking about the small impacts of monetary policy also answers concerns about whether it was appropriate to consolidate bonds held by the BOJ into the government accounts. If one believes that some day the BOJ will have to sell off its entire stock of JGBs (worth 80 trillion yen in 2002), an action that would entail a 93 percent contraction in base money, this still would only imply that $\lambda_t m_t = -0.18$, a very small implication for the sustainable tax rate.

This underscores an important reason why long-run bond rates are so low. Whatever your forecast is for the future expenditure path of the Japanese government, knowing what the inflation rate may be in the next five years will have almost no impact on sustainability. In the long run, if Japan chooses a high benefit path, the only way that it will be able to pay for these expenses is through higher taxes. Put simply, a key message from our long-run fiscal sustainability exercises is that the fiscal problem that Japan faces is future liabilities not current liabilities, and as such, inflation is not the answer to Japan's fiscal issues.

5 Conclusions and Policy Implications

This paper has argued that fiscal policy debates in Japan have been fraught with confusion over current and future liabilities. Data on current net liabilities of the Japanese government suggest that these liabilities are large not enough to be dangerous. The fact that past liabilities have not amounted to a high net debt level implies that inflation is not an answer to Japan's fiscal issues. This probably explains why Japanese interest rates have remained low in the face of sometimes shrill discussions of Japan's gross debt levels.

The relatively minor impact of large changes in Japan's net debt level on its sustainable tax rate also suggests that concerns about long run demographic transitions probably should not have much influence on short run fiscal policy. Moving the net debt level up or down by as much as 50 percent has only relatively minor effects on long-run sustainable tax rates. In other words, while fiscal stimulus packages in all countries imply some increase in future taxes, there is little evidence that these policies would push Japan over some critical sustainable tax level. However, the analysis in this paper abstracts from unsustainability that arises because of political reasons for default or self-fulfilling prophecies, either of which may depend on the short-run behavior of fiscal policy.

The final policy implication is that Japan's demographic transition is manageable. The Japanese government's target of trying to restore a primary balance of zero by 2012 is a particularly painful way of handling the transition for the current generation of workers. We have considered other approaches that smooth the transition over more generations and thus would entail lower taxes in the short run (and higher rates later).

Although we don't know how generous today's young Japanese are going to be towards their parents and what their demands for public expenditures will be, we can be fairly certain of what will happen in the long run. If the Japanese want to have generous expansions in government expenditures for themselves and the elderly, then Japanese government outlays and receipts will look a lot like those in Europe today. If they want to keep the real growth rate of per capita expenditures positive but only equal to GDP growth, then Japanese government outlays and receipts will look like those in the United States today. The bottom line is that we could construct no scenario in which Japanese tax rates needed to rise above those found in many other high income countries.

The message, then, is clear. If Japanese voters want more benefits for the young and old, then they will have to pay for them, but Japan's future in this regard does not look any different than that of a typical OECD country.

Acknowledgments

We wish to offer special thanks to Takatoshi Ito and Hugh Patrick for providing us with tremendously detailed comments on an earlier draft. We also wish to thank Donald Davis, Rick Katz, Kenneth Kuttner, David Lebow, Robert Masden, Peter Morgan, Adam Posen and Cedric Tille for helpful comments. David Weinstein wishes to thank the Center for Japanese Economy and Business for providing research support for this project. The views expressed here are those of the authors, and do not necessarily reflect the position of the Federal Reserve Bank of New York, the Federal Reserve System, or any other institution with which the authors are affiliated.

Notes

1. See, for example, Asher and Dugger (2001), Dekle (2002), Madsen (2002), and Fukao (2003).

2. Ideally, we would like to know the value of long-term government debt in private hands. Unfortunately, we were not able to locate this information.

3. For example, Fukao (2002) writes, "They [holders of Japanese bonds] are blindly buying government-backed financial assets even though the credit worthiness of the government is rapidly deteriorating. This negative bubble is clearly unsustainable."

4. Note that our analysis cannot address unsustainability that may arise even if the fundamentals suggest it is sustainable. Unsustainability might occur because of irrational actions by markets, multiple equilibria (for example, a default arising because everyone expects default even though the government could honor its obligations if people continued to believe that it would), and political reasons for default.

5. A different approach has been suggested by Auerbach and Kotlikoff (1995) who uses generational accounting to assess fiscal sustainability. This methodology compares tax burdens of current and future generations and defines a tax rate as sustainable if future generations need not pay higher tax rates than current generations. The two approaches are conceptually similar in that they are both based on the government's intertemporal budget constraint.

6. Unlike the infinite horizon case, the level of outstanding debt in period n discounted to today (i.e., the last term in equation (4)) is not zero.

7. A different indicator could be the level of initial debt, b^*_0, such that, for a given path of fiscal and monetary policy $\{\lambda_t, g_t, h_t, \tau_t\}|_{t=1,\ldots,n}$, (4) is satisfied. We could then compare this level of debt to the actual level of debt to have a sense of the extent of fiscal adjustment that is needed.

8. The same approach could have been used to compute a sustainable spending rate given the forecast of government revenues.

9. See Abel et al (1995) and Frisch (1995) for a discussion of issues related to dynamic efficiency.

10. The same is true for the average of OECD countries. During the 70s and most of the 80s the average difference across countries between nominal interest rates and nominal growth rates was negative. For a simple explanation of dynamic efficiency see Romer (1996).

11. This is subject to a caveat raised by Abel et al. They show that under uncertainty the condition for dynamic efficiency differs from the condition that interest rates have to exceed growth rates. In particular, they demonstrate that a negative $i_t - \eta_t$ does not necessarily imply that the economy of major industrialized countries is dynamically inefficient. Obviously, if Japan's long-run growth will exceed the interest rate, then Japan's fiscal situation will be brighter than what we discuss in this paper.

12. Formally, the condition for sustainability when n goes to infinity implies that the limit of the second term of the RHS of (4) is equal to zero.

13. Technically we should add non-financial assets to the balance sheet. We do not because we assume that the government will never sell any of its real estate holdings or other real assets.

14. This number is calculated by summing together the net debts of the Japanese government, postal savings, and government financial institutions as reported in the BOJ Flow of Funds website. Net debt of social security and the central and local governments in these accounts is 70% of GDP for fiscal year 2002. This is very close to the OECD's number of 71% for *calendar* year 2002 as reported on the OECD website. By contrast, the OECD reports net debt to GDP ratios for Belgium, Italy, and the US are 96%, 94%, and 44%.

15. Lebow (2004) provides a more detailed analysis of the interaction between net debt and monetary policy.

16. Numbers are from the BOJ's flow of funds website, spreadsheet fys1100e.xls. Bond holdings are "Central government securities and FILP bonds" held by the BOJ. Operating surplus is "Financial surplus or deficit (Transactions)"

17. Takayama and Kitamura (1999) arrive to a similar conclusion using a different approach called "Generational Accounting". They find that most of the generational imbalances are due to future demographic change rather than the existing level of debt.

18. It is important to bear in mind that although "shakai hoken" is translated in most government publications as "social security" the better translation is "social insurance" as these data include a large amount of benefits, such as unemployment benefits and child welfare benefits, that would not be included in a US definition of social security. This difference means that one cannot simply compare US "social security" payments with the Japanese ones.

19. All "real" expenditure levels are deflated by the GDP deflator. 1986 marks a break point in the series because a number of cost control measures were introduced in that year to contain growth in benefits for the elderly. Data is from Faruqee and Muhleisen (2001).

20. Studies that use simple indicators of fiscal sustainability (e.g., Alexander (2000) and Dekle (2001)) use current levels of expenditure as their baseline assumption and do not separate the cyclical and trend component of government expenses. These studies tend to find much bigger required tax increases because cyclical policy is mixed together with long-run policy.

21. The difference between the birth rate and fertility rate is important, and our concern is primarily with the latter. The fertility rate is the number of children a woman has over her reproductive life. The replacement level—the fertility rate necessary to sustain a constant population—is about 2.1, the 0.1 covering those who do not themselves procreate. The birth rate refers to the ratio of births to current total population, and thus is affected by the proportion of women of childbearing age in the population.

22. The National Institute of Population and Social Security Research Medium Variant Forecast is the standard one used in government publications and in academic research such as Dekle (2002).

23. PPP per capita GDP data was taken from the World Bank's World Development Indicators Database for the year 2001. Fertility data reported in the WDI is from the United Nations (2003).

24. This corresponds to e^{10}. While one should not make too much of the precise location of the trough, it is clear that decline in fertility tapers off and appears to rise.

25. As one can see from equation (5) the discount factor depends only on the ratio of one plus the interest rate to one plus the growth rate. For small growth rates, this ratio is al-

most independent of the actual growth rate, and hence we focus on the interest rate gap. In practice, we used a GDP growth rate of 2 percent per year and assumed per worker income growth equaled the growth rate less the growth rate in the labor force. Changing the growth rate from 2 percent to 0 percent change our sustainable tax rates by less than 0.1 percentage points in our base case scenarios.

26. Blanchard et al (2000) assume that the non-elderly expenditures grow at the same rate as GDP. This assumption implies that per-capita expenditure to people below 65-years of age is monotonically increasing over time as a share of GDP. As suggested above (see Figure 2.3), this has not been the behavior of per-capita expenditures on this age group in the last 20 years. In their study of OECD countries, Dang et al (2001) recognize that education and child/family benefits fluctuate with the number of young but, in the case of Japan, do not have enough data to correct their expenditure forecasts. Dekle (2002) assumes a constant share of GDP is spent on education per young. Blanchard et al (2000) and Dang et al (2001) assume that the percent change in the ratio of public pension expenditure to GNP is the same as the percentage change in the old-age dependency ratio. This amounts to an implicit assumption that the ratio of the average pension to the average gross wage remains unchanged over time, and is similar to having elderly outlays grow with GDP per capita.

27. Transfers to the elderly per old, H_0/n(old), and rest of expenditures per young, G_0/n(young) are assumed to be at their average level between 1980–2000. Using the NIPSSR population projects we would face even more dramatic changes in the per-capita expenditure levels over time.

28. For the time being, we are going to assume that taxes are the only means of attaining sustainability. We will return to monetary policy later.

29. Revenue and expenditure data are from Faruqee and Muhleisen (2001). Government revenue in 2000 was 31 percent of GDP. They obtain their data from the system of national accounts.

30. Data is from SourceOECD website. As the OECD explains, "current receipts consists mainly of taxes on production and imports, property income receivable, current taxes on income and wealth receivable, social contributions and other current transfers."

31. In robustness checks we found that assuming the same interest rate gap and a real GDP growth rate of 0 percent did not affect the first three digits of the numbers so we do not report those results here.

32. Adjustments of this magnitude periodically do occur. Between 1970 and 1997, 16 out of 23 OECD countries for which we have data raised or lowered their tax rates by 9 percentage points or more. Of these cases, 9 countries raised government current revenues by 9 percentage points of GDP in ten years or less.

33. The path of expenditures in this case corresponds to Figure 2.6.

34. Interestingly, in these scenarios it still is the case that the spreading the benefits over 100 years is worse than over 40 years because the demographic transition takes a long time to complete and we are assuming very generous benefits for people in future generations.

35. Since tax rates are assumed to be constant over the entire horizon, a higher tax rate than the sustainable tax rate implies that debt-to-GDP ratios are smaller in the end of the sustainability horizon than at the beginning. In the case depicted in Figure 9, Japan moves from a net debtor position to a net creditor position around the year 2090.

36. Since our analysis is concerned with long-run sustainability we assume that changes in money supply are equal to inflation rates.

References

Abel, A., N. Mankiw, L. Summers, and R. Zeckhauser. 1989. Assessing Dynamic Efficiency: Theory and Evidence. *Review of Economic Studies* 56 (185): 1–20.

Asher, D. and R. Dugger. 2000. "Could Japan's Financial Mount Fuji Blow its Top?" MIT Japan Program, Working Paper No. 00-01 (May).

Auerbach, A. and L. Kotlikoff. 1998. *Macroeconomics: An Integrated Approach.* 2nd Edition Boston, MA: MIT Press.

Bank of Japan. 2004. http://www.boj.or.jp/en/stat/stat_f.htm

Blanchard, Olivier J. 1990. "Suggestions for a New Set of Fiscal Indicators." OECD Department of Economics and Statistics Working Paper 79.

Blanchard, Olivier J., Jean-Claude Chouraqui, Robert P. Hagemann and Nicola Sartor. 1990. "The Sustainability of Fiscal Policy: New Answers to an Old Question." OECD Economic Studies 15.

Doi, Takero and Takeo Hoshi. 2002. "Paying for the FILP." NBER Working Paper 9385.

Dang, T., P. Antolin, and H. Oxley. 2001. "Fiscal Implications of Aging: Projections of Age-related spending." OECD Economics Working Paper 305.

Dekle, Robert. 2002. "The Deteriorating Fiscal Situation and an Aging Population." NBER Working Paper 9367 (December).

Economic and Social Research Institute. www.esri.cao.go.jp/en/sna/qe0332/gdemenuea.html

Faruqee, Hamid and Martin Mühleisen. 2001. "Population Aging in Japan: Demographic Shock and Fiscal Sustainability." IMF Working Paper 01/40 (April).

Fischer, S., K. Kuttner, J. Makin, and A. Posen. 2001. The Great Recession: Lessons for Macroeconomic Policy from Japan. *Brookings Papers on Economic Activity* 2: 93–186.

Frisch, H. 1995. "Government Debt and Sustainable Fiscal Policy." *Economic Notes* 24(3): 561–80.

Fukao, Mitsuhiro. 2003. "Financial Strains and the Zero Lower Bound: the Japanese Experience." Keio University. BIS Working Paper 141.

Hsieh, C., M. Hori, and S. Shimizutani. 2001. Helicopter Drops of Money: Assessing an Unusual Experiment in Japanese Fiscal Policy. Manuscript. Princeton University.

Kotlikoff, L. and B.Raffelhuschen. 1999. Generational Accounting Around the Globe. *American Economic Review* 89 (2): (May) 161–166.

Kuttner, K. and A. Posen. 2002. Fiscal Policy Effectiveness in Japan. *Journal of the Japanese and International Economies* 16: 536–558.

Lebow, David. 2004. "The Monetization of Japan's Government Debt." Mimeo. Monetary and Economic Department, Bank of International Settlements.

Madsen, Robert. 2002. "Japan: Game Over." MIT Japan Program, Working Paper Series 02.05.

Mylonas, P., S. Shich, T.Thorgeirsson, and G. Wehinger. 2000. "New Issues in Public Debt Management: Government Surpluses in Several OECD Countries, The Common Currency in Europe and Rapidly Rising Debt in Japan." OECD, Economics Department Working Paper 239.

Muhleisen, M. 2000. "Sustainable Fiscal Policies for an Aging Population." In: Japan-Selected Issues, IMF Staff Country Report 00/144.

National Institute of Population and Social Security Research Medium Variant Forecast http://www.ipss.go.jp/index-e.html

Organization of Economic Cooperation and Development. 2003. *OECD Economic Surveys: Japan*. Paris: OECD.

Organization of Economic Cooperation and Development. 2004. Source: OECD http://www.columbia.edu/cu/lweb/eresources/databases/3003554.html

Posen, Adam. 1998. *Restoring Japan's Economic Growth*. Washington: Institute for International Economics.

Romer, D. 2000. *Advanced Macroeconomics*. 2nd Edition. Columbus: McGraw Hill.

Tufte, Edward R. 2001. *The Visual Display of Quantitative Information*. Cheshire, CT: Graphics Press.

Takayama, N. and Y. Kitamura. 1999a. Lessons from Generational Accounting in Japan. *American Economic Review, Paper and Proceedings* 89:2 (May) 171–180.

Takayama, Noriyuki, Yukinobu Kitamura, and Hiroshi Yoshida. 1999b. Generational Accounting in Japan. In *Generational Accounting Around the World,* editors Auerbach, Alan J., Laurence J. Kotlikoff, and Willi Leibfritz. Chicago: The University of Chicago Press.

United Nations. 2003. *World Population Prospects 1950–2050: The 2002 Revision*. Database. Department of Economic and Social Affairs, Population Division. New York.

3

Lost Decade in Translation: Did the United States Learn from Japan's Post-bubble Mistakes?

James Harrigan

and

Kenneth N. Kuttner

1. Introduction

In 1991, the Japanese economy ended a historic expansion and entered a period of stagnation, from which it has yet to fully recover. Japan's "lost decade" was marked by slow growth, falling prices, and persistent financial system dysfunction. This sad tale is made more poignant by Japan's extraordinary economic performance in the four decades that preceded the collapse of the bubble economy in the early 1990s. Indeed, during the 1980s Japan was seen as a model to be emulated, and nationalistic voices in the United States worried about being eclipsed by the Japanese.[1]

While the 1990s were a lost decade for the Japanese economy, this same period was a triumph for the American economy. Following the shallow recession of 1990–1991, the American economy expanded, picking up steam in the latter half of the decade. As the United States stumbled in 2001, however, a number of commentators noticed some uncomfortable similarities between the end of the American boom and the end of the Japanese boom a decade earlier.[2] The concerns about emulating the Japanese were changed from envy in the late 1980s to a sense that the United States had not learned enough from Japan's mistakes to avert a similar fate of stagnation and deflation.

In this paper, we look closely at the similarities and differences between the ending of the two booms, Japan's in 1991 and the United States' in 2000. We begin by analyzing macroeconomic similarities and differences, with results that are both reassuring and discomfiting for the United States. We then turn to a detailed comparison of monetary policy, and we show that the Federal Reserve was far more aggressive after the end of the American boom than the Bank of Japan was a decade earlier at the onset of its recession. The Federal Reserve's sharp rate cuts seem to have worked: the American economy avoided, perhaps narrowly, a fall into deflation in 2003. Nonetheless, the United States faces economic challenges in the coming years that in some ways are more daunting than those faced by Japan in the early 1990s.

2. Macroeconomic Similarities: Too Close for Comfort?

In this section, we look closely at how the American and Japanese economies behaved as their respective booms went bust. Our method is to examine comparable time series from the two countries, in each case converting calendar time to periods (quarters or years) relative to the respective business cycle peaks. For the Japanese data, we examine windows around the business cycle peak of the second quarter of 1991, while for the United States data the analysis is centered on the cyclical peak in gross domestic product (GDP) of the fourth quarter of 2000.

Figure 3.1 illustrates the similarities in overall GDP growth. In the decade before the cyclical peaks, the American economy grew a cumula-

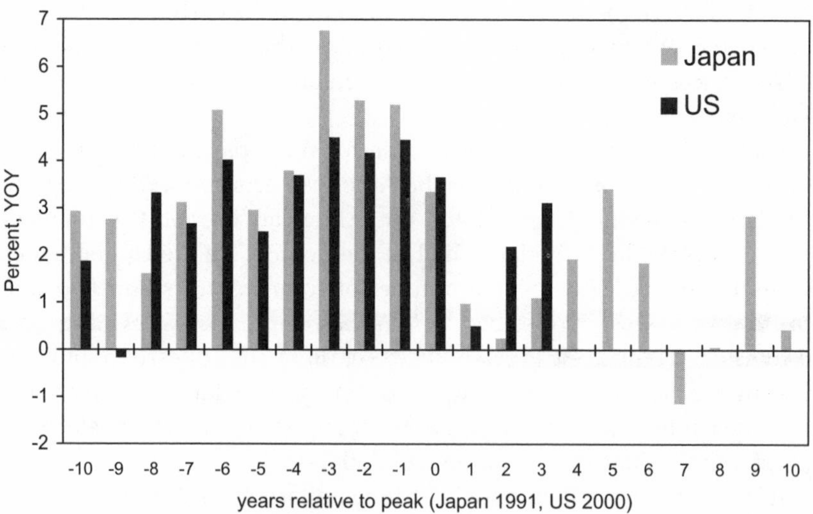

Sources: US and Japanese national accounts.

Figure 3.1
Real GDP growth

tive 38%, while Japan's grew 48%. Neither country saw GDP decline in the year after the peak, though growth fell sharply, from 3.4 to 1.0 percent in Japan and from 3.7 to 0.5 percent in the United States. But two years after the end of the boom, growth was recovering in the United States, while Japan's growth stayed low, as its economy grew a mere 12% cumulatively in the decade after the 1991 peak.

In Figure 3.2, we set real investment and real GDP equal to 100 in the peak year. The figure shows that in both countries, the boom and bust cycles were led by real investment: investment grew much faster than GDP in the years before the peak, and plunged in the years following the peak. Two years after the peak, the American and Japanese experiences were remarkably close, but in the third year real investment in the United States picked up, a year earlier than when Japan's investment recovery began.

The best-known similarity between the Japanese and American booms is the extraordinary bull market that accompanied fast GDP growth in both countries. But as illustrated in Figure 3.3, the timing and magnitude of the stock market booms are quite different. The Nikkei peaked a full six quarters before the peak in GDP, while in the United States the GDP and stock market peaks were almost concurrent, with

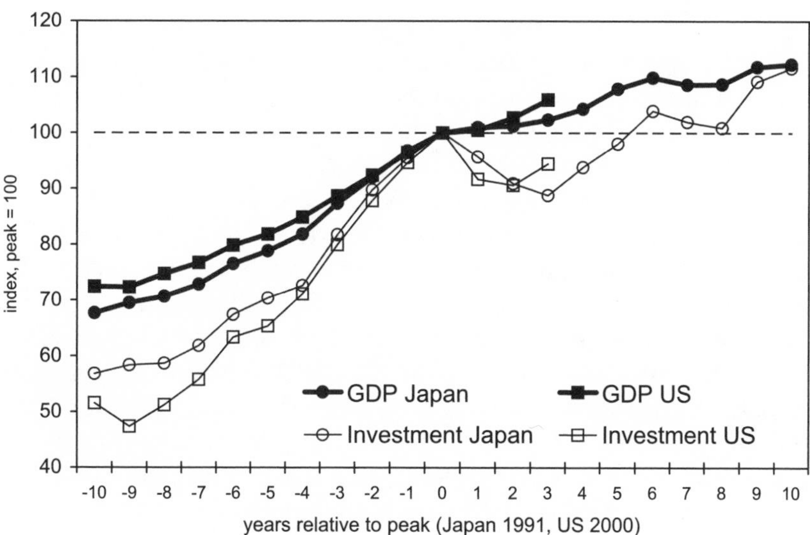

Sources: US and Japanese national accounts.

Figure 3.2
GDP and investment

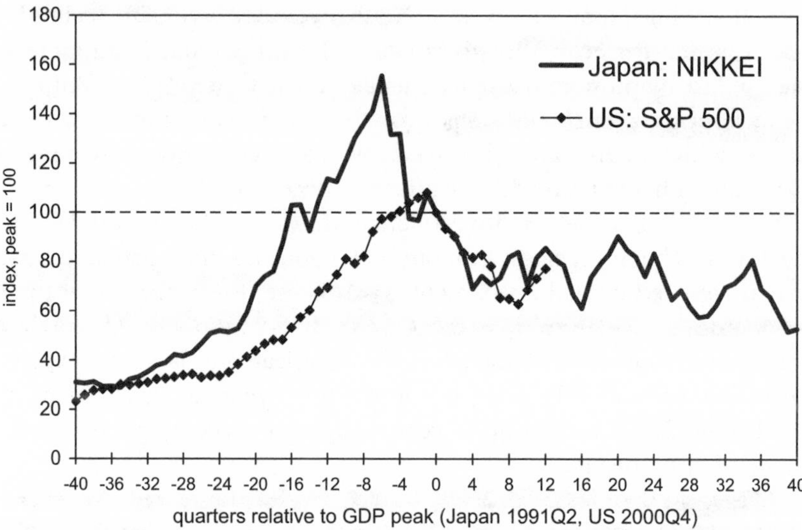

Sources: Federal Reserve Bank of New York database.

Figure 3.3
Stock markets

the Standard & Poor's (S&P) 500 peaking just one quarter before the GDP peak. More importantly, though, the broad Japanese stock market rose higher faster, and fell farther, than did the American market. Looking at troughs and peaks in the stock market rather than in GDP, the Nikkei grew 275% in the five and one-half years before it peaked in 1989Q4, while the S&P 500 grew "only" 225% in the six years preceding its peak in 2000Q3. After the Nikkei peaked, it plummeted 38% in a year, rendering insolvent much of the Japanese banking sector in the process and contributing to the end of the GDP boom. The drop in the S&P 500 was similar in magnitude but slower, falling over 40% before bottoming out (for now) in 2003Q1 and then recovering. It is sobering to note that, as illustrated in Figure 3.3, the Nikkei also bottomed out roughly two years after the GDP peak before staging a comeback, yet to this day it stands at a fraction of the level reached at the end of 1999.

Besides the stock market bubble, Japan also experienced a property market bubble in the late 1980s, which continues to affect balance sheets (especially of banks) today. Did the United States experience a similar bubble? Probably not. International comparisons of property markets are difficult to do, and for the United States and Japan there are no broad time series which are internationally comparable. With that caveat, Figure 3.4 shows the overall urban land price index for Japan, together with two measures of housing prices in the United States (all indices are divided by the country's GDP deflator). The Japanese experience is unambiguous: a vertiginous climb followed by a steep collapse which has yet to stop. The first American index is the repeat-sales index from the U.S. Office of Federal Housing Oversight, which shows no trend at all in the pre-peak years but a very sharp move upward since the peak, growing 18% since 2000. The second index is a constant-quality index produced by the U.S. Census Bureau; this index also shows no trend in the pre-peak years and a more modest climb since 2000, rising just 8% in three years. McCarthy and Peach (2004) argue persuasively that the latter index is more appropriate for evaluating whether there is a bubble in the housing market, a hypothesis they reject.[3] Whichever price index is superior, it is clear that in the United States property prices experienced nothing like the bubble that Japanese land prices did.

On growth and asset markets, then, the post-boom experience in the United States looks superior to Japan's episode. But other comparisons are more worrying. Figure 3.5 illustrates the fiscal positions of the two countries, using comparable figures for the primary surplus and net

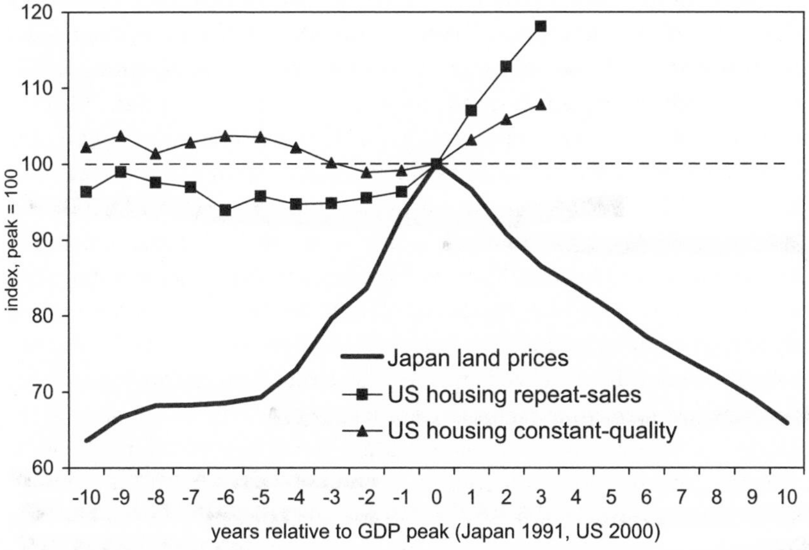

Sources: US Office of Federal Housing Oversight, US Census Bureau, and Japan Real Estate Institution.

Figure 3.4
Relative price of real estate

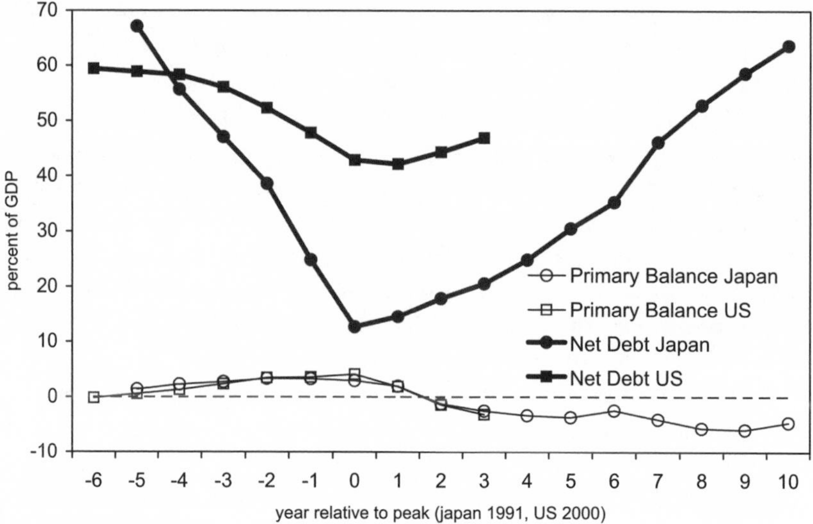

Source: *OECD Economic Outlook*, Annex Tables 30 and 34.

Figure 3.5
Government debt and deficit

government debt as a share of GDP.[4] As the chart illustrates, both countries were in excellent fiscal shape as the boom peaked, with primary surpluses of 3 to 4 percent of GDP. These surpluses evaporated rapidly as the economy slowed, and the paths are remarkably similar, although the United States fiscal deterioration, –7.3 percentage points of GDP in three years, from 4.1 to –3.2, was sharper than Japan's, –5.5 percentage points of GDP. The United States looks significantly worse, however, when debt levels are compared: as the boom peaked, Japan's net government debt had been falling sharply for years and was less than 13% of GDP, while the fiscal consolidation in the United States had gone less far, with debt at 43% of GDP when the boom ended.

As the economies slowed in both the United States and Japan, the fiscal policy response was remarkably similar. Figure 3.6 shows the change in the cyclically-adjusted budget deficits, a standard measure of fiscal stimulus, for both countries. Japan and especially the United States shifted quickly from fiscal consolidation in the last years of the boom to substantial stimulus, on the order of 1% of GDP in the first year after the GDP peak to almost 3% of GDP in the following year. In both countries fiscal stimulus slowed, but remained positive, in the third year after the boom.

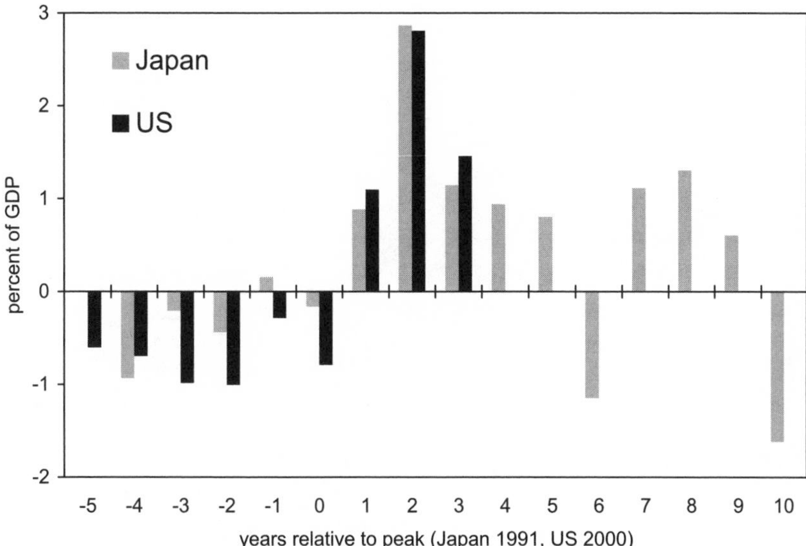

Source: *OECD Economic Outlook*, Annex Table 26.

Figure 3.6
Fiscal stimulus (change in structural deficit)

While the United States looks worse with respect to government debt, the biggest negative comparison has to do with foreign indebtedness. Figure 3.7 illustrates the respective current accounts, depicting the well-known fact that Japan persistently runs surpluses while the American deficit has soared in recent years. The United States' large current account is not sustainable, and adjustment is likely to be a substantial policy challenge in the coming decade (see, for example, IMF 2004).

3. A Detailed Look at Monetary Policy

We now turn to a detailed examination of the similarities and differences between the Bank of Japan's policies since the onset of its recession in 1991 and the Federal Reserve's response to the recession that began in the first quarter of 2001. The analysis focuses initially on the three and one-half years following the two countries' respective business cycle peaks. There are two reasons for concentrating on this period. First, there is broad agreement that the first half of the 1990s was a critical time for the Japanese economy, for it was during this period that what might have been a normal cyclical downturn began its decade-long stagnation. The second reason for focusing on this three

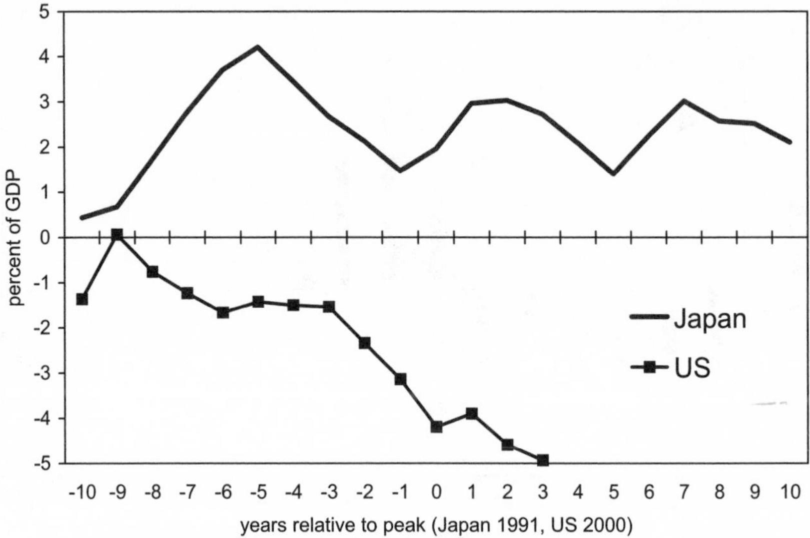

Sources: US and Japanese national accounts.

Figure 3.7
Current account balance

and one-half year interval is that it takes the United States up through mid-2004, when economic conditions, and monetary policy, began to diverge sharply from those in Japan; thus, it is only for this period that a direct comparison of the two countries' monetary policies makes sense. A subsequent subsection discusses Japan's post-1994 monetary policy, comparing it to what the Federal Reserve *might* have done, had it faced continuing deflationary pressures.

Monetary Policy in the Early Stages of the Recessions

Monetary policy followed broadly similar paths in Japan and the United States in the years leading up to, and immediately following the onset of recession in the two countries. As shown in Figure 3.8, short-term nominal rates were rising in the two years leading up to the peak, and generally falling in the years following the peak. In both countries, a period of rapid rate reductions was followed by a period of more gradual rate cuts. The overall level of interest rates was consistently one to two percentage points higher in Japan than in the U.S., however—at least until Japan's call rate was cut to 50 basis points (.5 percent) in 1995, four years after that country's cyclical peak.

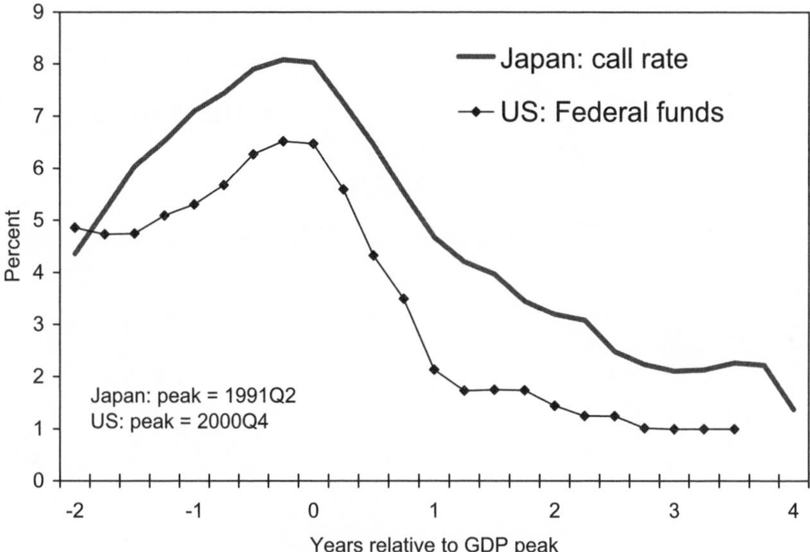

Sources: Bank of Japan, and Board of Governors of the Federal Reserve System.

Figure 3.8
Nominal short-term interest rates in Japan and the U.S.

Higher inflation can partly explain Japan's higher level of nominal interest rates, at least during the period surrounding the peak level of economic activity. As shown in Figure 3.9, Japan's inflation rate rose rapidly in 1990, and by the peak of the expansion core consumer price index (CPI) inflation reached nearly three percent. Inflation then began a rapid decline, reaching zero by early 1995, four years after the peak.[5] In the U.S., meanwhile, inflation remained relatively quiescent, and growth in the core personal consumption expenditure (PCE) deflator remained in the 1.0–1.5 percent range throughout both the expansion and the recession. Inflation finally began to drift down in 2003, two years following the business cycle peak. Even though inflation only began its decline *after* the recession was officially over (at least according to the NBER), its pronounced downward trend raised the specter of Japanese-style deflation in the United States.

Taking inflation into account accentuates the differences between the two countries' monetary policies as measured by the real short-term interest rate. Figure 3.10 plots a simple, *ad hoc* gauge of real interest rates in Japan and the United States: the difference between the nominal overnight interest rates and the previous year's core inflation rate. As shown, the rise and subsequent fall in inflation attenuated both the

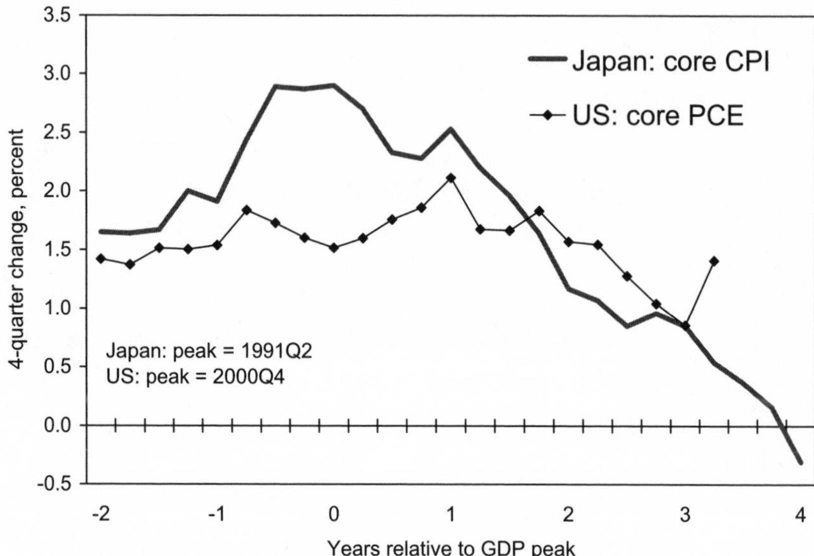

Sources: Statistics Bureau of the Ministry of Public Management, Home Affairs, Posts, and Telecommunications; and the Bureau of Economic Analysis. Japanese core inflation is calculated by FRBNY staff, removing the effects of changes in taxes, energy, and food prices.

Figure 3.9
Inflation in Japan and the U.S.

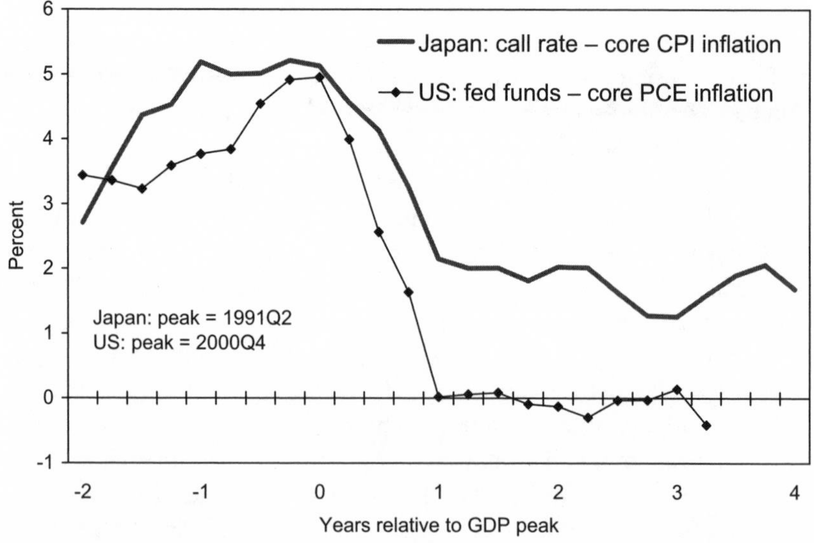

Sources: Same as those for figures 9 and 10, and authors' calculations as described in the text.

Figure 3.10
Real interest rates in Japan and the U.S.

rise in the real rates prior to the peak, and the decline in the real rate as the economy entered the recession. Consequently, the Bank of Japan's policies of tightening in 1989 and 1990, and easing after 1991, were not as aggressive as the path of nominal interest rates would suggest. Indeed, because the Bank of Japan's rate reductions from mid-1992 to mid-1995 barely kept pace with the decline in the inflation rate, the real rate of interest (at least as gauged by lagged inflation) remained within a relatively narrow 1.5–2.0 percent range for a period of three years. In contrast, because the impact of the Federal Reserve's 2001 rate cuts on the real interest rate was not offset by disinflation, the real federal funds rate fell to virtually zero by the end of the year. After 2001, however, the Federal Reserve's more measured rate cuts only sufficed to overcome the decline in inflation, and as a result the real federal funds rate did not fall appreciably below zero.

Was Japan's Disinflation Anticipated?

The path of Japan's inflation-adjusted call money rate, as depicted in Figure 3.10, suggests that a delay in cutting short-term interest rates very likely contributed to the severity of the recession, at least in its early stages. But in this context an important issue arises over the extent to which Japan's disinflation of the early 1990s was anticipated. The question is crucial for assessing the contribution of monetary policy to the economic downturn: to the extent that the disinflation was *un*anticipated, it would not have translated into higher *ex ante* real rates of interest; a monetary policy that seemed too tight *ex post* would have seemed less so at the time. By the same token, to the extent that the disinflation was anticipated, it would have increased *ex ante* real interest rates, and increased the likely contribution of monetary factors to the recession's severity and duration. In this case, the failure to cut interest rates more aggressively would have represented a serious policy mistake.

It is no coincidence that the same issue arises in assessing the role monetary factors played in the United States during the Great Depression of the 1930s; indeed, this question generated a lively debate between Hamilton (1987, 1992) and Cecchetti (1992).[6] With a decline in the overall price level of 5 percent in 1930, the problem of disinflation was obviously much larger than it was for Japan in the 1990s. Nonetheless, the three percentage point decline in Japan's inflation rate during the critical 1991–95 period was of sufficient magnitude to make a difference between a neutral and an accommodative policy stance.

Since no universally-accepted measure of inflation expectations exists, it will never be possible to provide the definitive answer to the question of whether Japan's disinflation was anticipated. But the evidence from statistically-based and consensus forecasts reported below indicates that during the first two years of the recession inflation was somewhat lower than anticipated. By mid- to late-1993, however, disinflation had become firmly embedded in both statistical and market forecasts.

The statistical model used to forecast inflation is simply a regression of the four-quarter inflation rate on lagged inflation, and current and lagged estimates of the output gap. The question then becomes what to use for the output gap—a very difficult issue, in light of what appears to have been a break in trend output growth in or around 1991. As discussed by Kuttner and Posen (2004), what one assumes about the evolution of potential output is critical to any assessment of monetary policy, especially during this period.

Clearly, in order to approximate what expectations were likely to have been at the time, the estimate of the output gap used as an input must be based on information comparable to what observers would have had available contemporaneously. For this reason, many procedures commonly used to calculate potential output proxies, such as the Hodrick-Prescott (HP) filter, are inappropriate, as they use information from the entire sample. As a result, measures of potential output derived from these procedures tend to turn down well in advance of the onset of the recession. This tends to reduce the measured severity of the recession, and exaggerate the magnitude of the preceding business cycle peak.[7]

Instead, we construct an output gap proxy as the difference between the logarithm of real GDP and a linear trend fitted to the logarithm of real GDP, recursively estimated over a rolling, 40-quarter window. In a crude but nonetheless plausible way, this procedure captures the idea that initially observers likely expected the downturn to be transitory, but revised down their assessment of trend real GDP growth gradually as sluggish growth persisted.[8] This pattern is consistent with the behavior of the consensus private-sector forecasts for year-over-year real GDP growth displayed in Figure 3.11: those forecasts stubbornly in the 2.5–4.0 percent range until the end of 1993, when they were finally revised sharply downward.

Figure 3.12 depicts our estimate of the *ex ante* real call money rate in Japan from 1990 to 1995. For comparison, the figure also shows the call rate minus the four-quarter lagged inflation rate (also plotted in

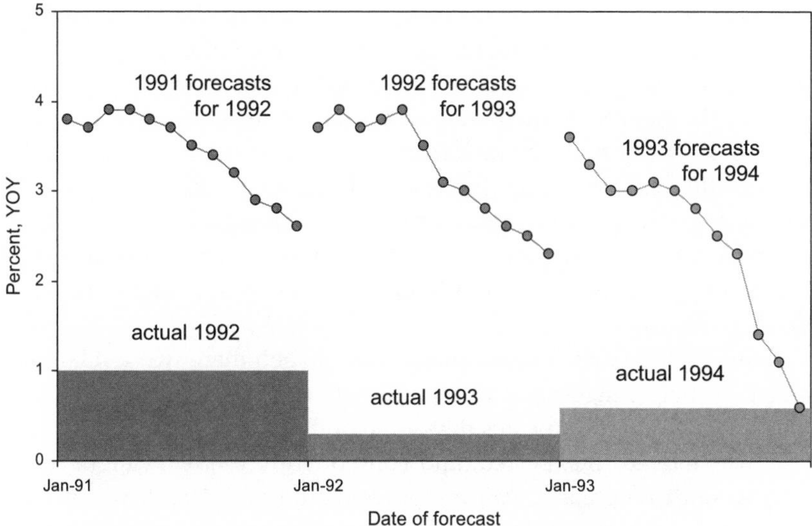

Sources: Consensus Economics Inc., and Economic and Social Research Institute.

Figure 3.11
Consensus real GDP growth forecasts, Japan

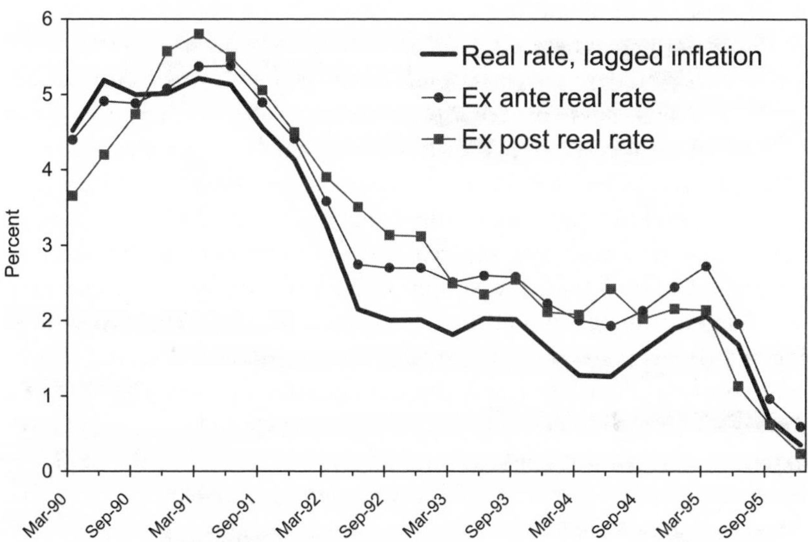

Sources: Same as those for figures 9 and 10, the Economic and Social Research Institute, and authors' calculations as described in the text.

Figure 3.12
Alternative real interest rate measures, Japan

Figure 3.10), and the *ex post* real rate. Not surprisingly, all three capture the overall downward trend in real interest rates, and consequently the three look quite similar at first glance. There are, however, some important differences in the *timing* of the real rate reductions. One key difference is that both the *ex ante* and the *ex post* measures exceed the simple difference between the nominal rate and lagged inflation by 1.0–1.5 percentage points between mid-1992 and mid-1995. This is of course a natural consequence of the fact that in an environment of rapidly-falling inflation, lagged inflation is a poor proxy for future inflation expectations.

A more subtle difference occurs in 1992, when there was a relatively large, .75 percentage-point difference between the *ex ante* and *ex post* measures. This gap indicates that some of the disinflation over this period was indeed unexpected, and consequently the real rate of interest was not as high as *ex post* measures would indicate. (It was higher than indicated by the difference between the nominal rate and lagged inflation, however.) This gap between the *ex ante* and *ex post* real interest rates narrowed in 1993; in the third quarter of that year both were close to 2.5 percent, suggesting that the disinflation had by then become largely anticipated. This pattern is reflected in the consensus private-sector forecasts in Figure 3.13, which show a systematic overprediction of inflation up until late 1993.

The overall conclusion to be drawn from this analysis is that while the disinflation was to some extent unanticipated in the early stages of Japan's recession, by late 1993 disinflationary expectations were likely to have been pretty firmly entrenched. This conclusion holds both for private-sector survey expectations, and for econometric forecasts designed to mimic expectations that observers might have formed at the time. As a result, *ex ante* real interest rates were in all likelihood somewhat higher than the simple difference between nominal rates and lagged inflation would have indicated. In this light, the Bank of Japan's decision to leave the call money rate unchanged at 2.25 percent through all of 1994 and the first quarter of 1995 seems all the more surprising. By keeping the call rate unchanged even as inflation expectations fell, the Bank of Japan effectively allowed the stance of monetary policy to become slightly tighter—a decision which could very well have contributed to the further weakening of economic conditions.

In this dimension too, the Federal Reserve's policy over the 2001–03 period provides a revealing basis for comparison. Figure 3.14 displays the *ex ante* real federal funds rate for the United States,using inflation

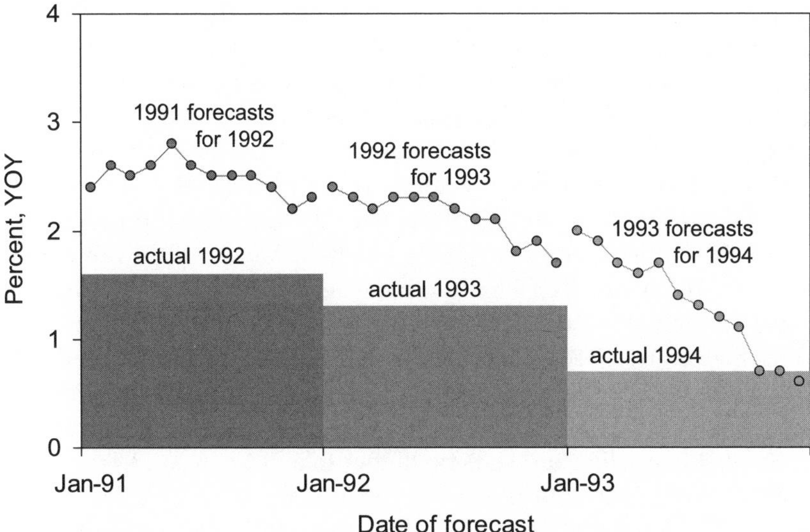

Sources: Consensus Economics Inc., and Statistics Bureau of the Ministry of Public Management, Home Affairs, Posts, and Telecommunications; and the Bureau of Economic Analysis.

Figure 3.13
Consensus CPI inflation expectations, Japan

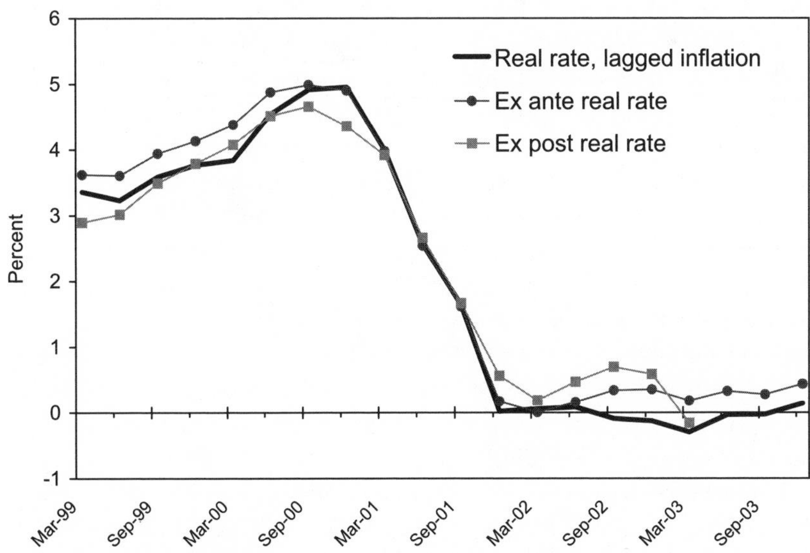

Sources: Board of Governors of the Federal Reserve, Bureau of Economic Analysis, and authors' calculations as described in the text.

Figure 3.14
Alternative real rate measures, U.S.

forecasts computed in a procedure analogous to that used for Japan; also plotted are the *ex post* real funds rate, and the difference between the nominal funds rate and lagged four-quarter inflation that was plotted in Figure 3.9. As the figure clearly shows, from the beginning of the easing cycle in January 2001 up through mid-2002, there is virtually no difference between the various measures of the real interest rate; with so little change in the inflation rate over this period, all three gauges tell basically the same story. Yet the picture changes a little as inflation begins to decline in 2003. Now, with the Federal Reserve's rate cuts not quite keeping up with the pace of disinflation, the *ex post* real rate rises from the neighborhood of zero to as much as 0.7 percent. But this disinflation was to some extent unanticipated, at least on the basis of our simple forecasting model. Consequently, the rise in the *ex ante* real rate of interest is smaller, and goes no higher than 0.4 percent. In any case, the differences between *ex ante* and *ex post* rates are dwarfed by the magnitude in the decline in the real interest rate, however measured.

What If the Bank of Japan Had Acted Like the Federal Reserve?

As demonstrated above, Japan's monetary policy stance, as measured by the real overnight interest rate, was considerably less expansionary than it was in the United States at a comparable stage in the downturn. The question remains, however, as to how expansionary policy *should* have been in light of economic conditions as perceived at the time.

A definitive answer to this question would, of course, require using a fully-articulated quantitative model to evaluate the Japanese economy's likely response to counterfactual interest rate paths. Such an undertaking is beyond the scope of this paper, and in any case the results from this kind of exercise would inevitably be sensitive to the assumptions underlying the model. The approach we take instead is to evaluate the Bank of Japan's monetary policy using empirical reaction functions—essentially we ask how the Bank of Japan's policy during this period compared with its "normal" reaction to output and inflation, and with the reaction of the Federal Reserve if it had faced a similar set of economic conditions.

This method has been a popular one in discussions of Japanese monetary policy: see, for example, Ahearne et al. (2002), Okina and Shiratsuka (2002), Taylor (2001), Jinushi et al. (2000), McCallum (2000, 2003), and Bernanke and Gertler (1999) to name a few. The approach is not without its hazards, however, and conclusions drawn from it are often sensitive to exactly how potential output is estimated, as discussed in detail in Kuttner and Posen (2004). But as discussed above, one major pitfall can be avoided simply by not using a retrospective method, like the HP filter, to estimate trend output.[9]

With this caveat in mind, we use the recursively-estimated trend method described above to estimate potential output; thus, the output gap and inflation expectations used as inputs in the reaction function are mutually consistent, and as argued above, plausibly correspond to policymakers' real-time assessment of economic conditions in Japan. This procedure yields an output gap proxy that works well in our inflation equation, and yields forecasts similar to the private-sector survey expectations.

The specific form of the reaction function used for the comparisons below is

$$i_t^* = \bar{\imath} + \alpha(y_t - y_t^*) + \beta\pi_t^e \qquad (1)$$

where $(y_t - y_t^*)$ and π_t^e are, respectively, our estimates of the output gap and four-quarter-ahead expected inflation. The equilibrium real interest rate and the target inflation rate are both absorbed into the intercept term, $\bar{\imath}$. Estimated versions of equations like (1) typically also include a partial adjustment mechanism in order to capture central banks' apparent preference for interest rate smoothing. For our purposes, however, the inclusion of a lagged interest rate term would only obscure the underlying policy response to output and inflation, so in the results below we display only the path of the desired, or target nominal interest rate, i_t^*.

Figure 3.15 displays the Japanese call money rate, and the target interest rate path implied by (1) for two sets of parameters. One uses the reaction function parameters reported by Ahearne et al. (2002) for Japan, which put very little weight on the output gap: specifically, $\alpha = 0.05$ and $\beta = 2.31$.[10] As shown in the figure, this configuration of parameter values tracks Bank of Japan policy quite well over this period, even without the partial adjustment mechanism. Rates in 1992 were actually cut slightly more aggressively than implied by the rule. The Bank of Japan deviated in a contractionary direction when it left interest rates unchanged in 1994, however; application of the rule would have led to a nominal rate of virtually zero by the first quarter of 1995. (The Bank of Japan did eventually reduce the call rate to zero, but not until the second quarter of 1999.) Thus by the standards of the estimated reaction function, the Bank of Japan's failure to cut rates in 1994 is hard to explain.

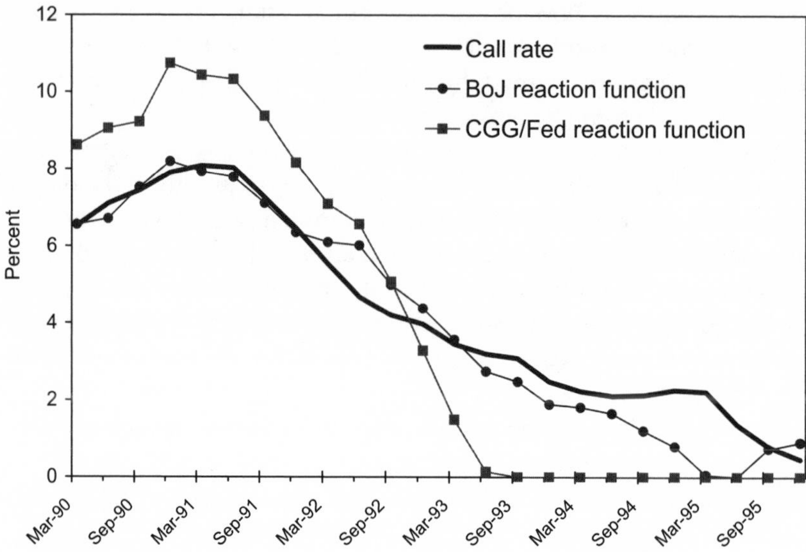

Sources: Same as those for Figure 12, and authors' calculations as described in the text.

Figure 3.15
Implications of alternative monetary policy reaction functions, Japan

Also plotted in Figure 3.15 is the path of the overnight interest rate implied by (1), but with the parameters reported in Clarida et al. (2000) for the Federal Reserve for the 1979Q3 to 1996Q4 period (i.e., with Paul Volcker and Alan Greenspan as Federal Reserve Chairmen): $\alpha = 0.93$ and $\beta = 2.15$. The difference between this and the path given by the Bank of Japan's estimated reaction function is striking: had the overnight rate been set according to the Federal Reserve's policy rule, it would have been reduced to zero by mid-1993, and remained there at least through 1995. It is also interesting to note, however, that prior to 1992, the rate implied by the Federal Reserve's rule is somewhat *higher* than the rate actually set by the Bank of Japan, and the rate implied by the estimated Bank of Japan rule.

The source of these differences is, of course, the larger weight on the output gap in the estimated Federal Reserve rule: 0.93 versus 0.05. This is consistent with the findings of Jinushi et al. (2000), who argued that the Bank of Japan in the late 1980s shifted its emphasis to managing the exchange rate and asset prices, and as a result appeared to lose sight of its core macroeconomic objectives. It consequently tended to *under*-react to output fluctuations—not only relative to the Federal Reserve, but also compared with the Bank of Japan's own response in the pre-bubble period. It is this shift in policy objectives, therefore, that potentially explains the weak response to the collapse in the early 1990s, and the failure to head off the excesses of the late 1980s.

The Federal Reserve's response to the 2000–01 recession, on the other hand, turns out to have followed the rule estimated by Clarida et al. (2000) quite closely. Figure 3.16 depicts the rule's implied federal funds rate path, along with the actual nominal funds rate. The most conspicuous deviation from the rule comes in 2002, when the Federal Reserve cut rates more sharply than it would have had it followed the rule mechanically. The Federal Reserve did not, however, cut rates quite as quickly in the first and second quarters of 2003 as the rule would have suggested. But the deviation between the implied and actual funds rate over this period is only on the order of 50 basis points, and by September the gap between the two had closed.

Anti-deflation policies in Japan and the United States

Three and one half years after their respective business cycle peaks, the monetary policy landscapes in Japan and the United States were similar, at least superficially. At the end of 1994, short-term interest rates

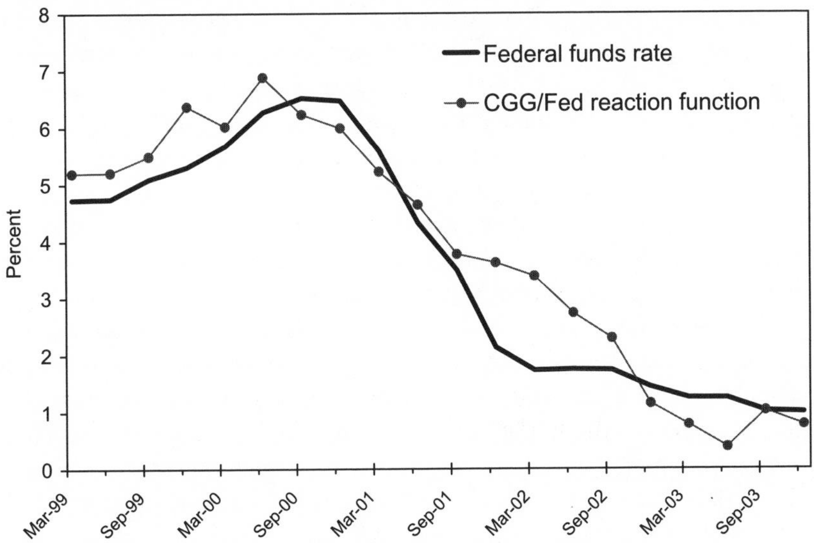

Sources: Same as those for figure 14, and authors' calculations as described in the text.

Figure 3.16
Implications of Clarida-Gali-Gertler rule for the U.S.

in Japan stood at 2.25 percent, well above the zero lower bound, and roughly where they had been since late 1993. In mid-2004, the federal funds rate was 1 percent, and had been at 1.25 percent or less for one and a half years.

Underlying economic developments in the United States and Japan had already begun to diverge sharply by this point, however. After two quarters of modest growth in mid-1994, the Japanese economy contracted in 1994Q4 and 1995Q1. Consequently, the Bank of Japan allowed the call rate to fall to 0.5 percent over the April to September 1995 period. In the United States, on the other hand, the sustained, highly expansionary monetary policy stance seems to have had a significant economic impact, and by mid-2004 any lingering concerns about the recovery's sustainability and deflation had been dispelled by the acceleration in GDP and the stabilization in consumer price inflation. Responding to these developments, the Federal Reserve in June 2004 began the process of raising the funds rate target from the 1 percent level it had reached in June of the previous year. Thus, four years following its business cycle peak, monetary policy in the United States began heading in an entirely different direction from that in Japan in 1995.

It is impossible to know, of course, what the Federal Reserve would have done had economic conditions continued to deteriorate, as they did in Japan. But in mid-2003, it was not at all clear that robust growth was going to resume in the United States, and there seemed to be a very real, albeit small, probability that deflation would also become a problem. It is, therefore, informative to compare the Bank of Japan's post-1994 policy with what the Federal Reserve might have done in response to an intensification of deflationary pressures.

Following its last round of rate cuts in mid-1995, the Bank of Japan's policy went through what might be characterized as three distinct phases.[11] The first is a nearly three-year period of stasis, in which the call rate remained at or near 0.5 percent. This period included a modest recovery in 1996, a renewed recession in the summer of 1997, and various domestic financial breakdowns as well as the onset of the Asian financial crisis in the fall of 1997. While the Bank of Japan did provide several emergency injections of liquidity to the banking system during this period, it did not change the call rate, much less introduce any unconventional monetary policy measures.

This first phase ended in late 1998 and early 1999 with the reduction in the call rate to first to .25 percent, and then to virtually zero.[12] This second phase, the so-called Zero Interest Rate Policy (ZIRP), is characterized by the Bank of Japan's initial, tentative efforts to influence expectations of the path of future policy. Specifically, the minutes of the April 9, 1999 Policy Board meeting, released a month later, stated that "it was important to maintain the current decisive easy stance of monetary policy, firmly underpinning economic activity until deflationary concerns were dispelled." Also under ZIRP, the Bank of Japan initiated outright purchases of short-term government securities, and expanded the range of government securities eligible for repo operations.

The Bank of Japan's highly expansionary setting of short-term interest rates, however, may have been counteracted by the statements of senior officials especially by those of then-Bank of Japan Governor Hayami. The most well-known of these comments was a speech given on March 21, 2000, in which Hayami contended that Japan's deflation was beneficial, or at least benign, and argued strenuously against policy measures intended to combat it. In reference to an explicit inflation target, Hayami stated that "such a proposal is tantamount to artificially creating inflation ... at any cost," and warned that "inflation is most likely uncontrollable, once triggered."

The ZIRP phase of the Bank of Japan's policy came to an abrupt end on August 11, 2000, when, in apparent contradiction to its stated policy, the Bank of Japan increased the call rate target to .25 percent. The Policy Board cited the "improvement of the economy" as a factor in its decision, but said nothing about deflationary pressures. Long-term Japanese Government Bond rates fell steadily during the six months following the rate hike, suggesting a further decline in inflation expectations. In fact, Kuttner and Posen (2004) identify this as the most distinct of several "deflation scares" occurring over the 1996–2003 period. And Orphanides (2004) likens the Bank of Japan's August 2000 rate increase to the Federal Reserve's disastrous policy tightening of 1937, which is widely blamed for extinguishing the incipient recovery that was then taking place.

The Bank of Japan reversed itself in early 2001 with the reduction of the call rate, in two steps, to zero. On March 19, the Bank of Japan announced a change in the main operating target to the outstanding balance of current accounts (i.e., total reserves), initiating the third, "quantitative easing" phase of monetary policy. The central element of this policy was the introduction of a gradually-increasing target for current account balances, along with a steady expansion in the range of assets eligible for purchase by the Bank of Japan. But perhaps more importantly, the policy change was accompanied by the announcement that "the new procedure will be kept in place until the CPI registers a stable zero percent or increase year-on-year." The specificity of this statement makes it a much more explicit effort to influence expectations than the less-precise "until deflationary concerns were dispelled" statement that accompanied the ZIRP. After a three-year delay, a false start, and a reversal, the Bank of Japan was finally on a path towards what might be described as "unconventional" monetary policy.

Many of the anti-deflation policy measures contemplated by the Federal Reserve in 2003 turned out to be quite similar to those that were eventually adopted by the Bank of Japan. But unlike the Bank of Japan, senior Federal Reserve officials floated proposals for unconventional monetary policy measures very early. In fact, public consciousness of deflation was raised in November 2002, by Federal Reserve Governor Ben Bernanke in a speech provocatively titled "Making Sure 'It' Doesn't Happen Here" (Bernanke 2002).

With year-over-year core CPI inflation still running at a 2 percent annual rate, deflation was hardly an imminent danger when Bernanke made his speech. Nonetheless, the speech forcefully articulated the view that monetary policy was not, in fact, powerless once the short-term nominal interest rate reached zero, and that the central bank still had a number of tools at its disposal. The specific tools mentioned in the speech included expanding the monetary base, targeting interest rates farther out on the yield curve, and instructing the Open Market Desk to purchase privately-issued securities. Some of these policy options were also mentioned as possibilities in a subsequent speech by Federal Reserve Chairman Alan Greenspan [Greenspan (2002)].

While the Federal Reserve did not commit publicly to any specific course of action, over the course of 2003 the evolution of Federal Reserve officials' thinking could be gleaned from FOMC statements, officials' speeches, and from published reports. Perhaps the most telling policy shift came at the May 6, 2003 meeting. Although the FOMC left the funds rate target unchanged, it departed from its conventional balance of risks assessment and stated that "the probability of an unwelcome substantial fall in inflation, though minor, exceeds that of a pickup in inflation from its already low level." By acknowledging that the FOMC was prepared to act to prevent further disinflation, the statement had a strong impact on expected future short-term rates. This was reflected in the bond rates: although yields did not fall immediately, in the five weeks following the FOMC's statement, the yield on 10-year Treasury notes fell by more than 50 basis points.[13]

While repeating its concern about an "unwelcome fall in inflation," the announcement accompanying the August 12, 2003 FOMC meeting provided an even stronger hint about future policy, stating that policy accommodation could "be maintained for a considerable period." This statement did not, however, have the same effect on long-term interest rates as the May 6 announcement—in fact, the 10-year Treasury yield *rose* in the weeks following the meeting—perhaps because of uncertainty regarding exactly what was meant by a "considerable period."

Other hints of the FOMC's intentions also emerged from press reports, such as that of Ip (2003). According to that article, senior Federal Reserve officials had largely discarded as unworkable some of the more interventionist proposals, such as the direct targeting of long-term interest rates, as impractical. Ip reports that the more conventional of the unconventional policy options, such as quantitative measures and the commitment to a future path of interest rates, were reportedly still under active consideration by the FOMC.

Ip's report turns out to have been largely consistent with the thinking of FOMC members, as outlined in Bernanke and Reinhart (2004). The FOMC appears to have been leaning towards an approach entailing a conditional commitment to keeping the funds rate low for an extended period of time, combined with quantitative measures of some sort—a strategy quite similar to what the Bank of Japan eventually adopted in 2001. But perhaps because it had learned from the Japan's experience, the Federal Reserve was prepared to implement a vigorous anti-deflation policy into place much more quickly than the Bank of Japan. Moreover, this intention was consistently backed up by statements and speeches by Federal Reserve officials emphasizing the seriousness of the deflation threat (however small), and pledging to do whatever was necessary to prevent it. In these respects, the contrast with Bank of Japan policymakers' statements on the topic could not be starker. One lesson that seems *not* to have been learned by the Federal Reserve, however, is that statements intended to affect expectations of future policy are most effective when they are specific—hence the mixed reaction to the FOMC's "considerable period" statement of August 2003.

4. Conclusions

The popular American attitude toward Japan's economic performance has evolved from fearful envy in the late 1980s, to smug superiority in the late 1990s, to a nervous "there but for the grace of God go I" feeling in the new millenium, for the boom in the United States ended in ways that seemed all-too-similar to the beginning of Japan's "Lost Decade." In this paper, we have looked more closely at the analogies between the Japanese and American experiences. Our conclusions for the United States are somewhat reassuring: the American recovery from post-boom-recession seems more solid, and Japan's problems resulting from imprudent bank lending during an asset price bubble are absent in the United States. More worrying, however, are the Americans' fiscal and current account imbalances, which are far larger than Japan's were at a comparable stage.

A major difference between Japan and the United States is in the response of monetary policy. As boom turned to bust, we have shown that Federal Reserve policy was far more aggressive than Bank of Japan policy was a decade earlier, and the Federal Reserve's decisive response may have helped the American economy recover more quickly than Japan's did. The attention within the Federal Reserve to Japan's experience, as seen in Ahearne et al (2002), may be evidence that the FOMC did indeed translate Japan's lessons into a usable prescription for averting deflation in the United States.

An important question left unaddressed in this paper is *why* Japanese policymakers in general—and the Bank of Japan in particular—responded so slowly and so erratically in the face of deteriorating economic conditions. Theories abound, but none provides an entirely satisfactory explanation. The simplest one is that the Bank of Japan behaved appropriately given the information it had available at the time, but was caught off-guard by the severity and speed of the disinflation. This may explain part of the delay in the early stages of the recession, but, as argued above, this story becomes less convincing after 1993.

One possible explanation emphasizes the conflict between the Bank of Japan and the Ministry of Finance, and attempts to explain suboptimal policy as the result of a noncooperative game between the two institutions. Bank of Japan policymakers have, at various times, voiced concern that aggressive central bank purchases of JGBs would "erode fiscal discipline" [see, e.g., Hayami (2000)]. In this case, monetary policy may have been distorted in an attempt to use it as leverage against the Ministry of Finance.[14]

A second candidate explanation focuses on the Bank of Japan's independence, which was formally granted in April, 1998. [Posen (2003) argues that the Bank of Japan achieved a large degree of *de facto* independence far earlier.] Conventionally, central bank independence is seen as a means to eliminating the problem of inflation bias—not as a source of *deflationary* bias. But as pointed out by Eggertsson (2003), the familiar time inconsistency problem of Barro and Gordon (1983) also applies in a deflationary environment, as it means any promise to create above-target inflation would not be credible. A related hypothesis, advanced by Cargill (2001), is that the fear of losing its newly-won independence kept the Bank of Japan from pursuing a more expansionary policy, thus falling into an "independence trap."

The explanation favored by Posen (2003) is simply that the Bank of Japan's policies were constrained by a rigid adherence to certain economic doctrines—ideas which, while appropriate (or at least not damaging) under normal economic conditions, became obstacles to the pursuit of more expansionary policy. One such doctrine is that because monetary policy transmission occurs exclusively through the overnight interest rate, other measures would be ineffective. Another is the "liquidationist" view that that low interest rates would retard the process of structural reform of the public sector, and creative destruction in the private sector.[15]

Which of these explanations best accounts for the conduct of Japanese policy in the 1990s remains unsettled, as does the extent to which more decisive monetary policy would have lifted the Japanese economy out of its recession. But if there is a fundamental lesson to be learned it is that monetary policy should not neglect output stabilization in its pursuit of inflation stabilization.

Acknowledgments

This paper has benefited from the comments of the pre-conference participants in New York in August 2003, from the detailed suggestions of Hugh Patrick, and from colleagues at the Federal Reserve Bank of New York. Christina Marsh was our research assistant. The views expressed in this paper are those of the authors and do not necessarily reflect the position of the Federal Reserve Bank of New York, the Federal Reserve System, or the NBER.

Notes

1. This tendency was exemplified by Michael Crichton's best-selling xenophobic mystery-thriller *Rising Sun*, published (ironically) in 1992.

2. See, for example, Krugman (2001) and DeLong (2002).

3. The McCarthy-Peach argument is that the repeat-sales index fails to control for quality upgrading in the housing stock, which they argue has been substantial.

4. As Broda and Weinstein argue persuasively elsewhere in this volume, the gross debt figures often cited as an indicator of the fiscal position of the Japanese state hugely overstate the extent of the net financial claims by the private sector on the government. The data used here are from the OECD. The definition of primary surplus is the general government surplus excluding debt interest payments.

5. The measure of Japan's core CPI used in this analysis is constructed by subtracting the food and energy price contributions (the food and energy price sub-indexes, multiplied by their weights) from the overall CPI. Very similar pictures are obtained using alternative price indices. Inflation as measured by the implicit GDP deflator, for example, exhibited a similar pattern, although the increase in 1990 was somewhat less pronounced. The decline in the GDP deflator was somewhat more severe, registering a –1 percent year-over-year change in the second quarter of 1995.

6. According to the chronology of the National Bureau of Economic Research, the U.S. experienced two recessions in the 1930s: one lasting from 1929Q3 through 1932Q4, and a second lasing from 1937Q2 through 1938Q1.

7. Kuttner and Posen (2004) point out that applying the HP filter in this way would lead one to conclude that trend growth began to turn down in 1988, and that the output gap remained *positive* until well into 1993.

8. This idea is captured more precisely by the unobserved-components specification used by Posen (1998), and Kuttner and Posen (2001), which yields an estimate of potential output broadly similar to that obtained from the recursive trend. All of these statistical methods are based on the questionable assumption that output reverts to potential over horizons normally associated with business cycles, however, and none captures the underlying microeconomic determinants of the nation's productive capacity. Thus, it is fair to say that the output gap proxy used in this analysis captures the decline in Japan's trend growth rate, but fails to provide an explanation for the slowdown. A more extensive discussion of alternative approaches to estimating the output gap can be found in Kuttner and Posen (2004).

9. Okina and Shiratsuka (2002), for example, use the full-sample HP filter, and consequently conclude that Bank of Japan policy deviated very little from a conventional reaction function.

10. Kuttner and Posen (2004) reported parameter estimates for Japan that are very similar to those of Ahearne et al. (2002).

11. This account of Bank of Japan policy draws heavily on section 3 of Kuttner and Posen (2004).

12. While not literally a zero call rate target, the ZIRP was implemented by way of a new guideline for money market operations that called for the Bank of Japan to "provide more ample funds and encourage the uncollateralized call rate to move as low as possible."

13. Much of this decline was reversed in June, after the FOMC cut the funds rate target by a less-than-expected 25 basis points. A further rise in long-term interest rates occurred immediately following Greenspan's congressional testimony on July 15 (Greenspan (2003)), which was widely viewed as discounting any imminent implementation of unconventional policy measures.

14. To our knowledge, no one has as yet developed a model that delivers this result under assumptions relevant to the Japanese case. The general outlines of such a model would presumably be similar to those of Nordhaus (1994) or Dixit and Lambertini (2003).

15. Ample evidence of both can be found in the published statements and speeches of Bank of Japan officials; see Posen (2003) for references.

References

Ahearne, Alan, Joseph Gagnon, Jane Haltmaier, and Steve Kamin. 2002. "Preventing Deflation: Lessons from Japan's Experience in the 1990s." Board of Governors of the Federal Reserve System, International Finance Discussion Paper 729. (June).

Barro, Robert and David Gordon. 1983. A Positive Theory of Monetary Policy in a Natural Rate Model. *Journal of Political Economy* (91) 4: 589–610.

Bernanke, Ben and Mark Gertler. 1999. Monetary Policy and Asset Price Volatility. Federal Reserve Bank of Kansas City, *Economic Review*, 4th Quarter.

Bernanke, Ben. 2002. "Making Sure 'It' Doesn't Happen Here." Speech presented to the National Economists Club, Washington, D.C., November 21.

Bernanke, Ben and Vincent Reinhart. 2004. "Conducting Monetary Policy at Very Low Short-Term Interest Rates." Speech presented at the Meetings of the American Economic Association, San Diego, January 3.

Broda, Christian and David Weinstein. 2004. Happy news from the dismal science: reassessing Japanese fiscal policy and sustainability. In *Reviving Japan's Economy: Problems and Prescriptions*, Chapter 2. Cambridge, MA: MIT Press.

Cargill, Thomas. 2001. Monetary Policy, Deflation, and Economic History: Lessons for the Bank of Japan. *Bank of Japan Monetary and Economic Studies.* (Special Edition) February.

Cecchetti, Stephen G. 1992. Prices During the Great Depression: Was the Deflation of 1930–1932 Really Unanticipated? *American Economic Review* (82) 1: (March) 141–56.

Clarida, Richard, Jordi Galí, and Mark Gertler. 2000. Monetary Policy Rules and Macroeconomic Stability: Evidence and Some Theory. *Quarterly Journal of Economics* 115: (February) 147–80.

Consensus Economics, Inc., London. *Consensus Forecasts*, various issues.

DeLong, Bradford. 2002. America's Date with Deflation. *Financial Times*, August 21.

Dixit, Avinash and Luisa Lambertini. 2003. Interactions of Commitment and Discretion in Monetary and Fiscal Policies. *American Economic Review* (93) 5: 1522–42.

Eggertsson, Gauti. 2003. "How to Fight Deflation in a Liquidity Trap: Committing to Being Irresponsible." International Monetary Fund Working Paper 03/64 (March).

Greenspan, Alan. 2002. "Issues for Monetary Policy." Speech presented to the Economic Club of New York, New York City, December 19.

Greenspan, Alan. 2003. Testimony before the Committee on Financial Services, U.S. House of Representatives. Federal Reserve Board's semiannual monetary policy report to the Congress, July 15.

Hamilton, James D. 1987. Monetary Factors in the Great Depression. *Journal of Monetary Economics* 19 (2): (March) 145–69.

______. 1992. Was the Deflation During the Great Depression Anticipated? Evidence from the Commodity Futures Market. *American Economic Review* 82 (1): (March) 157–78.

Hayami, Masaru. 2000. "Price Stability and Monetary Policy." Speech presented to the Research Institute of Japan, Tokyo, March 21.

International Monetary Fund. 2004. "United States: 2004 Article IV Consultation—Staff Report." IMF Country Report No. 04/230.

Ip, Greg. 2003. Fed Weighs Alternative Ways to Create Economic Stimulus. *Wall Street Journal*, April 9.

Jinushi, Toshiki, Yoshihiro Kuroki, and Ryuzo Miyao. 2000. Monetary Policy in Japan Since the Late 1980s: Delayed Policy Actions and Some Explanations. In *Japan's Financial Crisis and Its Parallels to U.S. Experience*, editors Ryoichi Mikitani and Adam S. Posen. Washington, D.C.: Institute for International Economics.

Krugman, Paul R. 2001. The Fear Economy. *New York Times Sunday Magazine*, September 30.

Kuttner, Kenneth, Adam Posen, 2001. The Great Recession: Lessons for Macroeconomic Policy from Japan. *Brookings Papers on Economic Activity* 2: 93–198.

Kuttner, Kenneth and Adam Posen. 2004. The difficulty of discerning what's too tight: Taylor rules and Japanese monetary policy. *North American Journal of Economics and Finance* 15: (March) 53–74.

McCallum, Bennett T. 2000. Alternative Monetary Policy Rules: A Comparison with Historical Settings for the United States, the United Kingdom, and Japan. Federal Reserve Bank of Richmond, *Economic Quarterly* 86: (Winter) 49–79.

______. 2003. Japanese monetary policy, 1991–2001. Federal Reserve Bank of Richmond, *Economic Quarterly* 89: (Winter) 1–31.

McCarthy, Jonathan and Richard Peach. 2004. Home Prices: Are they the next 'Bubble'? Federal Reserve Bank of New York, *Economic Policy Review* 10 (3) (December).

Nordhaus, William. 1994. Policy Games: Coordination and Independence in Monetary and Fiscal Policies. *Brookings Papers on Economic Activity* 2: 139–217.

Okina, Kunio and Shigenori Shiratsuka. 2002. Asset Price Bubbles, Price Stability, and Monetary Policy: Japan's Experience. *Bank of Japan Monetary and Economic Studies*, (October) 35–76.

Orphanides, Athanasios. 2004. Monetary policy in deflation: the liquidity trap in history and practice. *North American Journal of Economics and Finance* 15: (March) 101–124.

Posen, Adam and Debayani Kar. 2002. "Japanese Macroeconomic Policy: Unusual?" Mimeo. Institute for International Economics.

Taylor, John B. 2001. Low Inflation, Deflation, and Policies for Future Price Stability. *Bank of Japan Monetary and Economic Studies* 19: 35–51.

4 Monetary Policy in Japan: Problems and Solutions

Takatoshi Ito

and

Frederic S. Mishkin

There is no doubt that Japan's economy is in deflation. The GDP deflator has been declining since 1995, while the consumer price index (CPI) has been falling since 1998. Land prices have been declining since the early 1990s. Important questions about this long deflation are how much of it is due to demand factors and how much to supply factors; and whether it is a result of a stagnant economy or a cause of the stagnation?

Inflation or deflation is ultimately a monetary phenomenon. In theory, when the growth rate is below potential and prices are dropping, monetary policy should be eased without hesitation. It is thus natural that the conduct of monetary policy by the Bank of Japan (BOJ) has been a source of controversy for several years.

This chapter reviews theoretical and practical issues surrounding the controversy. Although an economic recovery began in 2003, it faltered in the second and third quarters of 2004 when economic growth again turned negative, while the fourth quarter of 2004 displayed only a 0.5% growth rate. Additional monetary policy steps to exit deflation and stimulate the economy therefore are necessary for the economy to reach its full potential.

The chapter is organized as follows. The first section outlines the extent of Japan's deflation, explores its causes, and reviews some of the consequences. The second part raises issues regarding monetary policy during the deflationary period from 1998 to the time of this writing (Spring of 2005). The chapter then presents possible solutions to various problems exacerbated by the deflationary environment and offers recommendations for monetary policy.

A monetary policy that can help return the economy to health is a hybrid strategy of both price-level and inflation targeting. This strategy goes several steps beyond the current policies of the Bank of Japan. Given that the interest rate cannot go below a floor of zero, to supplement the hybrid targeting strategy, various unconventional policies should be utilized. We examine four such measures: quantitative easing, open-market operations in long-term bonds, foreign exchange rate intervention, and open-market purchases of private assets. All of these strategies have various problems, and purchasing private assets should be undertaken only as a last resort. However, we believe that if these additional policies had been employed in a multifaceted approach sometime in 2001 and 2002, the Japanese economy would have started a sustained recovery much earlier than 2003.

1 Japan's Deflation

Figure 4.1 shows Japan's deflation as measured by the CPI and by the GDP deflator. (Both are adjusted to take out the temporary effects of the consumption tax rate increases in April 1989 and April 1997, so the rates shown are different from those seen elsewhere in the literature.) Both measures moved in tandem until the mid-1990s. After that, the GDP deflator has implied greater deflation than the CPI inflation rate.

Although the CPI has been declining since 1998 (since 1995 for the GDP deflator), deflation worsened from 2001 to 2003, and in 2003 it was running at about 1% for the CPI measure and more than 2% for the

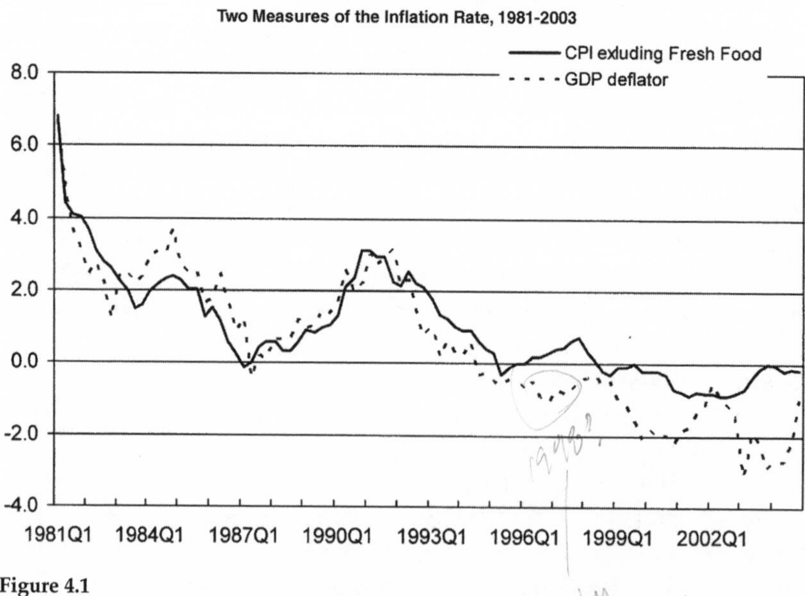

Figure 4.1

GDP deflator. At the end of 2003, the CPI's level was about 4% lower than its peak in 1998, and the level of the GDP deflator was about 10% lower than its peak in 1994. Although 1% to 3% annual deflation may not be serious for a short period, the cumulative magnitude of Japan's prolonged deflation has become quite large, and concern about the effect of this has been voiced with increased frequency.

The reasons and possible cures for disinflation and deflation in Japan are controversial. In the beginning stage, from 1997 to 1999, some economists in Japan argued that deflation might be good for consumers and even for the macroeconomy. Advocates of "good deflation" noted that it was a world-wide, supply-side phenomenon, and cited technological advances and competitive pressures from China as causes. In particular, the New Economy argument in the United States provided an explanation for a combination of high economic growth without inflation, with advances in information and communication technologies (ICT) driving down prices not only in the ICT sector, but also in other sectors through the use of cheaper ICT goods. For example, Bank of Japan former Governor Masaru Hayami repeatedly mentioned that price declines due to technological innovations and their use in the distribution sector are good for consumers. As late as March 2000 he was maintaining that technology-induced price declines "cannot necessarily be regarded as pernicious price declines" (Hayami's speech to the Research Institute of Japan, Tokyo, March 21, 2000).

Advocates of good deflation also have argued that lowering prices benefits consumers as their real incomes grow, pointing out that Japanese consumer prices had been higher than those in comparable large cities in the world.

However, most economists regard the "good deflation" view as inconsistent with economic theory. First, citing the ICT revolution mistakenly generalizes the need for relative price changes among sectoral prices to inflationary-deflationary macroeconomic forces. It is true that innovation brings down the prices of ICT goods, but that is relative to all other goods. The average price of all goods and services can go up or down depending on all other economic factors, including monetary policy and household income. Second, basic economics teaches that a shift of the aggregate supply curve to the right should cause prices to decline and output to rise, so that the price decline should be accompanied by output expansion—but this clearly has not been the case in Japan. The average growth rate in the past ten years was barely above 1%, much below the potential growth rate.

The evidence suggests that Japan's deflation is due to declining demand. This is seen in Figure 4.2, which graphs the relationship between the growth rate and the inflation rate. (In view of sticky price responses to demand-supply conditions, the growth rate is lagged four quarters. In other words, we assume last year's growth rate affects this year's prices.) The figure clearly shows the positive relationship between the growth rate and the inflation rate (a variant of the Phillips curve). Thus, the decline in economic growth is associated with deflation.

ICT effects may explain the productivity increase in the United States, but comparable effects were not observed in Japan or in Europe. Productivity increases were not observed in Japan's ICT industry, nor did they occur in other industries, unlike in the United States. Some rigidity in labor markets (lay-offs are very difficult) in Japan may explain why ICT has not been widely employed to reduce costs and increase productivity in various industries. Imports from China are only 2% to

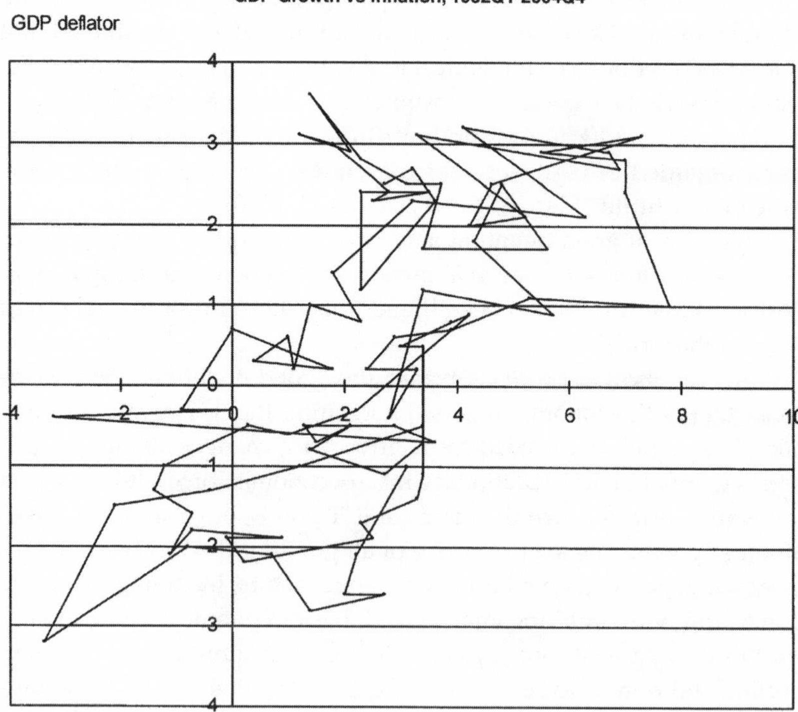

Figure 4.2

3% of GDP and so, alone, these cannot have a large impact on the GDP deflator. Moreover, the effects of ICT and Chinese imports are as important in the United States as in Japan, but the United States has not fallen into deflation.

1.1 Potential vs. Actual GDP

After examining the various arguments over whether deflation was due to insufficient demand or ever-expanding supply, our view is that the demand side has been more responsible for Japan's deflation and stagnation. Annual GDP growth from 1973 to 2003 averaged about 4%, while from 1993 to 2004 it was 1.2%. If one thinks that the trend growth rate reflects the supply side, then one concludes that Japanese productivity suddenly declined sharply. Another possibility is that demand was too low and the economy was not achieving its potential beginning in the early 1990s.

Economic common sense leads to an educated guess that America's boom with high growth rates and disinflation was driven by ICT industries, while the Japanese stagnation with deflation was due more to a lack of aggregate demand. Jorgenson and Motohashi (2003) have shown that a contribution of TFP growth to overall growth is as large in Japan as in the United States. This implies that supply side shocks to Japan and the United States have been similar but demand shocks have been vastly different.

As measured by nominal GDP, in 2003 the Japanese economy was about 4% smaller than its peak of 520 trillion yen in 1997. A shrinking economy causes problems in many aspects of the macroeconomy. Tax revenues decrease more than proportionately due to the nominally fixed tax brackets. The real burden of nominally contracted debt increases, so major debtors—the government and corporations—suffer from ever-increasing real debt. As a consequence, deflation has caused a severe strain on the macroeconomy. To illustrate, suppose that nominal GDP in Japan had grown at 3% annually since 1997: the hypothetical economy in 2003 would have been 25% larger in nominal terms than the actual economy. Tax revenues would have been higher, corporate profits would have been higher, and nonperforming loans would have been lower.

1.2 Monetary Policy and the Zero Interest Rate

The nominal interest rate cannot become negative because, at a negative interest rate, cash dominates holding any debt instrument. Thus, a lower bound for the interest rate is 0%. (Actually, rates on extremely liquid debt instruments such as Treasury bills can go very slightly negative because they may have liquidity advantages over cash. Indeed, this happened in Japan in November 1998 when 6-month Treasury bills had an interest rate of –0.004%. However, for all practical purposes, the floor for interest rates is zero.)

When the rate of deflation rises, then the real interest rate (that is, the difference between the nominal interest rate and the inflation rate) rises. The worse deflation becomes, the higher the real interest rate rises, thus leading to an unintended tightening of monetary policy.

A higher real interest rate and the expectation of future deflation has discouraged investment and consumption in Japan. Lower aggregate demand widened the GDP gap, contributing to a further lowering of prices. This is the first part of a deflationary spiral. Since the nominal interest rate cannot be lowered below zero, the traditional monetary policy instrument—the short-term interest rate—loses its effectiveness in combating the deflationary spiral. In textbooks, this situation is described as a liquidity trap, but we prefer to refer to it as a deflationary trap, because we do not take the view, as will be clear below, that monetary policy, particularly of the unconventional variety, is ineffective in this situation, as it is in the liquidity trap of the conventional Keynesian model.

The real burden of debt is another important result of a deflationary cycle. Most debt contracts—bonds, bank loans, mortgages, etc.—call for nominal payments denominated in a fixed amount of yen. If the actual inflation rate turns out to be lower than the expected inflation rate at the time of the contract, debtors have a windfall loss because the real debt burden has increased. Although there is no precise measure of expected inflation, an educated guess suggests that from 1992 to 2003, Japan's inflation rate continuously turned out to be lower than the inflation rate that had been expected three or more years earlier. This meant debtors continuously suffered unexpected real burdens and lower rents, dividends, sales, or income to service these debts. Some went bankrupt due to deflation. The process is commonly known as debt deflation (Fisher 1933).

Conventional monetary policy, using short-term interest rates, is not effective in combating the deflationary cycle and debt deflation after the short-term interest rate has reached zero because the policy instrument cannot be lowered further. Should the central bank just watch things deteriorate in the cyclical process and hope that improvement in the economy occurs as a result of positive external shocks? Or should it use tools that are beyond conventional policy instruments to get the economy out of a deflationary cycle? What are the risks and the likelihood of success in employing unconventional policy tools? These questions have been hotly debated from 1998 to now.

2 The Monetary Policy Challenge

A new Bank of Japan law became effective in April 1998, making the Bank independent of the Ministry of Finance. A new Governor, Masaru Hayami, age 72, and two new Deputy Governors were appointed around the same time. The Monetary Policy Board was enhanced with additional members. (Previously, the nine-member Board was regarded as just rubber-stamping decisions essentially made by senior Bank staff. But under the new law, the Bank's senior staff meeting was abolished and the Board itself debates and decides monetary policy. In order to do this a Board member must now be qualified as an expert in monetary policy matters.) The edited summary of the discussions is disclosed about six weeks after the Meeting. This section explores whether these institutional changes help the Bank of Japan make timely, well-informed decisions.

The Japanese economy was performing poorly at the time this change was made. The Asian currency crisis, which started with the collapse of the Thai baht in July 1997, had become a full-blown regional economic crisis, and Japan's banking crisis was getting worse. The official discount rate (ODR) at the time was 0.5%, and the call rate was in the range of 0.4% to 0.5%. Throughout the third quarter of 1998, economic conditions were deteriorating, and the discussion of legislation to strengthen the financial system was becoming as hot and sticky as Tokyo's summer weather. Interest rates policies were maintained until September 9, when the target for the call rate was reduced to 0.25%, without any accompanying change in the ODR.

With further bad economic news during the rest of 1998, the Bank of Japan announced additional action on February 12, 1999:

> The Bank of Japan will provide more ample funds and encourage the uncollateralized overnight call rate to move as low as possible. To avoid excessive volatility in the short-term financial markets, the Bank of Japan will, by paying due consideration to maintaining market function, initially aim to guide the above call rate to move around 0.15%, and subsequently induce further decline in view of the market developments. (Bank of Japan, Announcement of Decisions, February 12, 1999)

The call rate became very close to zero by the end of March. This was the beginning of the zero interest rate policy (ZIRP). In April, Governor Hayami declared that the ZIRP would continue "until deflationary concerns are dispelled". It was clear that the economy was in a very weak condition. According to statistics at the time, GDP was thought to be registering five consecutive quarters of negative growth, from 1997:IV to 1998:IV.

The economy showed some recovery from mid-1999 to 2000, mainly due to the IT boom in the stock market. Exports and consumption became engines of growth. Stock prices rose from a low of 13,000 (Nikkei 225 index) in the first quarter of 1999 to 20,000 in the second quarter of 2000. As stock prices rose, the economy also recovered. The economic growth rate of 2000 exceeded 3% (according to the GDP statistics at the time).

Several indicators showed brighter prospects in the second quarter of 2000. Against this background, the Bank of Japan decided to lift the ZIRP in August 2000, on the grounds that deflationary concerns were over. The call rate immediately shot from 0.01% to 0.25%. The government (at least, the Cabinet Office and the Ministry of Finance, both sending non-voting representatives to the Monetary Policy Meeting) opposed the decision, submitting a proposal, as provided by law, to delay the vote lifting ZIRP but was overruled by the Monetary Policy Board. Two of the nine Board members cast nay votes to the increase in the interest rate (with only one nay vote to overruling the government proposal). The decision to raise the interest rate was severely criticized by many economists as an unnecessarily hasty decision to get away from ZIRP. Although there were signs of increasing output activity and a consumption increase, there were no sure signs of an investment increase. Moreover, the CPI inflation rate was still negative in the third quarter. The Bank of Japan's decision to terminate the ZIRP indeed turned out to be premature. The IT boom was ending, and stock markets in major countries were declining, while the American economy was entering a recession. The Japanese business cycle hit a peak in October 2000, and Japan again fell into recession.

The growth rate in 2000:III turned negative, and the economy weakened substantially toward the end the year. Many economists urged changes in monetary policy. Some economists recommended a return to ZIRP, while others recommended quantitative easing or unconventional tools such as increasing the amount of regular purchases of long-term government bonds, as well as new purchases of exchange-traded funds (ETF) of stocks, foreign bonds, and, in some cases, even real estate investment funds. These measures were opposed by Bank of Japan economists.[1]

With continuing weakness and worsening deflation, the Bank of Japan decided to ease rates. In February 2001, the Bank adopted the Lombard lending facility, and the official discount rate (ODR) was cut from 0.5% to 0.35%. The Lombard facility was to lend automatically to banks with collateral at the official discount rate, hence capping the interest rate at 0.35%. However, the market rate was in the range of 0.20% to 0.25%, so there was little real impact. Pressure to ease monetary conditions did not cease because of these measures.

Within a month, the Bank of Japan decided to take further action. On March 19, it lowered the ODR to 0.25% from 0.35%, and changed the policy instrument from the short-term interest rate to the current-account balance (reserves) at the Bank of Japan. The target of the current-account balance was set at 5 trillion yen. The required reserve was about 4 trillion yen at the time, so targeting 5 trillion yen was effectively providing enough liquidity for banks so that excess reserves would be accumulated in the Bank of Japan account without earning interest. Therefore, this was effectively a return to ZIRP as far as the interest rate was concerned. The Bank also announced the conditions under which it would terminate the ZIRP: ZIRP would not be abandoned until the CPI inflation rate became stably above zero (what that meant was further clarified in October 2003).

Deflation, whether measured by the CPI or GDP deflator, became worse in 2000–01. The CPI inflation rate dropped to around minus 1%, while the GDP deflator inflation rate became close to minus 2%. As the duration of the deflation became longer, and the degree of deflation became more significant, the expectation of future deflation was strengthened. The yield curve started to flatten.

Quantitative easing beyond the ZIRP has taken three different forms since March 2001. First, the amount of long-term government bonds that the Bank of Japan purchased was expanded in several steps. In August 2001, outright purchases were raised from 400 billion yen per month to 600 billion yen. The amount was raised to 800 billion in December 2001, to 1 trillion yen in February 2002, and to 1.2 trillion yen in October 2002. Second, the current account target (effectively, excess reserves) was raised to 6 trillion yen in August 2001, to 10–15 trillion yen in December 2001, to 15–20 trillion yen in October 2002, to 17–22 trillion yen on April 1, 2003, to 22–27 trillion yen on April 30, 2003, to

27–30 trillion yen in May 2003, to 27–32 trillion in October 2003, and 30–35 trillion yen in January 2004. Third, assets that could be purchased by the Bank of Japan were expanded to qualified corporate bonds, commercial paper, and asset-backed securities.

These changes are shown in Figures 4.3 and 4.4. It is certain that quantitative easing contributed to an expansion of the monetary base. However, expanding the monetary base did not result in a sharp increase in the money supply. Bank credit to corporations continued to decline. Therefore, the regular transmission mechanism did not work.

Those who advocated quantitative easing pointed out that, despite the failure in expanding bank credit, easing did have two distinct positive effects. First, it contributed to financial systemic stability. There was no panic reaction to news of the failure of some commercial banks, such as Resona Bank and Ashikaga Bank in 2003. Second, the easing, combined with the commitment to the ZIRP, seems to have contributed to a flattening of the yield curve. The lower long-term interest rate encouraged banks and non-financial investors to take more risk in the stock market and in foreign-currency-denominated assets. Therefore, although its transmission channel was not clear-cut, quantitative easing may have contributed to an economic recovery toward the end of 2003.

Japan's economy seemed to turn around in 2003. The economic growth rate exceeded 2%, and the degree of deflation was diminishing. The Nikkei stock index rose from below 8000 in April to the 10,000 mark toward the end of the year. How much of the recovery has been due to monetary policy is difficult to assess, but a firm commitment to ZIRP seems to have worked under the new Bank of Japan's Governor, Toshihiko Fukui, who took over in March 2003. From March 2003 to January 2004, the target amount of the Bank of Japan's current account (effectively, excess reserves) was raised to strengthen quantitative easing, and in October 2003, the necessary conditions for an exit from the ZIRP were further clarified.

The history of Japan's monetary policy over the past decade has created two basic problems for the Japanese monetary authorities today. First, the Bank of Japan's policies have left the economy in a prolonged deflationary environment in which conventional monetary policy through lowering the short-term interest rate is no longer effective because the policy rate has hit the floor of zero. Second, past policy, particularly under Governor Hayami, has left the Bank with

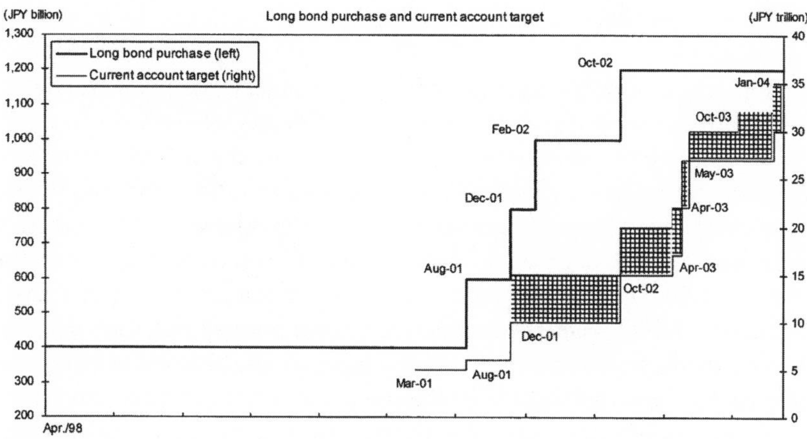

Figure 4.3

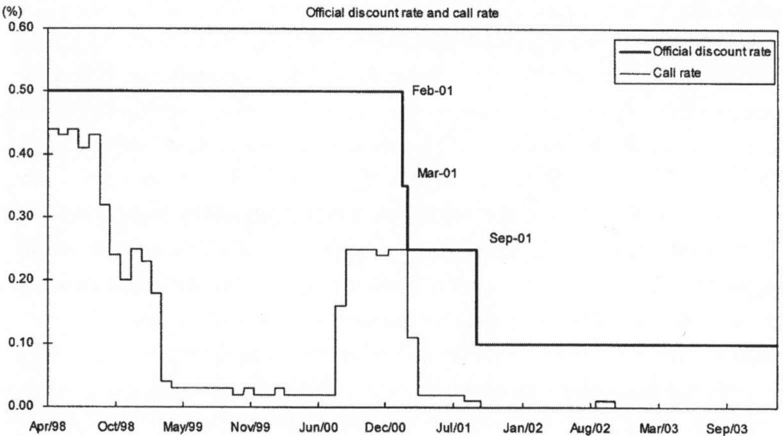

Figure 4.4

a severe credibility problem in which the markets and the public are unconvinced that monetary policy will be committed to a sustained expansion that returns the economy to health. Both problems present the Bank with particular challenges in getting the economy out of deflation quickly. We address how they can do this in the next section. [For a fuller treatment of monetary policy, see Ito and Mishkin (2004); for a political economy explanation of why the Bank of Japan rejected inflation targeting, see Ito (2004).]

3 Price-Level and Inflation Targeting

At first blush, it might appear as though monetary policy cannot be effective in escaping the deflation trap because there is no way to drive the standard interest-rate instrument below zero. Indeed, this claim has been raised repeatedly by the Bank of Japan (for example, Okina 1999a, 1999b; Oda and Okina 2001) to explain why it has been unable to stimulate the economy. However, a number of studies (Krugman 1998; Ito 1999; Cargill, Hutchison, and Ito 2000; Eggertsson and Woodford 2003; Auerbach and Obstfeld 2003; Svensson 2003) suggest that there is a solution: management of expectations. If the central bank can convince the markets and the public that there will be higher inflation, then even with the interest rate at a floor of zero, the real interest rate will fall and this will stimulate aggregate demand through the usual channels (Mishkin 1996). Let us consider how the central bank can do this.

One way to manage expectations to stop a deflation is by having the central bank announce a positive inflation target, as suggested by Krugman (1998), Posen (1998), and Bernanke (2000). Clearly, an announcement of a positive inflation target by itself is far from sufficient because it may not indicate to the markets that the central bank has a strong commitment to this policy, thus leaving expectations unchanged. This is why advocates of inflation targets stress that central banks need to do much more than simply announce an inflation target in order to make this policy credible. For successful inflation-targeting, central banks have to put a lot of effort into increasing transparency and improving communications by publishing inflation forecasts, testifying publicly, and putting out inflation reports in which the bank explains how it is to achieve its target and why it has or has not been able to achieve it in the recent past (Bernanke, Laubach, Mishkin, and Posen, 1999). A committed inflation-targeting regime thus can be helpful in managing expectations and preventing further deflation.

However, once an economy has entered a prolonged deflationary period, as it has in Japan, lowering the real interest rate to stimulate the economy requires a substantial increase in expected inflation. This is why Krugman (1998) made the radical suggestion that the Bank of Japan adopt an inflation target of 4% for a 15-year period. However, a high inflation target, as suggested by Krugman, is unlikely to be credible for two reasons.

First, it is too much at variance with a goal of general price stability. No inflation-targeting central bank in an industrialized country has chosen an annual inflation target above 3%, whether using a core or an all-items CPI measure (usually referred to as "headline inflation"). Indeed, we suspect that Krugman's proposal may have increased the Bank of Japan's resistance to inflation targeting because his suggested level of inflation was well above what officials in the Bank believed was consistent with price stability. Furthermore, once the economy has emerged from a deflationary spiral and starts to recover, the central bank will be tempted to renege on its commitment to a high inflation target because it would like the economy to return to an inflation rate consistent with price stability.

Thus, as pointed out by Eggertsson (2003), a central bank in a deflationary environment is subject to a time-inconsistency problem: it cannot credibly commit to "being irresponsible" and so continue to shoot for high inflation. The result of the time-inconsistency problem is that markets will not be convinced inflation will remain high, so inflation expectations will not be sufficiently high to lower real rates enough to stimulate the economy out of the deflation trap.

Another problem with an inflation target is that it is not "history-dependent" because it is purely forward-looking (Woodford 2000, 2003). An inflation target is not adjusted depending on the past outcome of inflation: in other words it lets bygones be bygones. As Eggertsson and Woodford (2003) have shown, such a purely forward-looking target will not be effective in extricating an economy from a deflation trap. When the interest rate hits a floor of zero, a deflationary shock that lowers the price level and puts the economy even farther below its potential output requires an even higher expected inflation rate to lower the real interest rate and make it even more stimulative. Since such an inflation target is not revised when it is under-shot because of the deflationary shock, it will not generate the required increase in expected inflation.

On the other hand, a CPI price-level target does generate higher expected inflation when a deflationary shock hits. A price-level target means that monetary policy is attempting to hit a particular set path of the price level, and bygones are not allowed to be bygones. That means when a deflationary shock occurs, the price level has to rise even further in order to get back to the target. In other words, the target is "history dependent" because the desired medium-term inflation rate is affected by what has happened in the past. Thus, with a price-level target when there is a deflationary shock, future inflation will be expected to be higher, and this produces exactly the right response of a lower real interest rate and more stimulative monetary policy.

The theoretical argument for a CPI price-level target when an economy is in a deflationary environment is thus quite strong. But there is a further reason why a price-level target is needed in Japan's current environment, even if its economy continues to have a solid recovery. Japan is currently experiencing a severe balance-sheet problem that prevents the financial system from working properly (Posen 1998; Mishkin 1998; Hoshi and Kashyap, this volume). Non-performing loans have weakened bank balance sheets, and the lack of capital has meant that banks have been forced to cut back on lending, particularly for new investment. The result is that the financial system is unable to allocate capital to productive investment opportunities, and this is a key element in Japan's stagnation.

Deflation also has weakened the balance sheets of firms that have found their debt increase in value in real terms while their assets have not (the debt-deflation phenomenon described by Irving Fisher in 1933). The resulting loss in net worth makes lenders less likely to lend to firms, particularly small and medium ones for which information about their activities is harder to get, because, with less at stake, these firms are more likely to engage in risky (moral hazard) behavior that will make it less likely the lender will be paid back (Mishkin 1997). As a result, even if these firms have productive investment opportunities, they may not be able to get the funds to pursue them. Thus restoring both financial and non-financial balance sheets is crucial to helping the Japanese economy achieve a more efficient allocation of capital that will restore it to health.

A price-level target that gets the price level to what it would have been if the economy had not experienced deflation is one way to help restore firms' balance sheets. A higher price level will lead to lower real indebtedness of Japanese firms, thereby increasing their net worth and making it more attractive to lend to them when they have productive investment opportunities. The improvement in balance sheets also will help reduce non-performing loans, with positive effects on bank balance sheets, thus making it easier for the banks to lend.

Beyond these medium-term measures, both the Bank of Japan and outside commentators have stressed the need for restructuring the Japanese economy if it is to return to health. Indeed, the Bank has continually argued that Japan's economy cannot recover without restructuring, and has worried that expansionary monetary policy, perhaps seen as a compromising alternative to the needed restructuring, may be counterproductive. Closing inefficient firms and financial institutions may be exactly what the economy needs in the long run, but in the short run it might lead to severe dislocations and unemployment. Indeed, this is probably why there has been so much resistance to restructuring on the part of Japanese politicians. Here is where a price-level target comes in: a higher price level would help restore financial and non-financial balance sheets, and would help the financial system to start working again to allocate capital efficiently, which is critical to a restructuring process.

Contrary to a belief among some Bank of Japan Board members, restoring a low but positive inflation rate is not bailing out the debtors that are the source of non-performing loans, inflating away debtors' problems, or further slowing structural reforms. Price stability means a low, but positive inflation rate that encourages a normal level of investment. Also, to the extent that a commitment to a higher price level by the monetary authorities helps raise aggregate demand, the short-term negative effects of the restructuring process are cushioned.

A price-level target that encourages a more expansionary monetary policy is more sensibly viewed as a complement to restructuring than as an impediment. Indeed, we argue that a recovery with an annual growth rate at only around 2% will still leave the Japanese economy below the potential it could reach if the necessary restructuring occurs. Raising the price level back to where it would have been if deflation had not occurred is needed to help the restructuring to occur.[2]

The logic of our analysis leads us to the following recommendation for the conduct of Japanese monetary policy:

> Japanese monetary authorities should announce that monetary policy will be conducted to raise the price level to the path that it would have achieved if deflation had not started in October 1997.

To see how this would work, consider that Japan's CPI, excluding fresh food, fell from a peak of 101.1 in October 1997 to 97.4 in March 2005; this was about 3.7% decline. This certainly understates the amount of deflation because, as is well known, measured inflation is likely to be upwardly biased compared to true inflation. Most estimates of measurement error in CPI inflation in industrialized countries are around 1%. Shiratsuka (1999) estimated that the bias in Japan was about 0.9%, although the subsequent redefinition of the CPI may mean the bias is now lower.

We regard a 1% annual increase in measured CPI as absolute price stability. Suppose that the long-run price target is increasing at an annual rate of 1% after 1998. That would put the target level in March 2005 at 108.8, about 11.4% higher than the actual level of 97.4. This target level is the result of cumulative increase in the long-term target by 1 percent a year (7.7%) and the actual decline in the prices by 3.7%. The long-term target is increasing at 1%. In order to catch up with the moving target, the medium-range target has to be higher. Suppose that the Bank of Japan sets the medium target so that the price level would catch up with the long-term target after five years, in March 2010. An annual inflation rate of 3.3% from March 2005 is what it would take to get the price level to its target. If this target is credible, even with a nominal interest rate of zero, the real interest rate falls to minus 3.3% which is highly stimulative, exactly along the lines that Eggertsson and Woodford (2003) suggest is appropriate. To illustrate the moving target and the catch up process, Figure 4.5 shows the actual price level changes from 1990 to 1997, the path of the price level target, 1% inflation after October 1997, and the hypothetical path of 3.3% inflation after March 2003.

The Bank of Japan also needs to make it clear that the commitment to a price-level target is also a commitment to price stability. Although achieving the price-level target might result in temporarily modest inflation, returning to the price level that would have occurred without deflation is actually more consistent with a price stability goal then just letting the price level remain at a permanently lower level. Thus, achieving the price-level target should increase the credibility of the Bank of Japan's long-term commitment to price stability.

3.1 *After the Price-Level Target Is Achieved*

This brings us to the question of what to do once the price-level target is achieved. One strand in the literature suggests it is optimal to continue with the target. In models with a high degree of forward-looking behavior (for example, Clarida, Gali, and Gertler 1999; Dittmar, Gavin and, Kydland 1999; Dittmar and Gavin 2000; Eggertson and Woodford 2003; Svensson 1999; Svensson and Woodford 2003; Vestin 2003; Woodford 1999, 2003), a price-level target produces less output variance than an inflation target. However, empirical evidence (for example, Fuhrer 1997) does not clearly support forward-looking expectations formation, and models with forward-looking behavior have counter-intuitive

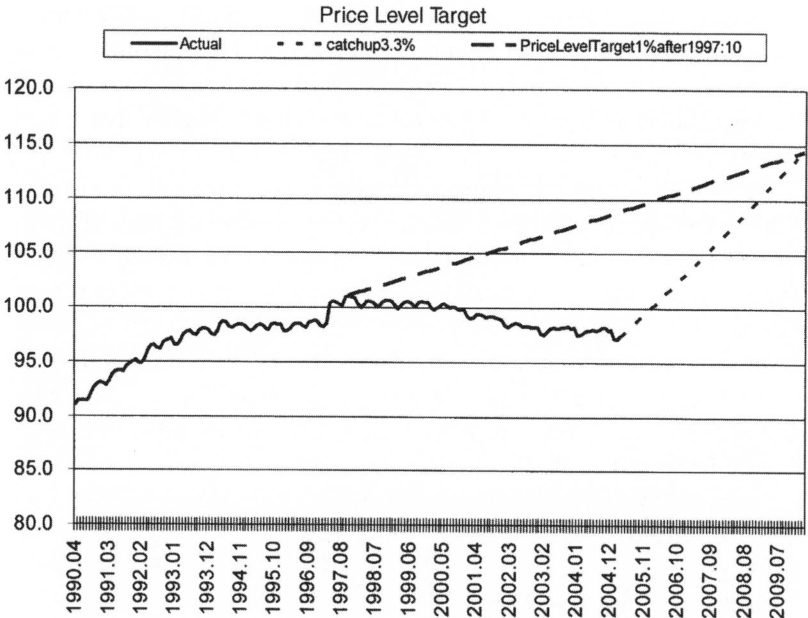

Figure 4.5

properties that seem to be inconsistent with inflation dynamics (Estrella and Fuhrer 1998).

The traditional view, forcefully articulated by Fischer (1994), argues that a price-level target might produce more output variability than an inflation target because unanticipated shocks to the price level are not treated as bygones and must be offset. Specifically, a price-level target requires that an over-shoot of the target must be reversed, and this might require quite contractionary monetary policy which, with sticky prices, could lead to a sharp downturn in the real economy in the short run. Indeed, if the over-shoot is large enough, returning to the target might require a deflation, which could promote financial instability and be quite harmful. Our suspicion is that this traditional view has strong supporters in central banks in most countries and is the reason why no central bank currently has adopted a price-level target. [A price-level target was used in the 1930s in Sweden (Berg and Jonung 1999).]

Note that this criticism of a price-level target does not argue against it when an economy is in a deflationary trap and is far from the appropriate target, as is Japan's current situation. In such a case, the price level is necessarily below the target, and so the target promotes higher expected inflation, which in turn lowers real interest rates; this process works in exactly the right direction to get the economy back on track. (See Ito and Mishkin (2004) for a more detailed discussion of the choice between an inflation target and a price-level target.)

Taking the traditional view into account suggests that a conservative strategy is to abandon the price-level target once it is achieved, and replace it with a more conventional inflation target. Indeed, this is close to the position advocated as a general rule by the United States Federal Reserve Governor Ben Bernanke (2003). However, he is agnostic about keeping to a price-level target or going to an inflation target once the price-level target is achieved.

Another reason an inflation target may be more desirable after the price-level target is achieved is that it is a little easier to explain to the public, because it is not a moving target. Because increased transparency and accountability is a highly desirable attribute for the conduct of monetary policy, it seems sensible to follow the KISS principle ("keep it simple, stupid").

3.2 *Setting an Inflation Target*

Setting a target inflation rate requires taking a stance on what price stability means. Alan Greenspan has provided a widely cited definition of price stability as a rate of inflation sufficiently low for households and businesses not to have to take it into account in making everyday decisions. This is a reasonable definition and, operationally, any inflation number between 0% and 3% seems to meet this criterion.

Some economists, Martin Feldstein (1997) and William Poole (1999) being prominent examples, argue for a long-run goal of 0% inflation, which has the psychological appeal of the "magic number" zero. Indeed, one concern is that an inflation goal greater than zero might lead to a decline in central bank credibility and instability in inflation expectations, which could lead to an upward creep in inflation. However, the evidence suggests that maintaining an inflation target above zero, but not too far above (less than 3%), for an extended period, does not lead to instability in the public's inflation expectations or to a decline in central bank credibility (Bernanke, Laubach, Mishkin, and Posen 1999). It also provides a cushion against deflation, which *both of us* believe has potentially harmful effects on the economy. Bernanke et al advocate a target rate for true inflation of 1%, which is a 2% CPI inflation target if the CPI is subject to a measurement bias of 1 percentage point.

Having an inflation target above zero does not appear too costly. In addition, there are two arguments why it is beneficial to have an inflation target above zero.

First Akerlof, Dickens, and Perry (1996) believe that setting target inflation at too low a level produces inefficiency and increases the natural rate of unemployment. They argue that the evidence indicates there is a downward rigidity in nominal wages, which means that reductions in real wage increases can occur only through inflation. The implication of their thesis is that a very low rate of inflation might prevent real wages from adjusting downward in response to declining labor demand in certain industries or regions, thereby leading to increased unemployment and hindering the re-allocation of labor from declining sectors to expanding sectors. However, we do not find their argument totally convincing. As pointed out by Groshen and Schweitzer (1996, 1999), inflation not only "greases" labor markets and allows downward shifts in real wages in response to declining demand along the lines of Akerlof, Dickens and Perry (1996), inflation can also inject "sand" into the economy by increasing the noise in relative real wages. This noise reduces the information content of nominal wages regarding what is happening to relative real wages, and hence the efficiency of the process by which workers are labor is allocated across occupations and industries.

The second, and we believe, more persuasive argument against an inflation goal of 0%, as opposed to, say, 1%, is that it makes it more likely that the economy will experience episodes of deflation. We have argued above that deflation can be highly dangerous because it promotes financial instability. The implication is that under-shooting a zero inflation target (thereby inducing deflation) is potentially more costly than over-shooting a zero target by the same amount. The logic of this argument suggests that setting an inflation target a little above zero is worthwhile because it provides some insurance against deflationary episodes. The analysis here thus leads to a second recommendation for Japanese monetary policy:

> Japanese monetary authorities should announce that they will move to an inflation targeting regime with a long-run goal for inflation once the price-level target is achieved.

Committing to an inflation target once the price-level target is achieved also is crucial to strengthening the credibility of the monetary authorities. One possible danger from a price-level target is that inflation has to be temporarily high in order to get the price level back up to its target rate. To make sure that this does not weaken the credibility of the Bank of Japan's commitment to price stability, the Bank must make it clear that it will be extremely aggressive in fighting inflation once the price-level target is achieved. The commitment to an inflation target helps do this.

3.3 *The Inflation Target: A Point or Range?*

If there is a commitment to an inflation target, the next question is whether it should be a point target (say 2% plus or minus 1%) or a target range (say 1% to 3%). The Bank of England adopted a point target, while the Bank of Canada and the Reserve Bank of Australia have adopted a target range. Presumably, a central bank with a point target has a utility function with a peak at the target point and declining utility around it, while it is possible that a central bank with a target range feels indifferent so long as the inflation rate is within the range. However, a central bank with a target range could take the view that it has a utility function with a peak at the center of a target range.

Those who favor a point target cite its strong effect on inflation anchoring. The Bank of England notes that the inflation expectations for the next 10 years (measured by the difference between yields of straight bonds and inflation-indexed bonds) has converged to its inflation target point, 2.5% (under the old RPIX measure). Those who favor a target range worry that the point target may suffer from fine-tuning. Because we do not have a strong view on whether a point target would be better than a target range, and the difference may not be that great depending on the central bank's communication strategy, we do not make a recommendation on which should be adopted.

4 Unconventional Monetary Policies

Critics of inflation targeting (Friedman 2003) have argued that managing expectations is problematic. Why would announcing an inflation rate or a price-level target pin down expectations? Are not actions more important than words? We agree that words by themselves are not enough. But neither are actions. It is words plus actions that is critical to successful monetary policy. Also, when there are doubts among market participants about the precise interpretation of price stability, announcing the intention is quite important.

This concern raises the issue of what actions actually influence the economy and help make a price level or inflation target credible, particularly when the policy interest rate has hit a floor of zero and thus cannot be driven lower. We look at four types of unconventional measures: quantitative easing, open-market operations in long-term bonds, foreign exchange rate intervention, and open-market purchases of private assets.

4.1 *Quantitative Easing*

The unconventional monetary policy tried by the Bank of Japan has been "quantitative easing." This involves expanding the monetary base, either through open-market purchases of government debt or through unsterilized purchases of foreign currency. The Bank began conducting such a policy in March 2001, and has pursued it more aggressively since December 2001.

The monetary base (MB) had indeed expanded quickly from the end of 2001, but with little effect on money supply (M2+CD, hereafter in this paper simply M2). How to explain the deviation between MB and M2 is a challenge, as is the question of whether an expansion of the MB without an expansion of M2 has positive effects on the economy. The MB includes the current account balance at the Bank of Japan, which measures the amount of excess liquidity in the system.

Normally, excess reserves are unlikely to help stimulate the economy. However, an expansion of MB might be beneficial, even if it does not produce a significant increase in M2, when the interest rate is zero. First, ample liquidity in the system may help avoid a potential financial crisis (a concern in 2002–03). Second, liquidity may encourage financial institutions to take more risk in portfolio management, particularly positions in long-term bonds, equities, and foreign bonds, any of which contributes to stimulating the economy indirectly. Japan's economic recovery in 2003 may have been due to ample liquidity in the system.

Yet the data does not favor this approach. The growth rate of monetary base fluctuated between 20% and 40% in the period of 2002 and 2003 and yet deflation did not stop. As discussed in Ito and Mishkin (2004), the Bank of Japan under Governor Hayami created the market expectation that even if an expansionary monetary policy was pursued for a time, it would soon be reversed. So it is no surprise that easing did not work. Given the very different rhetoric under Governor Fukui, there is the possibility that quantitative easing may be more successful.

However, there also are good theoretical reasons why it might be ineffective. Conventional liquidity-trap analysis suggests that when the short-term interest rate hits zero, short-term bonds become a perfect substitute for money, so expanding the monetary base has no effect on the economy. Eggertsson and Woodford (2003) show that this result can even hold if short-term bonds and money do not become perfect substitutes, although the conclusion is based on specific features of their model. Still, as they emphasize, quantitative easing might help stimulate the economy if it provides a signal that the monetary base will be higher than it otherwise would be once the deflation is over. This is the position taken by Auerbach and Obstfeld (2003).

Given the theoretical arguments against quantitative easing being effective and the fact that, at least under Governor Hayami, it did not work to stimulate the economy and stop deflation, there is clearly a strong case that the Bank of Japan needs to look at other approaches.

4.2 Open-Market Operations in Long-Term Bonds

Alternative unconventional monetary policies involve the monetary authorities conducting open-market operations in assets besides short-term bonds. The most conventional of these approaches is a shift toward central bank purchases of long-term bonds: the Bank of Japan could engage in even larger purchases of Japanese government bonds (JGBs) relative to Treasury bills. Long-term interest rates are more likely than short-term rates to figure in household and business decisions about spending, so it seems that open-market purchases of JGBs might succeed in lowering long-term interest rates, thereby stimulating the economy.

In order for purchases of long-term bonds to work, there has to be significant portfolio-balance effects, so that a shift in the supply of long-term versus short-term publicly-held government debt as a result of these purchases would affect risk (term) premiums and thereby result in falling long-term rates. The evidence that risk (term) premiums can be affected by changing the supply of long-term bonds relative to short-term bonds in the hands of the public is, unfortunately, far from clear. One episode when this was tried was "Operation Twist" in the United States in the early 1960s: the Federal Reserve bought long-term bonds in order to lower long-term rates relative to short-term rates. This policy has generally been viewed as a failure, with only a very small, if any, effect on relative interest rates [see Meulendyke (1998) for a summary of the literature and Fujiki, Okina, and Shiratsuka (2001, p 106–07) for a negative appraisal of Operation Twist and of any increase in long-term bonds at the time of their writing].

Bernanke (2002) has suggested that the apparent failure of Operation Twist does not mean that the central bank could not drive long-term bond rates down as long as the central bank announced it would peg interest rates on long-term bonds at a very low level (possibly zero) and stood ready to purchase any amount of the bonds at this low rate. The peg could certainly work, because the commitment is easily verifiable: the price and interest rates on long-term bonds are immediately known. However, it might require the central bank to purchase the entire stock of long-term bonds, which it might not be fully comfortable doing.

Another way for the central bank to lower long-term bond rates is to convince the markets that it will continue to pursue a zero-interest-rate policy (ZIRP) for a considerable time even after the deflation is over (Orphanides and Wieland 2000). Then, as suggested by the expectations hypothesis of the term structure, because long-term bond rates are an average of expected short-term rates, long-term interest rates would necessarily fall. Indeed, this strategy is complimentary to Bernanke's because it is a way of committing to more expansionary policy in the future, even after the economy has bounced back.

Earlier Bank of Japan economists were skeptical, if not negative, regarding increasing JGB purchases. [See the Goodfriend (2000) recommendation and negative reactions to it from Fujiki, Okina, and Shiratsuka (2001).] However, the Bank gradually increased the amount of JGB purchases from 400 billion yen per month prior to August 2001 to 1.2 trillion yen per month in October 2002. In addition, the Bank of Japan had made it clear that ZIRP will be maintained. These actions contributed to JGB yields dropping below 1% in late 2002 and mid-2003.

4.3 *Committing to the Zero Interest Rate Policy*

The Bank of Japan's announcements under Governor Fukui, in particular the one in October 2003, about conditions for lifting the ZIRP have some elements of a strategy that commits to continuing the ZIRP for a considerable time even after the deflation is over, but these do not go nearly far enough. The Bank has announced it will not reverse the ZIRP policy until there is clear-cut evidence that deflation is over and it is unlikely to recur. In particular, the October 2003 announcement states that a condition for changing the current quantitative easing policy is that the inflation rate should be above zero "for a few months" and would not return to negative territory (deflation) again. However, this is a far weaker commitment than the commitment strategy outlined above suggests.

We would like to see the Bank commit to stay with the ZIRP not just until deflation is clearly over, but until there is a prospect of achieving the price-level target described above, in which the CPI rises by around 3% for the several years it takes to get to the target. In order not to over-shoot, ZIRP has to be abandoned a bit before the target is reached, but for all practical purposes, this is a commitment to keep ZIRP for a substantial period after deflation is over.

There is the problem that an announcement of this type might not be believed by the markets because the Bank, under Governor Hayami, reversed the ZIRP as soon as it looked as if the economy might be recovering in August 2000. This is where the purchase of JGBs might help. The Bank could buy substantial amounts of JGBs as a sign of its confidence that their prices will remain high, because the ZIRP will be continued well after the deflation ends. If the Bank has concerns about its balance sheet, buying long-term bonds provides incentives for it to stick with the ZIRP after deflation is over because prematurely abandoning the ZIRP would lead to losses on the JGBs it has bought. However, as will be argued later, we believe the Bank of Japan's balance sheet should not be an important consideration in its conduct of monetary policy.

There is a concern that a premature rise in the nominal long-term interest rate may harm the balance sheets of commercial banks that hold a large amount of long-term bonds. First, the average maturity on bonds held by commercial banks is being shortened. Second, a long-term interest rate rise is most likely when the economy is showing a strong recovery accompanied by rising stock prices. While the share of equities in assets has fallen, Japanese commercial banks still hold a substantial amount of equities, so capital gains on stocks likely will offset partly, if not completely, any capital losses in the long-term bonds. Furthermore, a stronger commitment to the ZIRP and purchases of JGBs are likely to prevent a premature rise in long-term interest rates. Finally, held to maturity, there should be few losses on commercial banks' holdings of JGBs.

4.3 Foreign Exchange Intervention

Currency depreciation provides an additional way of exiting a deflation trap. A fall in the domestic currency's value makes imports more expensive and exports cheaper. The result is expenditure switching, in which exports rise and imports fall, thereby increasing the demand for domestically produced goods, which stimulates aggregate demand. Intervention in the foreign exchange market—the selling of yen and purchase of foreign currency—thus has been suggested as a powerful way of getting the Japanese economy moving again (Bernanke 2000; McCallum 2000a, 2002, 2003; Meltzer 2001; Orphanides and Wieland 2000; Svensson 2001, 2003).

The Ministry of Finance and Bank of Japan have indeed been intervening to keep the yen from appreciating against the American dollar, but they have not engineered a depreciation. The intervention has become very large: monetary authorities sold 20 trillion yen in 2003 and 15 trillion yen in the first three months of 2004. However, against the dollar the yen appreciated from 120 in January 2003 to 103 in March 2004. Ito and Yabu (2004) show that the effects of intervention were much smaller in 2003 compared to earlier periods.

One problem with this exchange rate transmission mechanism is that it also requires portfolio-balance effects be operational. An exchange rate intervention in which the purchase of foreign-denominated assets (such as United States Treasury bills) are bought with yen, thereby increasing the supply of yen-denominated assets relative to foreign-denominated assets, only affects the exchange rate if domestic and foreign assets are imperfect substitutes. As was the case for short-term versus long-term bonds, the evidence for portfolio-balance effects are not strong (see the survey in Sarno and Taylor 2001).

However, here is where a price-level target and the management of expectations can again come to the rescue. Svensson (2001, 2003) has advocated that, along with an announcement of a price-level target similar to the one described above, the Bank of Japan and Japanese government should commit to an exchange rate peg consistent with the target. This involves a commitment to an immediate depreciation of the yen, which would then be allowed to appreciate at the rate of the foreign interest-rate differential (so that the expected return on foreign and domestic assets is equalized). The peg would be abandoned once the price-level target has been achieved and a price-level or inflation targeting regime would be put into place. Commitment to the peg is also committing to the higher price-level target and to a continued expansionary monetary policy even after the deflation is over. This dual strategy solves the commitment problem that the Bank of Japan has faced in the past when there were doubts that it would continue to pursue expansionary policy.

Clearly, implementing such a peg requires cooperation between the Bank of Japan and the Ministry of Finance because it is the government that has the ultimate authority over the exchange rate and exchange rate interventions in Japan. Also, because the policy calls for a substantial depreciation of the yen from current levels, it requires that Japan stand ready to buy a large amount of foreign-denominated assets and to ensure that these are a good investment relative to yen-denominated assets. This means an even larger accumulation of international currency reserves for Japan, which is always feasible. This situation is in contrast to a case where a country wants to prop up the value of its currency, and thus must sell foreign assets, thereby losing international reserves which may run out and thus force the abandonment of the peg.

An incentive for the central bank and the government to stick with the peg until the price-level target is achieved is that early abandonment leads to an appreciation of the yen, which would result in substantial losses on Japan's international reserves.

Although we agree with Svensson that his "foolproof way" to escape the deflation trap would work, we do have doubts about the strategy, which suffers from two difficulties. First, Japan's trading partners would likely be up-in-arms if an exchange-rate peg of this type is announced. We have seen strong American complaints against the Chinese peg of the yuan at a depreciated rate, and we expect the outcry would be even harsher if Japan adopted Svensson's suggestion. The yen appreciated substantially in September 2003 when the G7 called for "flexibility in the exchange rate" without naming countries. The outcome of a depreciated peg might be trade sanctions against Japan and a rise in protectionism that could be disastrous for the world trading system.

Globalization and free trade have become dirty words for many politicians, and these issues could get much worse if Japan adopted a highly depreciated exchange-rate peg. In 2002 and early 2003 when the Japanese economy, stock market, and financial system were at lows, the chance of a depreciation strategy winning the tacit approval of Japan's trading partners might have been reasonably high—if Japan had argued that this was a temporary strategy to prevent the economy falling into another crisis, and that a strong Japanese economy would be beneficial to the rest of the world. However, this logic has since lost its appeal, as the economy has recovered somewhat and stock prices have risen by 50% from the trough.

A second problem is that adopting an exchange-rate peg might cause a shift of the nominal anchor away from the price level or inflation to the exchange rate. We do not dwell on this here because we discussed it extensively elsewhere (Ito and Mishkin 2004). Inflation-targeting central banks have gotten into trouble when they have included an exchange-rate peg as part of their monetary policy strategy—Chile, Hungary, and Israel immediately come to mind. The exchange rate ends up as the dominant influence over monetary policy, and this results in monetary policy not focusing sufficiently on domestic considerations, with poor economic outcomes the result.

The bottom line is that we believe that the Svensson plan would be a serious mistake for Japan, not because we disagree with Svensson's logic, but because the political economy of such a plan could be disastrous. Svensson's "foolproof way" would be a red flag to protectionist and anti-Japanese elements in the rest of the world and would likely hinder a communication strategy based on the price-stability objective. Nonetheless, we do think that a more subtle approach makes sense.

We advocate Japanese intervention in the foreign exchange market to depreciate the yen as one element of unconventional monetary policy, but no precise exchange-rate target should be announced. Instead the Bank of Japan and the Ministry of Finance should emphasize that exchange-rate interventions, along with other measures, are being conducted to achieve a higher price level and a stronger Japanese economy, outcomes which are highly beneficial for Japan's trading partners. Thus, the interventions should be unsterilized as a signal that their primary purpose is to produce an expansionary monetary policy that raises the price level.[3]

4.4 *Open-Market Purchase of Private Assets*

An even more radical step for the Japanese monetary authorities would be to purchase private assets such as stocks, corporate bonds, or real estate. Purchasing these assets directly raises their prices and leads to expansion in aggregate demand though a number of monetary transmission channels (Mishkin 1996; Ito 1999). Purchasing private assets also directly helps restore balance sheets in the economy and helps get the financial system working again, which is crucial to Japan's recovery.

However, the Bank of Japan's purchase of these assets is not without problems. Government purchases of private assets can be highly politicized. Different elements in the private sector would lobby for asset purchases that make them profits. This concern can be partly mitigated by the Bank buying broad-based bundles of assets or market indices so that specific private firms do not benefit over others. Ito (2001) proposed that the BOJ buy Japanese exchange-traded funds, which can include bonds or stocks. The question of how much of each asset class to buy is also important. Decisions on what to buy have important distributional consequences, which would put the BOJ under intense political pressure. Not only might this result in distortionary decisions, but it could politicize the BOJ and interfere with the independence it has worked so hard to get.

Another problem with the Bank of Japan's purchase of private assets is that it involves the government in ownership of the private sector. The trend in recent years has been toward privatization because it is believed that the private sector has better incentives to produce efficiently than does the government sector. Substantial purchases of private assets by the BOJ, which after all is a government entity, goes against this belief. These conflicts can be reduced by announcing that the BOJ will have no involvement in running the companies or real estate investments in which it has a position. For example, the BOJ could simply abstain from voting as a shareholder. However, political pressures may make the BOJ's non-involvement hard.

We have a real concern that if the BOJ's purchases of private assets are sizeable, there would be adverse consequences both for the BOJ and the economy. Therefore, we are reluctant to advocate a policy of purchasing private assets, at this point, but it should not be ruled out entirely. If nothing else works, this more radical step might be necessary as a way of stimulating the economy and achieving a higher price level. But it should be a monetary policy of last resort.

4.5 The Bank of Japan's Balance Sheet

The Bank of Japan has expressed concern about its balance sheet in response to suggestions that it purchase large amounts of long-term bonds, equities, and foreign assets. Governor Hayami and Bank economists have argued that such unconventional policies put the Bank's balance sheet at risk because of possible losses. Theoretically, this argument is specious. The Bank of Japan, despite being legally independent, is still part of the public sector. Any profits (seigniorage) are paid to the government and any losses beyond the seigniorage should be offset by a government fiscal injection. However, politically, the Bank of Japan may not be comfortable asking for government money if its losses become too large.

This potential hesitation is understandable and relates to the Bank's concern for its independence. The old Bank of Japan law explicitly stated that the Ministry of Finance would cover its losses, but this clause was eliminated in the 1998 law, presumably to make the Bank take responsibility for its independent decision-making. Yet independence can be said to have come at the wrong time if it makes the Bank of Japan more timid in adopting policies that may cause losses on its balance sheet. We make the following recommendation:

If the Bank of Japan achieves the price-level target with losses in its balance sheet, the Ministry of Finance will inject money to restore the Bank's capital position without assigning responsibility for such losses to the Governor or other Policy Board members. This policy should be announced unilaterally by the Ministry.

4.6 *Taking Ownership of Monetary Policy*

There are two reasons why in the past unconventional monetary policies may not have worked in Japan. First is that these were not coordinated with managing expectations using a price-level target of the type recommended here. On the contrary, particularly under the Hayami regime, the Bank of Japan was unwilling to commit to raising the price level, and, as in August 2000, reversed its expansionary monetary policy as soon as there was a glimmer of an economic recovery. Second, when the Bank has conducted unconventional policies, as it did after March 2001, it has not taken ownership of these decisions: that is, it has been reluctant to say that these policies would work. For example, when quantitative easing was implemented in March 2001, the Bank did not explain why the policy change would be effective; this action was particularly important because the Bank had not been positive on the effectiveness of quantitative easing in the past. In addition, as the following quotation indicates, high officials in the Bank have argued that other unconventional policies would be unlikely to be effective:

"Three options for further monetary easing can be considered when money market interest rates are near zero. . . . Third, the BOJ can carry out unconventional operations by purchasing assets other than short-term Japanese government securities. . . . The third policy option is for a central bank to purchase non-traditional assets such as government bonds, foreign currencies, corporate bonds, stocks, or real estate which are more imperfectly substitutable for base money than are short-term government securities. . . . [C]entral bank operations that amount to the exchange of perfect substitutes produce little effect on the economy. Such non-traditional operations are effective because they directly alter the prices of the assets in question. Possible benefits and costs of this monetary policy option, however, are extremely uncertain." (Kazuo Ueda, member of the Policy Board, at the semi-annual meeting of the Japan Society of Monetary Economics, Fukushima University, Sep 29, 2001. Full remarks are posted in English at www.boj.or.jp/en/press/01/ko0112a.htm#0301. Also see Okina 1999.)

Our discussion in this chapter has indicated that all of the unconventional monetary policy strategies have problems. Thus, we advocate a multifaceted approach in which many unconventional policies are tried to see which work best. For unconventional policies to work, the Bank of Japan needs to take ownership of its monetary policy through the following recommendation:

The Bank of Japan will commit to using different unconventional policies until deflation is ended and its price-level target is achieved.

To supplement this announcement, the Bank needs to declare that it is accountable for achieving its price-stability goals and that it HAS the tools to lead the economy out of deflation.

4.7 Overcoming Timidity

Uncertainty about the impact of different approaches might make it harder for the Bank to be sure what might be the outcome of using unconventional policies. One response could be paralysis and then not trying any of them. Indeed, in the past the Bank has defended doing nothing because it was unsure what the effects of unconventional policies might be (Okina 1999). The Bank, particularly under Governor Hayami, has been concerned that unconventional policies might lead to uncontrollable inflation.

There are two responses to these concerns. The first is that having clear-cut price-level and inflation targets to ground/fix expectations can make it highly likely that less-conventional tools will achieve the goal of price stability and that inflation will not spin out of control. In recent years there have been major successes in the ability of monetary policy to control inflation in many industrialized countries. We argue that this is not because central banks have become more knowledgeable about the transmission mechanisms of monetary policy: there still is tremendous ignorance on this score. What has changed is that central banks in industrialized countries have been able to put in place much stronger nominal anchors (targets or goals that tie down the price level). The result is greatly improved performance on both the inflation and output fronts. One method has been adopting inflation targets, as in New Zealand, Canada, the United Kingdom, Sweden, and Australia, as well as, to some extent the European Monetary Union. (The European Central Bank does not like to call its strategy "inflation targeting", but it is pretty close: there is a strong commitment to price stability and an explicit inflation goal of less than, but close to, 2% has been announced.)

Alternatively, a strong nominal anchor can be put into place without a formal inflation target, using direct communication with the public about the commitment to price stability and taking actions that are consistent with this goal. This is the strategy pursued by the United States Federal Reserve. It has as strong a nominal anchor as inflation-targeting central banks, albeit one embodied in an individual, Alan Greenspan (Mishkin 2000). Adopting a price-level target and committing to an inflation target in Japan would make it highly unlikely that inflation would spin out of control thereafter.

Conclusions

We have argued that the Bank of Japan can end deflation with two steps: 1) managing expectations by announcing a price-level target and an inflation target once the targeted price level is achieved; and 2) taking ownership of monetary policy and indicating that it will conduct whatever unconventional monetary policy actions are needed to achieve its price stability goals. The most obvious reason why the Bank of Japan needs to take these steps is that these policies will directly stimulate the economy and help restore it to health.

The currently declared (Monetary Policy Board, October 2003) necessary conditions for exiting the zero-interest-rate policy (ZIRP) and quantitative targeting are (1) when the year-on-year CPI (excluding fresh food) inflation rate registers zero or is positive for a few months; and (2) a majority of Board members forecast that inflation (as measured by both the CPI and GDP deflator) will stay above zero in the coming year. Yet we worry that these conditions may prompt premature tightening. In the Spring of 2005 semi-annual Outlook for Economic Activity and Prices, the Policy Board members of the Bank of Japan predicted that the deflation would be ending in fiscal year 2006, and they might thus be tempted to end ZIRP in the not too distant future. We instead recommend that the Bank of Japan raise the price level to what it would have been if deflation had not occurred, and then move to a forward-looking inflation target of 2%. This would surely involve maintaining ZIRP for a long time, and is needed to ensure a strong economic recovery.

The second reason why the Bank of Japan, in concert with the Ministry of Finance, needs to pursue more radical actions to stimulate the economy is that the weakness of Japan's financial sector and the need for massive restructuring of the Japanese economy requires extraordinary measures. Clearly, monetary policy by itself cannot solve Japan's economic problems. Indeed, we believe that financial and non-financial restructuring is probably far more crucial to restoring Japan's economic health than are changes in Japanese monetary policy, and this is the subject of other chapters in this book.

However, monetary policy is crucial to making the restructuring process more successful and palatable to the Japanese public. Using monetary policy to reflate the economy will promote restoration of balance sheets that will help the financial system recover. Expansionary monetary policy that increases aggregate demand will make it easier to deal with the disruptions that will necessarily be caused by restructuring: it will make it easier for workers in a displaced sector to move to a sector where they will be more productive.

It is a tragedy to see the once-great Japanese economy fall below its potential. Japan has tremendous strengths and a highly educated work force, an incredibly hard working population, and superb engineers. This is manifested in Japan's incredibly vibrant export sector, which is the envy of the world. Japan should not be satisfied with growth rates of 2% to 3% when it has fallen so far behind where it would be if years of deflation and financial instability had not set in. There is room for the Japanese economy to grow even faster until it reaches its full-employment level of resources (see Hashimoto and Higuchi in this volume). In addition, if monetary policy can help in the restructuring of the financial, as well as the non-financial, sectors of the economy, higher productivity growth could result.

The analysis here provides some guidance on how monetary policy can be effective in unleashing Japan's enormous potential. However, fear of the consequences of positive action has meant almost a decade of hesitation and doubt—non-action that has exacerbated Japan's economic malaise, including the deflation. There is a theoretical and practical basis for using a range of tools to supplement those already being used. For Japan's deflation to be defeated, a committed, broad-based approach that includes non-standard policies is needed.

Notes

*For presentation at the U.S.-Japan Conference on the Solutions for the Japanese Economy, sponsored by the Center on Japanese Economy and Business, Columbia Business School and Research Center for Advanced Science and Technology, The University of Tokyo, June 19–21, 2004. Any views expressed in this paper are those of the authors only and not those of University of Tokyo, Columbia University or the National Bureau of Economic Research. We thank Hugh Patrick, David Weinstein, Anil Kashyap, Hiroshi Fujiki, Kunio Okina and participants at the conference and at the Economic and Social Research Institute (ESRI) Conference. The authors are grateful to Shoko Nakano and Emilia Simeonova for their excellent research assistance.

1. In September 2002, the Bank decided to purchase equities from commercial banks at market prices. This was an operation to contribute systemic stability, rather than monetary policy, since commercial banks were trying to shed large equity portfolio in the adverse market conditions. Therefore nothing legal prevents the Bank from purchasing stocks as monetary policy.

2. At the press conference after deciding the end of ZIRP in August 2000, Governor Hayami mentioned two side-effects of ZIRP were firms not taking up innovative production processes and not restructuring due to the ready availability of free money. (Posted, in Japanese only, at www.boj.or.jp/press/00/kk0008a.htm)

3. Some may remember that Japanese prices in the late 1980s were regarded as too high, and argue that declining prices must be a good thing, converging to the international norm. However, price-level parity does not work for many reasons. Specifications for the environment and climate as well as taste explain most of price differentials. Few Japanese at this point complain that quality-adjusted prices of most goods and service in Japan are too expensive. Fifteen years ago, hotels and taxis in Tokyo were extremely expensive relative to New York, but this is no longer the case.

4. Under ZIRP, unsterilized intervention becomes equivalent to sterilized intervention because the interest rate is not affected. Therefore, the difference is mainly through the intervention's effect through increasing the monetary base. Bank of Japan economists are skeptical of this argument (see Fujiki, Okina, and Shiratsuka 2001).

References

Akerlof, George, William Dickens, and George Perry. 1996. The Macroeconomics of Low Inflation. *Brookings Papers on Economic Activity* 1: 1–59.

Auerbach, Alan J. and Maurice Obstfeld. 2003. "The Case for Open Market Purchases in a Liquidity Trap." University of California, Berkeley Working Paper C04-135.

Berg, Claes and Lars Jonung. 1999. Pioneering Price Level Targeting: The Swedish Experience 1931–1937. *Journal of Monetary Economics* 43: 525–551.

Bernanke, Ben. 2000. Japanese Monetary Policy: A Case of Self-Induced Paralysis? In *Japan's Financial Crisis and its Parallels to U.S. Experience,* editors Ryoichi Mikitani and Adam Posen. Washington, D.C.: Institute for International Economics.

______. 2002. "Deflation: Making Sure 'It' Doesn't Happen Here." Speech before the National Economists' Club, Washington, D.C., November 21.

______. 2003. "Some Thoughts on Monetary Policy in Japan." Address to the Japan Society of Monetary Economics, Tokyo, Japan, May 31.

Bernanke, Ben, Thomas Laubach, Frederic Mishkin, and Adam Posen. 1999. *Inflation Targeting: Lessons from the International Experience.* Princeton, NJ: Princeton University Press.

Cargill, Thomas, Michael Hutchison, and Takatoshi Ito. 2000. *Financial Policy and Central Banking in Japan.* Cambridge, MA: MIT Press.

Clarida, Richard, Jordi Gali, and Mark Gertler. 1999. The Science of Monetary Policy: A New-Keynesian Perspective. *Journal of Economic Literature* 37: 1661–1707.

Dittmar, Robert and William Gavin. 2000. What Do New-Keynesian Phillips Curves Imply for Price-Level Targeting? Federal Reserve Bank of St. Louis *Review* 82 (2): (March–April) 21–30.

Dittmar, Robert, William Gavin, and Finn E. Kydland. 1999. The Inflation-Output Variability Tradeoff and Price-Level Targets. Federal Reserve Bank of St. Louis *Review* 81 (1): (January–February) 23–31.

Eggertsson, Gauti. 2003. "Fighting Deflation at Zero Nominal Interest Rates: Committing to Being Irresponsible." IMF Working Paper 03/64 (March 1).

Eggertsson, Gauti B. and Michael Woodford. 2003. "Optimal Monetary Policy in a Liquidity Trap." NBER Working Paper 9968.

Estrella, Arturo and Jeffrey Fuhrer. 1998. "Dynamic Inconsistencies: Counterfactual Implications of a Class of Rational Expectations Models." Federal Reserve Bank of Boston Working Paper 98/05 (July).

Feldstein, Martin. 1997. "Capital Income Taxes and the Benefits of Price Stability." NBER Working Paper 6200 (September).

Fischer, Stanley. 1994. Modern Central Banking. In *The Future of Central Banking,* editors Forest Capie, Charles Goodhart Stanley Fischer, and Norbert Schnadt. Cambridge, U.K.: Cambridge University Press.

Fisher, Irving. 1933. The Debt-Deflation Theory of Great Depressions. *Econometrica* 1 (4): 337–357.

Friedman, Benjamin. 2003. "Discussion of 'Inflation Targeting: A Critical View." Speech to the Federal Reserve Bank of St. Louis Annual Conference on Inflation Targeting: Prospects and Problems, October 16–17.

Fuhrer, Jeffrey. 1997. The (Un)Importance of Forward-Looking Behavior in Price Specifications. *Journal of Money, Credit, and Banking* 29 (3): (August) 338–50.

Fujiki, Hiroshi, Kunio Okina, and Shigenori Shiratsuka. 2001. Monetary Policy under Zero Interest Rate: Viewpoints of Central Bank Economists. Bank of Japan, *Monetary and Economic Studies*, (February) 89–130.

Goodfriend, Marvin. 2000. Overcoming the Zero Bound on Interest Rate Policy. *Journal of Money, Credit, and Banking* 32 (4): 1007–1035.

Groshen, Erica L. and Schweitzer, Mark E. 1996. The Effects of Inflation on Wage Adjustments in Firm-Level Data: Grease or Sand? Federal Reserve Bank of New York, *Staff Report* 9 (January).

______. 1999. Identifying Inflation's Grease and Sand Effects in the Labor Market. In *The Costs and Benefits of Price Stability*, editor, Martin Feldstein. Chicago: University of Chicago Press.

Higuchi, Yoshio and Masanori Hashimoto. 2005. Problems in Japanese Labor Market. In *Reviving Japan's Economy: Problems and Prescriptions*. Cambridge, MA: MIT Press.

Hoshi, Takeo and Anil Kashyap. 2005. Solutions to Japan's Banking Problems: What might work and what definitely will fail. In *Reviving Japan's Economy: Problems and Prescriptions*. Cambridge, MA: MIT Press.

Ito, Takatoshi. 1999. Introducing Inflation Targeting in Japan. *Financial Times*, October 19.

______. 2001. How to Rescue Japan. *Financial Times*, October 23.

______. 2004. "Inflation Targeting and Japan: Why has the Bank of Japan not adopted Inflation Targeting?" Presentation to the Conference on the Future of Inflation Targeting at the Reserve Bank of Australia, August 9–10.

Ito, Takatoshi and Frederic Mishkin. 2004. "Two Decades of Japanese Monetary Policy and the Deflation Problem." Presentation to the NBER 15th East Asian Seminar on Economics, Tokyo, Japan, June 25–27.

Ito, Takatoshi and Yomoyoshi Yabu. 2004. "What Prompts Japan to Intervene in the Forex Market? A New Approach to a Reaction Function." NBER Working Paper 10456 (April).

Jorgenson, Date W. and Kazuyuki Motohashi, 2003. "Economic Growth of Japan and the United States in the Information Age" RIETI Discussion Paper Series 03-E-015, July.

Krugman, Paul. 1998. It's Baack! Japan's Slump and the Return of the Liquidity Trap. *Brookings Papers on Economic Activity* 2: 137–187.

McCallum, Bennett. 2000a. Theoretical Analysis Regarding a Zero Lower Bound on Nominal Interest Rates. *Journal of Money, Credit and Banking* 32 (2): 879–904.

______. 2002. Inflation Targeting and the Liquidity Trap. In *Inflation Targeting: Design, Performance, Challenges*, editors N. Loayza and R. Soto. Santiago: Central Bank of Chile.

______. 2003. Japanese Monetary Policy 1991–2001. Federal Reserve Bank of Richmond, *Economic Quarterly* 89.

Meltzer, Allan H. 2001. Monetary Transmission at Low Inflation: Some Clues from Japan. Bank of Japan, *Monetary and Economic Studies* 19 (S-1): (February) 13–34.

Meulendyke, Ann-Marie. 1998. The Federal Reserve and U.S. Monetary Policy: A Short History. In *US Monetary Policy and Financial Markets*. New York: Federal Reserve Bank of New York.

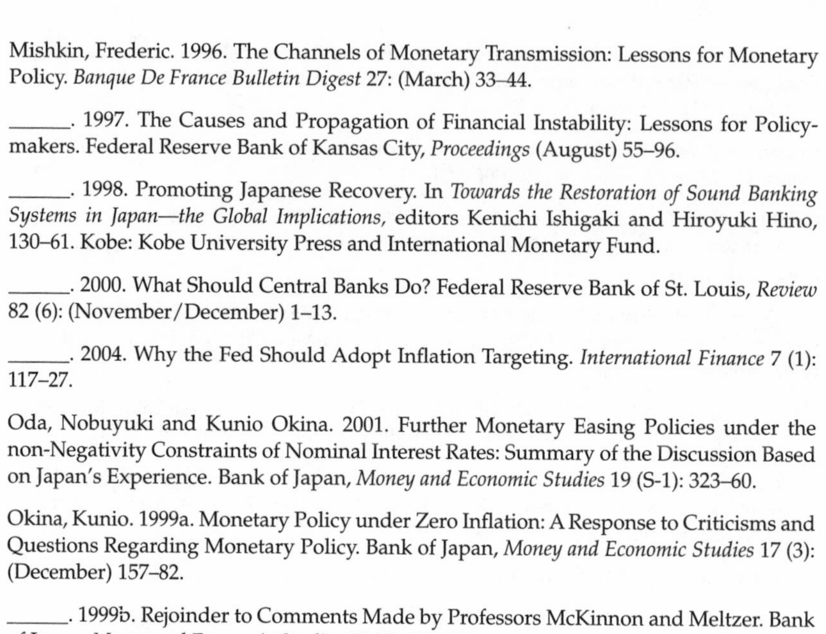

Mishkin, Frederic. 1996. The Channels of Monetary Transmission: Lessons for Monetary Policy. *Banque De France Bulletin Digest* 27: (March) 33–44.

______. 1997. The Causes and Propagation of Financial Instability: Lessons for Policymakers. Federal Reserve Bank of Kansas City, *Proceedings* (August) 55–96.

______. 1998. Promoting Japanese Recovery. In *Towards the Restoration of Sound Banking Systems in Japan—the Global Implications,* editors Kenichi Ishigaki and Hiroyuki Hino, 130–61. Kobe: Kobe University Press and International Monetary Fund.

______. 2000. What Should Central Banks Do? Federal Reserve Bank of St. Louis, *Review* 82 (6): (November/December) 1–13.

______. 2004. Why the Fed Should Adopt Inflation Targeting. *International Finance* 7 (1): 117–27.

Oda, Nobuyuki and Kunio Okina. 2001. Further Monetary Easing Policies under the non-Negativity Constraints of Nominal Interest Rates: Summary of the Discussion Based on Japan's Experience. Bank of Japan, *Money and Economic Studies* 19 (S-1): 323–60.

Okina, Kunio. 1999a. Monetary Policy under Zero Inflation: A Response to Criticisms and Questions Regarding Monetary Policy. Bank of Japan, *Money and Economic Studies* 17 (3): (December) 157–82.

______. 1999b. Rejoinder to Comments Made by Professors McKinnon and Meltzer. Bank of Japan, *Money and Economic Studies* 17 (3): 192–97.

Orphanides, Athanasios and Volker Wieland. 2000. Efficient Monetary Policy Design near Price Stability. *Journal of Japanese and International Economies* 14: 327–56.

Posen, Adam. 1998. *Restoring Japan's Economic Growth.* Washington, D.C.: Institute for International Economics.

Poole, William. 1999. Is Inflation Too Low? Federal Reserve Bank of St. Louis, *Review* 81 (4): 3–10.

Sarno, Lucio and M.P. Taylor. 2001. Official Intervention in the Foreign Exchange Market: Is it Effective and, If So, How Does It Work? *Journal of Economic Literature* 39: 839–68.

Shiratsuka, Shigenori. 1999. "Measurement Errors and Quality-Adjustment Methodology: Lessons from the Japanese CPI." Federal Reserve Bank of Chicago, *Economic Perspectives* 23 (2): (2nd Quarter) 2–13.

Svensson, L.O. 1999. Price Level Targeting vs. Inflation Targeting. *Journal of Money, Credit and Banking* 31: 277–295.

______. 2001. The Zero Bound in an Open Economy: A Foolproof Way of Escaping from a Liquidity Trap. Bank of Japan, *Monetary and Economic Studies* 19 (S-1): (February) 277–312.

______. 2003. "Escaping from a Liquidity Trap and Deflation: the Foolproof Way and Others." NBER Working Paper 10195.

Svensson, L.O. and Michael Woodford. 2003. "Optimal Policy with Partial Information in a Forward-Looking Model: Certainty-Equivalence Redux." NBER Working Paper 9430.

Vestin, David. 2003. "Price-Level Targeting Versus Inflation Targeting in a Forward-Looking Model." Central Bank of Sweden Working Paper 106.

Woodford, Michael. 1999. "Optimal Monetary Policy Inertia." NBER Working Paper 7261.

______. 2000. Pitfalls of Forward-Looking Monetary Policy. *American Economic Review* 90 (2): 100–104.

______. 2003. *Interest and Prices: Foundations of a Theory of Monetary Policy.* Princeton, NJ: Princeton University Press.

Part II

Reforming the Financial System

5

Solutions to Japan's Banking Problems: What Might Work and What Definitely Will Fail

Takeo Hoshi

and

Anil Kashyap

The Japanese banking sector recorded operating losses in each of the ten fiscal years from 1993 and 2002. The losses have eroded the capital base of banks, but only a handful have been closed, and there have not been widespread panics. The economic recovery that began in 2003 may allow the Japanese banking sector to post the first operating profits in a decade, but as we document below, the banking sector's problems are far from over. A consensus has gradually emerged regarding causes and implications of these problems. In this paper we seek to build on this consensus and analyze the question of what steps might be taken to fully resolve these long-standing problems. We argue that an examination of the past Japanese policies that have failed, together with a study of the successful policies in other high-income OECD countries that have overcome banking crises, provides a roadmap for resolving Japan's ongoing problems.

The chapter is divided into four parts. Section 1 briefly reviews the current conditions and describes the consensus on the problems plaguing the banking system. We distill these into four basic troubles. The first is that most Japanese banks are severely under-capitalized when their condition is properly evaluated. The second is that the nation's banks are not currently allocating credit efficiently, and instead are directing many loans to borrowers that will not be able to repay them. The third is that Japan's banking sector is too large (in terms of assets) to make adequate returns. The final problem is that the banks' lack of profitability is partly related to their inability to offer the high margin products that are commonplace among their foreign competitors. We use these four observations as a point of departure for all the subsequent analysis.

Section 2 explores the implications of these observations for the long-run condition of Japan's banking industry. In particular, a natural way to define the end of the problems is when the following three conditions are satisfied. First, the banking sector has shrunk to a level where it can profitably operate. Second, the banks are once again adequately capitalized. Third and finally, the banks no longer ever-green loans to deadbeat borrowers. Recognizing this constellation of conditions as the eventual equilibrium for the industry is helpful because it identifies the set of problems that a successful policy must confront. We conclude the section with a menu of choices that contains the necessary ingredients to resolve the problems.

Section 3 evaluates these competing policy solutions by comparing them against international experiences and the outcomes in Japan thus far. We find that the main policies pursued to date in Japan—regulatory forbearance, liquidity support for distressed banks, and liability guarantees for depositors—have been tried in most banking crises over the last twenty-five years. The evidence from other countries suggests that these policies do not typically lead to lower taxpayer costs or speedier resolution of the problems. We explain why these also seem to have failed in Japan. Accordingly, we propose some alternative solutions that have been effective elsewhere.

Section 4 makes these arguments more tangible by focusing on the rescue of Resona Bank. We demonstrate the specific ways in which existing policies fall short and lay out a set of alternatives that can be used instead to foster the desired long-run equilibrium of the Japanese banking industry. Section 5 uses our framework to assess the merger between Mitsubishi Tokyo Financial Group and UFJ. Section 6 concludes.

1. A Stylized Description of Japan's Banking Problems

There are a number of recent, excellent summaries of the conditions of Japan's banking sector [including, Bank for International Settlements (2002), Fukao (2003a), International Monetary Fund (2003), Kashyap (2002), and Organization for Economic Cooperation and Development (2001)]. Rather than rehash these articles, we focus on the research consensus, which we see as pointing to the four major observations mentioned in the introduction. This section documents these facts.

In taking this approach we necessarily side-step a number of financial system issues, most notably the problems of Japan's insurance companies and government-sponsored financial institutions (see the chapters by Fukao and Doi, respectively, on these sectors). We make this choice to keep the scope of this chapter manageable, but we recognize that there is some important interdependence among the various sectors that together comprise Japan's financial services industry.

1.1 *Under-capitalized Banks*

The first chronic condition for the Japanese banks is the low level of capitalization. Fukao (2003a) and Japan Center for Economic Research (2004), which is edited by Fukao, have shown that the conventionally reported data for Japanese banks overstate their capital because the figures fail to correct for two important factors. These are under-reserving against acknowledged problem loans and how deferred tax credits are treated. Fukao's adjusted data are in Table 5.1.

Japan's banks have many more loan losses than they have acknowledged, but have failed to provision for. If Japan's banks were following standard international procedures they would have much higher loan loss reserves. The increases in loan loss reserves cause a corresponding decrease in capital. Importantly Fukao's adjustment is only for under-reserving against *acknowledged* problem loans. These are the loans that the banks themselves rated as "substandard" "doubtful" or "uncollectible," following the Financial Supervisory Agency's (FSA) *Bank Examination Manual*. The FSA collects these data but does not publish the numbers for individual banks.

The adjustment proposed by Fukao is a very conservative correction. This is because it is widely agreed that there are in fact many more bad loans than the banks have voluntarily revealed to the FSA. It has often been the case that the bad loans that are uncovered by FSA inspections far exceed the amounts that had been previously reported. For example, the FSA inspection of Ashikaga Bank in late 2003 uncovered ¥48 billion more of "doubtful" loans (category III) and ¥21 billion more of "uncollectible" loans (category IV) than Ashikaga's own internal assessment. The amount of additional loan losses was large enough to make Ashikaga insolvent, and this bank was subsequently nationalized.

The second adjustment is necessary because the official figures count deferred tax assets (tax credits from past losses that the bank expects to claim in the future) as a part of core capital. Compared with American tax rules, Japanese rules limit more severely the types of loan losses that can be deducted from taxable income. Thus, banks that generate more loan losses than can be deducted from current-year profits accumulate

Table 5.1
Official and Adjusted Capital in the Banking Sector (trillion yen)

	Market Value of Shares A	Book Value of Shares B	Official Capital (Core capital) C	Deferred Tax Assets D	Estimated Under-reserving E	Adjusted Capital C + (A – B) × 0.6 – D – E	Equity Capital Held by the Government G	Nikkei225 Index
Mar-86	46.9	11.9	12.3	0.0	NA	33.3	0.0	15860
Mar-87	63.7	13.4	13.8	0.0	NA	44.0	0.0	21567
Mar-88	77.6	17.6	17.2	0.0	NA	53.2	0.0	26260
Mar-89	97.1	23.2	22.5	0.0	NA	66.8	0.0	32839
Mar-90	88.6	29.7	28.6	0.0	NA	63.9	0.0	29980
Mar-91	77.7	33.1	30.2	0.0	NA	57.0	0.0	26292
Mar-92	56.4	34.5	31.3	0.0	NA	44.4	0.0	19346
Mar-93	56.4	34.5	31.8	0.0	NA	44.9	0.0	18591
Mar-94	61.9	36.5	32.3	0.0	NA	47.5	0.0	19112
Mar-95	52.0	39.8	32.3	0.0	NA	39.6	0.0	15140
Mar-96	64.3	43.0	27.9	0.0	NA	40.7	0.0	21407
Mar-97	54.1	42.9	28.5	0.0	15.0	20.2	0.0	18003
Mar-98	50.8	45.7	24.5	0.0	5.1	22.5	0.3	16527
Mar-99	47.1	42.7	33.7	8.4	4.6	23.4	6.3	15837
Mar-00	54.5	44.4	35.2	8.1	6.6	26.6	6.9	20337
Mar-01	44.5	44.3	36.7	7.3	7.6	21.9	7.1	13000
Mar-02	34.4	34.4	29.3	10.7	6.9	11.7	7.2	11025
Mar-03	23.2	23.2	24.8	10.6	5.4	8.8	7.3	7873
Mar-04	28.5	28.5	29.0	7.2	5.1	16.7	9.2	11715

Source of data: Fukao (2003a) and JCER (2004), based on Federation of Bankers Associations of Japan, "Analysis of Bank Financial Statements," various issues; securities reports for individual banks. Both market and book values represent listed shares only. The Table pertains to banking accounts of all banks in Japan.

Note: Core capital, sometimes referred to as Tier I capital, includes equity capital and capital reserves. The market value of stock portfolios was not published prior to March 1990, so Fukao imputed it using the Nikkei 225 share price index. However, the figures for 1985–86 should be discounted, because bank stock portfolios have been gradually increasing, so that values estimated from the end of fiscal 1990 will have an upwards bias the farther back one goes. A 40% corporate tax rate is assumed in the adjusted-capital calculation.

deferred tax credits that they hope to use in the future. As Fukao notes, however, these credits are only usable if the banks can regain profitability quickly—they must claim the tax credits within five years after the losses occur. We discuss the issue of deferred tax assets in detail in our case study of Resona Bank. We follow Fukao's approach and remove all the credits from core capital figures.

The first two columns of Table 5.1 show the unrealized capital gains in bank portfolios. As of March 1989, a little before Japan's stock market peaked, the market value of the shares held by banks far exceeded book value (which was their purchase price). However, by 2001 this gap had disappeared. Nonetheless, the fact that their equity holdings in other firms are still about equal to their own equity capital leaves the banks very exposed to changes in the stock market.

The remainder of the table shows how the official bank capital figure reported in the third column should be adjusted for unrealized capital gains and other factors to get an estimate that better reflects the banks's true capital position. The fourth column shows that deferred tax assets now account for roughly forty percent of the adjusted book value of capital. The banks were not counting them in the capital positions prior to 1999 (which makes sense given that these assets serve no buffering role). The next column shows Fukao's (probably conservative) estimates of under-reserving by banks against bad loans, which represents about one-fifth of book capital.

The sixth column shows the adjusted level of capital that accounts for the unrealized capital gains (net of the taxes that would be owed), the under-reserving for non-performing loans, and the sham deferred tax credits. By March 2003, when the problem was most serious, the adjusted capital figure was just under 9 trillion yen and therefore far below a prudent level of equity.[1]

In fact, even the adjusted level paints an overly optimistic picture of the banks' financial condition. One consideration (shown by column 7) in the table is that most of this capital represents funds from past government transfers. In other words almost no private capital remains in the banking sector.

Even our adjusted figure exaggerates the true private capital, because of the "double gearing" between banks and life insurance companies. Banks hold a significant amount of insurance company debt (usually in the form of subordinated loans or surplus notes), and the life insurance companies also hold large amounts of subordinated bank debt and stock. Indeed, banks raise money by selling their securities to the life insurance companies, but use the proceeds to buy the securities issued by the life insurance companies, so that the life insurance companies can buy the banks' securities in the first place. As of March 2003, ten major life insurance companies owned ¥6.3 trillion of bank equity and subordinated bank debt (Fukao 2003b). At the same time, banks provided ¥1.9 trillion of surplus notes and subordinated loans to the ten major life insurance companies. (The numbers were ¥10.5 trillion and ¥2.0 trillion respectively as of March 2001.) The net effect of this practice is to boost reported capital levels. Many of the life insurance companies are also in a very precarious financial position. Thus, the double gearing makes both the banks and the insurance companies appear better capitalized than is in fact the case.

The important conclusion is that the amount of bank core capital is currently very small and mostly consists of public funds. There is almost no private capital in Japan's banking sector. As detailed below, even using optimistic forecasts for near-term macroeconomic performance we find a substantial capital shortage.

1.2 Ever-greening

Given these extremely low levels of capital, the banks have been hesitant to recognize any more losses than they are required to do. Japanese regulators have been complicit and allowed the banks to avoid reporting true figures. To cover things up, the banks have taken to rolling over loans, giving interest concessions, and partially forgiving loans to firms with grim repayment prospects, because calling the loan would require the banks to recognize losses. We call all these actions by banks that continue support for customers with poor repayment prospects "ever-greening."

There is a growing literature examining the potential misallocation of bank credit in Japan [see Sekine, Kobayashi, and Saita (2003) for a survey]. Early studies looked at the profitability of industries that attract more bank loans. For example, in the first paper to directly investigate this issue, Hoshi (2000) found that bank loans to real estate developers continued to grow in the 1990s, well after the industry's profitability declined following the collapse of land prices, while loans to manufacturers steadily declined. He suggested this situation may have resulted from banks repeatedly making new loans to real estate developers so that these borrowers could cover the interest payments on past loans and make the past loans appear to be performing. Sakuragawa (2002, Chapter 5) shows that the positive relationship between a given region's land price increases and the importance of real estate loans to the banks headquartered in the same region broke down after 1992, when banks became concerned with their capital ratios.

Fukao (2000) calculated the average amount of loans per firm and found it increased in the late 1990s in the industries that had been affected most by the collapse in land prices: construction, real estate, and non-bank financial institutions. He interpreted this as evidence that banks were lending more to already heavily indebted firms to prevent their loans from becoming classified as non-performing.

Hosono and Sakuragawa (2003) also examined loans to these three under-performing sectors. They find the banks with a low "market-based" capital ratio, which they define as the market value of their shares divided by the sum of the book value of debt and the market value of shares, tend to increase their loans to these three industries (their debt measure includes the subordinated debt that is counted as part of regulatory capital). They interpret this finding as showing that banks with weak capital positions roll over non-performing loans to hide the true picture of their health.

Sekine, Kobayashi and Saita (2003) estimate a bank loan supply function using data for individual borrowers, and show that there was a break in the connection between loans received and bank debt-to-asset ratios. They find that loans grew more at firms with high bank debt-to-asset ratios starting only after 1993, and that these increases were most pronounced among construction and real estate industries. They also find that the increase in lending was concentrated in what appears to be the rollover of short-term loans, rather than the extension of new long-term credits. The Sekine et al. approach encounters all the usual difficulties in separating loan supply from loan demand. In this case, the question is whether one accepts their assumption that a firm's bank debt-to-asset ratio is only related to subsequent borrowing because of its influence on banks' willingness to lend (and not because of the firm's demand for bank loans).

Nishimura, Nakajima, and Kiyota (2003) examined entries and exits of Japanese firms between 1994 and 1998 using METI (Ministry of Economy, Trade, and Industry) data from the *Basic Survey of Business Structure and Activity*, and found the average productivity for exiting firms was often higher than the surviving firms, especially in construction, wholesale and retail trade. Since many exit decisions are presumably related to the availability of working capital, their result indirectly suggests a misallocation of funds.

Peek and Rosengren (2003a,b) conducted what is arguably the most systematic study to date on the potential misallocation of bank credit. In the first of these papers, they find that aggregate credit flows do not follow the patterns that are associated with a credit crunch during the mid-1990s. In particular, aggregate bank credit did not decline and credit extensions by Japanese banks with weak balance sheets expanded more than they did for banks with stronger balance sheets. More importantly, they find that bank credit to poorly performing firms often increased between 1993 and 1999. Main banks are more likely than other banks to lend to these firms when their profitability is declining. This pattern of perverse credit allocation is more likely when the bank's own balance sheet is weak, or when the borrower is a *keiretsu* affiliate. Importantly, non-affiliated banks do not show this pattern.

Rolling over loans is not the only way for a bank to help weak borrowers. For instance, banks can also refinance the loans at lower interest rates or forgive a part of the principal. Banks may decide to restructure the loans rather than just rolling these over, especially if the borrowers are publicly known to be in trouble. Without such restructuring, banks would be forced to classify these borrowers' loans as "at risk", which usually would require the banks to set aside 70 percent of the loan value as loan loss reserves. With loan restructuring, the banks need only move the loans to the "special attention" category, which requires reserves of at most 15%.

There are some studies showing that many Japanese firms are receiving very low interest rate spreads, especially since the mid-1990s. For example, Smith (2003) finds that loan spreads for Japanese borrowers are, on average, lower than those for American, British, or German borrowers in the 1990s. Moreover, Japanese lenders to Japanese corporations charge lower risk-adjusted spreads and vary credit terms less than foreign lenders do to Japanese corporations. Schaede (2003) finds that the loan rates for most Japanese firms are extremely low or extremely high (for some firms that need to rely on loan-sharks such as *shōkō loan* lenders) with no middle ground between these two extremes.

Figure 5.1, taken from Jerram (2004), shows that even through April 2004, Japanese banks were charging less than 3% on the vast majority of their loans. Indeed, Jerram also emphasizes the fact that interest rates on short term loans (those with a maturity under one year) have continued to decline despite the upturn in the macroeconomy. For example, the average rate on new short-term loans in April 2004 was 1.534 per-

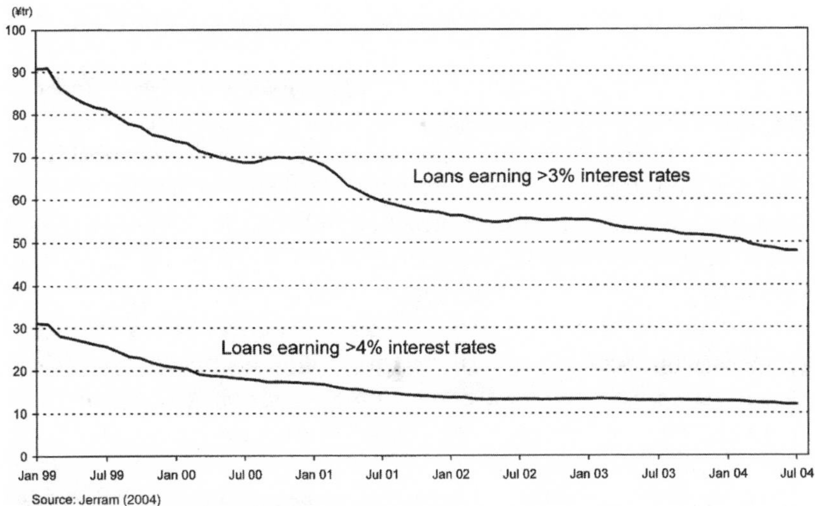

Figure 5.1
Loans Earning Premium Interest Rates

cent, compared to 1.664 percent in April 2003. By February 2005, the average rate dropped to 1.255 percent.

Caballero, Hoshi and Kashyap (2003) attempt to quantify the amount of subsidized lending that is occurring for publicly traded firms in the manufacturing, services, retail and wholesale (excluding the nine general trading companies), construction and real estate sectors. They do so by comparing the actual interest payments that are reported by each of these firms to a notional lower bound that would be paid by an extremely creditworthy firm. The lower bound for each firm is calculated supposing that all bank borrowing takes place at the prime rate, and all bonds financing takes place at the minimum rate that is recorded for any bonds issued in the last five years. Commercial paper is assumed to have been issued at a zero interest rate. This approach to identifying subsidized lending by banks yields two noteworthy results.

First, the level of subsidized lending for publicly listed firms in all these industries increased markedly during the 1990s. For this universe of firms, the fraction (weighted by assets) of firms receiving subsidies tripled from around 4.7 percent (1981–93 average) to 14.5 percent (1996–2002 average). Their approach is conservative in that it does not identify firms whose interest payments are not extremely low but still lower than is appropriate for their risk. In this sense, these numbers should be considered lower bounds for the amount of subsidized lending being done by the banks.

The second key conclusion is that the subsidies were far more common for non-manufacturing firms than for manufacturing firms. In the manufacturing sector, the asset-weighted percentage of subsidized firms rose only from 3.6 percent (1981–93 average) to 10.1 percent (1996–2002 average). In the construction industry, the index increased from 4.4 percent (1981–93 average) to 20.3 percent (1996–2002 average). Similar large increases occurred for the retail and wholesale sector, and services and real estate industries. These patterns confirm the conventional view that lending distortions have been most pronounced in the parts of the economy that have been most protected by regulation and from external competition. These same sectors also seem to have the strongest political protection.

The effort of supporting weak borrowers not only hurts bank profitability, it also harms the rest of the economy. As Caballero, Hoshi, and Kashyap (2003) argue, the unprofitable borrowers that are protected by banks (called "zombies") distort competition throughout the economy. The zombies' distortions act in many ways, including depressing market prices for their products, raising market wages by retaining workers whose productivity at the current firms declined, and, more generally, congesting the markets in which they participate.

Effectively, the growing Japanese government liability that comes from guaranteeing the deposits of banks that support the zombie firms is serving as a very inefficient program to sustain employment.[2] Thus, the normal competitive outcome whereby the zombies would shed workers and lose market share is being thwarted. More importantly, the resulting low prices and high wages reduce the profits that new and more productive entrants can earn, discouraging their entry. Thus, even solvent banks see few good lending opportunities.

1.3 Over-banking

Another factor that has kept bank profitability low is the excessive size of the Japanese banking sector. By essentially all conventional measures, Japan has far more intermediated lending than the other advanced industrial economies. This should mean that loan spreads are low in Japan, and in fact Japanese banks are less profitable than their peers in other countries, and have been for over 20 years.

Table 5.2 shows the profitability of commercial banks in France, Germany, Japan, the United Kingdom, and the United States. The second and third rows of the table show that after-tax profits in Japan are much lower than in these countries, and actually were negative over the five years between 1997 and 2001. These losses reflect the large loan losses that were realized over this period. The bottom two rows in the table, however, show that even the unadjusted earnings for Japanese banks (that do not depend on loan losses) are much lower than in other countries.

The low profitability of Japanese banks has persisted for ten years. As Fukao (2003a) stresses, Japan's banking industry did not have a *net operating* profit from fiscal year 1993 to fiscal year 2002. Until late in the 1990s, the banks offset these losses by realizing capital gains on long-held stocks (cross-shareholdings) and land holdings. By 2000, little more could be squeezed from these sources. Since 1995, Japanese banks have recorded net losses in more years than not. Fukao shows that the cumulative loan losses incurred and recognized by the banks from April 1992 to March 2002 is ¥91.5 trillion (18 percent of Japanese GDP in 2002).

These losses are too large and persistent to be blamed solely on the sudden decline in asset prices in the 1990s. Indeed, as the Bank of Japan (2002) has pointed out, the losses amount to 80 percent of the increase in loans during the asset price boom (1986 to 1990)! Thus, it is implausible to suggest that the continued losses can be attributed only to misguided lending decisions during the late 1980s. Rather, these are indicative of deeper underlying problems facing the banking industry, including the problem of over-banking.

Table 5.2
Size and Profitability of Commercial Banking Sector for Selected Countries

	France	Germany	Japan	United Kingdom	United States
Number of banks (2001)	355	199	124	42	8130
Profits After Tax (2001) / Assets	0.64%	0.16%	–0.71%	0.75%	1.18%
Profits After Tax (1997–2001) / Assets	0.37%	0.31%	–0.41%	0.85%	1.22%
Net Income (2001) / Assets	0.96%	0.60%	–0.06%	1.34%	2.45%
Net Income (1997–2001) / Assets	0.61%	0.84%	0.28%	1.45%	2.35%

Source: Organization for Economic Cooperation and Development (2003).

The size of the Japanese banking sector is a legacy from the 1960s and 1970s when the choices of corporate borrowers were constrained by capital controls that hindered overseas lending possibilities and other regulations that limited domestic non-bank financing options (see Hoshi and Kashyap 1999, 2001). The savings options for households were also limited by various regulations. While the savings options have steadily expanded, and as of 2001 been fully liberalized, Japanese consumers have not yet substantially rebalanced their portfolios. Given the poor performance of the stock market and continued deflation, this has not been an unwise decision. Meanwhile, Japan's banks have struggled to find profitable uses for the funds that they have retained. Many of their largest borrowers left the banks in the 1980s when corporate financing choices were greatly enhanced by deregulation, giving them access to bonds, commercial paper, and other non-bank financing both domestically and abroad. Japan's movement away from bank financing is not yet complete. More and more firms will eventually migrate to capital-market financing. Indeed, Hoshi and Kashyap (1999) calculate that if Japanese corporate borrowing patterns move toward American patterns, Japanese bank assets could shrink by 25 to 50 percent. In the five years since those calculations were done, the quantity of bank loans in Japan has dropped by only 10 percent. It seems likely that much more adjustment is needed.

1.4 *Backward Banks*

The low profitability of Japanese banks reflects the outdated business model many of them still follow. Japanese banks still rely heavily on traditional banking business—that is, taking deposits and making loans. The proportion of income from non-traditional products is much smaller in comparison with global banks in other advanced economies. Table 5.3 compares the income structure of major banks in six countries. Compared with the major banks in the other countries, Japanese banks have low fee income and high dependence on interest income.

Hoshi and Kashyap (2001, Tables 8.3 and 8.4) compared the percentage for fee and commission income between Japanese banks and American banks. For Japanese banks in aggregate, fee and commission income as a percentage of total income was essentially identical in 1976 and 1996. During this same period American banks increased their percentage of fee and commission income by 150 percent. This disparity was partially attributable to regulations that handicapped Japanese banks.

Table 5.3
Backward Japanese Banks

Number of Large Commercial Banks (2001)	France 5	Germany 4	Japan 7	United Kingdom 42	United States 10	Switzerland 3
Units for next 8 rows are as a percent of assets						
Net interest income	0.46	0.89	1.09	1.77	2.87	0.97
Total net non-interest income	1.76	1.17	–0.61	1.37	2.23	1.49
Fees and commissions receivable	0.82	0.67	0.25	1.09	0.73	1.03
Fees and commissions payable	0.28	0.10	0.09	0.20	NA	0.12
Net profits (or loss) on financial operations	0.78	0.30	–0.77	0.48	0.43	0.50
Other non-interest income	0.44	0.30	0.00	0.00	1.07	0.07
After tax profits	0.44	0.21	–0.88	0.75	0.97	0.47
Ratio of net non-interest income to net interest income	3.86	1.31	–0.56	0.77	0.78	1.54
Growth rate of fees and commissions receivable (1996–2001)	122%	149%	7%	48%	NA	63%

Source: Organization for Economic Cooperation and Development (2003).

For instance, until 1998 Japan's banks were barred from many activities, such as providing loan commitments, conducting over-the-counter derivatives transactions and brokerage activities, and underwriting corporate bonds and equities. Some of the gap is also attributable to the slow development of the syndicated lending market in Japan, since loan syndications move revenue from the form of interest payments to fees. But even after Japan's bank deregulation that was completed along with a larger financial "Big Bang" on April 1, 2001, the gap persists, and Japanese banks remain overly reliant on lending revenue.

Since non-traditional products and their associated revenue streams are central to the business strategies of most global banks, this deficiency is a huge problem for Japanese banks. Indeed, as the table indicates, bank fee income has grown substantially in all the other countries.[3] There are few product lines, if any, in which the Japanese banks are world leaders. We know of no examples where Japanese banks and their global rivals have competed for business on a level playing field and the Japanese banks have emerged as market leaders. Instead, the recurring pattern is that Japanese banks are late to enter markets or slow to offer new products and, consequently, their profitability lags.

The critical fact is that low profitability was present even in the 1980s when the Japanese economy was booming, as this suggests that there is little reason to believe that macroeconomic recovery alone will restore the banks's profitability. Indeed, the low profit rates are symptomatic of a more fundamental problem: Japanese banks have not innovated and evolved like their global competitors. As we have stressed elsewhere (Hoshi and Kashyap 1999, 2001), the stunted evolution was in part due to regulatory barriers. But regardless of the cause, the consequence is that at this point in time the major Japanese banks have a rather different business model, product mix, and set of competencies than major banks elsewhere.

2. Long-run Equilibrium and How to Get There

We have just documented the four major problems that the Japanese banking sector currently faces: capital shortages, ever-greening of loans to zombie firms, over-banking, and an outdated business model. This section and the following one discuss some alternative strategies to deal with these problems.

We will consider the banking problems to be over once the banks are well capitalized, stop ever-greening non-performing loans, and are earning rates of return that are comparable to their global competitors. We see these as the three minimal necessary conditions that must prevail if Japan's banking sector is to reach any type of long-run equilibrium. If one accepts this definition of the eventual condition of the industry, four important conclusions for fostering solutions follow.

First, a successful policy must have components that permit all three problems to be overcome. Proposed solutions that ignore one or more of these problems can be immediately spotted as being partial at best, and likely to fail absent luck or some subsequent policy that remedies the shortcomings.

Second, it may not be necessary for a policy to tackle the product mix problem of the banks. To achieve rates of return that are comparable to global banks in other industrialized countries, it is necessary to solve the over-banking problem. If the banking sector becomes sufficiently small so that every bank can find enough borrowers to overcome the low margins from the traditional banking business, they will be able to return to profitability without changing their business model. This would be quite unusual given the experience of banking in other countries, and would require a substantial downsizing of the industry, but nonetheless it is possible. More likely, however a successful policy will address both the over-banking and product mix problems simultaneously. The case study of Resona Bank discussed below offers a useful illustration of the difficulty of achieving both goals.

Third, no policy will succeed without a return to macroeconomic normalcy. The stagnation that accompanies deflation continues to erode the quality of bank portfolios and capital. We view the cessation of deflation as minimum condition that will be associated with a return to macroeconomic normality. No modern industrial economy has ever shown sustained growth along with deflation: we assume that Japan will not do so either. Without some macroeconomic improvement, it is impossible for banks to regain profitability either in the traditional banking business or in non-traditional areas. Throughout the rest of this chapter, we assume that macroeconomic policies are implemented to stop Japan's deflation, so that we can focus on policy alternatives that are geared specifically toward the banking industry. (At the end of this section we explain why an improvement in the economy alone seems unlikely to be sufficient to resolve the banking problems.)

The fourth and most important conclusion is that we can use these long-run necessary conditions to come up with alternative strategies to solve the problems. There are multiple ways to achieve each long-run condition, and we can evaluate the likely success of these alternative policies. In the rest of this section, we list several approaches to achieve each of the three long-run conditions and briefly evaluate them. The discussion here focuses on Japan, but it can be applied to any economy in a similar developmental stage that faces similar problems. Although Japan may have some specific institutional characteristics that require special attention, it is by no means unique.

2.1 Recapitalization

Many Japanese banks are under-capitalized and some of them are insolvent under a stricter (and more reasonable) definition of what constitutes capital. The shrinkage of bank assets, which needs to happen to address the over-banking problem, does not by itself seem to be enough to solve the capital shortage problem. Thus, Japanese banks need to be recapitalized in some way. There are several alternative ways to do this.

First, one can encourage the banks to rebuild capital through accumulated profits. As the deflation stops and the economy recovers, many banks will gradually recover profitability and by retaining profits they will rebuild their capital. However, given the size of the capital deficit and the historical profit rates of Japanese banks, this process would likely take many years before proper levels of capital are in place. Thus, this "solution" requires a long period of regulatory forbearance. As we shall argue in the next section, this approach, which constitutes part of Japan's actual policy so far, has never been successful elsewhere.

Alternatively, the regulatory agency can force the banks to recapitalize immediately. This approach can be classified further by the source of funds and by the required level of recapitalization.

Looking at the source of funds for recapitalization, we can distinguish between recapitalization using private funds and recapitalization using public funds. Private solutions require the banks to raise funds in the capital market (through new share issues, for example). Recapitalization with public funds, in contrast, draws on government funds (and hence taxpayer money). We can also consider hybrid programs that rely on both private and public funds. For example, recapitalization in capital markets may be supplemented by funding from the government. Finally, public funds may be "given" or "loaned" to the banks.

Japan essentially has already tried all of these options. In March 1998 and March 1999, the government used public funds to buy subordinated debt and preferred shares of major banks. The banks were not forced to recapitalize, but were strongly encouraged to apply for these funds. The banks, however, are expected to "return" the public funds eventually by accumulating enough internal funds to buy-back their shares and debt. The Bank of Tokyo Mitsubishi, Sumitomo Trust and Banking, and Yokohama Bank have already bought-back the government's holdings of their subordinated debt and preferred shares, and Mizuho has also started the buy-back.

In early 2003, many major banks recapitalized themselves by issuing new shares. In many cases, this was not really a public offering in the market. Rather the shares were bought by the banks's borrowers or foreign investment banks that are business partners of the particular Japanese banks. The 2003 recapitalization was not forced by the government, but the banks certainly felt pressure from new Financial Services Minister, Heizo Takenaka, who started in late 2002. The announced merger between UFJ and Mitsubishi Tokyo Financial Group is another private-sector solution to the capital shortage that UFJ faced. We will discuss the likely effectiveness of this deal in section 6.

The level of required recapitalization is the final critical parameter, and it can differ among alternative recapitalization policies. Banks could be recapitalized to the minimum necessary levels. In this case, small negative shocks in the future (an unexpectedly short-lived economic recovery, a further increase in non-performing loans, etc.) would necessitate repeated rounds of recapitalization. Alternatively, banks could be required to raise their capital to a sufficiently high level so that they can withstand small adverse shocks without any additional assistance.

The Japanese government has repeatedly tried to recapitalize the banking sector during the last decade, but none of these attempts was large enough to solve the problem. The most recent attempt was Resona Bank where public funding superficially "solved" Resona's problems based on a comparison of capital after the injection and reported loan losses at that time. But many observers suspected under-reporting of the true size of the losses. After a re-examination of the books by the new management, Resona increased its estimates for loans losses and, in doing so, consumed all the capital that been supplied by the government. Thus, even in a case where the support levels may have looked sufficient at first, in the end the government had not provided adequate funding.

2.2 *Stopping Ever-greening*

Ever-greening occurs when weak banks continue to lend to zombie borrowers. There are two ways to approach the problem: one focusing on the banks and the other focusing on the borrowing firms.

The bank-centric approach supposes that if banks can successfully get rid of non-performing loans, the incentive to keep ever-greening these loans will disappear. This approach, therefore, assumes that once the bad loans are disposed of, the banks will have enough creditworthy borrowers to resume operating normally. (However, as we note below, this need not be the case.)

Loan disposal can be accomplished in several ways. One method is for the regulators to force banks to fully disclose non-performing loans, sell them in the market, and recognize the losses. Stricter enforcement of the capital ratio regulation might be a way to convince the banks to unload their non-performing loans. In this case, any restructuring of the borrowers would be done by the purchasers of the loans.

Alternatively, or in addition, the government can set-up an asset management company to purchase the non-performing loans directly from the banks. Many countries have used such companies to deal with banking crises. One potential problem of this method is that the company can serve merely as a warehouse for non-performing loans. If this happens, ever-greening can continue at the asset management company—in which case, zombie distortions persist. To solve the ever-greening problem, it is important to force the asset management company to collect or get rid of non-performing loans quickly (after restructuring if necessary). We will review the Japanese experience with various asset management companies in the next section.

Yet another bank-centric approach is to patiently wait for the banks to accumulate enough profits to write off non-performing loans. This may work if the Japanese economy recovers rapidly and banks suddenly become very profitable. Banks then would have enough profits to pay for the losses from writing off non-performing loans without worrying about their capital positions. As indicated earlier, if the zombie problem is sufficiently pervasive, this possibility is very unlikely to work. Perhaps more importantly, profit increases from the economic recovery may be severely constrained by the over-banking problem.

Instead of focusing on the bank side, one can also try to fix the ever-greening problem on the borrower side. The borrower-centric approach tries to stop ever-greening loans by making a case-by-case decision as to whether to revive or liquidate every weak borrower.

A critical question under this approach is how many weak (and perhaps even currently insolvent) borrowers would be viable under normal macroeconomic conditions. If one believes that most firms would be profitable if normal macroeconomic conditions prevailed, large-scale debt relief (financed by the government) may be sufficient to solve the current problem. Under this scenario, when the economy recovers, most firms will recover and past-due loans will start performing again. Note that, if this is indeed the case, ever-greening is actually a long-run rational strategy and there is no reason to force banks to stop it.

If one believes that a substantial number of these underperforming firms would not be viable even under normal macroeconomic conditions, it is important to have a mechanism to sort out the borrowers that will be revived and the corporations that will eventually be liquidated or otherwise sold. In this case, ever-greening for all weak borrowers is clearly sub-optimal and creates serious problems. Setting up an agency like the Industrial Revitalization Corporation of Japan (IRCJ) , which helps banks rescue viable customers, is one form of the borrower-centric approach to stop ever-greening.

2.3 *Ending Over-banking*

The elimination of over-banking is a necessary condition for Japanese banks to restore their profitability. The size of this adjustment will depend on how successfully the banks can change their business models to catch up with their counterparts in the other advanced economies. If many banks fail to adjust, and continue the traditional banking business model, the Japanese banking sector must go through a massive downsizing.

One can consider alternative policies to eliminate the over-banking problem. At one extreme, the Japanese government may wait for the banking sector to reorganize itself through voluntary mergers and acquisitions. To help the reorganization during a recession, the government may actually relax normal prudential regulations so that even the weakest banks can be reorganized without being closed.

At the other extreme is a policy to eliminate the over-banking problem swiftly by closing non-viable banks. Given the general shortage of capital, closing down non-viable banks by strictly enforcing the supervisory rules would not be technically difficult. The policy could be further differentiated by the method chosen for closing non-viable banks. Is a closed bank (temporarily) nationalized and later sold (after restructuring if necessary)? Is a closed bank liquidated?

2.4 *Updating the Banking Business Model*

It may not be necessary for most Japanese banks to move out of traditional banking to restore profitability. In this case, however, the required shrinkage of the banking industry is very large. Thus, it probably is more desirable for surviving Japanese banks to update their business models.

The role of government policy in this process, however, is not clear. The government certainly should refrain from discouraging banks from innovating, as the Japanese government used to do under the convoy system before the 1990s. (See Hoshi and Kashyap, 2001, pp. 111–112 for a more detailed discussion of the convoy system.) It is certainly a good idea to allow foreign banks to enter the Japanese market so that they will bring both innovative products and competitive pressure to bear. Other than these obvious points that derive from a general principle that the government should allow (and even encourage) private markets to work, we do not see important government policy alternatives on this issue.

2.5 *Relying on a Macroeconomic Miracle*

A sustained period of macroeconomic growth offers one appealing solution to all of these problems. Growth not only helps improve borrowers' creditworthiness, leading to a drop in non-performing loans, but also raises the demand for borrowing, thereby creating profitable new lending opportunities for the banks. The fact that many of Japan's major banks reported profits for the fiscal year that ended in March 2004 and are expected to do so again for March 2005 raises the question of how much growth might help Japan's banking sector. In particular, could realistic amounts of macroeconomic improvement be sufficient to resolve the problems?

The following rough calculation suggests that even with a rosy-scenario growth forecast, macroeconomic improvements alone are unlikely to be sufficient to end the banks' problems. The calculation asks how many years of *extraordinary* performance by the banks and the economy are needed to eliminate the current problems. The essence of the exercise is, therefore, a comparison of the level of capital that the banks could build from the profits and other balance sheet improvements that come with very strong levels of growth with the level of capital called for by existing regulations.

As of March 2004 Japanese banks had ¥423 trillion of loans. Assuming banks need to hold core capital of at least 4% of their loans, they should have roughly ¥17 trillion of core capital to be adequately capitalized (assuming no unprovisioned loan losses). Table 5.1 shows that this amount is about what they reported as of March 2004; between March 2003 and 2004 they doubled their adjusted capital. Assessing their true condition, of course, requires us to take a stand on the size of the loan losses that are still hidden on the books and are not adequately provisioned for on the banks' balance sheets.

Obtaining realistic estimates for such losses is difficult. On the one hand, it is neither in the interest of the regulators or the private sector analysts who have to deal with the regulators and bank management to discuss or acknowledge that these losses still exist. On the other hand, the experience of UFJ suggests that there are still likely to be some losses. Kashyap (2002) reports estimates for the true size of loan losses, and concludes that Japan's banks were probably not acknowledging at least another ¥20 trillion in losses as of March 2003. So we take that figure as the starting pointing for the capital shortage.

The change in this gap since March 2003 depends on several factors. First, as shown in Table 5.1, the banks still have large holdings of other publicly traded firms. According to UBS Investment Research (Sasajima 2004) the major banks reported ¥3.2 trillion in capital gains on their stock portfolios between March 2003 and March 2004. But since March 2004 the stock market has been flat (actually down slightly as of May 2005) so this channel has not contributed anything further. Extrapolating using the Table 5.1 data implies that for each subsequent 10% increase in stock prices, banks as a group stand to gain another ¥2.85 trillion (before taxes). Therefore, if share prices rose substantially bank capital would directly improve as well.

The economic recovery since 2003 has also improved the quality of bank loan portfolios. There are various ways that one might try to estimate these effects. We rely on the special inspections done by the FSA in the first quarter of 2004 (FSA 2004), which involved detailed examinations of 133 of the largest customers of the large banks with total loans of ¥10.5 trillion. These customers were chosen because their "stock prices, external ratings, and other indicators had been experiencing significant changes." These data are particularly well-suited for our exercise because similar inspections were conducted in the third quarter of 2003, thus permitting a comparison and estimates of the improvement (or deterioration) of these borrowers between September 2003 and March

2004. The key finding from the FSA analysis is that loans totaling ¥1.3 trillion (12.6% of the total) showed improvement over this period. Most of these loans actually remain in one of the sub-standard categories: only ¥0.8 trillion were classified as normal quality as of March 2004, up from ¥0.6 trillion in September 2003. Moreover, the percentage of loans to bankrupt or near-bankrupt firms also increased, rising by ¥1.8 trillion.

We believe one can argue, based on these data, that there has been very little improvement in loan portfolios so far: in fact the fraction of loans being upgraded is below the fraction being downgraded. However, in the spirit of the exercise, let us assume that there has been a 25% improvement in the condition of the loan portfolio. This is almost twice the 12.6% observed rate, and we believe it is the most optimistic scenario that one can justify.

With a 25% improvement in loan quality, bank capital improves for two reasons. First, the under-reserving problem in Table 5.1 becomes less acute; a proportionate reduction adds another ¥1.275 trillion to bank capital. If we assume that the unacknowledged ¥20 trillion loan losses improved in a like manner, the capital shortage is reduced by another ¥5 trillion.

Finally, if the banks can become profitable again, some of the deferred tax assets that we assume to be worthless can be claimed. The scope for gains here are uncertain as the maximum that can be claimed depends on reported profits (over the next five years) and the timing of the profits, because some of the tax credits expire each year. To get an upper bound on this effect, we start by constructing an upper bound forecast for profits.

For the year ending in March 2004 net income for all major banks was –¥700 billion, but this includes the ¥2 trillion in losses by UFJ and Resona; the remaining large banks made profits of ¥1.3 trillion. The major banks were forecasting net income for the fiscal year ending in March 2005 of ¥1.4 trillion. (The final figures for the fiscal year ending in March 2005 are not yet available as of this writing (May 2005).) Smaller banks have risk-weighted assets amounting to roughly two-thirds of the assets held by major banks. By most accounts as a group the smaller banks are less far along in restructuring than the large banks. So we believe that forecasting increases in net income for these banks equal to two-thirds of the major banks is very optimistic. Under this scenario, the smaller banks show net income of no more than ¥0.87 trillion for the year ending in March 2004, and ¥0.93 trillion for the year ending in

March 2005. This implies total industry profits of ¥2.3 for the year ending in March 2005.

In the spirit of calculating an upper bound, we suppose that profits increase by 35% per year for the next three years. This means that net income rises to ¥3.105 trillion, ¥4.192 trillion, and ¥5.659 trillion in March 2006, March 2007, and March 2008 respectively. For comparison, net income for the industry in March 1989 (during the boom) was only ¥4.9 trillion (and assets at that time were ¥790 trillion, as opposed to the current level of ¥740 trillion).

With these very generous assumptions, the undiscounted sum of total industry profits for the five fiscal years starting in March 2004 is roughly ¥15.4 trillion. This allows the banks (assuming that the banks making the profits have usable credits) to claim deferred tax credits of ¥6.2 trillion.

Collectively these improvements suggest that the banks' capital position could be forecast to improve by roughly ¥27.85 trillion (¥15.4 from profits plus ¥6.25 trillion from improved loan portfolios plus ¥6.2 trillion in deferred tax credits). Under this scenario, we expect the stock market would rally even further and the loan portfolios would improve further, so the banks would more than cover the presumed ¥20 trillion shortage.

There are, however, several reasons to doubt that this kind of miracle can occur. First, a sustained economic recovery anywhere near this magnitude is not likely. Indeed after the remarkable growth of 2003 and the first quarter of 2004, the Japanese economy hardly grew during the rest of 2004. For every ¥1 trillion less in profits that does not materialize, the estimate of the usable tax credits drop by ¥0.4 trillion. We also have ignored the expiration of tax credits, and as most of the profits even under this scenario do not occur until 2007 or 2008, it is likely that many of the credits will expire before they can be used.

Second, there is the earlier evidence regarding ever-greening which suggests that the banks are still extending some low quality loans. Without stopping this kind of credit extension, there is little hope of reaching record profitability quickly (or of economic growth actually continuing).

Third, achieving record profitability requires more attractive lending spreads. Figure 5.2, also from Jerram (2004) shows that so far this has not occurred. The interest rate spreads on new loans have not shown any sign of increasing, even after the economic recovery started.

Finally and perhaps most importantly, if the growth scenario does occur, it would presumably be accompanied by an increase in the level

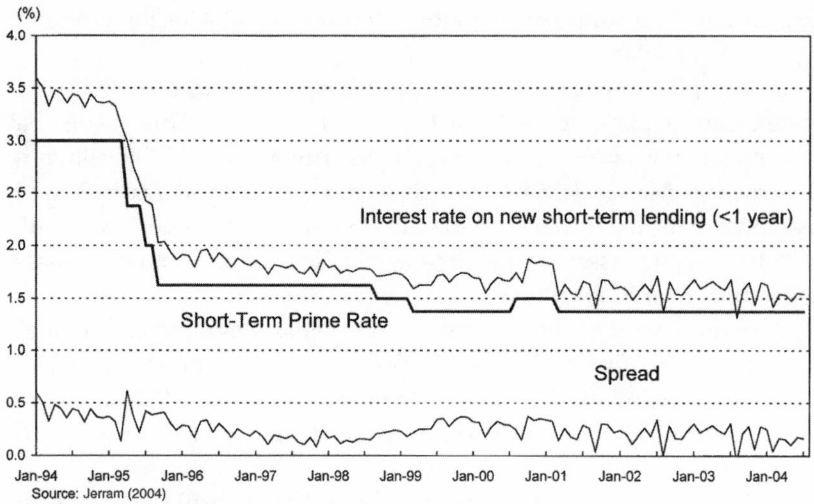

Figure 5.2
Interest Rate on New Short-Term Lending

of interest rates. The banks have substantial bond holdings which they are required to value at market prices when such prices are available (regardless of whether the bonds are going to be sold). Therefore, the banks will suffer capital losses on these holdings when interest rates rise. As a benchmark, Lehman Brothers Equity Research (Senoguchi 2004, Figure 3) estimates that the major banks have ¥104 trillion in bond holdings, with an average duration of 3.9 years. This means that a 1 percentage point rise in interest rates generates capital losses of over ¥4 trillion; recall the major banks' net income forecast for the year ending in March 2005 was ¥1.4 trillion. In other words, a one percentage point rise in interest rates wipes out several years worth profits for the major banks! Another way to benchmark the size of the effect is to compare the losses on the bond holdings due to an increase in interest rates with the capital gains that the banks realize from an increase in stock prices. Our estimates imply roughly that an across-the-board increase in interest generates losses that require a 15% increase in share prices. This is in line with estimates by Ned Akov at Macquarie Securities (Japan) (communicated via private correspondence) and Morgan (2004).

Against this background we see the growth miracle scenario for ending these problems as being very unlikely. The only way it could happen is if growth persists and accelerates for several years without any increase in interest rates—essentially the deflation has to persist, otherwise the banks will take huge losses on their bond holdings. As mentioned earlier, no industrial economy has ever been able to show sustained growth in a deflationary environment.

3. Strategies for Managing the Transition

In picking among the alternatives just discussed, it is instructive to consider both their theoretical properties and their success in other countries. To develop the empirical evidence, we consider both explicit cross-country comparisons and detailed country-specific evidence.

The onerous data requirements involved in undertaking large-scale cross-country studies have been a serious barrier to research of this type. To our knowledge Honohan and Klingebiel (2003) and Claessens, Klingebiel, and Laeven (CKL) (2003) are the only available studies using comparable data and methods to analyze the success of alternative resolution strategies in a number of banking crises. The two papers suggest three robust results.

First, there is a great deal of similarity in the policies adopted in the most crises. In particular, the three most common policies are (i) extensive liquidity support for banks, (ii) guarantees to bank creditors that bank liabilities will be paid, and (iii) regulatory-forbearance whereby normal rules regarding capital adequacy, loan classification, and loans loss provisioning are suspended. For instance, of the 35 banking crises (the universe of crises from 1977 to the present) analyzed by CKL, 80% of the countries used at least two of these policy options. Thus, even though every crisis differs in the details, there are enough important similarities to justify this kind of comparative analysis.

The other two general findings relate to the policies selected by the countries and the success of these policies. Together, these results suggest that there is no magic bullet, in the sense of a dominant policy that unambiguously lowers costs or expedites recovery.

There is no clear correlation between the choice of policies and the size of the ultimate fiscal cost borne by taxpayers in restoring a banking system to solvency. Banking crises are costly, and taxpayers inevitably bear at least some of the costs. Some resolution policies, however, may allocate larger proportions of existing losses from the crisis to taxpayers, or generate additional deadweight losses during the process, than other policies. The research so far fails to find any clear patterns. Further, the policy choices do not seem to correlate with the speed with which a country recovers. We (and the authors of the papers) recognize that these correlations need not be causal; it is possible that the countries with the most severe crises are more likely to try these policies.

3.1 Use of the Major Tools

Japan has used all three of the above polices (as well as some others discussed below). It is doubtful that the failure of forbearance, liquidity support, and liability guarantees to reverse the problems in Japan can be ascribed to their late deployment in the wake of increasingly large shocks. Instead, the record shows that Japan turned to these tools early, and these were clearly in place before Japan's problems developed into a crisis. Thus, the fact that Japan's financial sector problems have persisted must be due to the failure of these policies to adequately address the issues.

Recall the opening paragraph of the summary of the IMF's Executive Board assessment of Japan in August 1997:

> "Executive Directors welcomed the robust growth of the economy in 1996, which reflected the impact of policies to support aggregate demand and the correction of imbalances that had contributed to the prolonged downturn. Directors broadly endorsed the staff's view that the recovery was becoming self-sustaining, although some speakers pointed to uncertainties in the short term, including the effects of the recent consumption tax increase and continuing financial sector problems. Most Directors observed that the central challenge for policymakers was to return the fiscal balance to a more sustainable level over the medium term. Directors believed that the current easy stance of monetary policy should be maintained for the time being, but that it would likely be desirable to begin tightening later in the year, when the full effects of tax increases on activity would be apparent. While important steps had been taken to resolve the strains in the financial sector, Directors noted that a clear framework was needed for dealing with problems among financial institutions. They emphasized the importance of deregulation and structural reform in ensuring robust growth in Japan over the longer term, particularly in light of the aging of the population."

The assessment later turned out to be drastically incorrect, but we believe it was in line with the consensus view (including our own) at the time. It paints the picture of a recovering economy that had definite financial problems, but not ones that could be described as a crisis. Therefore, to the extent that the three policies (extensive liquidity support, guarantees to the bank's creditors, and regulatory forbearance) were already being pursued, we can conclude that these were not invoked because of the response to adverse shocks, but instead were policies in place at the time of the shocks that have repeatedly failed to work.

As of mid-1997 Japan's forbearance policy was already firmly in place. This can be most easily seen in the handling of the mortgage-lending institutions known as *jusen* in the early 1990s. Although *jusen* were not deposit-taking institutions, they were owned by banks and other financial institutions and financed by loans from these parent organizations and other small deposit-taking institutions, notably agricultural coops. Thus, failure of the *jusen* would have caused serious problems for depositary institutions. As Milhaupt and Miller (1997) note, after the economy slowed and asset prices began to decline, the *jusen* were clearly in trouble. In 1991, a series of Ministry of Finance inspections showed that 38% of their loans were non-performing. Yet, the *jusen* continued to operate for several years while the regulators tried to arrange various recapitalization and debt forgiveness programs. These loans were finally liquidated in 1996. Opposition parties heavily criticized the government's handling of the *jusen* resolution, which used ¥680 billion of public funds. This experience may have made the government even more reluctant to use public funds to resolve the banking crisis later in the decade.

Forbearance was also practiced in the case of Hyogo Bank. Based in Kobe, Hyogo was one of the larger regional banks. The Kobe earthquake of January 1995 exacerbated and exposed the bank's problems. When a run began against Hyogo, the Ministry of Finance announced it would be liquidated. This was the first bank failure in Japan in the post-war period. But Hyogo's viable operations, because of their importance to the Kobe area, would be preserved in a new bank, called Midori ("green"), that had as shareholders the large city banks and the BOJ, which provided fresh capital under Ministry of Finance guidance. Established on 27 October 1995, Midori began operations on 29 January 1996. Yet, less than two years later Midori was in trouble, and the regulators had to arrange for another merger and capital infusion. Clearly, through hoping that a recovery would ensue, the regulators had been lax in enforcing rules.

By the last half of 1997 Japan's macroeconomic environment had deteriorated much faster than the IMF (and most observers, including us) had expected. Several large financial institutions, notably Hokkaido Takushoku Bank and Yamaichi Securities, failed. By early 1998 it was becoming clear that the banks were much more seriously undercapitalized than had previously been thought. At the same time, the government was finding more and more ways to forbear (see Hoshi and Kashyap, 2001, chapter 8). One change involved adjusting accounting rules to improve the appearance of the public financial reports. A second was to delay the imposition of prompt corrective action requirements. These rules were intended to prevent regulatory delay from attending to bank capital shortages. As planned, these prompt corrective action requirements started in April 1998 for the handful of internationally active banks, but the application was delayed by one year for the rest.

By early 1998 there was absolutely no doubt that forbearance was being practiced on a large-scale in Japan. Indeed, by the August 1998 IMF Article 4 consultation, the IMF's Executive Directors were calling for much more aggressive action by the government: "Rigorous enforcement of the self-assessment framework is needed so that banks recognize and provision against the full extent of bad loans. Several Directors suggested that these results be published for individual banks to increase transparency." In the seven years since that time, forbearance has continued, although the supervisory stance for major banks has been tightened somewhat after late 2002. One simple indicator of this is that every time a major bank failed, the losses uncovered were substantially above those expected based on the most recent regulatory review.

By 1997 it was also clear that the government was guaranteeing the banks's liabilities. As part of the overhaul of the financial regulatory framework in 1996, which included the scheme to clean-up the *jusen* as its centerpiece, the Diet reformed the Deposit Insurance Act. Under the amended law, the existing 10 million yen limit deposit insurance was temporarily lifted; all deposits were covered under the amended Act. The limit was supposed to be reintroduced on 1 April 2001, but it was later postponed to 1 April 2002, and even then was only gradually lifted. Non-interest bearing demand deposits and (low interest) ordinary deposits were still fully protected until 1 April 2005. After that date, newly introduced non-interesting bearing deposits called "settlement deposits" continue to be fully protected.

The Bank of Japan's provision of liquidity to failed (or failing) financial institutions has been a long-standing policy. The Bank has always been permitted to provide liquidity to distressed financial institutions when it sees this as necessary (mainly for financial stability); this is specified in Article 25 of the old Bank of Japan Act and in Article 38 of the new (1998) Bank of Japan Act. This scheme was first used in 1965 to help Yamaichi Securities. More recently, the Bank of Japan used Article 25 loans to provide liquidity to Hyogo Bank, Kizu Credit Union, and Cosmo Credit Union in the summer of 1995. This category of lending was subsequently extended to other banks that failed or were rescued (including Hokkaido Takushoku and Yamaichi in November 1997).

The preceding discussion makes it clear that, as the financial crisis unfolded, Japan already had the three main tools in place. These were used both before the crisis was fully evident and then repeatedly and aggressively after the crisis became clearly evident in late 1997. It seems difficult to believe that a mere continuation of these policies will help end the problems in Japan's banking sector.

3.2 *Other Tools*

In addition to these three policies, Japan has repeatedly relied on the use of asset management companies. The first of a series of such companies was the Cooperative Credit Purchasing Company (CCPC) established in December 1992. As described in detail by Packer (2000), from its very beginning the CCPC was unusual. In August 1992, the government floated the idea of creating a government-financed institution to buy-up the collateral of non-performing loans. Faced with criticism from other industries that this would be using public funds to rescue banks, the government scrapped the idea. The private sector banks then created the CCPC, presumably with encouragement from the government. The CCPC's goal was to remove non-performing loans from bank balance sheets by purchasing them. The funds used to do this were lent to the CCPC by the founding banks. The CCPC was then supposed to collect on or sell the purchased loans. If the CCPC incurred a loss when a loan was sold, the originating bank was supposed to pay for the additional loss. This scheme left the banks with ongoing exposure to the loans transferred to the CCPC; in other words, the loan sales did not help the bank reduce their credit risk.

The banks, however, motivated by tax considerations sold substantial amounts of loans to the CCPC: ¥15.3 trillion (face value) during December 1992 to March 1998. The Japanese tax authority does not allow banks to deduct loan losses from taxable incomes until a borrower's bankruptcy procedure starts. A loan sale to the CCPC was an exception: the banks were allowed to deduct the difference between the appraised and the face value of the loans. During 1992–98, the banks claimed ¥9.15 trillion of such losses from loan sales to the CCPC and deducted them from their taxable income. Packer (2000) estimates the tax saving for the banks was as large as ¥4.6 trillion. Recall from Table 5.1 that official capital was between ¥25 and ¥30 trillion during this period.

The disposal of the loans by the CCPC did not proceed smoothly. By the end of March 1998, CCPC had sold 6,847 loans and associated collateral for a total of ¥1.1 trillion. This was only about one-third of the total number of loans that CCPC purchased (19,391) and the revenue was only 19% of the total appraisal value (¥5.8 trillion). The sales were slow partly because of the recourse that CCPC had against the original lender bank when the sale price of the collateral was below appraised value. With declining land prices, the loan often had a market price far lower than the appraised value. The banks typically opposed such transactions.

Another source of delay was (for reasons that are unclear to us) that the CCPC decided the debtor also must agree to the sale of the property. The debtor had no reason to agree because a new creditor might prove to be more aggressive in demanding payment or, in the case of a real estate loan, seek eviction.

The CCPC was allowed to buy loans until the end of March 2001, but in fact very few loans were purchased after 1998. The total amount of loans sold to the CCPC from 1992 to March 2001 (¥15.4 trillion in face value and ¥5.8 trillion in appraisal value) was hardly different from the total as of March 1998 (*Nihon Keizai Shimbun*, 25 April 2001). The sale of collateral seems to have picked up somewhat after 1998, and as of March 2001, the CCPC had collected 80% of the total appraised value of the assets that it purchased. The CCPC was liquidated at the end of March 2004.

Another asset management company, Tokyo Kyodo Bank, was set up in January 1995 to deal with the assets left by the December 1994 failure of two credit unions in Tokyo, Tokyo Kyowa Credit Union and Anzen Credit Union. More than 90% of ¥21.5 billion of capital of Tokyo Kyodo was financed using Article 25 loans from the BOJ. The rest of the capital was raised from private-sector banks. Tokyo Kyodo later absorbed assets of other failed credit unions, such as Kizu and Cosmo (both of which failed in August 1995), and changed its name to the Resolution and Collection Bank (RCB) in September 1996.

The Housing Loan Administration Corporation (HLAC) was established in 1996 to collect loans of failed *jusen*, and started with ¥6.8 trillion of *jusen* loans. Both the RCB and HLAC specialized in dealing with the loans and associated collateral of failed financial institutions.

Unlike the CCPC, they therefore could only act once an intermediary was closed, so regulatory closure policy was an important factor in determining which loans they ended up servicing. Given the forbearance policy of the 1990s, this limited the scope for these agencies to push for wide-scale restructuring.

In April 1999, the RCB and the HLAC merged into a new entity called the Resolution and Collection Corporation (RCC). Unlike its predecessors, the RCC is allowed to buy non-performing loans from solvent banks, though it cannot force the solvent banks to sell. The RCC also accepts loans from failed insurance companies and agricultural coops. Unlike the CCPC, the RCC does not have recourse against originator banks for losses incurred when selling any collateral associated with a loan. As of the end of March 2004, the RCC had acquired ¥9.311 trillion of loans (appraised value) from failed financial institutions (including those inherited from the RCB and the HLAC), of which ¥6.892 trillion (74%) were collected. The RCC has also purchased ¥327 billion of non-performing loans (appraised value) from solvent banks, of which ¥222 billion (68%) have been collected. Starting in 2001, the RCC began discussing the importance of revitalizing the borrowers while they service the non-performing loans. Thus, the division of labor between RCC and the later IRCJ is not as clear as it is often discussed. See the RCC web site (www.kaisyukikou.co.jp/intro/intro_0064.html).

In April 2003, Japan established yet another government-funded asset management company. The Industrial Revitalization Corporation of Japan (IRCJ) also buys non-performing loans from the banks, but instead of selling them, the company aims to restructure and turn around the troubled borrowers.

The IRCJ had two years (until March 2005), during which it bought distressed loans. It helps borrowers reorganize their business and regain profitability, often in cooperation with their main banks. Thus, the IRCJ can be especially effective when the main bank has trouble convincing other lenders to participate in the rescue operation of a troubled borrower. The IRCJ can buy-up the loans from the other lenders and work with the lead lender to reorganize the company. Initially, the IRCJ was expected to tackle loans to relatively large borrowers, which typically involve numerous lenders. In the end, however, most of the forty-one companies that the IRCJ decided to restructure were small. (One of the few exceptions is Kanebo, which the chapter by Iwaisako examines in detail.)

The overall picture that emerges is one where specific events forced the Japanese government to confront various problems. None of the asset management companies were pro-active, with a possible exception of RCC's attempt to buy non-performing loans from solvent banks. Some of these asset management companies did absorb large quantities of loans and eventually sold the majority of them, while others did not. Only since 2003, however, did they focus on restructuring and rehabilitation of the underlying borrowers.

Klingebiel (2000) studied seven other country episodes and concludes that the Japanese experience with asset management companies is common. In a majority of the cases she studies these vehicles did not succeed in meeting their objectives. Importantly, the two most clear-cut successes (the Resolution Trust Corporation in the United States and the Swedish restructuring organizations) both actively disposed of their assets. For instance, the Swedish asset management organization, Securum, was very quick in disposing of the loans that it acquired, selling 98% of them within five years.

The final hallmark of the Japanese policy has been repeated incomplete and inadequate recapitalizations. The initial recapitalization attempt was in March 1998, when ¥1.8 trillion was disbursed almost equally to twenty-one major banks. Although ¥1.8 trillion is a substantial amount, it was not sufficiently large to convince the market that it would solve the capital shortage of Japanese banks. The Japan premium, the extra interest paid by Japanese banks compared to other large banks in the international inter-bank market, which had increased after the crisis of November 1997, showed no sign of coming down after this recapitalization.

Following enactment of the Prompt Recapitalization Act of 1998, a more sizable recapitalization was done in March 1999. Public funds of ¥7.5 trillion were injected into fifteen major banks. The capital shortage of smaller banks, however, was never properly addressed. Only twelve regional banks applied for and accepted public funds, receiving ¥0.5 trillion. Even for large banks, the stability was fleeting: capital shortages were again apparent by 2003.

When the Prompt Recapitalization Act expired in March 2001, the revision of the Deposit Insurance Act allowed the government to still provide funds to failing banks. In particular, Section 102 of the new Deposit Insurance Act allowed the government to use public funds to nationalize failed banks or help troubled (but not failed) banks in order to prevent a potential financial crisis. This was the scheme used for the rescue of Resona that we describe in the next section. The scheme was also used to nationalize Ashikaga Bank, which FSA judged to be insolvent in November 2003.

In June 2004, the Diet passed the Act for Strengthening Financial Functions, which sets up another mechanism of injecting public funds. The law, which became effective in September 2004, allows capital transfers without justifying them as being necessary in order to prevent a financial crisis. The FSA hopes to use the authority to provide government funds to regional banks, which have been slow to deal with their non-performing loan problems, to encourage mergers among them that involve substantial restructuring. These mergers could reduce overcapacity while creating better-capitalized banks. The law is set to expire at the end of March 2008.

3.3 *Policy Assessment*

The five policies discussed above, namely (i) extensive liquidity support for banks; (ii) guarantees to bank creditors; (iii) regulatory forbearance; (iv) the use of asset management companies to deal with nonperforming loans; and (v) repeated recapitalization, still characterize the approach of Japanese regulators. Charitably interpreted, this combination of policies can indirectly tackle the problems of capital shortage, ever-greening, and over-banking. In principle, the regulatory forbearance and the guarantee of credits give banks time to rebuild their capital base. In critical periods, the government also uses liquidity support and direct recapitalization. The banks can gradually remove non-performing loans from their balance sheets using asset management companies. With sufficient problem loans off of bank balance sheets and restructured, evergreening incentives fall. When normal macroeconomic growth resumes, no new non-performing loans emerge, and the ever-greening stops. Over-banking is solved by restructuring of banks in return for public capital. Voluntary reorganization through merger and acquisitions also helps eliminate the over-banking. With the macroeconomic recovery, the banks are profitable again. Or so the theory goes.

Unfortunately, these policies have been in place in Japan for a long time and have not worked. Over-banking and ever-greening continue, and bank profitability remains low. There is no reason, based on global historical experience, to believe that these problems will disappear on their own. More importantly, there are several clear differences between the policies being pursued in Japan and the ones that have been successful in other countries.

While there are many potential comparisons that can be made, we believe the most relevant lessons for Japan come from the Nordic banking crises in the 1990s and the American Savings and Loan crisis of the 1980s. The conventional wisdom is that these crises were in large part due to deregulation (Nakamura (2002), Drees and Pazarbasioglu (1998), and Barth and Litan (1998)). We have argued elsewhere that deregulation was also one of the triggers in Japan, but we concentrate on these cases for two other reasons. One is that all these countries have similar levels of development as Japan. In many emerging market crises, the quality of legal institutions precludes certain options. This is not the case in Japan, nor was it in the United States or in the Nordic countries. These are the only systemic crises that have occurred in rich, mature industrialized countries in the last twenty years. Second, the American and Nordic crises have been successfully and completely resolved, so we know how things turned out.

There are several stark differences between the approaches pursued in the American and Nordic cases and the ones tried thus far in Japan. The single biggest difference is that the asset management companies formed in those other countries were much more aggressive in disposing of, and restructuring, troubled loans. For instance, Klingebiel (2000) reports that the percentages of assets transferred by the asset management companies in Finland, Sweden, and the United States were 64, 86, and 98 percent respectively; in each case the initial amount of assets transferred was about 8% of GDP. All three of these asset management companies accomplished their loan disposals within five years of establishment.

A second important contrast was the willingness to shrink the amount of assets in the industry. For instance, Barth and Litan (2002, Table 9.2) show that assets (as measured for regulatory purposes) in the American savings and loan industry shrunk by 43% between 1988 and 1993. In Finland, total domestic bank assets fell by 33% between 1991 and 1995, while in Sweden domestic commercial bank assets dropped by 11% between 1991 and 1993.[4] In stark contrast, total domestic bank assets in Japan fell less than 1% (¥739 trillion to ¥736 trillion) in the ten years from December 1993 to December 2003.

Finally, during the period when the downsizing and loan disposal was occurring, the financial institutions in these other countries were decisively recapitalized and management typically was changed. For instance, as of 1988 only 14% of the S&L's assets resided in institutions that had (true) capital above 6% of assets (Barth and Litan (2002)). By 1993, 51% of assets were in such institutions and the remaining institutions essentially all had at least 3% capital. In the Nordic countries, similarly large capital infusions took place. Undoubtedly the macroeconomic recoveries that occurred in the Nordic countries and the United States facilitated these adjustments, but we believe that these kinds of policies will eventually need to be pursued in Japan as well.

3.4 *Policy Recommendations*

To start the necessary adjustment process in Japan, we recommend a set of strict bank inspections by the FSA with a consistent standard that closely monitors the health of borrowers and loan collateral. The scope of special inspections that the FSA has been conducting for major banks and their largest customers should be extended to cover regional banks and smaller borrowers. Such inspections will uncover many more undisclosed under-performing loans.

We next suggest moving simultaneously to restructure the bad loans that are uncovered and to close the most insolvent banks. Thus, we seek to attack the ever-greening problem from both the bank and the borrower sides. This policy will be contractionary, and the money that would have been spent propping up the banks should be used to provide unemployment and other transitional assistance to the workers displaced by this process. The banks and the bad loans should be sold, to foreign investors if they are willing to pay highest prices, but promptly in any case.

We also favor selective and aggressive recapitalization for the healthiest banks. Instead of marginal increases in capital, we propose sufficient public assistance to remove any doubts about the solvency of the remaining institutions.

These policies would take the necessary steps to start the financial system on the road to recovery. This would also put an end to the zombie firms that have been holding down growth, to the extent the systemic problem derives from the banks' ever-greening of loans. It is a bold program, but we believe one that is particularly appropriate now that there is a bit of aggregate growth. Large scale restructuring has a better chance now than at any time in the last several years.

4. The Rescue of Resona Bank

This section reviews the restructuring of Resona Bank (and its predecessors) with the goal of tangibly showing several of the problems with the current "muddling through" strategy of dealing with Japanese banks.[5]

Resona Bank was created by the merger of two weak large banks on 1 March 2003. Daiwa Bank and Asahi Bank, both of which were parts of Resona Holdings, merged to create Resona Bank and Saitama Resona Bank (which took over Asahi Bank's operations within Saitama prefecture). Resona Holdings also had three other banks, Kinki Osaka Bank, Nara Bank, and Resona Trust Bank, but Resona Bank was by far the biggest.

Both Daiwa and Asahi had been in trouble for quite a while. In the public capital injection of March 1998, each issued subordinated debt of ¥100 billion, which was bought by the government. Both accepted public support again in March 1999, when the government provided public funds with differentiated arrangements for individual banks according to the perceived health of each bank. At that time Daiwa was regarded as being especially weak and was forced to accept relatively severe conditions. Daiwa issued ¥408 billion of preferred shares with a dividend of 1.06% to the government. The government was allowed to start converting the preferred shares into common shares after three months. If all the preferred shares were converted the government would own more than 50% of Daiwa. Asahi issued ¥300 billion of preferred shares (with a dividend of 1.15% and conversion starting after 39 months), ¥100 billion of preferred shares (with a dividend of 1.48% and conversion starting after 51 months), and ¥100 billion of subordinated debt (with a coupon of LIBOR+1.04%). The conditions for Asahi were less favorable than those granted to other banks. For example, the Industrial Bank of Japan, considered healthier than Daiwa Bank and Asahi Bank, issued ¥175 billion of preferred shares (with a dividend of 1.00% and conversion starting after 54 months), ¥175 billion of preferred shares (with a dividend of 0.43% and conversion starting in 52 months), and ¥250 billion of subordinated debt (with a coupon of LIBOR+0.98%). Kinki Osaka Bank, also a part of the Resona Financial Group, issued ¥60 billion of preferred shares to the government in April 2001. These infusions meant that, upon its creation, the government already had a stake of ¥1.168 trillion in the Resona Financial Group.

The financial condition of Resona was shaky from the start. In its first accounting year (ended 31 March 2003), write-offs from acknowledging capital losses on stock holdings and nonperforming loans turned out to be so large that Resona would have been insolvent if the credit for deferred tax assets was excluded from its capital calculation. The bank initially planned to follow industry practice and claim that all the tax liability for the next five years would be offset by the tax credits for the past losses. This would have given the bank sufficient capital not only to make it solvent, but also to allow it to meet the minimum regulatory level for capital. Both Daiwa and Asahi had terminated all their overseas operations by this time, so that they were required to satisfy only the "domestic standard" for capital, which is 4% of their risk assets. When the bank tried to get approval from its auditors, Asahi & Co. (the auditor of the former Asahi Bank) and Shin Nihon & Co. (the auditor of the former Daiwa Bank), each balked.

According to *Kin'yū Business* (August 2003) Asahi & Co. simply refused to allow Resona to count any deferred tax assets as capital because the balance sheet without deferred tax assets would be insolvent, a decision undoubtedly influenced by its recent experience. Among Japanese auditors Asahi had the closest ties to Arthur Andersen, which collapsed following its involvement in the Enron case, and had been forced to pay fines to settle a lawsuit concerning its audits of a former *jusen*, Nippon Housing Loan. Resona had no plans for recapitalization and insisted that it should be allowed to count the deferred tax credits without proposing a restructuring plan; consequently Asahi & Co. refused to certify Resona's books. The lead auditor for Asahi committed suicide two days after informing his superiors that Resona's books were not in order.

Shin Nihon took a different approach, reportedly looked only at Resona's forecasts of expected future taxable income to determine the level of permissible tax credits. Even with this criterion (which overlooked the incongruity between the profit forecasts and the condition of the existing balance sheet), Shin Nihon decided that five years' worth of tax credits would be too much. They were still, however, willing to allow Resona to count three years' worth of losses as deferred tax credits.

Resona was dissatisfied with the Shin Nihon ruling because it made Resona's capital ratio lower than the regulatory minimum level. After a couple of weeks' unsuccessful negotiation, which reportedly involved the FSA, Resona had no choice but to apply for recapitalization using public funds. The government immediately convened the Financial Crisis Response Council and decided to inject ¥1.96 trillion into Resona, on the basis of Section 102-1 of the Deposit Insurance Act (DIA), which allows the government to provide public capital to a healthy but undercapitalized bank "to prevent a financial crisis." The summary minutes of the meeting suggest that the council quickly decided that failing to rescue Resona Bank would destabilize the financial system, and approved the recapitalization. The minutes show no serious discussion took place about the future viability of Resona Bank. (See http://www.fsa.go.jp/news/newsj/14/ginkou/f-20030613-2.html)

Since DIA Section 102-1 allows recapitalization only at the bank level, not at the financial holding company level, the injection occurred with Resona Bank issuing new shares (¥0.30 trillion of common shares and ¥1.66 trillion of preferred shares) that were bought by the government. After the issue, the new shares were then swapped into shares of Resona Holdings. The prices paid by the government (¥52 for the common shares and ¥200 for the prepared shares in Resona Holdings) were comparable to the prevailing market prices. Remarkably, the existing shareholders of Resona Holdings were not wiped out!

Resona submitted a revitalization plan to the FSA in June, 2003. Table 5.4 compares some performance goals under the old plan (submitted when Daiwa and Asahi were recapitalized in 1999 and updated thereafter) as of May 2002, and the new plan. Compared with the old plan, the new plan shows somewhat more aggressive disposal of non-performing loans (which shows up in higher level of loan losses), lower loan levels, lower ROE, lower ROA, and higher non-interest income, such as fee income. The plan, however, continues to look optimistic, as it predicts only slightly lower after-tax profits than did the old plan and much higher revenue growth (12.6% over two years rather than 4.8% under the old plan). The new plan also expects to continue counting substantial amounts of deferred tax assets as capital. The new plan, however, deviated from the old plan in some potentially important ways. Most of the old directors were replaced by new ones, many from outside the bank, including the new chair, Eiji Hosoya, who had been serving as vice president of JR East, a railroad.

To tackle the problem of non-performing loans, the new plan proposes dividing the balance sheet into two parts: a "revitalization account" that consists of non-performing loans and the "new account." This was in keeping with the FSA's policy on how banks accepting government help under the DIA Section 102 should proceed. The FSA sent in a management monitoring team, which was supposed to oversee the process of the balance sheet separation and monitor the new management. For

Table 5.4
Comparison of the May 2002 and June 2003 Revitalization Plans for the Banks in Resona Holdings (billion yen)

June 2003 Plan			May 2002 Plan			
March 2004	March 2005	March 2006	March 2004	March 2005	March 2006	
46,290	47,789	48,552	44,200	44,200	44,200	Total Assets
28,847	29,811	30,502	31,300	31,500	31,600	Loans
505	489	472	694	594	481	Deferred tax assets
731	793	823	852	885	893	Business income
677	731	752	824	847	848	Interest income
67	72	73	60	58	63	Fee income
300	372	415	348	419	444	Business profit
147	107	97	142	90	90	Loan losses
59	168	238	77	154	175	Profit after tax
12	17	104	74	157	166	Dividend payment
19.35	18.90	18.57	17.32	17.16	17.68	Non-interest income ratio (%)
15.93	15.44	16.23	23.53	27.56	28.28	ROE (%)
0.64	0.77	0.85	0.82	0.99	1.05	ROA (%)

more details on the separation of the balance sheet, see the FSA document on http://www.fsa.go.jp/news/newsj/14/ginkou/f-20030404-5.html.

In July 2003, the new management asked Deloitte Touche Tohmatsu (DTT) to reexamine Resona's books as part of the preparation for separating the balance sheet. In October, following submission of the DTT report, the new management decided to record a loss of ¥1.76 trillion for the period between March and September 2003. In doing so, more than 90% of the capital provided by the government was written off. The bank claimed that the write-offs allowed it to stabilize the balance sheet and that going forward it would become profitable. The newly realized losses included a ¥266 billion reduction in the deferred tax asset (counting only one year worth of credit rather than three years), a write-down that exceeds the bank's Tier I capital (¥246 billion). Thus, the reexamination seems to have confirmed that Resona was indeed insolvent when it applied for the capital injection, as many observers suspected.

Following the DTT examination, Resona also changed its revitalization plan. The revised plan, filed in November 2003, gives a more realistic outlook of Resona's near future. Table 5.5 compares the revised plan to the original plan in June 2003. The November plan forecasts a small decline in total assets and loans, and thus this revised plan looks a bit more realistic than the June 2003 plan. The deferred tax assets claimed are also lower. The prospect for business income growth is less optimistic, but the dependence on non-interest income is higher. Finally, the much larger loan losses in the November plan suggest an acceleration in the write-off of non-performing loans.

The November 2003 plan only briefly describes the separation of the balance sheet into "revitalizing" and "new" accounts; it does not provide any details. The success of the November plan seems to hinge on a successful reorganization of the bank's balance sheet. The assets that will be restructured are separated from those that will be producing profits, thereby clearly distinguishing the new management's responsibility from the old management's mistakes. This presumably will allow an independent assessment of the competence of the new management and the progress toward creation of a viable bank.

Unfortunately, the revised plan does not disclose how many assets were moved to the revitalization account and how many are in the new account, making it impossible for outsiders to calculate the rate of return on the new account that management is targeting. The plan is also

Table 5.5
Revitalization Plans (for Resona Bank only): June 2003 and November 2003 (billion yen)[1]

November 2003 Plan		June 2003 Plan		
March 2004	March 2005	March 2004	March 2005	
29,810	28,890	32,562	33,789	Total Assets
20,000	19,370	20,988	21,781	Loans
34	34	392	392	Deferred tax assets
438	468	502	556	Business income
440	432	524	539	Interest income
52	57	51	56	Fee income
119	234	216	274	Business profit
1,077	88	108	72	Loan losses
–1,439	116	37	134	Profit after tax
0	75	0	0	Dividend payment
14.14	21.17	13.42	12.89	Non-interest income ratio (%)
20.46	31.79	13.42	12.89	ROE (%)
0.55	0.85	0.66	0.81	ROA (%)

[1]The June 23 Plan in Table 5.5 covers Resona Bank only, while the June 23 Plan numbers in Table 4 are those for all the banks in Resona Holdings (Resona, Resona Saitama, Kinki-Osaka, and Nara). Thus, June 2003 numbers in two tables are not identical.

silent about the role played (if any) by the management monitoring team sent by the FSA in preparing the plan. This lack of transparency and accountability undermines the credibility of the process.

Summing up, the Resona rescue exemplifies many of the problems with Japan's current policy to address its banking problems. First, recapitalization using public funds was done primarily to avoid the failure of a large bank. The government did not thoroughly examine the long-run viability of the rescued bank. It may not have been practical to conduct a detailed examination of books before the government provided funds to Resona, but it could have paid more serious attention to any signals from the financial market about the future promise of Resona Bank.

Second, the Japanese government continues to protect a wide set of creditors of failed banks, not only the depositors but also other creditors (such as subordinated debt holders), as well as shareholders in the Resona case.

Finally, the bank restructuring continues to be piecemeal and uncoordinated. The problems at Resona were revealed only after the auditors refused to approve unreasonable amounts of deferred tax assets. The FSA, which had been conducting special inspections of Daiwa and Asahi, did not act before they were forced by the auditors.

Our recommended strategy would have been very different. It is doubtful Daiwa should have received public funds in the first place in 1999. Instead, the money saved would have been concentrated on the stronger banks in the late 1990s. Daiwa's loan portfolio would have been restructured long ago. The supervisory expertise developed in this restructuring would have been valuable in the subsequent cases that have emerged and still remain untreated.

After the 1999 recapitalization, the government could have forced management changes at Daiwa much sooner. From 1 July 1999, the government had an option of converting preferred shares of Daiwa into common shares, thereby practically nationalizing the bank. Although Daiwa repeatedly failed to meet the profitability targets set out in the revitalization plan, the FSA did not even mention the possibility of converting preferred shares into common shares.

Even after the problems at Resona were publicized in May 2003, there was a preferable alternative strategy that the FSA could have pursued. Before applying the provisions of DIA Section 102-1, the FSA could have reviewed more carefully the Asahi & Co judgment that Resona was insolvent. If Resona had been insolvent, nationalization (DIA 102-3) or liquidation with financial assistance from public funds (DIA 102-2) would have been better options for avoiding a potential financial crisis. During the restructuring, the FSA's management monitoring team could have played a more visible role in evaluating Resona's plan and progress under the new management.

5. Bigger Begs Better

Aside from Resona, the only other capital-impaired major bank in Japan is UFJ. By June 2004, UFJ's capital shortage apparently became so severe that the bank began looking for a merger partner.[6] In August it announced its intent to merge with MTFG. If consummated, a merger would avoid the need for any taxpayer support to resolve the capital shortage at UFJ. This is commendable, but we see no particular reason to believe it will solve UFJ's long-standing structural problems. Simply creating a larger organization does not mean that UFJ will cut its lending to zombie firms which it has continued to support. If the capital supplied by MTFG is used to support restructuring, that would be a favorable development.

Moreover, for this combined banking firm to succeed without subsequent government assistance, it must find a way to improve its profitability. Both management groups reportedly believe that the combination makes sense because their branch networks are centered in different parts of Japan. This ignores the fact that these branches are not particularly profitable. The largest bank in the world is not going to succeed if all it aspires to do as a business is taking deposits and recycling them as low margin consumer loans.

Indeed, for the new bank to prosper there will have to be big cost-savings. The combined organization will have redundant management, branches, back office operations and operating divisions, especially around Tokyo. If the new bank can eliminate this duplication, it could be much more efficient. Table 5.6 shows the difficulties encountered by UFJ in achieving these kinds of savings. The table contrasts the changes in employment for UFJ's banking operations and the rest of the holding company. The table covers the period since March 2002 because that is when the full holding company figures become available. Column 3 indicates that from March 2002 to March 2004, UFJ cut bank personnel by 13% (28,256 to 24,667). This is in line with the reduction in the number of bank employees that UFJ reports in its "Progress Report on Plan to Revitalize Management," that it is required to file with the FSA semiannually as a result of raising capital by selling shares to the government several years ago. These numbers, reported in Column 2, are the ones typically cited in the press and by analysts. They cover only the full-time employees in the two major UFJ banks along with the holding company management staff. Looking at either the column 2 or column 3 numbers suggests an impressive amount of restructuring since the regional overlap between Sanwa Bank (based in Osaka) and Tokai Bank (based in Nagoya) was not very large.

However, the remainder of the table shows that these figures are likely to overstate the cost reductions for a pair of reasons. One offsetting factor is that the banks themselves have increased part-time employment (column 4). A second is that the number of full-time employees in the other subsidiaries in the holding company has risen sharply (column 5). The net effect is that the number of total full-time employees at the holding company is essentially unchanged, while total part-time employment rose.

Table 5.6
Number of Employees at Various Entities within UFJ Holdings: March 2002 to March 2004

End of month	Individual data for UFJ Holdings + UFJ Bank + UFJ Trust	Consolidated data for all UFJ Banking entities: Regular employees	Consolidated data for all Banking entities: Part-time employees	Consolidated data for the rest of the UFJ subsidiaries: Regular employees	Consolidated data for the rest of the UFJ subsidiaries: Part-time employees
March 2002	24,205	28,256	6,586	6,442	694
March 2003	22,327	25,817	9,068	9,986	864
March 2004	20,395	24,667	8,326	9,602	1,176

Sources: Column 2 figures come from the *Progress Report on Plan to Revitalize Management (July 2004)*, remaining columns are from *Yūka Shōken Hōkokusho* (various years).

The optimistic interpretation of these data is that the bank is consolidating and achieving cost savings, while the rest of the holding company is branching out into new business lines that will raise future profits. The pessimistic reading is that employees are merely being shuffled around with the intent of pleasing regulators who tend to focus mostly on the banking operations. The fact that there are no increases in profits so far and no visible evidence of thriving new subsidiaries makes us lean toward the pessimistic interpretation.

If the merger is to be successful, the progress on cutting costs will have to be much less ambiguous and more transparent. Likewise, this combined bank will face significant challenges to integrate its personnel policies and computing operations. Early in its operations Mizuho had so many problems on this front that it was sanctioned by the FSA for failing to solve its computing problems.

Given all these challenges, it will be some time before one can conclude whether this deal actually does help the industry recover. The worst case is that the merger, by creating the largest bank in the world, spawns an organization that is "too big to fail" and thus perpetuates Japan's over-banking problem. For instance, if UFJ had been officially declared undercapitalized, then it would have been possible to force the restructuring of its bad loans and carve out the healthy parts to be resold. As a rule, we strongly prefer voluntary private sector solutions to government ones, so we would not block the merger. If this deal does go sour and the government is forced to intervene we hope that the mistakes in the handling of Resona are not repeated.

6. Conclusion

Japanese banks have experienced a decade of low or negative profits and ever-increasing non-performing loans. Loan losses, combined with low profitability, gradually eroded the capital of many banks and left them severely undercapitalized. The weak banks continued to lend to weak borrowers at low interest spreads to hide the problems, which exacerbated the problems by nurturing zombie firms. This paper has discussed some alternative approaches to dealing with Japan's banking problems. Drawing heavily on the experience of other countries, we have explained why the current policy is not likely to end the problems any time soon.

Now that macroeconomic conditions are improving, one might hope that the Japanese banks can finally grow out of their problems. However, it would take several years of miraculous growth, along with very low interest rates, for the banks to accumulate sufficient profits to become adequately capitalized. Economic recovery alone is highly unlikely to resolve Japan's banking problems.

We recommend instead a more aggressive policy approach, one that forces the banks to clean up their balance sheets and restructure their loans to distressed borrowers. The macroeconomic improvements underway since 2003 make this the best time since 1996 to implement aggressive restructuring. We also favor a policy of recognizing Japan's capital shortage and insisting that the banks be sufficiently capitalized to withstand a slowdown in growth. The Act for Strengthening Financial Functions may prove useful in providing capital to banks that are serious about implementing massive restructuring. We should note, however, that past attempts involving recapitalization using public funds, such as the Rapid Recapitalization Act, failed to generate sufficient restructuring.

Success of the approach we propose requires active participation and coordination by the FSA, the RCC, and the IRCJ. For the major banks, the FSA under Heizo Takenaka seems to have stepped up its inspections and started to focus on the restructuring of large troubled borrowers. We view this as a useful first step, but one that must be followed up with further inspections of regional banks and smaller borrowers. Once these additional inspections begin, an important part of the process is to insure the consistency of classification of borrower risk across banks. This should mean that the banks are holding adequate amounts of capital to cover the risks of these firms.

One tangible indication that this is taking place is that, unlike the Resona and Ashikaga cases, there should not be huge revisions to the estimated condition of failed banks that are closed; ideally the regulators will have accurate assessment of banks conditions so that closures are not accompanied by big surprises. Likewise, in cases where government funds are provided to keep a bank operating, repeated capital injections should not be required.

Acknowledgments

Anil Kashyap thanks the Center for Research in Securities Prices and the Stigler Center both at the University of Chicago Graduate School of Business for research support. We thank Hugh Patrick, Frederick Mishkin and other participants in the Solutions project for helpful conversations and comments. All errors here are our own.

Notes

1. The Basel capital standards that Japan and other countries use to assess capital adequacy include a requirement that Tier 1 capital exceed four percent of a risk-adjusted definition of assets. As of March 2003, total risk-adjusted assets for all banks in Japan were ¥435 trillion (Bank of Japan, 2003). Thus, adjusted capital is only 2% of risk-adjusted assets.

2. Omura et al. (2002) estimate the amount of employment that is sustained because the banks are not forced to write off bad loans. They estimate that writing off ¥1 trillion of bad loans leads to 41,600 job losses in one year, of which 14,200 remain unemployed, 20,400 will find new jobs within a year, and 7,000 leave the labor force. As of the time of their study the major banks had ¥10.1 trillion of loans that were rated as "doubtful" or worse. Accordingly, Omura et al estimate that unemployment would rise by 143,000 and 72,000 more people would become discouraged and drop out of the labor force if all these problem loans were written off. The cost of directly compensating all the additional unemployed and discouraged workers would be ¥860 billion a year (assuming an average wage of ¥4 million a year).

3. The OECD does not include time series information for American banks. But, net noninterest income did nearly double for the top 100 U.S. banks over this period.

4. These figures were computed by the authors using data reported in OECD (1997). For Finland, the figures are deduced by summing the assets of commercial and savings banks and subtracting foreign commercial banks. For Sweden the figures are computed by summing commercial, savings and cooperative banks and subtracting foreign commercial banks.

5. This section draws on accounting information and press releases on the web sites of Resona Holdings (www.resona-hd.co.jp) and the Financial Services Agency (www.fsa.go.jp), and articles in *Kin'yū Business (The Financial Business Review)*.

6. In keeping with past cases, this capital shortage arose despite the fact that the official figures as of March suggested that the bank was adequately capitalized.

References

Bank for International Settlements. *BIS 72nd Annual Report*. Basel, Switzerland. July 8, 2002.

Bank of Japan. 2002. Japan's nonperforming loan problem. *Bank of Japan Quarterly Bulletin* 10(4).

______. 2003. *2002-nendo Kessan kara mita Zenkoku Ginkō no Keiei Jōkyō* (Business Condition of Japanese Banks: Fiscal 2002). (In Japanese)

Barth, James R. and Robert E. Litan. 1998. Lessons from Bank Failures in the United States. In *Preventing Banking Crises: Lessons from Recent Global Bank Failures*, editors Gerard Caprio Jr., William C. Hunter, George G. Kaufman, and Danny Leipsiger. Washington: Economic Development Institute of the World Bank.

Caballero, Ricardo J., Takeo Hoshi, and Anil Kashyap. 2003. "Zombie Lending and-Depressed Restructuring in Japan." Mimeo. MIT.

Claessens, Stijn, Daniela Klingebiel, and Luc Laeven. 2003. "Resolving Systemic Crises: Policies and Institutions." Mimeo. World Bank.

Drees, Burkhard and Ceyla Pazarbasioglu. 1998. "The Nordic Banking Crises: Pitfalls of-Financial Liberalization?" IMF Occasional Paper 161.

Financial Services Agency. 2004. "Results of Special Inspections." April 27, 2004 press release.

Fukao, Mitsuhiro. 2000. Kin'yū Fukyō no Jisshō Bunseki. (Empirical Analyses of Financial Recession). Tokyo: Nihon Keizai Shimbun-sha. (In Japanese)

________. 2003a. Financial sector profitability and double gearing. In *Structural Impediments to Growth in Japan*, editors Magnus Blomstrom, Jenny Corbett, Fumio Hayashi, and Anil Kashyap. Chicago: University of Chicago Press.

________. 2003b. Kigyō, Ginkō, Seiho no Shūeki-ryoku. (Earning Power of Corporations, Banks, and Life Insurers). Tokyo: Japan Center for Economic Research. (In Japanese)

Gilsen, Stuart C. 1998. "Chase Manhattan Corporation: The Making of America's Largest Bank." Harvard Business School Case No. 9-298-016.

Hoshi, Takeo. 2000. Naze Nihon wa Ryūdōsei no Wana kara Nogarerareainoka? (Why is the Japanese Economy Unable to Get Out of a Liquidity Trap). In *Zero Kinri to Nihon Keizai* (Zero Interest Rate and the Japanese Economy) 233–266, editors Mitsuhiro Fukao and Hiroshi Yoshikawa. Tokyo: Nihon Keizai Shimbunsha. (In Japanese)

Hoshi, Takeo and Anil Kashyap. 2000. The Japanese Banking Crisis: Where Did It Come From and How Will It End? In *NBER Macroeconomics Annual 1999*, editors Ben Bernanke and Julio Rotemberg. Cambridge, MA: MIT Press.

______. 2001. *Corporate Financing and Governance in Japan: The Road to the Future*. Cambridge, MA: MIT Press.

Honohan, Patrick and Daniela Klingebiel. 2003. The Fiscal Cost Implications of an Accommodating Approach to Banking Crises. *Journal of Banking and Finance* 27 (8): 1539–1560.

Hosono, Kaoru, and Masaya Sakuragawa. 2003. "Soft Budget Problems in the Japanese Credit Market." Nagoya City University Discussion Papers in Economics 345.

International Monetary Fund. 2003. "Japan: Financial System Stability Assessment." IMF Country Report 03/287.

Japan Center for Economic Research. 2004. Nenkin Kaikaku to Ginkō Seiho Keiei. (Pension System Reform and Management of Banks and Life Insurance Companies). Tokyo: Japan Center for Economic Reasearch.

Jerram, Richard. 2004. "Banks still not reflating." ING Financial Markets, June 2, 2004.

Kashyap, Anil K. 2002. Sorting Out Japan's Financial Crisis. Federal Reserve Bank of Chicago *Economic Perspectives* 26: (4th Quarter) 42–55.

Klingebiel, Daniela. 2000. "The Use of Asset Management Companies in the Resolution of Banking Crises." World Bank Policy Research Paper 2284.

Milhaupt, Curtis and Geoffrey Miller. 1997. Cooperation, Conflict, and Convergence in Japanese Finance: Evidence from the 'Jusen' Problem. *Law and Policy in International Business* 29: 1–78.

Morgan, Peter. 2004. Japanese Government Debt Endgame: The exit strategy and the bond Market. *HSBC Economics,* July 9. HSBC Securities (Japan) Limited.

Nakamura, Richard. 2002. "The Big Cleanse: The Japanese Response to the Financial Crisis of the 1990s Seen From a Nordic Perspective." European Institute of Japanese Studies Working Paper 149.

Nishimura, Kiyohiko, Takanobu Nakajima, and Kozo Kiyota. 2003. "Ushinawareta 1990-nen dai, Nihon Sangyō ni Nani ga Okottanoka?" (What Happened to the Japanese Industry in the Lost Decade?) RIETI Discussion Paper 03-J-002. (In Japanese)

Ohara, Yukiko. 2004. "Probability that this is last chance for recovery." *UFJ Holdings*. Credit Suisse First Boston Securities (Japan) Equity Research, June 4.

Omura, Keiichi, Hidehiro Iwaki, Shinji Mizukami, Takahide Sudo, Hiroki Sugeta. 2002. "Furyō Saiken no Shori to sono Eikyō ni tsuite II." *Disposal of Non-Performing Loans and its Effects II*. Cabinet Office Discussion Paper 02-4. (In Japanese)

Organization for Economic Cooperation and Development. 2002. *Economic Survey – Japan 2001*. Paris: OECD.

______. 1997. *Bank Profitability: Financial Statements of Banks 1997 Edition*. Paris: OECD.

______. 2003. *Bank Profitability: Financial Statements of Banks 2003 Edition*. Paris: OECD.

Packer, Frank. 2000. The Disposal of Bad Loans in Japan: The Case of CCPC. In *Crisis and Change in the Japanese Financial System*, editors Takeo Hoshi and Hugh Patrick. Boston, MA: Kluwer Academic Publishers.

Peek, Joe and Eric S. Rosengren. 2003a. "Crisis Resolution and Credit Allocation: The Case of Japan." University of Kentucky Working Paper. September 15.

______. 2003b. "Corporate Affiliations and the (Mis)allocation of Credit." University of Kentucky Working Paper. August 29.

Sasajima, Katsuhito and Shin Tamura. 2004. Major banks FY03 results: Sustained recovery and polarization. *Japan Daily Notes*, May 24. UBS Investment Research.

Sakuragawa, Masaya. 2002. Kin'yū Kiki no Keizai Bunseki. (Economic Analysis of Financial Crisis). Tokyo: Univeristy of Tokyo Press. (In Japanese)

Schaede, Ulrike. 2003. "Does Japan Need Specialized Small Firm Banks? The 'Middle Risk Gap' and Financial System Reform." Manuscript. University of California, San Diego, December 5.

Sekine, Toshitaka, Keiichiro Kobayashi, and Yumi Saita. 2003. Forbearance Lending: The Case of Japanese Firms. Bank of Japan, *Monetary and Economic Studies* 21 (2): 69–91.

Senoguchi, Junsuke. 2004. "Major Banks: Operating Results." Lehman Brothers Equity Research, May 25.

Smith, David C. 2003. Loans to Japanese Borrowers. *Journal of the Japanese and International Economies* 17 (3): 283–304.

6 Government Financial Institutions: What and How to Reform

Takero Doi

The government is a huge financial intermediary in Japan, but as the economy has matured, factors that once made government financial institutions useful have diminished. As private-sector financial firms have developed, government intermediation has become increasingly redundant, and it often competes unfairly with the private sector. The government's system is complex, and in some respects is non-transparent, inefficient, and wasteful. It is in dire need of reform. This chapter presents specific proposals to achieve a more relevant, accountable, and efficient set of government financial institutions.

In Japan the source of most government-intermediated funds is the Postal Savings System (PSS), the largest financial institution in the world. As of March 2004, the Postal Savings System held about 30% of total household deposits ¥227 trillion ($2.1 trillion). These funds are mostly lent through the Fiscal Investment and Loan Program (FILP), which had a fiscal 2003 budget of ¥311 trillion (net of ¥43 trillion loaned back to PPS). This is equal to some 62% of 2003 gross domestic product (GDP). Box 6.1 provides some additional background for and sources about government financial institutions and the Fiscal Investment and Loan Program. Table 6.1 lists the major government financial institutions with key aspects of their balance sheets. The historical scale of government financial institutions is illustrated in Figure 6.1, with underlying data in Tables 6.A1 and 6.A2.

Box 6.1
Fiscal Investment and Loan Program and Government Financial Institutions

The Fiscal Investment and Loan Program (FILP) has been called "the second budget," since the government initially used FILP to undertake projects it was unable to include in the general account budget because of a policy of not issuing deficit-financing bonds, a policy relaxed in 1965 and largely abandoned in 1975. In addition, until fiscal year 2000 FILP funds were used to make loans to borrowers in targeted areas, as well as to directly finance the government's budget deficit through bond purchases.

As of 2004 the FILP plan disburses funds to almost all local governments, and 54 other entities. Of the latter, 10 are central government accounts (these consist of the Japan Post, which has inherited a Postal Savings Special Account, 8 other special accounts, and Japan National Railways-related loans) and 44 are "Fiscal Investment and Loan Program agencies" (9 government financial institutions, 19 special public corporations, 10 independent administrative agencies, and 6 special firms. Special public corporations—*tokusho hojin*, or literally, "special legal entities"—are government-owned entities engaged in business activity on behalf of the government. Besides lending activities, government financial institutions also issue credit guarantees, especially for smaller businesses.

In April 2001, the government implemented a fundamental reform of the Fiscal Investment and Loan Program. The Trust Fund Bureau of the Ministry of Finance, which handled all the deposits from postal savings and pension reserves, was abolished. Postal savings and pension reserves now are not automatically deposited into the Fiscal Loan Fund, which has succeeded the Trust Fund Bureau. Instead, at their managers' discretion, these programs invest all their funds in the financial market. The Fiscal Loan Fund, unlike the Trust Fund Bureau, does not buy central government bonds. The FILP agencies raise funds through issuing bonds that do not come with a government guarantee.

Doi and Hoshi (2003) provide a good summary of the structure, components, and history of the FILP and the Postal Savings System, and provide estimates of the costs associated with these programs that taxpayers have had to bear and may have to bear in the future. Its appendix provides a further review of the literature [also see Cargill and Yoshino (2000, 2003)]. Other studies on the role of Japan's government financial institutions include Iwamoto (2001, 2002), Mitsui and Ota (1995), Okina (1999), and Nishigaki (2003). The Fiscal Investment and Loan Program Report, an annual publication available on the Ministry of Finance web site (http://www.mof.go.jp/english), is an official guide to the FILP, with basic information and data.

Table 6.1
Government Financial Institutes Balance Sheets, March 2004
(billion yen)

		Borrowing and Bonds			
	Loans	Total	from FILP[2]	Capital	Policy Costs[1]
Government Housing Loan Corp (GHLC)	60,510	61,765	58,827	–261	–81
National Life Finance Corp (NLFC)	9,647	9,768	9,000	–134	4
Japan Finance Corp for Small Business (JFS)	7,212	7,141	6,732	106	273
Japan Small and Medium Enterprise Corp[3] (JASMEC)	478	—	—	1,040	—
Agriculture, Forestry & Fisheries Fin Corp (AFC)	3,391	3,069	2,907	256	300
Japan Fin Corp for Municipal Enterprises (JFM)	24,888	22,632	17,284	2,153	8
Okinawa Development Finance Corp (ODFC)	1,431	1,417	1,367	45	12
Development Bank of Japan (DBJ)	14,390	13,184	12,242	1,779	107
Japan Bank for International Cooperation (JBIC)	19,043	11,954	11,457	7,896	692
Shoko Chukin Bank (SBC)	9,390	8,311	168	636	22
Total	150,380	139,241	119,984		

March 2004 is the end of fiscal 2003.

Most discussions (and data presentations) of FILP list Shoko Chukin Bank as a Special Firm. It was formed in 1936 to provide financial services to unions at small and medium enterprises. The Japan Small and Medium Enterprise Corp is a special public corporation , but its Credit Guarantee Division is included in the analysis here. For sources of additional data, see Box 6.1.

[1]Policy costs (subsidy costs) are the total present value (discounted present value) of subsidies and other expenditures to be invested by the central government (General Account, etc) in the future in conjunction with the implementation of projects using FILP funding. Policy costs are estimated by individual FILP agencies. Negative value means payment to the national treasury.

[2]Figures include government-guaranteed bonds approved in FILP plan.

[3]Credit Guarantee Division only.

Source: Ministry of Finance, *FILP Report 2004, Zaisei Kin'yu Tôkei Geppo (Ministry of Finance Statistics Monthly)*. Jul 2004; and the Administrative Cost Statements of each agency.

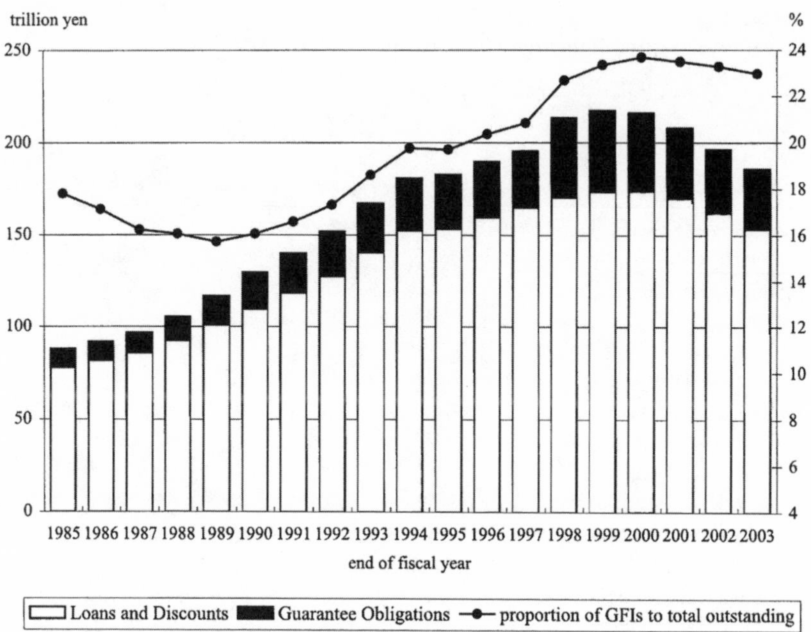

Source: Ministry of Finance, *Zaisei Kin'yu Tôkei Geppo* (*Ministry of Finance Statistics Monthly*), and Bank of Japan, *Financial and Economic Statistics Monthly*, various issues.

Figure 6.1
Loans, Discounts, and Guarantee Obligations Outstanding of GFIs

Since the early 1990s, financial intermediation through the public sector has increased, with postal savings' share of household deposits rising from 28.3% in March 1991 to a peak of 35.1% in March 1999 (28.5% in December 2004), and the government financial institutions' share of total loans and discounts outstanding jumping from 13.9% to a peak of 20.1% in March 2002 (19.8% in March 2004). In part this increase reflects the weakened state of private-sector financial institutions in the wake of the collapse of the 1980s bubble and the fourteen-year ongoing economic malaise. This shift to public sector financing is harmful to economic growth, since it crowds out private investment.

Funds intermediated by government financial institutions are not usually invested in activities that generate profits. Generally, funds collected in the public sector tend to remain in the public sector under the FILP. Moreover, when government financial institutions do lend to private companies, these often are companies that cannot borrow from private banks or are relatively less profitable. Hence, if the government does not itself reduce demand for funds, it is difficult to resolve the misallocation of investment.

The first part of this chapter provides overviews of government financial intermediation in Japan, and of the broad FILP reforms underway or under consideration. Problems common to all government financial institutions, special public corporations, and other recipients of FILP funds, and ways to address these issues, are then discussed. The core of the chapter takes each government financial institution in turn and puts forth a course of action for its reform. In connection with this, an analysis of the financing arrangements between the central and local governments and how they should be changed is also presented.

I stress that the general principles of reform are clarifying the appropriate roles of the public and private sectors, more efficient allocation of funds and operations by government financial institutions, and reducing the costs to the central government stemming from the activities of government financial institution and special public corporation. To achieve these goals, the current soft-budget constraint of unlimited government liability for deficits incurred by government financial institutions and special public corporation deficits should be terminated, and bankruptcy laws and procedures for these two programs should be established. In assessing each government financial institution, it is recognized that privatization or abolition is not the best course of action for every individual case.

1 Government Financial Intermediation

In Japan government financial institutions have economic rules, promote social goals, and can play political roles. The government can raise funds at a lower interest rate than a private intermediary, and thus offer those funds to borrowers at a lower lending rate than would a private lender. This below-market financing is a subsidy that can be economically appropriate in situations where there are large externalities, and acceptable for some socially desirable activities. Note that the government need not necessarily lose money from such intermediation.

Iwamoto (2001, 2002) summarizes in six points the economic reasons why government financial institutions have been created, These are to: 1) improve the operational efficiency of private financial institutions through their competition with government financial institutions; 2) produce credit information produced by government financial institutions, rather than relying on private financial institutions; 3) use short-term deposits to fund long-term projects; 4) generate externalities; 5) engage in risk-bearing; and 6) overcome asymmetric information problems. Among these, Iwamoto shows that only risk-bearing and asymmetric information are considered currently important rationales for these institutions.

Welfare losses due to asymmetric information are said to be mitigated by government financial institutions. Credit rationing takes place because lenders lack information about possible borrowers, and the costs of obtaining the information cannot reasonably be expected to be recovered. Government financial institutions have been more willing to lend in the absence of information than private financial institutions. This can be economically appropriate, presumed to be costless (at least directly) to taxpayers, and socially desirable. However, the lending also can be aimed at specific groups for political purposes.

Compared to private financial institutions, government financial institutions clearly can claim the "double-complementary role" proposed by Iwamoto (2001). That is, they can enhance both private intermediation and the functioning of capital markets. But there is a fine line between these activities and usurping the private market's role. In Japan, the scope of government financial institution activity has expanded into fields that are arguably inappropriate. Government financial institutions make loans to customers that private financial institutions could be lending to, and funding customers that should be financed in the capital market. Iwamoto (2001, 2002) shows that both these activities can lead to welfare loss.

The functions and competitiveness of private financial institutions and capital markets have been changing in Japan as a result of domestic deregulation and the global evolution of financial institutions and markets. It follows that the roles of government financial institutions should be required to adjust in accordance with these environmental changes. Government financial institutions were part of a segmented-market system, filling gaps arising in Japan's private financial sector. Now, these gaps are, or can be, filled by the private sector. As a specific example, large Japanese enterprises now tend to raise funds by direct finance, so the scope of the role played by all financial intermediaries is shrinking.

However, as a practical matter, the bad loan problems facing private Japanese financial institutions have contributed to their reluctance to lend. Thus, in the near-term there is room for complementary activity by government financial institutions in making loans to small- and medium-sized enterprises. But when the bad loan problem is resolved and the financial strength of private financial institutions improves, the scope of government financial institutions should naturally shrink, or end, in some cases.

2 Reforms Underway

The sheer size and ubiquity of the FILP has created tremendous vested interests, which have complicated attempts to introduce even such basic changes such as greater transparency and accountability. Yet slowly, recognition of the need for reforms spread, along with the resolve to undertake these measures. A revamping of the FILP began in April 2001. However, more needs to be done, and these additional efforts are underway. Doi and Hoshi (2003) summarize the reforms and illustrate the structure of the new FILP as shown in figure 2.2.

The Koizumi cabinet put forth a "Plan for Reorganization and Unification of Special Public Corporations" in December 2001. Under the overall guiding principle of "from government control to privatization", and the goals of properly managing the risk involved in loans and disclosing information related to reserves, the plan initiated studies and reviews of the existing system.

It was planned that the Council on Economic and Fiscal Policy would commence study at the beginning of 2002. Based on the results, the cabinet would then have a clear view of the economic situation and be able to make detailed proposals. The Council on Economic and Fiscal Policy was specifically charged with four things: studying the techniques used to evaluate policy-based financing, with specific attention to clearly indicating any subsidy costs estimating losses from redemption before maturity by borrowers from government financial institutions in calculating their subsidy costs; studying the structure under which the results are reflected in operations; and reviewing the organizational form of each special public corporation to determine whether it should be privatized, transformed into an independent administrative institution, or abolished. Although scheduled to be concluded no later than the end of 2002, the deadline was put off until the end of 2004.

Assuming office in 2001, the Koizumi cabinet had made a public commitment to the privatization of the postal system. To this end, a council was established to study the future modalities of the three postal businesses, namely to deliver the mail, operate postal savings, and operate a life insurance provider. The Council presented three approaches to reform in September 2002, and these, along with various other proposals, have been hotly debated. As of May 2005, privatization of postal services continues to be discussed in the Diet; its fate is beyond the scope of this chapter. Fukao's chapter in this volume addresses the life insurance industry component of the postal business.

A good deal of the discussion about reforming the government financial institutions and the Postal Savings System are in terms of how to privatize the system's components. In this regard, it must be stressed that if existing government financial institutions are simply privatized without scaling down and reducing the scope of their operations, the over-banking situation already besetting Japan will not be resolved but, on the contrary, could even be aggravated. Moreover, privatization is not the only solution. Some government financial institutions should simply be shut down because they are engaged in businesses that private financial institutions can carry on. A few government financial institutions are not suited for privatization, and should be retained as public institutions. In these cases, the scope of operation needs to be clearly delimited, and subsidies from the government will need to be curtailed, as is discussed in more detail in a later section.

3 General Issues

FILP activities represent a very large, open-ended liability of the government (hence taxpayers), and the system lacks transparency. This means that in reforming government financial institutions, four objectives are important: greater transparency, clarification of the roles of the private and public sectors, restraint on the fiscal burden government financial institutions impose, and increased business efficiency. To accomplish the last two goals, it is necessary for the soft-budget constraint problem to be fundamentally settled. Ways to address this problem—setting limits on government liability concerning capital contributions, restructuring FILP agencies including government financial institutions as "state-owned limited-liability companies," committing to using objective indicators such as "grant elements", and creating bankruptcy procedures—are presented in this section. The slowness with which FILP agencies have shifted their funding sources since the 2001 reform is also considered in this section.

FILP, "the second budget", uses Postal Savings System deposits as the equivalent of tax revenue in order to engage in activities that the government was unable to budget in the general account, which is financed primarily by taxes. However, unlike taxes, the deposits used have to be paid back, with interest. There have been many cases in which the revenue earned from the undertakings falls short of what is owed, and this difference must be covered by the general account. In such a manner, significant subsidies have been provided to government financial institutions on an unplanned, ex post, open-ended basis.

Table 6.2 shows the size of government subsidies to government financial institutions. This phenomenon is the soft-budget constraint originally formulated by Kornai (1979). At a time when outstanding Japanese government debt exceeds 400 trillion yen, a historically high level, it is not reasonable to provide the current level of subsidies.

3.1 *Limiting Capital Contributions*

In effect, the Japanese government, and ultimately taxpayers, has assumed almost unlimited liability for government financial institutions. With the government standing ready to cover any deficits, these institutions have little incentive to avoid creating deficits: the government bears the risks of their lending. Since the Japanese government has a huge amount of debt outstanding, such an ad hoc, open-ended commitment is not tolerable.

Proposed reforms seek to have Postal Savings System deposits flow into the private sector as much as possible. Currently, Postal Savings System funds are used mostly to purchase government bonds and FILP bonds. The central and local governments are issuing large amounts of bonds, and there continues to be a great demand for funds by government financial institutions and special public corporations. Thus, demand for public funds must be restrained if more funds are to flow to the private sector. To this end, the government must reduce its deficit. (In their chapter, Broda and Weinstein are more sanguine about the budget deficit.)

Moreover, regardless of the deficit situation, it is necessary to restrain the government financial institutions' demand for funds to make them more efficient and effective. That is, what is required in any meaningful reform of public finance is a hardening of soft budget constraints. In addition, the role of government financial instituions needs to be clarified, their operations limited to those in which public involvement is necessary, and their subsidies planned and limited within a framework possessing a more comprehensive control of expenditures than now exists.

Table 6.2
Government Subsidies to Government Financial Institutions, 1985–2003 (billion yen)

Fiscal year	GHLC	NLFC	JFS	JASMEC[1]	AFC	JFM	ODFC	DBJ	JBIC	SCB[2]	Total
1985	341.250	28.949	14.893	0	139.840	15.592	12.198	0.001	29.925	0	582.648
1986	343.250	46.068	29.759	0	143.432	15.910	12.528	0.004	35.501	0	626.452
1987	343.995	58.072	51.391	0	143.732	15.115	13.789	5.501	30.192	0	661.788
1988	343.995	48.373	36.825	0	144.141	13.604	13.201	3.287	36.587	0	640.013
1989	953.255	42.570	27.585	0	127.451	10.883	13.366	3.460	42.802	0	1,221.371
1990	353.995	34.548	28.828	0	119.751	9.436	12.798	0.011	43.528	0	602.894
1991	373.995	20.502	13.322	0	120.851	8.493	13.577	0.170	13.914	0	564.823
1992	393.995	16.004	12.923	0	118.321	7.644	12.459	0.309	8.675	0	570.330
1993	404.500	24.285	13.094	0	103.121	7.380	12.307	0.418	0.836	0	565.942
1994	404.500	60.426	28.491	0	100.835	6.192	11.702	0.444	0	0	612.590
1995	419.719	99.684	97.141	0	100.727	5.573	9.734	0.453	0	0	733.031
1996	526.600	60.206	39.455	0.010	99.297	5.016	8.659	0.388	0	0	739.632
1997	440.000	76.947	44.110	0.023	96.450	4.166	8.858	5.602	0	0	676.155
1998	560.000	80.960	64.228	0.028	85.635	2.900	8.852	16.840	0	0	819.443
1999	621.000	56.577	54.810	0.043	87.723	2.000	7.215	0.168	0	0	829.535
2000	518.500	50.973	60.585	0.079	72.709	1.400	5.592	0	0	0	709.838
2001	440.500	39.430	54.818	0.033	67.440	0	5.701	0	0	0	607.922
2002	375.900	27.508	38.863	0.022	53.717	0	5.262	0	0	0	501.272
2003	364.400	5.141	45.058	0.010	47.426	0	5.190	0	30.000	0	497.225

Fiscal years end Mar 31 of the following calendar year.
For full names of the Government Financial Institutions, see Table 6.1
[1]Credit Guarantee Division only.
[2]Shoko Chukin Bank.

Source: Ministry of Finance, *Explanation of settlement of Accounts,* various issues.

3.2 *Creating a New Corporate Structure*

Fiscal discipline of government financial institutions and other special public corporations is necessary. Establishing discipline will require ending the government's unlimited liability. A step in achieving this goal is changing the organizational form of government financial institutions and other special public corporations into "state-owned limited liability companies." Limited needs to mean exactly what it implies: as the primary (usually, sole) shareholder, the government will not cover deficits ex post. The government's fiscal burden needs to be clarified in advance, rather than remaining in its current ambiguous form. This is an important part of hardening what is now a soft budget constraint.

In Japan, state-owned limited-liability companies already exist and are functioning well. (The Japanese term is *tokushu kaisha*, which usually is translated as "special firm".) Examples are the regional spin-offs of the former Japan National Railways (JNR): JR Hokkaido, JR Shikoku, and JR Kyushu. Although these firms do not make enough profits and still are not sure when their shares will be listed on the Tokyo Stock Exchange, they have not received subsidies from the government since they were "privatized" in 1987. The government does not usually provide subsidies to such "privatized" firms. These companies operate with much more independence and self-support than in the age of JNR, which suffered massive losses that were covered by the government. If the government imposed a hard-budget constraint, government financial institutions would be more aggressive about collecting loans, and more careful about making new ones, because they would know the government was not going to cover any potential losses.

3.3 *Standards for any Grant Elements*

In terms of the medium- and long-term reform of government financial institutions, it is necessary to ensure the principle that government contributions of capital are made according to standards applied consistently across all recipients, and are not simply done on an ad hoc basis to fill ex post deficits. When the government financial institutions were created, there was an expectation that there would be a subsidy element involved in their operations. Yet the level and distribution of these subsidies is not being managed by the government to achieve its overall policies, or even to achieve the specific goals of each government financial institution in a cost-effective way. To ensure these goals finally are met, it is first necessary to establish a set of objective standards to measure their performance.

With objective performance standards, consistently applied across all government financial institutions, the subsidy element will be explicit and a clear constraint will be imposed on these institutions. The subsidy will be an explicit grant—hence it can be called the Grant Element. The concept and term are already used in the context of official development assistance as an indication of the degree to which the terms and conditions of loans have been eased.

The Grant Element is defined by the Development Assistance Committee of the Organisation for Economic Co-operation and Development as follows:

$$GE = \left(1 - \frac{R/A}{D}\right)\left(1 - \frac{\dfrac{1}{(1+D)^{A\times N}} - \dfrac{1}{(1+D)^{A\times M}}}{D(A \times M - A \times N)}\right)$$

where GE is the Grant Element stated as a percentage of the loan, R is the annual interest rate of the loan, A is number of payments, M is maturity (the period expressed in years from when the loan is made to final repayment of principal), I is a discount rate, $D = (1 + I)^{1/A}$ is the discount rate per repayment interval. N = G – 1/A, and G is the grace period. The more favorable the loan conditions are for the borrower, such as receiving a low interest rate or a longer term than would be available in the private lending market, the greater is the Grant Element. For example, in the case of a pure grant (where no repayment is expected), the Grant Element is 100%, and for a loan with a market rate of interest and other conditions, the Grant Element is 0%.

There is, of course, no obvious standard as to what the Grant Element should be in each case. (The Development Assistance Committee assumes a discount rate of 10% per annum, but it does not have to be 10%.) However, making loans through government financial institutions at a below-market interest rate is equivalent to granting the borrower a subsidy, which is income redistribution. As such, this is a policy issue that should be left in the hands of the politicians—that is, it should be settled in the Diet. It is important to have an objective basis for such decisions, and the Grant Element of a loan provides this criterion. In making the subsidies transparent, the Grant Element also fills the need for policymakers to be held accountable to the public.

3.4 *Comparing Policy Tools*

The comparison of administrative costs among alternative policy tools —loans, guarantees, subsidies, tax reductions—is important. Loans and guarantees have been the main instruments used by government financial institutions. However, the choice of tools may not be the best. For example, loans and guarantees have screening and monitoring costs, subsidies incur a range of costs, taxes preferences create distortions, and so on. Japanese government ministries have never compared the costs of their policy tools, and as a result, costs are not minimized.

Assuming the same result from a set of possible policies, the one with the lowest cost should be selected. The cost of lending through government financial institutions may be relatively higher than one associated with providing credit guarantees since the fiscal burden of the soft-budget constraint problem is hidden and large.

3.5 *Bankruptcy*

According to Yamamoto (2002), the legislation concerning the incorporation of government financial institutions, as well as other special public corporations, provides that their dissolution will be treated in other legislation that will be passed as separate acts. However, this "other legislation" has never been established. Therefore, at present, strictly speaking, provisions for bankruptcy proceedings of government financial institutions are not specified in statute law.

This situation needs to be remedied. As a part of hard budgeting, there needs to be a clear procedure for deeming government financial institutions bankrupt. This means establishing both a definition of what "bankruptcy" is as it relates to a government financial institution, as well as to a special public corporation, and a procedure for dealing with the bankruptcy. Otherwise, the Japanese government could find itself continuing to grant subsidies to cover operating deficits.

3.6 *Greater Transparency*

Greater transparency and clarity in the activities of FILP agencies are important in their own right, and are an essential element in hardening soft budget constraints. Thus, every fiscal year the government should publicly announce the details of its capital contributions to FILP agencies and other recipients. This includes disclosing the amount of any new capital contributions, and the cumulative amount of contributed capital, for each recipient. The level of disclosure phased in after the 2001 FILP reforms, which include computing "policy costs" for each recipient, is a first step toward this goal, but does not go far enough. Policy costs are defined as the present discounted value of the stream of net transfers from the government to an agency. This measure reveals the expected cost to the government (thus, the taxpayers) to sustaining the operation of a particular agency.

Moreover, every fiscal year, the government should make a close examination of whether a given government financial institution has a deficit, and whether payments to the national treasury can reasonably be made. The government would then take improving measures as the need arose.

As to making payments to the national treasury, the point is to keep a government financial institution from retaining profits to expand, or retaining cash flow to maintain its activities beyond a level consistent with overall government budget priorities and fiscal constraints. When government financial institutions are on the verge of making gains, it is because they have spent these excess funds to expand their businesses instead of paying these monies to the national treasury. Japan's central government requires government financial institutions to break even at least, not necessarily to earn profits. Even with the 2001 reforms, any profits that might be recorded in the administrative cost statements the public corporations are required to prepare using accounting principles accepted by private enterprises, or financial statements prepared under the Accounting Principles for Independent Administrative Agencies, can still be effectively determined. This is done simply by setting off the profits against reserves.

3.7 Funding FILP Agencies

The current sources of funds for FILP agencies are a mix of capital (contributed almost entirely by the government) and borrowing. The latter includes government-guaranteed bonds and FILP agency bonds. As expressed in the Framework of Fundamental Reform, each agency should "make utmost effort" to issue its own agency bonds in the market (Ministry of Finance 2001, p 28). Government guarantees are available if the market is otherwise unreceptive, and the FILP itself can issue bonds and distribute the proceeds to the agencies. The amounts of FILP agency bonds issued by individual agency are shown in Table 6.3.

Table 6.3
Issuance of FILP Agency Bonds
(billion yen)

2001	2002	2003	Fiscal year
200.0	600.0	350.0	GHLC
—	200.0	240.0	NLFC
—	200.0	200.0	JFS
14.5	22.0	22.0	AFC
—	10.0	20.0	JFM
100.0	220.0	300.0	ODFC
100.0	200.0	240.0	DBJ
100.0	200.0	240.0	JBIC
25.0	70.0	110.0	Urban Development Corp.
—	5.0	5.0	Japan Environment Corp.
45.0	55.0	—	Teito Rapid Transit Authority
10.0	28.5	32.7	Japan Regional Development Corp.
10.0	20.0	40.0	Social Welfare & Medical Service Corp.
6.0	6.0	6.0	Promotion & Mutual Aid Corp. for Private Schools of Japan
10.0	56.0	61.0	Japan Scholarship Foundation
—	4.0	4.7	Japan Green Resources Corp.
65.0	549.0	510.0	Japan Highway Public Corp.
—	50.0	40.0	Metropolitan Expressway Public Corp.
10.0	20.0	35.0	Hanshin Expressway Public Corp.
—	—	22.0	Honshu-Shikoku Bridge Authority
10.0	25.0	40.0	Japan Railway Construction Public Corp.
50.0	30.0	20.0	New Tokyo Int'l Airport Authority
10.0	25.0	25.0	Corp. for Advanced Transport & Technology
10.0	13.0	13.0	Water Resource Development Public Corp.
224.9	283.2	331.9	SCB
—	—	10.0	Kansai Int'l Airport Co. Ltd.
1,000.4	2,891.7	2,918.3	Total

For full names of the Government Financial Institutions, see Table 6.1 and 6.2
Figures are on a face value basis.

Source: Ministry of Finance, *FILP Report*, various issues.

Most government financial institutions have issued both government-guaranteed and agency bonds (which are not government-guaranteed). At present, however, private financial institutions buying government financial institution debt act as the though unguaranteed debt is in fact guaranteed. That is, these private institutions assume an implicit guarantee by the government to see that interest is paid and the bonds are redeemed at maturity. Therefore it is the resulting problem that FILP agency bonds do not function effectively as indicators of the market's perception of the issuer's creditworthiness. (See Doi and Hoshi 2003, p 62–64 for further analysis of the market's view of agency bonds.)

A second problem is that the shift to FILP agency bonds has been slow. It has been easier to continue old practices, even within the new structural framework. To overcome this inertia, the government must decide a schedule for fully phasing out direct loans to government financial institutions, and then for eliminating government-guaranteed bonds. Once a timetable is set, there also must be a credible commitment to the schedule.

4 Reforming Government Financial Institutions

This section offers workable plans for the reform of individual government financial institutions in ways that address the problems common to these institutions as a whole, as well as institution-specific issues. The Japan Finance Corporation for Municipal Enterprises is treated in a separate section analysizing how the financing arrangements between the central and local governments should be changed.

4.1 The Postal Savings System

What the Postal Savings System should become as a financial intermediary has been considered extensively (for example, Okina 2000, Inukai et al 2001, Cargill and Yoshino 2003, Japanese Bankers Association 2004). Taking into account this research and the current status of the Postal Savings System, I propose making it a narrow government-owned bank, which invests its deposits in central and local government bonds. This proposal is similar to that of Hoshi (2003).

Let us first discuss the environment surrounding Postal Savings System. Hoshi and Kashyap (2000) explain the current situation of overbanking in Japan's financial industry as follows. Corporate finance has been gradually liberalized, however, household asset diversification and deregulation enabling financial institutions to develop into universal banks lagged significantly behind during the 1980s, resulting in unbalanced liberalization. Large banks lost their traditional customers, which were large business enterprises, but the volume of their deposits was not reduced. Thus forced to develop new customers, banks increased lending to small- and medium-sized enterprises and to the real estate industry. Then, the bursting of the asset bubble in the early 1990s had a devastating impact on bank balance sheets.

Hoshi and Kashyap (2000 and in their chapter in this book) further insist that major Japanese enterprises will continue to move away from borrowing from banks, and that small- and medium-sized enterprises to some extent will also raise funds in the capital market. In other words Japan's traditional banking businesses will be forced to shrink; Hoshi and Kashyap foresee the banking business shrinking to 50%, or perhaps even just 30%, of its current size.

Meanwhile, bad loan disposals still have not been completed, as many banks simply lack the capital to offset these losses. Fukao (2003) examined the data and calculated that if the 15 major banks had made proper provisions for non-performing loans, did not count useless deferred tax credits as capital, and unwound their double-gearing with insurance companies, their net Tier 1 capital ratio as of the end of September 2002 would be a mere 0.86%.

Why do many Japanese banks have a negligible net worth? Establishing deposit insurance is a factor in this. Without deposit insurance, runs on banks having a negative net worth ought to weed them out of the system. But with insurance, depositors have no cause to stage a run. Phasing out the system of unlimited guarantees was deferred several times until April 2005, and even then settlement deposits for transaction purposes continue to provide unlimited coverage. This is despite the fact the existence of deposit insurance gives banks with inadequate capital an incentive to take more risks.

Hoshi (2003) proposes abolishing deposit insurance and making all deposits held by private financial institutions assets at risk. In this way, the issue of moral hazard at private financial institutions is settled because the absence of deposit insurance will discipline institutions through the possibility of a run by depositors. If it is unnecessary for banks to pay deposit insurance premiums, they can pay higher interest rates on deposits.

Under these circumstances, it is desirable for the Japanese government to protect the Postal Savings System by converting it to a narrow bank with assets limited to central and local government bonds. Virtually all of the funds the Postal Savings System collected in the past were passed on to the Ministry of Finance's Trust Fund Bureau, which then passed them on to various government financial institutions. With the 2001 reform, the Postal Savings System gained formal control over disposition of its funds, but it did not acquire the capability to do credit analysis. There is no reason to believe that the Postal Savings System can be readily transformed from an open conduit of funds to a sophisticated lending institution. Therefore, it is desirable to confine its activities to what it does well, which argues for a narrowing of its scope and activities.

Moreover, the Postal Savings System already has been investing a large part of its funds in government bonds. Given that the outstanding balance of government bonds already issued is enormous, it is hardly necessary to drastically change the present structure and activities of the Postal Savings System. This suggests there is little reason to privatize it entirely: it is sufficient to turn it into an institution specializing in handling Japanese government bonds and highly rated local government bonds. Among existing Postal Savings System financial products, from the individual holder's standpoint, fixed-amount postal savings (*teigaku chokin*) are similar in nature to government bonds.

A range of options for depositors will result. Thus, the Postal Savings System will offer its depositors low risks and low returns, while private financial institutions will offer higher risks and higher returns.

A reformed Postal Savings System should not be able to hold FILP agency bonds or even government-guaranteed bonds. Cut off from this funding source, FILP agencies will be exposed to greater market discipline. Agencies that find it difficult to raise funds by issuing bonds will have to be scaled down, or should be allowed to collapse. The latter course of action will require legislation to deal with agency bankruptcy.

Although still state-owned, a reformed Postal Savings System should be turned into a stock company with the discipline that this implies. The foregoing analysis suggests that it is not necessary to privatize the Postal Savings System to affect reforms in this system that will strengthen Japan's financial system directly and indirectly; however there is a strong political impetus to privatize the Postal Savings System entirely. If a private Postal Savings System then sought to evolve into a regular bank in competition with existing private financial institutions, the results could be very deleterious to the country's overall financial structure. First, Japan's over-banking problem would be exacerbated. Second, the Postal Savings System still would not have any internal capability to make loans or otherwise manage its assets. Although it could hire staff away from existing banks, this hardly makes the financial system better as a whole. Quite simply, at least until the over-banking problem is settled, the Postal Savings System should not be allowed to be more than a narrow bank, holding only government bonds and high-grade local government bonds, even if it is eventually completely privatized.

4.2 *The Government Housing Loan Corporation*

Under the 2001 "Plan for Reorganization and Unification of Special Public Corporations", the Government Housing Loan Corporation, which is the largest of the government financial institutions, is to be abolished within five years, by 2006. More specifically, the plan states: the Government Housing Loan Corporation's loan business is to shrink gradually from fiscal 2002 onward; interest subsidies should not be granted in principle; how the business is handled should be decided at the time of establishing a new, independent administrative agency, taking into account whether private financial institutions are smoothly taking over; and the new agency should assume the existing receivables of the Government Housing Loan Corporation. In December 2004, the Koizumi cabinet decided to abolish the Government Housing Loan Corporation in fiscal 2006, thereby ending its direct lending operations, and to set a new independent administrative agency to focus on securitizing housing loans after that. At present the loan business is being rearranged and related agencies are being reorganized in line with this plan. However, the curtailing of new loans by the Government Housing Loan Corporation has not progressed as much as expected.

Since fiscal 2001, the Government Housing Loan Corporation has issued FILP agency bonds without a government guarantee in the form of mortgage-backed securities. However, these schemes do not aggressively enhance the securitization of existing Government Housing Loan Corporation loans.

There are problems with how the Government Housing Loan Corporation makes loans. Seko (1998) finds that this agency decides the amount of a loan on the basis of floor area only. This means that the smaller the residence, the lower the interest rate. Therefore, there is a tendency to reduce floor area in order to obtain a lower lending rate.

Although this is partly offset by improving housing quality, Seko estimated the welfare loss caused by distorted resource distribution amounts to 14% of the Government Housing Loan Corporation entire loan portfolio.

As a context for the specifics of how the Government Housing Loan Corporation should be reformed, I have investigated the relationship between development of securitization and the role of government financial institutions. These institutions have shouldered the responsibility of supplying funds at a long-term fixed interest rate, a difficult task for private financial institutions as they were able to raise only short-term funds earlier. In this regard, there has been a place for government financial institutions, and the housing-finance market is such an example. However, the private-sector now has better tools to deal with term-mismatch, so this older rationale needs to be reconsidered in light of new market realities.

Interest rate risk, and the related advanced-redemption risk, is borne by the government financial institutions, and thus in effect is transferred widely to the public through taxation. If people can more or less equally bear this risk, improved efficiency in fund allocation can be expected. However, if the capacity to bear these risks significantly differs among people, a voluntary disproportional risk-bearing system is superior. Securitization offers just such a system. At present there is a strong evidence that the risk bearing capacity is significantly different among the Japanese, as noted in Mitsui (2004). Accordingly, it is desirable from an efficiency standpoint to mitigate the burden that government financial institutions assume in intermediating loans by implementing policies promoting securitization in the housing-finance market.

When the market for securitization mortgages is still undeveloped, government intervention to promote it is appropriate. This might even extend to granting government guarantees—although only after evaluating each specific case, rather than a blanket guarantee. Yet when the securitization market has been put in good order, continued public intervention at the same level as at the initial stage is an obstruction to the activities of private financial institutions. Moreover, even if the extent of public intervention is mitigated after the fact, because private financial institutions consider the possibility of public intervention continuing, their positive steps toward greater securitization will be weakened. Accordingly, it is important to show clearly in advance the schedule for phasing out public intervention—presumably through proclaiming easily identified mileposts—in order that private financial institutions fully fulfill their function in the securitization market.

With this context as background, the steps to reforming the Government Housing Loan Corporation can be outlined. First, securitization of its existing should be promoted. Next, at the initial stage of securitization, the institutional successor to the Government Housing Loan Corporation should stop making direct loans but continue to provide credit guarantees for housing loans. The successor to the Government Housing Loan Corporation should be abolished when two things have happened: existing Government Housing Loan Corporation receivables are completely securitized and the securities market is deemed mature. The latter occurs when the market readily accepts the absence of public guarantees, private financial institutions can hedge the risk involved in term-mismatch (as is happening already) and the risk from a mismatch between variable- and fixed interest rates. Finally all other government financial institutions should completely pull out of the housing loan market.

4.3 *Government Financial Institutions for Small- and Medium-sized Enterprises*

Three government financial institutions serve small- and medium-sized enterprises. These are the Japan Finance Corporation for Small Business, the National Life Finance Corporation, and the Credit Guarantee Division of Japan Small and Medium Enterprise Corporation. Public funds for small- and medium-sized enterprises also come as direct subsidies and as direct finance from these government financial institutions.

Loans outstanding to small- and medium-sized enterprises have been decreasing, but the government financial institutions' share of total loans to small- and medium-sized enterprises is increasing. The total outstanding loan balance was about ¥350 trillion in the mid-1990s, but had dropped to about ¥260 trillion at the end of March 2004. The share of government financial institutions was in the 8% range in the mid-1990s, and had risen to 10.5% by 2004. Loans included in these figures are those made by public and private financial institutions, while loans made by local governments are excluded.

In Japan, the central and local governments are involved in credit guarantees to small- and medium-sized enterprises. The Credit Guarantee Division of Japan Small and Medium Enterprise Corporation took over the credit insurance business operated until July 2001 by the Small Business Credit Insurance Corporation, the loan business of Credit Guarantee Corporation, and a machinery credit insurance business.

The Small Business Credit Insurance Corporation had been a government-affiliated agency subject to Diet budget resolutions. Credit Guarantee Division of Japan Small and Medium Enterprise Corporation's credit insurance operations shifted to Japan Finance Corporation for Small Business in July 2004. The rest of Credit Guarantee Division of Japan Small and Medium Enterprise Corporation's activities became part of the Independent Administrative Agency for Structural Improvement of Small and Medium Enterprises.

The credit guarantee system is structured as follows. There are 52 Credit Guarantee Corporations; they basically guarantee 100% of loans made by private financial institutions that meet certain requirements. The Credit Guarantee Division of Japan Small and Medium Enterprise Corporation underwrites, in a form of insurance, 70% to 80% of the liability for the loan guarantees. The fiscal burden involved includes central-government capital contributions to Credit Guarantee Division of Japan Small and Medium Enterprise Corporation and local-government subsidies. The central government also indirectly provides funds, including making good deficits, with subsidies to local governments and the Credit Guarantee Corporations.

During the 1990s economic malaise, the fiscal burden with subrogated performance by Credit Guarantee Corporations increased from 88.4 billion yen in fiscal 1992 to 579.2 billion yen in fiscal 2001. This reflected an increase in the amount of loans guaranteed, and a decline in the collection ratio of guaranteed receivables, and the implementation of a special guarantee plan. The fiscal burden with subrogated performance per unit amount of liability for guarantee went from 0.39% to 1.49% of the amount guaranteed.

Takezawa, Matsuura, and Hori (2004) investigated the effectiveness of measures to facilitate funding for small- and medium-sized enterprises, especially credit guarantees and institutional government lending, in the late 1990s. They find that Japanese small- and medium-sized enterprises are excessively indebted in terms of their ability to repay loans from earnings. These results suggest that fund-supply facilitation policies did nothing but delay the timing of small business bankruptcies, while adding high social costs. Small- and medium-sized enterprises' problems cannot be dissolved by temporary credit through programs such as these. What is really needed are measures to reorganize heavily indebted firms, not measures to promote unprofitable lending practices.

A financial structure for small- and medium-sized enterprises centered on indirect financing cannot be changed immediately without a recovery by the private banks. Under the current situation, a role for government financial institutions pertaining to small- and medium-sized enterprises remains, but is limited. To continue making loans to small- and medium-sized enterprises, government financial institutions should become state-owned limited-liability companies, as described earlier. Moreover, liquidation of their loans should be promoted. As private financial institutions settle their non-performing loans problem, any role for government financial institutions diminishes. To ensure this development takes place, sunset provisions should be included on new loans made by government financial institutions.

It is also necessary to review the role played by government financial institutions that are controlled by local governments. Local governments have granted loans at low interest rates directly to small- and medium-sized enterprises. These total loans amounted to about ¥10 trillion, making up 13% of the entire outstanding loans to extended to small- and medium-sized enterprises at the end of March 2004.

As an example, the May 2003 announcement that the Tokyo Metropolitan Government would establish a new financial institution, called Shin Ginko Tokyo, Limited (literally "New Bank Tokyo") to provide loans and credit guarantee to small- and medium-sized enterprises attracted much attention. Tokyo's reason for establishing a new bank was the assertion that private financial institutions are often reluctant to lend money and existing government financial institutions make insufficient loans to small- and medium-sized enterprises in Tokyo. However, any regional government could make this claim. More important, there is no robust evidence that the ability of a local government to engage in lending is better than that of a government financial institution controlled by the central government or of a private financial institution.

At present, the public sector's involvement in financing small- and medium-sized enterprises is being conducted without clearly defining the roles to be played by the central and local governments in the overall financial structure. This situation has to be rectified. Specifically, local government involvement should be abolished, or at least scaled back. Where there is a recognized need for public involvement that can be conducted at the national level, it should be provided by government financial institutions run by the central government. This means these government financial institutions should absorb many existing local activities and integrate them into national programs. For lending activities where there is a strong case for a regional or local approach, the majority of such business can be handled by regional financial institutions such as regional banks, *shinkin* banks, and credit cooperatives rather than local governments. This means local governments should make efforts to actively transfer loans they have made to regional financial institutions.

4.4 The Development Bank of Japan

The Development Bank of Japan was created in 1999 through the merger of the former Japan Development Bank and the Hokkaido-Tohoku Development Finance Public Corporation. The Development Bank of Japan's business is centered on three objectives: structural reform of the Japanese economy and hastening of economic vitality; the creation of self-reliant economic regions; and the development of an affluent lifestyle. Reform and a vital economy involve promotion of, and improvement in, social capital and intellectual infrastructure. The self-reliant regional goal includes improving the social infrastructure, creating a vital business climate, and promoting regional collaboration. Developing an affluent lifestyle relates to the environment, disaster prevention, welfare measures, traffic congestion alleviation, the distribution network, and the information and telecommunications networks. The Development Bank of Japan invests in and provides support to, debtor-in-possession financing and business rehabilitation funds. As part of creating self-reliant regions it has cooperative arrangements with more than 60 private financial institutions. The Development Bank of Japan's Japanese name—*Seisaku Toshi Ginko*—literally translates as "the policy-based investment bank," as these extensive goals stated on the bank's mission statement indicates.

Under the economic conditions of the last decade, the need for such a bank-oriented investment institution has been high. Thus, Iwamoto (2004) finds that the current activities of the Development Bank of Japan are justified as supplementing the activities of private financial institutions because private institutions cannot supply long-term funds. Further, private institutions neither assume adequate business risk nor make use of the most advanced financial technology. However, many of the Development Bank of Japan's areas of operation can take place in the private sector once private financial institutions become sounder, and some of these activities can readily be covered by private investment banks even now. This is particularly true in such areas as debtor-in-possession financing, the business rehabilitation fund, and the activities done in cooperation with private financial institutions. Iwaisako (this volume, ch 8) questions the Development Bank of Japan's role in restructuring private firms because the private sector can do that now.

In other words, what can reasonably be considered transitory problems in the private sector to provide near-term justification for the Development Bank of Japan? When private financial institutions have reduced their holdings of bad loans, improved the soundness of their management, and ceased being cautious in taking risk, the importance of the supplementary function of government financial institutions, including the Development Bank of Japan, will be reduced, and their role should be terminated or severely curtailed.

Yet simply shutting down the Development Bank of Japan is probably not practical, Therefore, it should eventually be privatized. Toward this end, the Development Bank of Japan should be reorganized into a state-owned limited company subject to taxation, and its activities made more subject to market conditions. These steps are necessary to ensure fair competition between (former) government financial institutions and private financial institutions.

4.5 The Japan Bank for International Cooperation

The Japan Bank for International Cooperation has two distinct operating units: the Overseas Economic Cooperation Operations and the International Financial Operations, which are strictly separated in terms of financial sources and accounts. Until the Japan Bank for International Cooperation was created in 1999 these two units were completely separate entities—the Overseas Economic Cooperation Fund was established in March 1961, and International Financial Operations was previously the Export-Import Bank of Japan, founded as the Export Bank in December 1950. The International Financial Operations promotes Japanese trade, as well as Japanese economic activities overseas, and contributes to the stability of the international financial order. The Overseas Economic Cooperation Operations provides Japan's official development assistance.

The scope of the International Financial Operations includes export loans, import loans, overseas investment loans, untied loans, and equity participation in overseas investment projects of Japanese corporations. In the face of the 1997–98 Asian currency crisis, the Japan Bank For International Cooperation extended untied loans to other Asian countries in order to stabilize the international financial order, and at the same time vigorously supported Japanese company in the region, which faced difficulties from deteriorating business conditions and a credit squeeze. One important source of funds for the Japan Bank for International Cooperation is the Fiscal Investment and Loan Program. Other funding comes from bond issues in international capital markets and retained earnings (net interest income) from past loans.

The Overseas Economic Cooperation Operations is the cornerstone of Japan's official development assistance policy, accounting for about 40% of Japan's official development assistance. The basic tenet of its operations is providing concessionary long-term, low-interest funds for self-help efforts in developing countries, including social infrastructure development and economic stabilization. More specifically, it provides official development assistance loans in various forms attuned to local needs, private-sector investment finance support, and development-related research. Official development assistance loans are a key form of financial assistance that are indispensable in putting in place the socioeconomic infrastructure necessary for the economic growth of developing countries. The sources of the Overseas Economic Cooperation Operations funds are grants from the central government's general account and borrowing from FILP and other agencies.

With regard to the business of the Japan Bank for International Cooperation, the following policies were presented in the 2001 "Plan for Reorganization and Unification of Special Public Corporations". For International Financial Operations, it was decided that outstanding loans are to be reduced by promoting liquidation (including securitization) of credited loans and so forth. In the export finance business, it was decided to actively utilize guarantees and discontinue business related to developed countries. In import finance, business not related to natural resources is to be discontinued, and in principle involvement will be limited to high-risk businesses outside of developed countries. For the business that will be continued, guarantees will be utilized, and will be available for both general investment (project development) and trade finance.

At the Overseas Economic Cooperation Operations, the overseas investment and the loan businesses are to be eliminated. From fiscal 2002 onward only projects approved before the end of the fiscal 2001 or those of a continuous nature are to be funded, and the yen-credit business is to be reviewed in line with the review of the official development assistance with the aim of reducing the scale of operations. The review is proceeding as planned.

Official development assistance must be operated by a government organization by definition, so the Overseas Economic Cooperation Operations arm of the Japan Bank for International Cooperation cannot be privatized. Nonetheless, it is necessary to reorganize the Japan Bank for International Cooperation into a state-owned limited company in order to reduce the inefficiency of official development assistance. For the International Financial Operations, the Japan Bank for International Cooperation should promote the liquidation of its loans and decrease outstanding loans, as stated in the "Plan for Reorganization and Unification of Special Public Corporations". However, the cabinet has not committed to a schedule for this plan. The government should commit to a deadline for liquidating and reducing outstanding loans. It is also useful to afix sunset provisions on new business projects operated by the Japan Bank for International Cooperation. Also necessary is clarifying intentions so that the international financing business does not degrade into providing interest-free loans and ex-post subsidies.

4.6 The Agriculture, Forestry, and Fisheries Finance Corporation

The Agriculture, Forestry, and Fisheries Finance Corporation supplies enterprises in the agriculture, forestry, fishery, and food industries with the funds necessary to ensure maintenance and promotion of production, and to ensure a stable supply of food. It is difficult for the Central Cooperative Bank for Agriculture and Forestry and other private institutions to supply long-term credit in this area at low interest rates. Outstanding Agriculture, Forestry, and Fisheries Finance Corporation loans were around ¥3.6 trillion at the end of March 2003. By industry, agriculture was 53%, forestry 27%, fisheries 3%, and the food industry 17%. Data by type of borrower are in Table 6.4.

Because losses accrue as a matter of policy, the Agriculture, Forestry, and Fisheries Finance Corporation is subsidized by the general account of the central government to cover its deficit every year. In addition, local governments and various associations, including agricultural cooperatives, are subsidized or given tax concessions through the general account and special accounts of the central government. Table 6.5 provides details on the financing sources to these primary-sector industries.

In addition to individual farms, agriculture ownership includes limited-liability companies (*yugen kaisha*), agricultural cooperative corporations, general (unlimited) partnerships (*gomei kaisha*), and limited partnerships (*goshi kaisha*). Until 2000, joint-stock companies (*kabusiki kaisha*) could not make capital contributions to an agricultural

Table 6.4
Loans by Type of Borrower, March 2004
(percentage distribution)

12.3	Individuals
27.6	Corporations
15.9	Land improvement districts
25.8	Local governments and Forestry Public Corporation
16.3	Cooperatives (agricultural, forestry, and fishery)
2.2	Others

Outstanding loans amounted to ¥3.4 trillion.

Land improvement districts are corporations that can be established by 15 or more farmers under the Land Improvement Act for the purpose of developing agricultural land, subject to approval of prefectural governors. A district has the authority to collect compulsory dues. The Forestry Public Corporation is a public utility corporation established by capital contributions from the prefectures that promotes reforestation and afforestation, including tree planting by owners of mountainland.

Source: Agriculture, Forestry, and Fisheries Finance Corporation, briefing material for investor relations, August 2004

Table 6.5
Sources of Finance for Primary-Sector Industries, March 2003
(percentage distribution)

12.1	Agriculture, Forestry, and Fisheries Finance Corporation
67.6	Agricultural cooperatives
5.4	Prefectural Credit Federation of Agricultural Cooperatives
4.3	Central Agriculture and Forestry Finance Corporation
0.6	Fishery cooperatives
2.9	Prefectural Credit Federation of Fishery Cooperatives
6.6	Banks and credit associations
0.5	Others

Outstanding loans amounted to ¥24,889.1 billion.

The various cooperatives are private organizations at the level of a municipality. As far as credit activities are concerned, for agriculture they are treated at the prefectural level as members of the Prefectural Credit Federation of Agricultural Cooperatives, and at the national level they are controlled by the Central Cooperative Bank for Agriculture and Forestry. Fishery cooperatives are members of the Federal Credit Federation of Fishery Cooperatives at the level of prefectures, and at the national level are controlled by the Central Cooperative Bank for Agriculture and Forestry.

Source: Central Agriculture and Forestry Finance Corporation (2004) "Financial Statistics of Agriculture, Forestry, and Fisheries in Japan."

production corporation. This meant funds could not be raised by issuing stock. Restrictions remain on joint-stock company involvement, and it cannot be said that a lot of funds are supplied to them through share issue.

Small-scale farming continues to be common in Japan, and much of it is inefficient. Even with large subsidies, rice farming on tracts under 2 hectares was unlikely to break even in 2000 according to a government study (Ministry of Agriculture, Forestry, and Fisheries 2002). More disturbing, at all farm sizes, break-even situations were less likely in 2000 than in 1995 (when even the smallest farms as a group made small profits).

Because of regional differences in what is an appropriate lending purpose, the Agriculture, Forestry, and Fisheries Finance Corporation obtains opinions on, or approval of, potential borrower's business plans from prefectural governments or municipalities. This means local governments are deeply involved in the lending process. In light of this involvement, the lending that has been done by the Agriculture, Forestry, and Fisheries Finance Corporation can be carried on through the prefectures, agricultural cooperatives, or the Central Cooperative Bank for Agriculture and Forestry.

The central government has been directly subsidizing from the general account a program to train the next generation of farmers and strengthen the base of agricultural management. This money flows first into the Special Account for Strengthening the Bases of Agricultural Management, which loans the money to the Agriculture, Forestry, and Fisheries Finance Corporation and special accounts of local governments, which in turn lend to farmers at a low interest rate. Consequently the central government provides an interest subsidy to farmers.

On examination, no great reason is found for government financial institutions to finance the primary food producing sector. Accordingly, the Agriculture, Forestry, and Fisheries Finance Corporation's operations that do not need to be subsidized by the government should be assigned to the Central Cooperative Bank for Agriculture and Forestry or agricultural cooperatives. The Agriculture, Forestry, and Fisheries Finance Corporation operations that require a subsidy should be transferred to local governments, with the central government providing these subsidies. In both cases, this will include liquidating (selling) existing outstanding receivables. After that takes place, the Agriculture, Forestry, and Fisheries Finance Corporation itself should be abolished.

This reform necessitates a review of the extent to which the government should grant subsidies, and how this role should be shared between Japan's central government and local governments. In any case, it is extremely important to cope with the problems which Japan's agriculture sector is facing, such as the inefficiency of small scale agriculture, and reducing subsidies as much as possible. (The need for agricultural reform to promote economic efficiency in the context of trade policy is covered by Urata's chapter in this volume.)

4.7 The Okinawa Development Finance Corporation

The Okinawa Development Finance Corporation is an agency that carries out, in a unified and comprehensive way in Okinawa, operations carried out by other agencies in the rest of the country, as shown in Table 6.6. That is, its activities are the same as the combined activities of the other government financial institution in other prefectures. This arrangement exists because Okinawa is a special case: it is the poorest prefecture and, because of geography, has never been as fully integrated into the nation as the other three main islands. In addition, Okinawa remained under American occupation much longer, reverting only in 1972, and continues to be a major base for United States forces.

The Okinawa Development Finance Corporation also independently finances enterprises in order to implement policies provided for in the Special Measures Act for Promoting Development of Okinawa. Some loans are made at a below-market rate that is even lower than interest rates provided in other prefectures. Some loans are subsidized from

Table 6.6
Relation of Other Government Financial Institutions to Okinawa Development Finance Corporation Operations

Government Financial Institutions consign operations	ODFC equivalent operation
Development Bank of Japan	Industrial Development Fund
Small Business Finance Corp	Funds for small & medium enterprises
National Life Finance Corp	Occupation fund; Public hygiene fund
Agriculture, Forestry, and Fisheries Finance Corp	Fund for agriculture etc
Govt Housing Loan Corp	Housing fund
Social Welfare and Medical Service Corp	Healthcare fund

Source: Okinawa Development Finance Corporation (ODFC), briefing material for investor relations.

the general account. The Okinawa Development Finance Corporation accounted for 33.5% of total outstanding loans made by all financial institutions, public and private in Okinawa at the end of 2002.

Although it makes loans independently, from a practical standpoint the Okinawa Development Finance Corporation can be said to be the collective regional office of the other government financial institutions. Therefore it is not necessary to organize it as one independent financial corporation. Rather, the Okinawa Development Finance Corporation should be treated in the same manner as all financial institutions elsewhere: activities that should continue to be performed by government financial institutions should be continued by the Okinawa branch of the appropriate institution, and those that should be abolished should assign their receivables and promote securitization in the same manner as elsewhere. In short, it is desirable to break the Okinawa Development Finance Corporation up.

5 Inter-Government Finance

This section looks at the financial arrangements between central and local governments. Proposals regarding the Japan Finance Corporation for Municipal Enterprises are then presented. Box 6.2 provides background on local government in Japan.

Box 6.2
Local Government in Japan

Local government refers to the 47 Japanese prefectures and the municipalities that comprise them. Unlike a federal system like in the United States, Japan has a unitary system like France. This means local jurisdictions depend on the central government financially and administratively, even though the prefectures have their own governors and assemblies.

Local tax revenues are almost entirely controlled by the central government, with the rates and sources of local taxes being basically determined by national laws so that local governments have limited discretion over them. The central government also distributes to each local government large amounts of Local Allocation Tax general grants and National Government Disbursements, treated as matching grants. Moreover, local governments must obtain advance permission from a minister of the central government when planning to issue local government bonds.

5.1 *Some Reforms and Changes*

The Koizumi cabinet has undertaken the "Trinity Reform Package" to address the fiscal relationship among the national and local levels of government. In this context, "trinity" refers to a decentralization reform that involves three elements: local taxes, Local Allocation Tax grants, and National Government Disbursements.

The incumbent Local Allocation Tax grant scheme allocates a certain percentage of national tax revenue to local governments without specifying the purpose of expenditure. Some 94% of the total allocations are "ordinary," that is, they are distributed according to a macro allocation rule, and 6% is appropriated as special Local Allocation Tax Grants used for special circumstances such as disasters. The macro rule considers the difference between standard financial need and standard financial revenue. Ordinary grants are made only to local governments whose standard financial revenue is less than their standard financial need. Standard financial revenue is the amount of tax collectable under normal circumstances, as calculated by the Ministry of Internal Affairs and Communications (the former Ministry of Home Affairs) according to a certain formula for each local government. Standard financial need is the amount of expenses necessary for local governments to carry out independently administrative work including debt service at an appropriate and rational level; the Ministry of Internal Affairs and Communications also calculates this figure.

As part of the Trinity Reform, there has been a reduction in Local Allocation Tax grants applied to payment of interest and principal of local bonds. However, because Local Allocation Tax grants still cover certain local bond repayments, the system undermines the sound issuance of local bonds. Therefore Doi (2004a) points out that there is a missing link in the "Trinity Reform Package".

In particular, the calculations determining a local government's standard financial need also includes repayment expenditures for certain types of bonds (depopulated area development bonds, revenue resource support bonds, and revenue-decrease compensation bonds). This suggests that local governments can raise funds for the kinds of projects these bonds are intended to finance even without sufficient ability to repay. If they do this, local governments enjoy the benefits of the projects and depend on future national tax revenue, including revenue collected in other communities, for debt repayment. In addition, if they focus on these sorts of projects, they will show a greater standard financial need and will receive a larger Local Allocation Tax grant! For example, a local government constructs facilities equipment, the cost of which are included in the standard financial budget but which is not strongly supported by local residents. This is because standard financial budget and therefore Local Allocation Tax grants to the local government increase due to the construction, and the costs to the local government become lower. More generally, because Local Allocation Tax grants implicitly cover debt service expenditures at the local level, the current system does not result in local awareness of being a debtor. To solve these problems, it is necessary to undertake local bond issuing reforms; this should be added to the "Trinity Reform Package". Neglecting such reforms will result in unsuccessful decentralization.

5.2 *The Use of Fiscal Investment and Loan Program Funds*

When issuing bonds, local governments in Japan need permission from the Ministry of Internal Affairs and Communications (for prefectures) or the prefectural governor (for municipalities). Before granting permission, the Ministry of Internal Affairs and Communications consults other parts of the central government and determines who will buy the local bonds. After this process, the Ministry of Internal Affairs and Communications announces the Local Bond Plan, which sets the size of local borrowing by project and allocates available funds to respective projects. In other words, the Ministry of Internal Affairs and Communications also largely determines who will be the bond buyers (creditors).

In connection with the 2001 FILP reforms, the cabinet decided to obtain FILP funds, including funds for loans to local governments, by issuing FILP bonds with the same face value as construction bonds and deficit-covering bonds in the general account. In the bond market, the increase in government bonds is identified with increases in FILP bonds. The implication is that the FILP is borrowing to buy local government bonds.

Because of the 2001 reform, funds no longer automatically flow into the general account under the deposit obligations of the Postal Savings System and public pension funds. The central government strongly desires that local Japanese governments borrow FILP funds, which have lower interest rates and longer maturities, rather than private funds. However, outstanding central and local government bonds have already reached historic levels. Given these circumstances, central government bond issues should not increase for the purposes of underwriting local government bonds through the FILP.

FILP purchased around 60% of newly issued local government bonds until fiscal year 2000, mostly through the Japan Finance Corporation for Municipal Enterprises. This amount fell somewhat after the 2001 reform, and was reduced to around 50% for fiscal 2004 under the Local Bond Plan. Fiscal 2004 loans to local governments by FILP were reduced by 27% compared to fiscal 2003.

There is a tendency for FILP funds to be allocated relatively more to buying bonds from rural prefectures than bonds issued by more urban prefectures. As a result, rural prefectures do not issue bonds in the market or borrow much from private financial institutions, as they can obtain lower interest rates borrowing from the FILP. This means an implicit interest subsidy is being granted to rural prefectures, and that there is income redistribution toward them through the allocation of FILP funds (Doi 2002).

If the administrative costs to FILP for issuing bonds to obtain funds to lend to local governments is less than directly subsidizing local borrowing, this program is justified in terms of cost. However, the extent to which local governments have been subsidized in this way has not been examined closely in deciding policy. If financing at a below-market interest rate by the central government is justified in terms of cost, after showing clearly how much of a grant element is involved, it is desirable to decide on a policy clearly showing the income redistribution effect.

Another important problem in local government finance is that, given how local government bonds are handled, it is difficult for the interest rate to become a signal of the financial condition of the local government.

5.3 *Local Government Solvency*

If a local government in Japan has been unable to curtail expenditures or ensure revenues, funds available for payments could fall short in the ordinary account. Under Japan's local government fiscal system, this situation takes the form of a net-balance deficit, which is the difference between the fiscal year's expenditures and revenue, after adjusting for items that should be carried over to the next fiscal year. This means it differs from the actual cash available for payments. When the size of a year-end net-balance deficit is small, payments for that year can nonetheless be completed by applying revenue properly attributable to the next fiscal year but already received. In such a case, the local government is technically insolvent but, because it is not illiquid it can continue to make payments. The time it takes to put receipts and expenditures in order and close the books after the fiscal year ends facilitates this.

However, when the scale of deficits is large, payments fall into arrears unless enough credit is provided to make good on these payments. Under the system of Local Bond Permits, local governments cannot issue deficit-covering bonds. In addition, local governments have to obtain advance permission to issue any bonds, which takes time. As a result, except to the extent there is unused authorization for bond issue, a net deficit cannot be made up by issuing local bonds.

Where the deficit is considerable, the problem is usually dealt with by applying provisions of the Special Measures Act for Promoting Local Fiscal Reconstruction. But this law provides for only limited fiscal support, such as limiting the issue of local bonds or subsidizing interest on temporary borrowing with a special Local Allocation Tax grant.

5.4 *Government Guarantees*

It is important to note that the central government does not explicitly guarantee local bonds legally. Rather, the central government simply contends that it guarantees the cash flow of local governments. However, the cash flow from the central government to local governments is not entirely secure because budgets are drawn up for just a single fiscal year. Under the Trinity Reform, the cash flows of some local governments will not be subsidized by the central government to the extent they have been in the past.

A similar situation exists in regards to local governments and the local public corporations and joint public-private ventures to which they have made capital contributions. In particular, the Financial Services Agency issued a manual for use in the financial examinations of local governments and public corporations in July 1999. The manual strictly states that a corporation to which a local government has made a capital contribution must be treated in the same manner as a general borrower; this means there is no implicit guarantee of local public-corporation debt. In April 2000 the former Ministry of Construction and former Ministry of Home Affairs jointly issued a notification that local governments must provide debt guarantees against the new long-term borrowing of a corporation to which the local government had made a capital contribution. This change was apparently done to address the reluctance of private financial institutions to lend to local public corporations because a number of them had fallen into financial difficulties. Government financial institutions had been unable to borrow funds easily unless local governments gave binding guarantees of the debt of the local public corporations to which the government financial institutions had lent. This is something local governments had not previously done.

Although debt guarantees by local governments regarding local public corporations may not have been offered in a formally legal way, there are indications that local governments did offer an implied guarantee to persuade private financial institutions. The local government was not directly obligated because the local public corporations and joint public-private ventures had not borrowed money in the name of the local government. Rather, as with the central government case, the guarantee was premised on ensuring cash flow to the actual borrower. When local governments failed to maintain cash flow, forsaking the implicit guarantee, private financial institutions were forced to waive debt. Although the debtor is not the local government itself, there has been a great effect on the revenue and expenditure of local governments.

Thus, the central government has used promised cash flow as an implied guarantee of local government debt, and local governments have done the same as regards local public-corporation debt. In both cases, the cash flows have proven to be insecure. Events suggest that, as sincere as the local governments may have been, when poverty comes in at the door, love flies out the window: the stopping of cash flows led to the non-payment of some obligations.

5.5 *The Mediation Law*

Debt restructuring under specific legal mediation applies to a local public corporation that is insolvent (illiquid) rather than completely bankrupt (having liabilities greater than its assets). However, as a legal concept, bankruptcy is simply being unable to pay one's debts as these come due. Because the specific mediation law applies to corporations that cannot meet their obligations on their own, it can be said that proceedings under the law are bankruptcy proceedings as a matter of fact.

Since 2003, a number of local public corporations—mostly prefectural housing corporations—have in effect declared bankruptcy by petitioning for debt restructuring under the specific mediation law. Specific cases were Hokkaido Housing Corporation and three joint public-private ventures of Osaka city in June 2003; Wakayama Land Development Corporation in July 2003; Nagasaki Housing Corporation in January 2004; and Chiba Housing Corporation in February 2004. Joint public-private ventures are sometimes referred to as "third-sector" companies.

Japan's ongoing economic difficulties have affected the revenues of local governments, with the result that they have been forced to cut back financial support of local public corporations and the joint public-private ventures. The situation is such that more local governments may petition for specific mediation proceedings.

Speed is important in debt restructuring, and specific mediation proceedings are generally quicker than a conventional bankruptcy proceeding. In cases so far, special mediation has taken about six months from the time of petition. However, this result may depend on the nature and results of any negotiations among the parties before a bankruptcy. A bankruptcy filing typically represents a failure of such discussions to resolve the problems, so the appropriate comparison may be between special mediation and pre-bankruptcy negotiations.

Special mediation also allows debt forgiveness to be negotiated with greater flexibility than in a bankruptcy. Yet this flexibility has an important drawback; very often it means that local governments employ an "ability to absorb losses" principle and seek greater debt forgiveness from healthy creditors than from others. In fact, some private financial institutions have been asked to waive debt or to reduce interest payments exceeding 50% of the subject debt. There also is a possibility that settlement choices are fewer in special mediation in that creditors cannot force the local government to increase taxes. But the same applies to debt restructuring under civil rehabilitation law or voluntary negotiation.

5.6 *Bankruptcy*

The assurance of revenue from the central government is taken to mean that local governments will not become bankrupt. However, detailed study of the actual budgeting process suggests that "the implied government guarantee" is not enough to prevent the "bankruptcy" of a local government. It is not desirable for a local government to become bankrupt, but the possibility exists.

There are no laws in which the "bankruptcy" of a local government is explicitly defined. The Special Measures Act for Promoting Local Fiscal

Reconstruction, which was enacted in 1955 and has not been basically amended, addresses some of the issues, but there are many things it does not provide for, so the existing law needs to be supplemented. Doi (2004b) investigates the prerequisites for building a new system of law relating to bankruptcy of local governments.

The first step is to reduce the risk of bankruptcy by setting restrictions on the issuance of bonds so as to ensure their redemption. Whether it is good to impose a balanced-budget rule like that used by state governments in the United States is not self-evident. However, a rule prohibiting reduction of the primary budget deficit by issuing local bonds is appropriate.

Furthermore, the new system should make reasonable increases in local taxes a requirement when a local government seeks postponement or reduction of interest or principal payments. Just what "reasonable" means will be left to case-by-case determination. However, the increase should be made in line with the benefit principle as much as possible. Governments allowed debt relief will be required to give priority to repayment of existing debt and face restraints on future bond issuance.

5.7 The Japan Finance Corporation for Municipal Enterprises

The Japan Finance Corporation for Municipal Enterprises supplies long-term funds at a below-market rate to municipal public enterprises managed by local governments. These include water supply, sewage, transportation, hospitals, and public housing, plus other borrowers that carry on operations deeply involved in life of residents. In addition, as part of the Local Bond Plan, the Japan Finance Corporation for Municipal Enterprises makes loans to local governments. Because the underlying obligation is made by the local government, the Japan Finance Corporation for Municipal Enterprises in effect substitutes for them in the bond market.

The Japan Finance Corporation for Municipal Enterprises raises the greater part its loanable funds by issuing bonds, including government-guaranteed and non-guaranteed FILP agency bonds. Most of these are 10-year bonds. Municipally operated gambling associations—which operate local horse, bicycle, motorcycle, and speedboat racing—also make payments to the Japan Finance Corporation for Municipal Enterprises.

If financing by the central government at a subsidized interest rate is justified, then it is desirable to clearly show the income redistribution effects, using the grant element described earlier, and to have an overall policy coordinating these effects. This would make the enterprise-related operations carried on by Japan Finance Corporation for Municipal Enterprises meaningless.

However there is a role for the Japan Finance Corporation for Municipal Enterprises. Since fiscal year 2001, FILP has lent funds to local governments, in principle at the same interest rate FILP pays on its bonds. The Japan Finance Corporation for Municipal Enterprises can be transformed into a joint-issuer of local-government bonds, thus eliminating borrowing from FILP. To the extent this increases the cost of the funds, the central government can provide explicit subsidies as part of the same comprehensive co-ordination of income distribution effects discussed earlier. In addition, it can jointly issue bonds with the public enterprises it lends to now. As a joint issuer, the Japan Finance Corporation for Municipal Enterprises should be divided into independent regional entities.

6 Conclusion

A good deal of Japan's record debt level is attributable to the actions taken by government financial institutions and special public corporations, as well as local public corporations. Because of the way these activities are funded, there is essentially no overall control of their deficits, and thus of their ultimate cost imposed upon Japanese taxpayers. Such open-ended liability is intolerable. This chapter has looked carefully at the government financial institutions to provide answers to the question of how to reform them. It has also offered some proposals regarding the related matter of the financial relationship between different levels of government. Several steps are necessary for reforming government financial institutions.

First is clarifying their role. All the government financial institutions should have their activities significantly curtailed, and some should be closed completely. This is in keeping with the recognition (and Koizumi cabinet policy) that economic efficiency and equity are best achieved when markets are allowed to do most tasks in allocating resources. But not all tasks, because a place for government financial institutions and their inherent subsidies does exist. One justification for government financial institutions is that they can be "doubly complementary": they can enhance both private intermediation and the functioning of capital markets. From such viewpoints, the important aims of reforming the government financial institutions are clarifiying the assigned roles between the private and public sectors, increasing the business efficiency of government financial institutions, and restraining the fiscal burden that government financial institutions impose on taxpayers.

Second, the soft-budget constraint problem must be fundamentally settled to accomplish these goals. As part of hardening budget constraints, it is important to establish a bankruptcy law covering the government financial institutions and local governments. The absence of the possibility of bankruptcy causes a soft-budget constraint problem and worsens the public finances. Agencies that continue to exist as government financial institutions should be reorganized with limits on future capital contributions. To this end, it is effective for government financial institutions to change into "state-owned limited companies" with a reduced scope of operations.

Third, to the extent subsidies are deemed appropriate for a government financial institution's activities, these should be budgeted in advance as part of an explicit, comprehensive redistribution policy for which policymakers can be held accountable. Policy regarding income redistribution should be set by the Diet, as it is a political matter.

There is a need for differentiated policies with regard to public involvement and competition. In the area of their business where government financial institutions compensate for market failure, public involvement is required, though the central government has to strictly monitor and restrain the operation. At the same time, it is necessary to reduce government intervention in those business areas that can be managed by private enterprises. Thus, it is better to confine government financial institutions to a smaller scope by limiting their business operations to instances of market failure, and to have them withdraw from businesses that private enterprises are now engaged in, than simply to privatize them. In some cases they should be terminated.

It is important to stress that simple privatization of government financial institutions could place them at an advantage to private enterprises in some ways, and at a significant disadvantage in other ways (especially in terms of staff not experienced in dealing with credit analysis and market discipline). In many cases the objective of reforming the government financial institutions can be better attained by restraining the business of public organizations in order to allow private companies to operate freely, rather than by simply transforming public organizations into private ones. In other words, privatization is not the same as reform—and in specific cases neither action is necessary nor sufficient to achieve the needed reforms.

There is widespread recognition that the complex and opaque system of government financial intermediation is in need of reform, and the Koizumi government has taken steps to achieve that end. The general and institutional-specific reforms proposed here, if adopted, will help the sound development of Japan's financial system and the orderly operation of its public finances.

Acknowledgments

The author thanks Professors Mitsuhiro Fukao, Takeo Hoshi, Toshihiro Ihori, Takatoshi Ito, Hugh Patrick, and Naoyuki Yoshino, as well as participants of the US-Japan Conference on the Solutions for the Japanese Economy held on June 19–20, 2004; a workshop held at the Ministry of Finance; and seminars at Tokyo Center for Economic Research and Institute of Statistical Research for helpful comments. I also thank Larry Meissner for careful editing. Any remaining errors are my own.

References

Cargill, Thomas and Naoyuki Yoshino. 2000. The Postal Savings System, Fiscal Investment and Loan Program, and Modernization of Japan's Financial System. In *Crisis and Change in the Japanese Financial System* 201–30, editors Takeo Hoshi and Hugh Patrick. New York: Kluwer Academic Publishers.

______. 2003. *Postal Savings and Fiscal Investment in Japan*. Oxford: Oxford University Press.

Council to Study on Future Modalities of Three Postal Businesses. 2002. *Final Report*. (In Japanese)

Doi, Takero. 2002. The System and Role of Local Bonds Permits in Japan. In *Government Deficit and Fiscal Reform in Japan* 121–51, editors Ihori, T. and M. Sato. New York: Kluwer Academic Publishers.

______. 2004a. "A Missing Link in Decentralization Reform in Japan: Trinity Reform Package." PRI Discussion Paper Series 04A-04. Policy Research Institute, Ministry of Finance, the Government of Japan.

______. 2004b. Local government bonds and a scheme for bankruptcy of local governments. *Financial Review* 71: 5–40.

Doi, Takero and Takeo Hoshi. 2003. Paying for the FILP. In *Structural Impediments to Growth in Japan* 37–69, editors Magnus Blomström, Jennifer Corbett, Fumio Hayashi, and Anil Kashyap. Chicago: University of Chicago Press.

Fukao, Mitsuhiro. 2003. Financial sector profitability and double gearing. In *Structural Impediments to Growth in Japan* 3–35, editors Magnus Blomström, Jennifer Corbett, Fumio Hayashi, and Anil Kashyap. Chicago: University of Chicago Press.

Hoshi, Takeo. 2003. "Road to state-owned narrow bank." *Keizai Kyoshitsu*, Nihon Keizai Shimbun, January 24 morning edition.

Hoshi, Takeo and Anil Kashyap. 2000. The Japanese Banking Crisis: Where did it Come from and How will it End? In *NBER Macroeconomics Annual 1999* 129–201, editors Bernanke, Ben and Julio Rotemberg. Cambridge, MA: MIT Press.

Inukai, Hideki, Tetsutaka Kawamura, Yuka Niwa, Masashi Miyazawa, and Makito Watanabe. 2001. Issues on privatization of the three postal businesses. In *Deflation and Financial System Reform*, editor Mitsuhiro Fukao. Tokyo: Japan Center for Economic Research.

Iwamoto, Yasushi. 2001. Japan's FILP. *Economic Review* 52(1): 2–15.

______. 2002. The Fiscal Investment and Loan Program in Transition. *Journal of the Japanese and International Economies* 16(4): 583–604.

______. 2003. Accelerate a privatization procedure of Government Financial Institutions excluding financing to small and medium enterprises. *Keizai Kyoshitsu*, Nihon Keizai Shimbun, September 11, morning edition.

______. 2004. Social benefit of Government Financial Institutions. *Public Debt Management and Government Financial Intermediation*, 81–97. Japanese Bankers Association.

Japanese Bankers Association. 2004. *Proposal on Privatization of Postal Services and the Future of Postal Saving*. February 3.

Kornai, Janos. 1979. Resource-constrained versus demand-constrained system. *Econometrica* 47(4): 801–819.

Ministry of Agriculture, Forestry, and Fisheries. 2002. *Food, Agriculture, and Village White Paper*. Government of Japan.

Ministry of Finance. 2003. *FILP Report 2003*. Government of Japan. (available at http://www.mof.go.jp/zaito/English/Zaito2003.html)

Ministry of Internal Affairs and Communications. 2003. *Policy Evaluation Report on Supply of Public Funds by Government Financial Institutions*. Government of Japan.

Mitsui, Kiyoshi. 2004. Securitization and roles of the government. *Public Debt Management and Government Financial Intermediation* 99–109. Japanese Bankers Association.

Mitsui, Kiyoshi and Kiyoshi Ota editors. 1995. *Productivity of Social Capital and Government Financial Intermediation*, Nihon Hyoron Sha

Nishigaki, N. 2003. *Government Financial Intermediation under Deregulation*. Ochanomizu Shobo Inc.

Okina, Yuri. 1999. Privatization of public organizations. *Japan Research Review*, 11–44. June.

______. 2000. Recent developments surrounding Japan's Postal Savings business and its future position in the financial system. *Japan Research Review*, 14–42. July.

Seko, Miki. 1998. *Economic Analysis of Land and Housing*, Sobun Sha.

Takezawa, Yasuko, Katsumi Matsuura, and Masahiro Hori. 2004. "Facilitation of Funds and Small Business Failures." *ESRI Discussion Paper Series* 87.

Yamamoto, H. 2002. Bankruptcy of Special Public Corporations. In *Laws for Aid of Civil Affairs*, Second Edition, editors Inoue, H., Y. Sagami, S. Sato, and H. Nakajima. Horitsu Bunka Sha.

Table 6.A1
Government Financial Institutions Loans and Discounts Outstanding, 1985–2003

Fiscal year	GHLC	NLFC	JFS	JASMEC	AFC	JFM	ODFC	DBJ	JBIC	SCB	Total
1985	25,001.5	5,668.8	5,249.0	316.9	5,156.4	9,669.1	784.8	8,532.5	9,201.6	8,235.1	77,815.7
1986	26,908.3	5,719.9	5,080.9	327.2	5,170.2	10,391.1	809.2	8,625.7	9,229.6	8,806.8	81,068.9
1987	29,569.5	5,841.6	5,085.9	355.5	5,254.1	11,117.5	826.2	8,823.7	9,361.3	9,332.8	85,568.1
1988	33,114.4	6,233.8	5,532.9	373.1	5,228.0	11,760.1	861.4	9,292.3	9,998.7	9,750.3	92,145.0
1989	37,007.5	6,926.1	6,625.3	388.0	5,251.3	12,409.6	923.6	9,858.6	11,034.8	10,321.4	100,746.2
1990	41,119.9	7,683.7	7,354.1	411.0	5,291.3	12,846.3	1,014.8	10,587.8	12,579.8	11,053.5	109,942.2
1991	44,338.7	8,287.5	7,849.4	428.0	5,321.5	13,371.6	1,118.3	11,689.3	14,404.5	11,382.9	118,191.7
1992	48,536.2	8,994.6	8,440.3	446.0	5,317.6	14,032.2	1,235.2	13,481.7	15,584.1	11,624.9	127,692.8
1993	55,312.1	9,930.9	9,235.5	498.3	5,244.0	15,150.1	1,378.4	15,357.6	16,438.7	11,847.9	140,393.5
1994	64,496.3	10,354.8	8,893.4	572.0	5,091.3	16,417.5	1,540.8	16,530.5	16,950.2	11,813.0	152,659.8
1995	64,736.2	10,112.9	7,789.4	648.8	4,748.9	17,540.0	1,582.9	16,986.0	17,629.7	11,719.2	153,494.0
1996	70,106.2	9,998.9	7,248.7	630.9	4,490.2	18,912.9	1,629.4	17,301.6	18,102.7	11,427.0	159,848.5
1997	72,440.1	10,249.7	7,215.5	594.3	4,317.8	20,224.4	1,697.4	17,730.3	19,209.5	11,326.4	165,005.4
1998	72,145.0	10,753.9	7,497.0	597.4	4,205.6	21,418.7	1,754.5	19,070.4	21,692.9	11,378.0	170,513.4
1999	74,541.3	10,956.8	7,627.2	584.8	4,081.0	22,534.2	1,772.0	18,754.4	21,521.2	11,169.3	173,542.2
2000	75,922.0	10,861.7	7,618.5	577.7	3,969.7	23,377.0	1,721.2	17,786.4	21,056.6	10,886.6	173,777.4
2001	72,651.6	10,705.3	7,570.2	576.4	3,797.3	24,047.1	1,664.1	16,803.9	21,582.1	10,539.3	169,937.3
2002	67,199.9	10,339.6	7,558.0	511.6	3,640.7	24,524.0	1,600.1	15,790.0	20,994.8	10,090.4	162,249.1
2003	60,594.7	10,069.4	7,592.1	534.9	3,442.9	24,888.4	1,504.9	14,840.8	20,412.6	9,811.1	153,691.8

Fiscal years end March 31 of the following calendar year.
For full names of the government financial institutions see Table 6.1

Source: Ministry of Finance, *Zaisei Kin'yu Tôkei Geppo (Ministry of Finance Statistics Monthly)*, and Bank of Japan, *Financial and Economic Statistics Monthly*, various issues

Table 6.A2
Government Financial Institutions Guarantee Obligation Outstanding, 1985–2003

Fiscal year	NLFC	ODFC	DBJ	JBIC	SCB	CGC[1]	Total
1985	261.6	10.8	137.2	8.1	53.3	9,266.0	9,737.0
1986	238.2	13.0	106.6	9.8	57.8	9,936.4	10,361.8
1987	228.1	15.0	34.0	9.3	51.6	10,773.6	11,111.6
1988	233.5	17.2	26.3	11.6	55.2	12,664.7	13,008.5
1989	248.4	19.1	19.7	13.4	61.0	15,601.2	15,962.8
1990	271.1	22.6	12.2	29.1	64.6	19,478.1	19,877.7
1991	296.1	25.9	6.6	47.1	66.4	21,549.1	21,991.2
1992	331.1	28.9	2.7	54.4	73.7	23,813.3	24,304.1
1993	360.4	34.1	0.6	66.1	68.8	26,175.7	26,705.7
1994	375.2	44.0	0	95.8	67.7	27,475.0	28,057.7
1995	363.0	48.2	0	113.7	68.9	28,624.3	29,218.1
1996	362.1	56.1	0.2	149.4	69.8	29,200.2	29,837.8
1997	365.4	60.3	1.6	201.7	66.3	29,558.9	30,254.2
1998	376.9	58.0	57.7	293.2	66.7	41,991.7	42,844.2
1999	0	54.4	104.1	342.5	66.5	43,019.1	43,586.6
2000	0	48.1	104.6	425.3	69.3	41,459.7	42,107.0
2001	0	42.2	78.1	555.6	69.5	37,012.0	37,757.4
2002	0	0.1	87.7	630.5	83.2	33,188.5	33,990.0
2003	0	0.1	76.8	724.9	96.7	31,102.2	32,000.7

Fiscal years end March 31 of the following calendar year.
For full names of the government financial institutions, see Table 6.1.
[1]Credit Guarantee Corporation

Source: Ministry of Finance, *Zaisei Kin'yu Tôkei Geppo (Ministry of Finance Statistics Monthly)*, and Bank of Japan, Financial and Economic Statistics Monthly, various issues.

7 Fixing Japanese Life Insurance Companies

Mitsuhiro Fukao

In Japan private life insurers comprise the second largest segment of the financial services industry after commercial banking, and in several respects these firms were in even worse condition than the banks in early 2000s. Weak control of interest-rate risk, excessive exposure to the stock market, and very weak supervision by regulatory authorities have contributed to the private life insurers' distress. The life insurance industry's biggest problem, which is most-widely discussed, is the consequence of mispricing their principal products during and immediately after the bubble period. The companies promised high minimum guaranteed returns on cash-value life policies and annuities sold during the 1980s and early 1990s, yet for some years they have been unable to actually earn those returns. The result has been a weakened private life insurance industry that has seen seven companies fail since the mid-1990s. The presence of a government-owned and subsidized competitor, the Postal System's Kampo which is the largest insurance company in the world, has further complicated the situation.

This chapter explores the origin and nature of the various problems facing Japan's private life insurance industry, and proposes policies to restore the life insurers to health. Although since the spring of 2003 the stock market recovery has improved the financial standing of the remaining companies, some are still very weak. In order to stabilize this sector, it is necessary to improve the quality of supervision and management. Government regulators still lack the will and the expertise to supervise large, complicated life insurance companies with significant political power. In addition, the weak corporate governance structure of policyholder-owned, mutual companies has to be significantly improved.

1 Industry Background on Japan's Life Insurance Industry

In the late 1940s, 14 Japanese life insurance companies started business again. At the encouragement of the Occupation authorities, all these firms took the form of mutual companies except for Heiwa, which was organized as a joint stock company. New entries were limited, so there were 20 established domestic companies before the current economic crisis began in the early 1990s. The industry was opened somewhat to foreign firms in the mid-1970s, and significantly more so since the mid-1990s. In 1996, 11 subsidiaries of Japanese non-life insurers started life insurance operations in return for the entry of 6 subsidiaries of Japanese life insurers into non-life insurance businesses. Deregulation also led to the establishment of some completely new companies during the 1990s. As a result of this activity, there were 40 life insurance companies in Japan as of April 2004. [Suzuki (1987, p 241–46) gives an overview of the industry as of the mid-1980s; Adams and Hoshii (1972, p 201–09) offer historical background, including the prewar period, and discuss the 1960s in more detail. In Japanese, Tone and Kitano (1993) and Maehara (2000) provide brief histories of the industry.]

Throughout the postwar period until the early 1990s, life insurers enjoyed fairly good profits due to limited competition under strict regulation and a robust Japanese economy. Competition was limited due to regulations mandating that premiums on similar policies should be virtually the same among companies. However, there were certain competitive elements in insurance policies. Most policies were issued as part of participating plans (because the insurers were mutual companies) and the companies distributed dividends to policyholders. Better-run companies could distribute more dividends than weaker companies, which helped them attract customers. Private insurers now are regulated by the Financial Services Agency (FSA); previously, this was done by the Ministry of Finance (MoF).

Private life insurance companies compete with the government's Postal Life Insurance (Kampo) and JA Kyosai. Kampo is a huge government-run insurer and part of the Postal System that includes Postal Savings; because of the very large number of post offices in Japan Kampo's services are more ubiquitous (and conveniently available) than any other Japanese insurance company or bank. Kampo's policies are explicitly guaranteed by the government, although the maximum coverage is limited by regulation. It is regulated by the Ministry of Public Management, Home Affairs, Posts and Telecommunications, into which the previous regulator, the Ministry of Post and Telecommunications, was merged. Kampo is thus independent of oversight by the regulator of private sector financial institutions. Although Junichiro Koizumi, the Prime Minister, has pledged to privatize the entire postal system, whether this actually takes place is very uncertain given the extremely strong opposition to this policy within Mr Koizumi's own Liberal Democratic Party (for further discussion see Doi's chapter in this volume on privatizing the Postal Savings System).

JA Kyosai is an insurance company run by the politically strong agricultural cooperatives and regulated by the Ministry of Agriculture, Forestry and Fisheries. While private life insurers cannot sell non-life insurance policies directly, JA Kyosai can sell both life and non-life policies. Moreover, agricultural cooperatives also run banks and other businesses that support farmers. Anyone can buy this company's insurance policies by becoming a nominal member of an agricultural cooperative, as actual involvement in agriculture is not a requirement to join these cooperatives.

Since the mid-1990s, the Japanese life insurance industry's financial health has deteriorated significantly, and seven private companies have failed. These failed companies were reorganized and bought by foreign or domestic companies.

As Table 7.1 shows, the 10 survivors of the original 14 postwar life insurance companies still dominate the private-sector part of the business. Only one newcomer (AFLAC) is among the top-10 based on market share of premiums. This chapter concentrates on analyzing the 10 major Japanese companies and Kampo, the Postal System's insurance company.

2 The Life Insurance Business in Japan

In order to understand the problem that Japanese life insurance companies have been facing, it is necessary to understand the basic conditions of the insurance business in Japan.

Until the mid-1990s Japanese life insurance companies primarily sold policies to salaried male workers who wanted to obtain protection for their wives and children. These policies were a package of whole-life insurance and a term-rider that was not renewable beyond 60 or 65 years old, by which time workers had retired. The premium for the term policy was raised periodically (often every five years), but the rate increases were set at the time of the initial contract.

Table 7.1
Japanese Life Insurance Market
Financial Year Ended March 2003

	Gross asset JPY 100 million	Market Share %	Premium JPY 100 million	Market Share %
Major Japanese Companies				
Nihon Life	436,865	12.8	54,207	12.1
Daiichi Life	289,105	8.5	35,621	8.0
Sumitomo Life	219,115	6.4	26,989	6.0
Meiji Life	162,431	4.8	21,847	4.9
Yasuda Life	94,841	2.8	12,953	2.9
Mitsui Life	76,692	2.2	9,530	2.1
Asahi Life	65,968	1.9	7,686	1.7
Taiyo Life	65,280	1.9	8,879	2.0
Daido Life	60,072	1.8	9,894	2.2
Fukoku Life	47,329	1.4	7,626	1.7
Sub total	1,517,698	44.4	195,232	43.6
Other Japanese Companies				
Orix Life	6,532	0.2	1,213	0.3
Sony Life	19,819	0.6	4,916	1.1
Sompo Japan Himawari Life	5,120	0.1	1,828	0.4
Tokyo Marine Nichido Anshin Life*	11,610	0.3	4,034	0.9
Sub total	43,081	1.3	11,991	2.7
Foreign Companies				
ING Life	6,239	0.2	4,611	1.0
Axa Life	3,402	0.1	1,815	0.4
Axa Group Life	24,452	0.7	6,186	1.4
GE Edison Life (former Toho Life)	23,149	0.7	2,833	0.6
Gibraltar Life (former Kyoei Life)	35,932	1.1	3,848	0.9
Hartford Life	2,954	0.1	2,450	0.5
Prudential Life	8,220	0.2	2,599	0.6
Manulife (former Daihyaku Life)	9,232	0.3	1,440	0.3
American Family Life (AFLAC)	40,550	1.2	8,328	1.9
Alico Japan	18,415	0.5	5,993	1.3
AIG Star Life (former Chiyoda Life)	17,775	0.5	1,996	0.4
Sub total	190,320	5.6	42,099	9.4
Postal Life (Kampo)	1,257,494	36.8	143,117	32.0
Japan Agricultural Cooperative (JA Kyosai)	409,443	12.0	55,252	12.3
Total	3,418,036	100.0	447,691	100.0

Source: Standard & Poor's (2004) and individual disclosure materials.
(1) Major Japanese companies, other Japanese companies, and foreign companies includes 26 companies that are rated by Standard & Poor's and AIG Star. These 26 companies covers about 96 % of total premium of the market excluding Kampo and JA Kyosai.
(2) Tokyo Marine Anshin and Nichido Life merged in October 2003 to create Tokyo Marine Nichido Anshin Life.
(3) JA Kyosai's full English name is "National Mutual Insurance Federation of Agricultural Cooperatives" and also known as Zenkyoren. JA Kyosai provides non-life insurace coverages. About one-third of its gross asset corresponds to non-life policies.

The annual premiums received by life insurers are used for three purposes: (1) the costs of operating the company, (2) the insurance (death) benefits paid out during the year, and (3) reserves for the future protection of policyholders. While the first two costs are paid out by the company, the third is the savings component of the policy, and it is invested by the company. The companies set the premium charged in reference to a fixed minimum return from that investment. In other words, the premium charged is reduced by the amount of estimated future returns from the savings component of outstanding insurance contracts.

Most life insurance policies have been participating plans because the companies are organized as mutuals (owned by policyholders). The companies have to pay dividends to policyholders when the premiums collected exceed the actual cost of discharging their contractual obligations. A minimum return is usually not explicitly promised to policyholders, but this commitment is implicit in the insurance policy that describes the insurance premium, the surrender value on cancellation, the maturity insurance amount, and so forth.

The maturity of most Japanese life insurance policies is quite long and insurers have to manage risk for adverse changes in mortality rates and interest rates, so the guaranteed rate of return and mortality rates are set conservatively. In practice, this means the minimum returns are kept low and the mortality rates are kept high. These basic rates were in fact set by regulators at the Ministry of Finance. Because of the safety margins, even uncompetitive life insurance companies could earn some profits and, after deducting operating expenses, most of these profits were distributed to policyholders. However, this system involved a perverse incentive for the management to increase operating expenses. Moreover, because the distributable profit is measured by historical cost accounting, firm managers could retain a large amount of unrealized capital gains in their equity portfolio and avoid distributions to policyholders.

Until the mid-1970s, the guaranteed minimum return for new policies was 4%, which was lower than the one-year bank-deposit rate at the time. However, when Japan experienced a rising inflation rate and higher nominal interest rates in 1972–74, many large companies were accused of profiteering by raising prices. Life insurers were no exception and these firms faced strong political pressure to reduce premiums. In this atmosphere, Kampo raised its minimum return to 5.5% in 1975 and private companies followed this lead in 1976 because they could not ignore the pricing policy of the giant postal insurance system.

In the mid-1980s the minimum rate was increased again, to 6%, and remained there until 1990, when it dropped back to 5.5%. As the Bank of Japan repeatedly cut interest rates in the 1990s, insurers also lowered policy rates, bringing the minimum return to 1.5% in 2001. (Kampo maintained slightly higher rates until 1994.) Despite the rapid cut in guaranteed rates on new life policies, the average insurance rate guaranteed on all policies did not fall rapidly. This is because most policies had long lives, were sold as installment plans, and the insurance companies had guaranteed a certain minimum return on all future cash inflows on the polices. For example, if a person signed a contract for a life-time annuity or whole-life insurance policy in 1992, the insurance companies guaranteed 5.5% on all payments. Clearly, a policyholder has had strong incentives not to cancel a policy.

Table 7.2 shows the average guaranteed return of the 10 major Japanese life insurance companies for fiscal 2001 and 2002; later data are not available. The return on fixed-rate contracts was about 4% in fiscal 2002 when 10-year bond rate yields were less than 2%. The floating rate contracts are mostly group annuity plans with yields mostly 1% to 1.5% in fiscal 2001 and 2002. While the share of floating rate contracts differs among companies, the average is about one quarter of their total reserves.

Table 7.2
Average Guaranteed Returns, in percents

2001	2002	Change[1]	2002 ex float[2]	Company
3.70	3.49	–0.21	4.16	Nippon
3.59	3.38	–0.21	4.13	Daiichi
3.60	3.40	–0.20	4.00	Sumitomo
3.20	3.06	–0.14	3.93	Meiji
3.20	3.07	–0.13	4.42	Yasuda
3.63	3.62	–0.01	4.35	Mitsui
4.00	4.17	0.17	4.25	Asahi
3.62	3.17	–0.45	3.39	Taiyo
3.08	2.86	–0.22	3.87	Daido
3.15	2.92	–0.23	4.12	Fukoku

Data are for fiscal years. Firms are listed by asset size.
[1]Change from 2001 to 2002.
[2]Guaranteed return excluding floating-rate contracts.

Source: Fukao and Japan Center for Economic Research (2004a).

2.1 *Negative Carry*

Because Japanese life insurance companies did not invest in long-term assets that matched the long duration of their liabilities, these firms started to incur losses in the second half of the 1990s. Generally, the average duration on the asset side has been about 5 years, while the average on the liability side has been 15 to 20 years. The gap between the return earned and the return promised is called negative carry (*gyakuzaya*). Most Japanese life insurance companies have been unable to cover the negative carry from profits elsewhere in their business, and some quickly depleted their capital. On the other hand, Kampo, JA Kyosai, Daido Life, and Taiyo Life did not sell very long-term contracts. These firms sold endowment plans with lives of 10 years or less, so their term mismatch has been limited.

Table 7.3 shows the market-value return ("fair-value return" in Financial Accounting Standards Board terms) on the assets of the 10 major life insurers. The annual return over the seven-year period ending March 2004 was only 0.81%. In spite of the massive negative carry, all 10 companies have reported a positive "basic profit" (*kiso rieki*) because this concept of profits does not take account of most capital gains and losses in equity and foreign-security portfolios. About 15% of these companies' assets were invested in stocks in the late 1990s, so until the spring of 2003 they incurred heavy losses due to falling equity prices.

2.2 *Profitability*

Table 7.4 decomposes the economic profit of the 10 major companies based on estimated market-value accounting. This table shows that in 2000–02 the companies would have earned about ¥3 trillion a year if there had been no negative carry. With negative carry, they averaged over ¥2.4 trillion in annual losses. In 2003, however, they earned ¥3.2 trillion reflecting the sharp recovery of stock prices.

The profitability of a life insurance policy depends on the three following factors:

1. The gap between assumed and actual operating costs;
2. The gap between assumed and actual death rates;
3. The spread between the assumed and actual rate of return.

Table 7.3
Market Value Return on Asset

%

	FY 1997	FY 1998	FY 1999	FY 2000	FY 2001	FY 2002	FY 2003	7-year Average**
Nihon	1.69	1.29	5.04	–1.00	–1.27	–0.89	5.12	1.39
Daiichi	0.51	2.09	4.73	–0.65	–1.43	–0.50	4.62	1.31
Sumitomo	0.25	1.33	3.94	–0.60	–1.07	0.18	2.71	0.95
Meiji	0.13	0.64	2.43	0.58	–1.04	–0.38	Merged to	0.39
Yasuda	0.99	1.39	4.73	–1.03	–0.21	–0.76	Meiji-Yasuda	0.83
Meiji-Yasuda*	0.43	0.90	3.26	0.00	–0.74	–0.52	4.04	1.04
Mitsui	2.46	0.18	4.94	–1.74	–1.19	–0.72	1.78	0.63
Asahi	0.90	1.19	4.40	–1.76	–1.92	–0.68	3.41	0.33
Taiyo	0.03	1.13	3.89	0.45	–0.55	1.11	3.98	1.00
Daido	2.35	2.27	2.82	0.58	0.08	1.57	3.55	1.61
Fukoku	0.29	2.72	3.52	1.06	–0.61	–0.47	4.47	1.07
Average	0.96	1.42	4.04	–0.41	–0.92	–0.15	3.74	0.81

	FY 2000	FY 2001	FY 2002	FY 2003
JA Kyosai	—	0.54	5.17	N.A.
Kampo	2.63	1.11	1.20	1.55

Source: Fukao and Japan Center for Economic Research (2004a).
Note:
*Pre-merger data for Maiji-Yasuda is the weighted average of Meiji and Yasuda.
**Average for Meiji and Yasuda is 6 years until FY 2003; when they merged.

Table 7.4
Economic Profit of Life Insurance Companies
Total of Ten Major Companies

			Billion yen, Percent	
	FY 2000	FY 2001	FY 2002	FY 2003
Gross Profit from Insurance (A)	6,171 (3.72)	5,997 (3.79)	5,663 (3.73)	5,478 (3.59)
Operating Expenses (B)	2,853 (1.72)	3,023 (1.91)	2,669 (1.76)	2,682 (1.61)
Negative Carry (C)	–5,753 (–3.47)	–6,209 (–3.92)	–4,573 (–3.01)	2,125 (1.39)
Economic Profit (A - B + C) before tax and dividend	–26,342 (–1.46)	–3,260 (–2.06)	–1,613 (–1.06)	4,921 (3.22)

Note: Numbers in the parentheses are the ratios against gross asset.
Source: Fukao and Japan Center for Economic Research (2004a).

Assumed operating costs and death rates tend to be higher than the actual rates, so a limited negative spread between the actual return and assumed return can be covered by the positive gaps in death rates and operating costs. For example, Japanese life insurance companies are required to use the standardized 1996 death rate table for regulatory accounting purposes. Because death rates are gradually falling in Japan, the long time lag will generate a profit margin. However, for many large Japanese life insurance companies, the negative gap in asset returns has been too big to cover, which means that capital has been depleted. Some companies were operating with little or no equity by the late 1990s. When they finally filed bankruptcy, most were deeply insolvent, as will be discussed later.

Reflecting the continuing negative carry, the net asset position of most Japanese life insurers eroded fairly rapidly until early 2003, as shown in Table 7.5. This table also shows the capital-asset ratio and the amount of deferred-tax assets within net assets at the end of March 2003 and March 2004. The net assets of some companies had been declining fairly rapidly. Although Nippon Life has maintained a capital ratio of more than 10%, Mitsui Life's ratio is less than 2%. Moreover, weaker companies show a relatively high deferred-tax asset, which is the net present value of the tax benefit created by the carry-forward loss rules. Under Japanese tax rules, no carry-back loss is allowed, and carry-forward is limited to five years. Therefore, unless a company expects taxable income in the near future, the company will not realize the value of the deferred-tax asset.

Table 7.5
Net Asset of Japanese Life-Insurance Companies

Billion yen, %

					Mar-03					Mar-04			
	Mar-00	Net asset Mar-01	Mar-02	Mar-03	Gross Asset Billion yen	Net Asset Ratio %	DTA Billion yen	Net Asset Ratio Excluding DTA %	Net asset Mar-04	Gross Asset Billion yen	Net Asset Ratio %	DTA Billion yen	Net Asset Ratio Excluding DTA %
Nippon	8,274	7,211	5,968	5,077	43,686	11.6	303.0	10.9	6,608	45,271	14.6	749	12.9
y-y change		−13	−17	−15					30				
Daiichi	3,940	3,151	2,410	2,062	28,911	7.1	282.0	6.2	3,103	29,653	10.5	422	9.0
y-y change		−20	−24	−14					50				
Sumitomo	1,930	1,520	980	844	21,911	3.9	262.0	2.7	1,178	21,124	5.6	250	4.4
y-y change		−21	−36	−14					40				
Meiji	2,170	1,937	1,628	1,362	16,243	8.4	248.0	6.9	} Merged to become Meiji-Yasuda Life				
y-y change		−11	−16	−16									
Yasuda	1,104	855	702	590	9,484	6.2	151.0	4.6					
y-y change		−23	−18	−16									
Meiji-Yasuda				1,952	25,727	7.6	399.0	6.0	2687.7	25329.8	10.6	455.3	8.8
y-y change									38				
Asahi	1,051	571	394	236	6,597	3.6	99.0	2.1	350	6,447	5.4	120	3.6
y-y change		−46	−31	−40					48				
Mitsui	730	379	278	118	7,669	1.5	77.0	0.5	211	7,509	2.8	80	1.8
y-y change		−48	−27	−58					79				
Taiyo	820	680	456	341	6,528	5.2	79.0	4.0	452	6,410	7.1	73	5.9
y-y change		−17	−33	−25					33				
Daido	728	619	471	515	6,007	8.6	52.0	7.7	633	6,018	10.5	91	9.0
y-y change		−15	−24	9					23				
Fukoku	522	471	375	316	4,733	6.7	52.0	5.6	474	5,005	9.5	64	8.2
y-y change		−10	−20	−16					50				

Note: DTA = Deferred Tax Asset; changes in percent.
Source: Fukao and Japan Center for Economic Research (2004b).

Another important factor that decides the fate of Japan's life insurance companies is the outstanding amount of insurance contracts, and the premiums being received, which are shown in Tables 7.6-1 and 7.6-2. Over the four years ending March 2003, contracts declined by 13.5% for the 10 major firms as a single group. In the case of Asahi, the drop was almost 23%; the only increases posted were at three of the smaller companies, with Fukoku's 4.4% the greatest increase.

Premiums received dropped even more than insurance contracts. With the falling income of Japanese workers under deflation and the declining need for traditional life insurance policies among an aging population, the sale of new contracts has been stagnant. A husband's death benefit is important when children are small and his wife has no income. As his children grow up and his wife enters the labor market, insurance policies with large death benefits are no longer necessary. The most-fragile companies, Mitsui Life and Asahi Life, have also experienced a rapid cancellation of existing contracts. The received premiums of these two companies declined more than 30%.

The Japanese life insurance industry's dire situation became brighter in 2003. Because of the sharp recovery of Japanese stock prices in fiscal year 2003, the net assets of life insurance companies recovered some-

Table 7.6-1
Outstanding Personal Insurance Contracts
Index Mar-99=100

	Mar-99	Mar-00	Mar-01	Mar-02	Mar-03	Mar-04
Nihon	100	97	94	90	87	82
Daiichi	100	97	95	92	89	85
Sumitomo	100	98	94	90	85	79
Meiji	100	94	93	90	84	Merged to
Yasuda	100	97	95	91	86	Meiji-Yasuda
Meiji-Yasuda	100	95	93	90	85	78
Mitsui	100	95	90	83	79	73
Asahi	100	95	91	83	77	68
Taiyo	100	99	98	100	103	114
Daido	100	100	99	99	100	100
Fukoku	100	101	103	104	104	104
Total	100	97	94	90	87	81

Source: Fukao and Japan Center for Economic Research (2004).
*Pre-merger data for Maiji-Yasuda is the total of Meiji and Yasuda.

Table 7.6-2
Insurance Premium Received Personal Contracts
Index Mar-99=100

	Mar-99	Mar-00	Mar-01	Mar-02	Mar-03	Mar-04
Nihon	100	90	88	87	87	80
Daiichi	100	88	85	86	89	78
Sumitomo	100	93	88	83	79	75
Meiji	100	89	85	82	81 }	Merged to
Yasuda	100	93	89	86	84 }	Meiji-Yasuda
Meiji-Yasuda	100	90	86	83	82	74
Mitsui	100	89	84	75	70	65
Asahi	100	90	85	74	62	57
Taiyo	100	91	85	80	74	67
Daido	100	97	97	94	96	91
Fukoku	100	91	91	89	90	84
Total	100	91	87	84	82	75

Source: Fukao and Japan Center for Economic Research (2004a).
*Pre-merger data for Meiji-Yasuda is the total of Meiji and Yasuda.

what. The Nikkei 225 index rose from 7973 at the end of March 2003 to 11,715 at the end of March 2004 so the capital-asset ratio rebounded by about 3 percentage points. However, these companies still have large amounts of high-yield debt. Unless these firms can earn more than a 2% market-value return, their capital will continue to erode.

3 Origins of the Problems

This section further examines three of the four fundamental factors that caused the crisis in the Japanese life insurance industry during the late 1990s. The first two problems, the design of insurance policies and the absence of asset-liability management, are discussed together. The third factor, the weak governance of mutual companies, is then taken up. A fourth factor, supervision, is discussed in the following section.

3.1 The Failure of Asset-Liability Management

Japan's life insurance companies have mostly sold whole-life insurance policies with a term rider, 10- to 20-year endowment plans, and personal pension policies. In addition, they have sold term policies to corporate employees as group plans. Except for the group life policies, most contracts have involved a long-term saving component. In other words, prior to the 1990s economic downturn the life insurance companies expected to earn more than the guaranteed minimum return over the contracted periods.

To properly hedge such contracts, the insurers had to invest in long-term securities such as 20-year government bonds. Some foreign companies in Japan did carry out such a strategy and effectively hedged the interest rate risk. However, most Japanese companies did not hedge their risks. There are several possible reasons why this did not take place.

First, these firms could not imagine a situation in which their investment assumptions were excessively optimistic. Certainly, nobody in the 1980s expected Japan would suffer economic stagnation and deflation in the 1990s, resulting in devastated equity portfolios and very low interest rates. Life insurers have a built-in margin of about 2 percentage points on policies after paying operating expenses, but this spread did not provide enough cushion to absorb the investment losses.

Second, in the 1980s Japan's life insurers had massive unrealized capital gains on their equity portfolios. At the end of 1990, the book value of their stock portfolios was 22% of their ¥127 trillion assets. According to my interviews with industry executives, the market value was about three times the book value. In other words, unrealized gains would have added over 40% to the companies' assets had they been included in the calculation. This was a substantial cushion.

Third, the management structure of Japanese life insurance companies was not designed to manage investment risks well. Fund managers looked at the asset side of their balance sheet and competed with conventional benchmark indicators. Actuaries looked at the reserves and the distribution of surplus to owners of participating policies. Most company directors came from sales, and were ill-prepared to perform asset-liability management at the top level. They did not appreciate the importance of hedging risks.

3.2 *Weak Governance of Mutual Companies*

Most large Japanese life insurers are mutual companies, and the corporate structure of mutual companies may have weakened the governance of these firms. All 10 companies in this data set were originally mutual companies, but some have since reorganized as joint-stock companies:

Daido (April 2002), Taiyo (April 2003), and Mitsui (April 2004). Five of the seven failed life insurance companies also were mutuals; these all reorganized as joint-stock companies after their bankruptcy proceedings.

At Japanese mutual companies, a meeting of representative policyholders elects the board of directors. Representative holders are chosen from all policyholders by a nominating committee. That committee is nominated by the sitting board and ratified by a policyholders meeting. In this circular process, the sitting board has a decisive role. The board nominates the members of the nominating committee and it prepares a short list for representative policyholders. Policyholders get a list of names of representative policyholders and vote for or against their ratification as their representatives. A nominee is removed if more than 10% of policyholders vote "no", which is extremely unlikely. Policyholders are given only the names, prefecture, and profession of the nominees. I am not aware of any rejected nominations from such votes.

Many representative policyholders are top managers of other companies. Often the life insurance company has a significant holding in the stock of the companies of these managers. Many "housewives" among representative holders are married to these managers; the pianist and organist of a theater owned by an insurance company also have been representative holders. Some representative holders bought policies only after being asked to become a representative. In this process, the governance of mutual companies tends to be particularly weak.

Much more broadly, certainly the corporate governance system of Japanese joint-stock companies as a whole is not particularly strong. In many cases, the directors and presidents are selected from senior managers of the company. Major shareholders are often silent because of the extensive cross-shareholdings. Thus, as a consequence governance of Japanese banks is especially weak (see Fukao 1998).

Furthermore, the major private life insurance companies are major shareholders of banks and other listed companies. The very weak governance of life insurers also weakens the governance of other Japanese companies. This means good prudential supervision was even more necessary and important.

3.3 *Options Not Used*

Until a major revision in the law governing the Japanese insurance industry was passed in 1995 and implemented in 1996, the laws to prevent insurance company failures dated to 1939 and were based on German insurance law of that time. Under this legislation, mutual life insurers were 100% equity companies. Theoretically, policyholders were nominal owners of the company. If a company had severe financial problems, it could reduce its insurance obligations to all policyholders through a resolution taken by a representative policyholders' meeting. Most policyholders do not read the articles of incorporation of the insurance company and do not imagine their policies actually constitute an equity stake in the company. Nippon Life has more than 10 million policyholders and most large companies have more than 1 million policyholders. Equityholder governance has little meaning under such circumstances.

Under the old law, the Minister of Finance could issue an executive order to reduce insurance obligations. For example, the Ministry could reduce the guaranteed return of all outstanding policies, but only the future return, not any accrued return or retroactively on paid returns. This power was invoked only once, in 1946, when in order to save life insurance companies in the wake of wartime devastation MoF raised the insurance premiums of existing policyholders. Some policyholders sued the government, saying the action violated the protection of property rights under the Meiji Constitution (effective until May 1947) because the government changed existing private contracts by executive order. The case went to Japan's Supreme Court, which ruled the measure constitutional in 1959. Given strong legal grounds to address the negative-spread issue, the question is why the life insurance companies in the early 1990s, did not use policyholder resolutions or ask MoF to provide relief. Top management may have been too complacent to take actions against their huge interest rate risks, but it is also true that both these escape routes were controversial among experts. The executive-order approach is regarded as unconstitutional by some Japanese jurists, despite the 1959 ruling. (And, there is now a different constitution.) In any case, the 1995 major overhaul of the law repealed these measures.

The 1995 law converted insurance policies from equity contracts to debt contracts. Representative policyholder meetings no longer can reduce benefits by resolution. MoF lost the power to change the contracts by decree. Effectively, the mutual companies were converted from 100% equity companies to ordinary limited-liability companies with small equity. (As discussed later, a 2003 change in the law restores the ability of companies to reduce the guaranteed rate on existing policies.)

With these changes, policyholders are both creditors and residual claimants. The surrender value of policies and the insurance benefits comprise the senior debt of the companies. At the same time, the future profit and retained earnings of mutual life companies are distributed to policyholders of participating plans. When a mutual company wants to reorganize as a joint-stock company, the company has to distribute new shares to policyholders. The distribution is based on the estimated contribution of individual policyholders to the total net assets of the company.

4 Weak Supervision

The life insurance industry's crisis has been exacerbated by the forbearance of its supervisory authorities, previously the Ministry of Finance and now the Financial Services Agency. Both MoF and the FSA have had very strong regulatory power. However, the high officials of these authorities have been very reluctant to use this power. I suspect they did not want to face very strong political headwinds unless strong actions were absolutely necessary. Because of extremely lenient capital requirements and a regulatory reluctance to shut down unhealthy insurers, most failed life insurance companies have had large negative equity by the time they failed.

4.1 Solvency Margin Requirements

The capital requirement of life insurers is measured by the solvency margin, which relates net assets to estimated risk. Net assets are defined as capital + risk reserves + general loan-loss reserves + 90% of unrealized capital gains – 100% of unrealized capital losses + excess reserves over surrender value of polices + a half-year of future profits + tax effect + subordinated debt. In this calculation, the deferred tax assets from loss carry-forward is included in the first item, "capital". The "tax effect" is calculated from the "possible future tax savings when the company has to use retained earnings to cover future losses". In other words, the net asset figure used for solvency margin calculation counts future profits in *three* ways: the tax effect, deferred-tax assets, and a half-year of future profit.

Estimated risk equals $[(\text{insurance risk})^2 + (\text{interest-rate risk} + \text{asset-value risk})^2]^{1/2}$ + management risk. Insurance risk is related to adverse movements in death rates.

Net assets are divided by estimated risk and multiplied by 200 to obtain the solvency margin. The minimum ratio for sound companies is 200. Below 200, regulators are required to take corrective actions.

This capital requirement was imported from American regulations, but Japanese regulators have made a number of modifications that weaken the rule considerably. Table 7.7 illustrates the major differences.

The Financial Studies Group of the Japan Center for Economic Research, which I head, has tried to adjust for the differences in the solvency margin requirements in Japan and the United States. The quality of disclosure by life insurance companies has improved considerably

Table 7.7
Comparison of US and Japanese Capital Requirements on Life-insurance Companies

	US RBC regulation	Japanese Solvency Margin regulation
Assets of no liquidation value in the net asset calculation		
Deferred tax asset	Not allowed	Allowed
Movable property	Not allowed	Allowed
Future profit	Not allowed	One year profit until March 2000
		Half year profit is allowed since then
Unrealized losses		
in domestic bonds	Deducted from asset	Not deducted from assets until March 2001
in foreign securities	Deducted from asset	Not deducted from assets until March 2001
Weights for market risk		
Stocks	22.5–45%	10%
Foreign bonds	10%	5%
Real estates	10%	5%
Trigger levels for prompt corrective actions		
No action	250%	200%
Submit plans for improvements	150–250%	100–200%
Stronger intervention	70–150%	0–100%
Authority takes over the control	Less than 70%	Less than 0%

Source: Prepared by the author.

since the mid-1990s, so we can do this from publicly available data. Based on what these firms disclose, all the major companies indicate they are above the 200% level—indeed, above 375%, with half over 600%—implying they are sound.

However, as noted, the reported solvency ratios are overstated in a number of ways. We have made three types of adjustments. The first uses American risk weights and adjusts for unrealized capital gains and losses, but allows inclusion of assets with no liquidation value. With these adjustments, all the firms have lower ratios, but remain above 250%, with six clustered between 250% and 300%.

The second adjustment is closer to, but still somewhat less stringent than, American standards. In addition to the first set of adjustments, we excluded assets with no liquidation value such as the deferred tax asset and future profits. This makes one company insolvent (negative solvency ratio) and puts three others under 200%. Under American rules, these four companies would face prompt corrective actions.

The third approach involves, in addition to the above two adjustments, removing subordinated debt from the capital base because its quality as capital is less than that of retained earnings and surplus notes (which are similar to the non-voting redeemable preferred shares of joint-stock companies). The number of companies below the 200% solvency margin remains four, but seven companies have lower ratios than with the second approach.

Subordinated debt is included in the numerator to calculate official solvency margins up to the amount of the net assets. Subordinated debt does play a limited role as capital because insurance policy contracts are senior to such debts in a bankruptcy procedure. However, when an insurance company runs out of genuine capital (net assets), the company is regarded as insolvent in bankruptcy court even if it still has some subordinated debt, and usually loses going-concern value. This loss is often very large and policyholders incur heavy losses when companies go bankrupt. Moreover, companies have continued to pay interest on subordinated debt to avoid default even when their financial condition is bad. Therefore subordinated debt is less qualified as capital than the other components. It also is an important part of the double-gearing with banks, a situation analyzed in the next section as a danger to the health of the financial system.

Table 7.8 shows the distribution of companies by solvency margins using the second approach. The ratios of most companies have been declining fairly rapidly. Two factors contributed to this trend: falling stock

Table 7.8
Adjusted Solvency Margin Ratios (Adjusted 2)

Number of Companies in each solvency-margin ranges

	Less than 0	0 to 70%	70 to 100%	100 to 150 %	150 to 200%	200 to 250%	250 400%	More than 400%	Nikkei 225 index
Mar-00	0	0	0	0	0	3	6	1	20,337
Mar-01	0	0	0	1	2	1	5	1	13,000
Mar-02	0	0	1	2	0	2	5	0	11,025
Mar-03	1	1	0	1	1	2	3	1	7,973
Mar-04	0	0	0	1	1	0	5	2	11,715

Source: Fukao and Japan Center for Economic Research (2004b).

prices and high guaranteed returns on insurance contracts. The recovery of stock prices after March 2003 helped pull all but one company back over 200% based as of their March 2004 reports, and other actions by the firms make the distribution better than in March 2002 when the Nikkei was about the same level.

4.2 Double-Gearing between Banks and Life Insurance Companies

Double-gearing occurs when banks and life insurance companies provide capital, broadly defined, to each other. Major Japanese life insurance companies are major shareholders of Japanese banks, collectively owning 10% or more of each city bank during the 1990s. Most major life insurance companies are mutual companies. Mutuals raise core capital by issuing "surplus notes" that are similar to non-voting preferred shares of joint-stock companies and most of them have been sold to banks. Between March 2000 and March 2001 the bankruptcies of Chiyoda, Kyoei, and Tokyo Life reduced the double-gearing of the industry as a whole, but it is still significant.

Tables 7.9-1 and 7.9-2 provide insight on the extent of double-gearing. At the end of March 2003, 10 life insurance companies collectively held ¥1.7 trillion of bank stock and ¥4.2 trillion yen of bank subordinated debt. At the same time, banks held ¥1.4 trillion of surplus notes and ¥1 trillion of subordinated debt of 7 life insurance companies. (The value of bank shares held by life insurance companies declined from ¥7.7 trillion in March 2000 to ¥1.7 trillion in March 2003. This is mostly due to the falling prices of major Japanese banks rather than the sale of bank shares by insurance companies, so there will have been some recovery since.) The insurers own stock in both the major banks and many of the smaller ones. Beyond double-gearing, a motive for these relationships is to obtain business from banks and their employees.

Double-gearing generates two serious problems: a weak capital structure in Japan's financial system, and weaker governance in banks and life insurance companies than in other listed companies.

As in regards to systemic risk, suppose a major life insurer files for bankruptcy. The banks that hold the company's subordinated loans and surplus notes lose money. The price of the stock of these banks falls to reflect the write-offs, which reduces the value of bank stocks held by insurance companies. This fall in stock value may even trigger a chain reaction of failures among Japanese financial institutions.

Table 7.9-1
Double-Gearing between Banks and Life-Insurance Companies I (March 2003)
Capital of Banks held by Life-Insurance Companies

100 million yen

Insurance Companies	UFJ HD	SMFG	Sumitomo Trust	Mitsui Trust HD	Mizuho FG	MTFG	Resona HD	Other banks	Sub Total	Sub-Debt of all Banks	Total
Nippon	171	392			183	654		2,631	4,032	5,400	9,432
Daiichi	41	76			338	396	67	2,263	3,181	6,975	10,156
Sumitomo	7	444	107		7	90		1,535	2,190	7,584	9,774
Meiji	61				12	221		3,352	3,645	5,385	9,030
Yasuda					85		29	1,490	1,603	4,523	6,126
Mitsui		163		38				298	499	3,801	4,300
Asahi					170		46	602	818	3,923	4,740
Taiyo	46	227						1,180	1,453	3,506	4,959
Daido	124						40	818	982	2,196	3,178
Fukoku								435	435	995	1,430
Total	450	1,301	107	38	795	1,361	181	13,226	17,461	42,383	59,844

Source: Fukao and Japan Center for Economic Research (2004a). Data are taken from disclosure materials of individual financial institutions. Shaded cell means the figures are not disclosed.

Example: Sumitomo Life holds 444 SMFG shares and 107 shares of Sumitomo Trust (in 100 million yen). Sumitomo Life holds 2190 shares and 7584 sub-debts of banks.

Table 7.9-2
Double-Gearing between Banks and Life-Insurance Companies II (March 2003)
Capital of Life-Insurance Companies held by Banks

100 million yen

	UFJ Group			Sumitomo-Mitsui			Mitsui Trust G		Mizuho Group			Mitsubishi-Tokyo			Resona Group							
Insurance Companies	UFJ HD	UFJ	UFJ Trust	SMFG	SMBC	Sumitomo Trust	Mitsui Trust HD	Chuo-Mitsui Trust	Mizuho FG	Mizuho CB	Mizuho	MTFG	BOTM	Mitsubishi Trust	Resona HD	Resona	Saitama Resona	SPCs	Others	Sub Total	Sub-Debt of LI held by Banks	Total
Nippon	0	0	0	0	0	0	0	0	0	0	0	0		0	0	0	0	3,000	0	3,000	0	3,000
Daiichi		176			176					264			88			88		800	708	2,300	1,000	3,300
Sumitomo		100			700	300				250			100					0	150	1,600	3,750	5,350
Meiji		170								90			260	150				0	275	945	0	945
Yasuda										100						50		300	450	900	1,000	1,900
Mitsui					811			415		30								0	169	1,425	2,030	3,455
Asahi										1,340						660		0	0	2,000	1,230	3,230
Taiyo		56	39		56													0	125	277	800	1,077
Daido	50	167	117													88		0	495	918	0	918
Fukoku	0	0	0	0	0	0	0	0	0	0	0	0	0	0	0	0	0	300	0	300	350	650
Total	50	670	157	0	1,743	300	0	415	0	2,074	0	0	448	150	0	886	0	4,400	2,373	13,665	10,160	23,825

Source: Fukao and Japan Center for Economic Research (2004a). Data are taken from disclosure materials of individual financial institutions. Shaded cell means the figures are not disclosed.

Daido Life was reorganized from mutual company to joint stock company on April 1, 2002. As a result, S notes for Daido are the value of shares at the time of listing.

The value of s-notes does not include those held by non financial companies.

Example: SMBC holds 176 of Daiichi Life's capital, 700 of Sumitomo Life's capital, and 811 of Mistsui Life's capital.

Regarding corporate governance, the cross-holding of capital tends to weaken the level of shareholder oversight. Often, top bank executives become representative policyholders of life insurance companies with which there is a cross-holding relationship. At the same time, the life insurance companies are often passive shareholders of banks with the same relationship.

In an effort to increase their capital, many banks have resorted to measures very similar to outright double-gearing. As an example, Mizuho Financial Group raised ¥1,082 billion in preferred equity in March 2003, mostly from its Japanese business borrowers and friendly life insurance companies. Of the 75 subscribers that bought more than ¥3 billion each, 32 have Mizuho Bank or Mizuho Corporate Bank among their top-three shareholders. The three largest subscribers were Daiichi Life (¥45 billion), Yasuda Life (¥33 billion), and Sompo Japan Insurance (a non-life insurance company created by merger of Yasuda Fire and Marine and Nissan Fire and Marine in July 2002, ¥31.5 billion). Mizuho Corporate Bank is among the two largest shareholders of these three companies.

The Financial Services Agency should restrict such double-gearing among banks, life insurance companies, and bank business customers. More generally, the FSA should pay careful attention to the capital structures of big financial groups rather than superficial Bank for International Settlements (BIS) ratios. Without the restoration of a sound financial sector, we cannot expect market forces to discipline banks and insurance companies in a constructive way.

4.3 Policyholder Protection

The Insurance Industry Act of 1995 changed policyholder protection rules. Under the old law, regulators tried to support even the weakest companies by limiting competition and using strong regulatory power. MoF could reduce guaranteed minimum returns by executive order and force a sound company to rescue a failing one. The new law ends these powers and seeks to create a more transparent regulatory regime. The law also introduced the solvency margin rule analyzed earlier.

Also newly created was a Policyholder Protection Fund. This was supposed to assist a failing company with up to ¥200 billion by future contributions from other life insurance companies. Membership in this Fund was not mandatory, but all companies contributed. However, when Nissan Life failed in April 1997, the Fund was depleted completely. Moreover, the scope of policyholder protection was not clearly defined. As a result, a new organization, the Policyholder Protection Organization, was created in December 1998 and all life insurance companies, including foreign ones that had a license to conduct insurance business in Japan, were required to participate. Contributions are determined by the amount of a company's responsibility reserves and the amount of annual premiums received. (The responsibility reserve is the present value of the estimated future insurance obligations of an insurance company. As such, it corresponds to the accumulated savings of all the policyholders.)

Although the scope of the policyholder protection was clarified, there still is large room for maneuver. The life insurers were required to contribute ¥460 billion over a 10-year period and the Policyholder Protection Organization could borrow for immediate use. When Toho Life failed in June 1999, ¥380 billion was used so the Policyholder Protection Organization in effect spent most of its future contributions. The FSA asked for more contributions, and the industry promised an additional ¥100 billion, which gives the Policyholder Protection Organization some ¥180 billion.

Table 7.10 shows the financial conditions of the seven life insurance companies that have failed, and the consequences to policyholders. Although these companies reported fairly high solvency margins before failing, all of them were found to be insolvent after their bankruptcy. This means that the solvency margin regulation is dysfunctional due to the factors discussed in section 3.1.

Stiff early withdrawal charges imposed after a life insurer fails mean that it is usually better for a healthy person to cancel a policy before the start of bankruptcy procedure, and get a new policy elsewhere. This is one reason companies with low solvency margins such as Asahi Life and Mitsui Life have seen larger declines in policies outstanding than have healthier companies. Because switching companies is not possible for an unhealthy person, the burden of these companies' failures is heavier on people who most need life insurance.

When an insurance company becomes under-capitalized, intervention by the FSA is desirable. Most life insurance policies are very long-term contracts, lasting more than 20 years. Many people who are not financially savvy rely on life insurance companies to keep their savings. Because insurance policies are less liquid than savings deposits, policy cancellations proceed more slowly than a bank run, and a weakened insurance company can operate for a long time with low or negative equity by window-dressing its financial statements. Most life insurers that failed, as listed in Table 7.10, aggravated their situations through this process.

Table 7.10
Failed Life Insurance Companies
Situations at the time of Bankruptcy

Name	Nissan	Toho	Daihyaku	Taisho	Chiyoda	Kyoei	Tokyo
Corporate structure	Mutual	Mutual	Mutual	LLC	Mutual	LLC	Mutual
Date of Failure	Apr-97	Jun-99	May-00	May-00	Oct-00	Oct-00	Mar-01
Asset (trillion yen)	1.82	2.19	1.30	0.15	2.23	3.73	0.69
Equity (trillion yen)	–0.32	–0.65	–0.32	–0.03	–0.60	–0.69	–0.07
Disclosed solvency margin	N.A.	154	305	68	263	211	447
Date of solvency margin	N.A.	Mar-98	Mar-99	Mar-00	Mar-00	Mar-00	Mar-00
Reduction of reserves by bankruptcy	0%	10%	10%	10%	10%	8%	0%
Average guaranteed return before failure	3.75–5.5%	4.79%	4.46%	4.05%	3.70%	4.00%	4.20%
Guaranteed return after failure	2.75%	1.50%	1.00%	1.00%	1.50%	1.75%	2.60%
Aid from Protection Fund (billion yen)	200	366	145	27	None	None	None
Early withdrawal charges (EWC)	15–3%	15–2%	20–2%	15-3%	20–2%	15–2%	20–2%
Period of EWC	7 years	8 years	10 years	10 years	10 years	8 years	10 years
Current names of reorganized companies	Aoba	AIG Edison	Manulife	Yamato	AIG Star	Gibraltar	T&D Finaicial

Source: Fukao and Japan Center for Economic Research (2004).
Note: LLC stands for limited liability company.

To sum up, the cost of resolving life insurance company failures has been very high for policyholders due to excessive FSA forbearance. The resolution costs also have been borne by healthier companies through their contributions to the Policyholder Protection Organization.

4.4 The Resolution Process for Failing Life Insurers

The FSA has improved the cumbersome bankruptcy procedures of life insurance companies under the 1995 insurance industry law. It introduced the Reorganization Order of Joint-Stock Companies Act (*Kaisha Kosei Ho*) for life insurance companies in June 2000. This is similar to Chapter 10, Corporate Reorganization, of the United States Bankruptcy Act of 1898.

Three companies have been through this new procedure: Chiyoda Life, Kyoei Life, and Tokyo Life. All three firms had significant negative equity at the time of their failures, but none used money from the Policyholder Protection Organization because it had already exhausted its resources taking care of Toho Life and Daihyaku Life. To get money for these three insolvent firms, the FSA would have had to go to the Diet to get a new resolution for authorization, so that no public or industry funds were used. Because such a procedure involves a lot of uncertainty, the court-appointed administrators of the failed companies did not want to use the Policy Protection Organization. Both core capital and subordinated debt were wiped out in these three cases, as was appropriate. The rehabilitation of Chiyoda Life is well documented in a book by its administrators (Chiyoda Seimei Kosei Kanzainin Dan 2002). Under the 2000 law, administrators can use innovative procedures to minimize the costs of bankruptcy for policyholders and the Policyholder Protection Organization.

In 2003, the FSA introduced a new law that allowed life insurance companies to reduce the promised return to policyholders. While a change of existing insurance contracts constitutes a default, under the new law the management of a weakened life insurer can take the following steps:

1. Management asks the FSA to allow it to change the contents of existing policies so as to improve its financial situation.
2. After obtaining FSA approval, management calls a policyholder meeting (if a mutual company) or a shareholder meeting to ratify the plan by a special resolution.

3. The FSA checks the plan in order to protect policyholders from an excessive reduction of their savings.

4. The insurer notifies all policyholders of the plan. Unless more than 10% object, the plan is approved.

Top management is not necessarily punished; incumbent company directors may retain their posts even after this process. It is not necessary to write-off the surplus notes or subordinated debt. Because insurance policies are the most senior debt of life insurance companies, this procedure clearly violates the absolute-priority rule of bankruptcy procedures. As such, if a weak company invokes this procedure, credit rating agencies may start to regard the "capital" of all life-insurance companies as an unreliable indicator of their solvency. Much of the subordinated debt and surplus notes are held by major banks, so this law tends to protect banks that provide capital to insurers at the expense of policyholders.

My analysis suggests that this law is clearly unnecessary and the regular reorganization order is better-suited for fair and quick resolution of insolvent life insurance companies. Fortunately, the law has yet to be invoked (as of March 2005) because of the recovery of equity prices and the likely loss of reputation for the invoking company.

5 Kampo and Market Distortion

The government-owned Japanese Postal Life Insurance System (*Kampo*) is the world's largest insurance company, with assets in March 2002 equal to more than 80% of Japan's 10 major private life insurers combined. Its very presence distorts the Japanese insurance market. Table 7.11 compares Kampo to the 10 major private life companies, providing the most recent data available.

Most Kampo funds are channeled into the Fiscal Loan and Investment Program to finance budget deficits, government lending agencies, and public investment projects. Its compound annual return on book value was 3.25% for the six years through fiscal 2002, significantly higher than the 1.84% of the 10 major private companies, and the subsequent returns have probably varied somewhat less. The cause of this superior performance is Kampo's conservative investment strategy; its share of equity holdings are less than a third of the average of the private companies. Nor did Kampo invest in real estate. Rather, it has

Table 7.11
Comparison of the Asset Structure of Postal Life and Private Life Insurance Companies March 2002

	Postal Life Insurance	Ten Major Private Companies
Deposits	7.6%	3.1%
Money in trust	0.0%	1.0%
Public Bonds	58.8%	30.3%
Stocks	4.5%	14.1%
Foreign Bonds	4.4%	9.1%
Foreign Stocks	1.6%	3.1%
Other securities	0.2%	1.0%
Loans	21.4%	29.1%
Real Estates	0.0%	4.8%
Other assets	1.5%	4.3%
Total	100.0%	100.0%
Amount in trillion yen	126.5	150.3
Notes		
Fixed income assets	87.8%	62.5%
Foreign assets	5.8%	9.4%

Source: Fukao and Japan Center for Economic Research (2003).

held most of its assets in long-term bonds and loans. This investment mix has performed considerably better than that of private companies under prolonged deflation in spite of low interest rates.

Kampo receives explicit and implicit subsides from the national government. The estimated value of such subsides for fiscal year 2001 are summarized in Table 7.12. The total subsidy from the government is about ¥495 billion a year. This amounts to 0.39% of gross assets, a significant advantage over private companies.

Kampo also benefits from more lenient regulation on its cross-selling of products. There are more than 24,000 post offices in Japan which offer, besides Kampo products, postal deposits and regular post office services. Even mail carriers routinely sell life-insurance policies. In contrast, Japanese life insurers cannot offer payment services, as the post office does, and Japanese commercial banks can sell only annuities and term insurance for housing-loan customers. Although the insurers together employ more than two hundred thousand sales people, Kampo is simply more widely and conveniently available.

Table 7.12
Estimated Benefits Received by Kampo from the Government, fiscal 2001 (billion yen)

388.9	Tax exemptions[1]
28.0	Waived Policy Protection Organization fees[2]
77.8	Excess return from FILP investments[3]
494.7	Total

Kampo is the government-owned Postal Life Insurance company.
[1]Kampo is exempted from all the central and local government taxes; it does not pay any corporate income tax, real estate tax or stamp duties.
[2]The amount Kampo would have to pay the Policyholder Protection Organization (PPO) if it were not exempt. Policyholders of Kampo have been fully protected by explicit government guarantees and this guarantee has been provided without any charge. Moreover, the government guarantee is much more comprehensive than the PPO. While the government fully guarantees all the benefits of Kampo policies, the PPO guarantees only 70% to 90% of the principal and accrued interest, and does not protect un-accrued interest. No estimate is made for the value of this more-comprehensive coverage.
[3]Kampo has received subsidized returns on its loans to the Fiscal Investment and Loan program (FILP). The interest rate on these loans has been higher than the government bond yield even though the loans are fully guaranteed by the government. Although the government stopped providing this subsidy beginning with new loans in fiscal 2002, Kampo still enjoys above-market yields from outstanding past loans.

Source: Fukao and JCER (2003)

As an insurance company, Kampo has a fairly sound balance sheet. The capital-asset ratio at the end of March 2002 was 11.2%. This was somewhat lower than the best private company, Nippon Life, at 13.2%. However, the estimated solvency margin of Kampo has been much higher than those of even the best private company due to its much lower risk exposure to the stock market (Table 7.13).

Given the advantages it enjoys from unequal tax treatment, policyholder protection schemes, and regulations on cross-selling, Kampo distorts the Japanese life insurance market.

Table 7.13
Estimated Solvency Margin Ratios of the Postal Life Insurace Company %

	March 2000	March 2001	March 2002
Disclosed	1146.9	1263.7	1328.1
Adjusted 1	791.2	924.8	934.1
Adjusted 2	780.5	912.3	920.0

Source: Fukao and Japan Center for Economic Research (2003)

6 Conclusions: To Stabilize the Life-Insurance Industry

To stabilize Japanese life-insurance companies, it is necessary to restore their profitability and install more effective risk-control mechanisms.

First, the operating costs of the major life insurance companies is still high. The cost of maintaining sales forces has been especially high, although it has been declining recently. The industry maintains about 250,000 salespeople, about a third of whom quit within one year. Moreover, the overall average per salesperson is just three contracts sold per month. It is necessary to modernize this strategy of deploying sheer numbers of sales people

Second, risk-control mechanisms have to be improved. The industry's top management needs to pay much more attention to market risk and insurance risk over a long period of time. Asset-liability management has to be strengthened.

Third, the Financial Services Agency should beef up regulation. The dysfunctional solvency margin requirement should be tightened considerably. At the very least, the FSA should remove deferred taxes from the definition of solvency, prohibit double-gearing among financial institutions, and raise the risk parameters on stock portfolios.

Fourth, it is necessary to remove the unfair competitive advantage that Kampo enjoys over the private companies due to favorable tax treatment, government guarantees, and cross-selling of deposits and insurance.

Fifth, the corporate governance of life insurance companies has to be improved. Ideally, mutual companies should be reorganized as joint-stock companies. If it is not possible to do so in the short run, the selection procedure of representative policyholders has to change. By choosing only independent policyholders without financial relationships with the companies, more effective oversight of the top life insurance executives can be expected.

The soundness of the remaining major life insurers has improved considerably due to the recovery of Japanese stock prices since the spring of 2003. If these firms can earn a 2% mark-to-market return on their assets, they should be able to cover the negative carry. Thus, if the average return on the bond portfolio rises to 2% and stock prices remain stable, the major life insurers can avoid further erosion of their equity capital. However, they always face the risk of another decline in stock prices. Moreover, this is not the end of the story. Most major life insurers maintain a number of old contracts with quite a large negative carry. As a result, these companies face a competitive disadvantage against new and foreign-owned competitors which are not burdened with such legacy contracts.

Because of the long duration of most contracts, the average guaranteed return on outstanding life insurance policies will fall only very slowly. As this analysis has shown, it is necessary to earn about 4% on assets to end the negative-carry problem. To realize such a return from a bond portfolio, long-term interest rates have to rise by 2 to 3 percentage points from the levels of early 2005. The only way to realize such prospects is to end the deflation that the Japanese economy has been suffering since the mid-1990s. Although higher interest rates will reduce the mark-to-market value of bond portfolios, the reduction of the net present value of the insurance companies' debt is much greater because the duration of the debt is much longer than the life of the assets.

Just as the present set of problems the life insurance industry faces involve the combined efforts and mistakes of the industry and its regulators, as well as the presence of a government-operated unfair competitor, so the industry and government must work together for solutions that will make the industry healthier and thus better able to serve both those who provide its capital and its policyholders. As this chapter suggests, the actual changes needed are rather straightforward. It is the willingness to act that is key.

Acknowledgment

The author thanks Professors Hugh Patrick, Takeo Hoshi, Takatoshi Ito, and an anonymous referee for their detailed comments on earlier drafts. The author has relied heavily on analysis of life insurance companies done by the Japan Center for Economic Research, including Fukao and Japan Center for Economic Research (2000, 2002, 2003a, 2004a, 2004b).

References

Adams, T.F.M. and Iwao Hoshii. 1972. *A Financial History of the New Japan*. Tokyo: Kodansha.

Chiyoda Seimei Kosei Kanzainin Dan. 2002. *Seiho Saiken* (Rehabilitating a Life Insurance Company). Toyo: Keizai Shimpo-sha. (In Japanese)

Fukao, Mitsuhiro. 1998. Zaisei Toyushi Seido No Gaikan To Mondai No Shozai (Overview of Fiscal Investment and Loan Program and its Problems). In *Zaisei Toyushi no Keizai Bunseki*, (Economic Analysis of Fiscal Investment and Loan Program) 1–23, editors Kazumasa Iwata and Mitsuhiro Fukao, Nihon Keizai Shinbun-sha. (In Japanese)

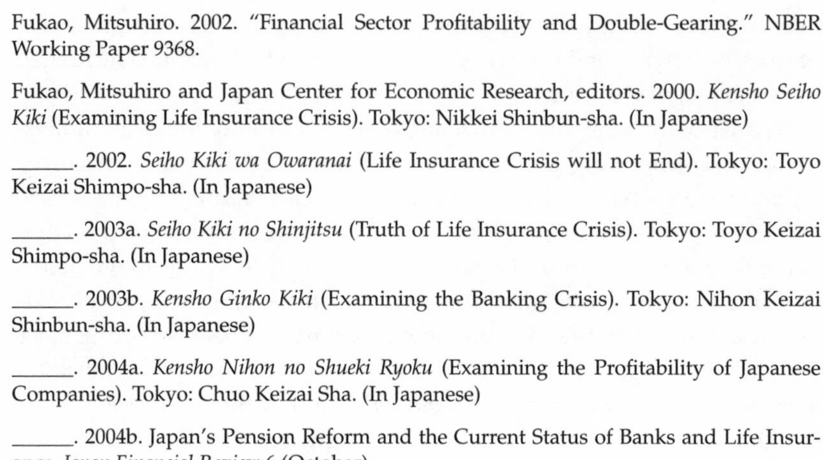

Fukao, Mitsuhiro. 2002. "Financial Sector Profitability and Double-Gearing." NBER Working Paper 9368.

Fukao, Mitsuhiro and Japan Center for Economic Research, editors. 2000. *Kensho Seiho Kiki* (Examining Life Insurance Crisis). Tokyo: Nikkei Shinbun-sha. (In Japanese)

______. 2002. *Seiho Kiki wa Owaranai* (Life Insurance Crisis will not End). Tokyo: Toyo Keizai Shimpo-sha. (In Japanese)

______. 2003a. *Seiho Kiki no Shinjitsu* (Truth of Life Insurance Crisis). Tokyo: Toyo Keizai Shimpo-sha. (In Japanese)

______. 2003b. *Kensho Ginko Kiki* (Examining the Banking Crisis). Tokyo: Nihon Keizai Shinbun-sha. (In Japanese)

______. 2004a. *Kensho Nihon no Shueki Ryoku* (Examining the Profitability of Japanese Companies). Tokyo: Chuo Keizai Sha. (In Japanese)

______. 2004b. Japan's Pension Reform and the Current Status of Banks and Life Insurance. *Japan Financial Review* 6 (October).

Tone, Toshio and Minoru Kitano. 1993. *Gendai no Seimei Hoken* (Contemporary Life Insurance). Tokyo: Tokyo University Press. (In Japanese)

Maehara, Kinichi. 2000. *21 Seiki no Seimei Hoken* Sangyo (Life Insurance Industry in the 21st Century). Tokyo: Kinyu Zaisei Jijo Kenkyukai. (In Japanese)

Standard & Poor's. 2003. *Nihon no Kinyu Sangyo 2004* (Financial Industry in Japan 2004). Tokyo: Toyo Keizai Shimpo-sha. (In Japanese)

Suzuki, Yoshio. 1987. *The Japanese Financial System*. (English translation of *Waga kuni no kin'yu seido*, 1986). New York: Oxford Univiversity Press.

Part III

Changing Markets and Business Investment

8 Corporate Investment and Restructuring

Tokuo Iwaisako

Investment has remained high relative to gross domestic product (GDP) since the collapse of Japan's bubble economy. At the same time, the return on capital invested has fallen to historically low levels. The only explanation that reconciles these two empirical facts is that Japanese firms and their creditors made bad investment decisions through the 1990s. In other words, the Japanese economy has been suffering both from the misallocation of capital and probable over-investment as a share of GDP.

In the 1950s and 1960s, Japan's rapid economic growth was based on the accumulation of physical capital and improvements in human capital. By the beginning of the 1980s, Japan had accumulated a substantial amount of physical capital stock per-capita. The mechanism enabling rapid growth had lost its effectiveness because Japan had caught up with the West.

There was very little room left in the early 1980s for Japan to grow by simply adapting to imported technology. Accordingly, it is realistic to focus on the lack of structural change since then, and on why Japan could not switch more quickly from capital intensive to research and development intensive growth. Given Japan's degree of industrialization and its level of per-capita GDP, I contend that the country's industrial structure should have changed more rapidly, and the proportional size of the service sector should have increased more dramatically since the early 1980s. This view emphasizes the lack of structural change and necessary structural reform (*ko-zo kaikaku*) during this period as being the root cause of many of Japan's current economic problems.

The first two sections of this chapter look at aggregate investment levels, excess capacity, investment returns, and the relationship between productivity and structural change, including the role of business cycles. Although there have been recessions in the post-bubble economy period, these have not resulted in a "cleansing effect," meaning the reallocation of resources to more efficient uses as companies restructure or close down and workers shift to other jobs. This failure reflects a malfunctioning of the financial system.

The evidence examined in the first two sections is illustrative rather than decisive. However, along with the related studies cited, this analysis concludes that there is little evidence to indicate that Japan's business investment slowdown from 1991 to 1997 was caused by a credit crunch. Even so, the series of banking failures in the last quarter of 1997 caused a sharp decline in bank lending and capital investment in 1998–99, so a credit-crunch might help explain the slowdown during these years.

During the 1991–1997 period, there had already been a significant decline in the ability of the financial system to reallocate resources. This is consistent with the argument based on macroeconomic data that the Japanese economy has been suffering from a misallocation of resources rather than from insufficient investment. The misallocated investment has contributed to the Japanese economy's difficulties throughout the 1990s and up to early 2005. Bank loans have been extended to many under-performing or insolvent companies to save them from liquidation rather than being lent to new and productive firms.

Turning to how corporate restructuring has been undertaken in Japan, the changing nature of the role of main banks and the new bankruptcy code are examined. Then, three specific restructuring cases are discussed. From this background, the reasons why Japan's restructuring process has been so ineffective and inefficient are derived and analyzed. The roles of two public financial institutions, the Development Bank of Japan and the Industrial Revitalization Corporation Japan are then explored. Finally, policy implications are presented.

1 Investment

Because of an assumed reluctance by banks to lend as a result of non-performing loan problems since the early 1990s, it is tempting to describe the Japanese economy's current situation in terms of under-investment brought on by a conventional credit crunch. However, the reality is considerably more complicated, and the explanation is quite different. Except during 1998–99, there is no sign a serious credit crunch occurred in Japan. Rather, as the data and analysis below will demonstrate, despite declining levels of investment, there probably has been over-investment in general, and a failure to reallocate resources away from inefficient industries and firms using resources inefficiently toward more productive uses [see Woo (2003) for more detailed evidence on the absence of a credit crunch in the Japanese economy before 1997 and Watanabe (2003) for evidence of a credit crunch in 1998–99].

1.1 *Aggregate Investment Levels*

Figure 8.1 shows the difference in the growth rates of real private non-residential investment and real GDP in Japan and the United States from 1981 through 2003. GDP growth rates have been subtracted from investment growth rates so that unusual increases and declines are more apparent.

The Japanese investment slowdown in 1992–94 is very significant. However, this should be considered a reflection of the extremely high growth rates of 1988–90 rather than an autonomous decline. Thus, the depth of the trough is not significantly different from the investment decline that the United States experienced in 2001–02 as its high-tech bubble deflated.

We know that private investment is generally more volatile and far more cyclical than other GDP components. Thus, the decline of

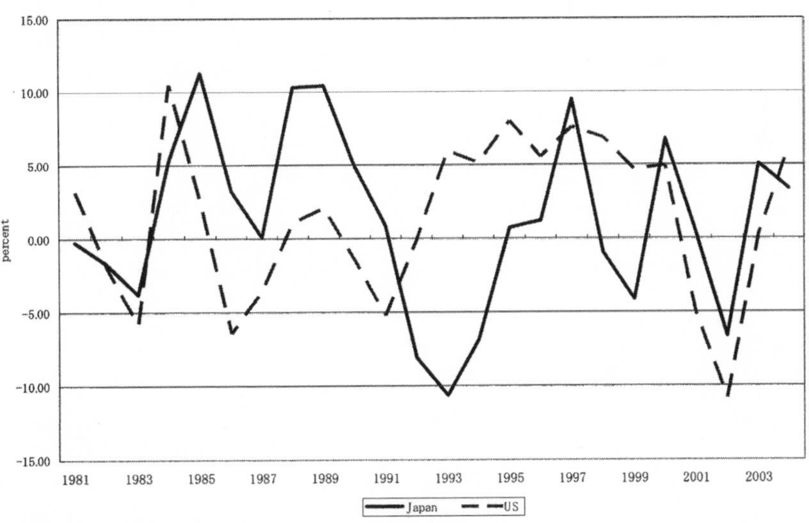

Data are for the private sector only.

Figure 8.1
Differences in Growth Rates between Real Non-Residential Investment and Real GDP: 1981–2004

Japanese private investment in the 1990s is more likely to have resulted from a slowing in output growth rather than the other way around. This is apparent in Figure 8.2, in which private investment is shown as a percentage of GDP.

Aggregate investment by the private sector declined quickly in the first three years of Japan's post-bubble economy, and private non-residential investment has hovered around 15% of GDP since 1994, which is the same level as during the first half of the 1980s. Japan's 1990–91 investment peak of 19% of GDP was much higher than the American peak of 13% of GDP in 2000. Although a direct comparison of aggregate investment levels in different countries is difficult, Japan has consistently been investing a much larger share of its GDP than has the United States.

The movement of Japanese investment in 1990s also is consistent with the diffusion indexes for "lending attitudes of financial institutions" in the Bank of Japan's *Tankan* survey. This suggests there was a credit crunch only in 1998–99, following the series of spectacular bank failures in late 1997 (see Figure 8.3).

Figure 8.4 implies that excess production capacity has been a problem for the Japanese economy since 1992, beginning immediately after the

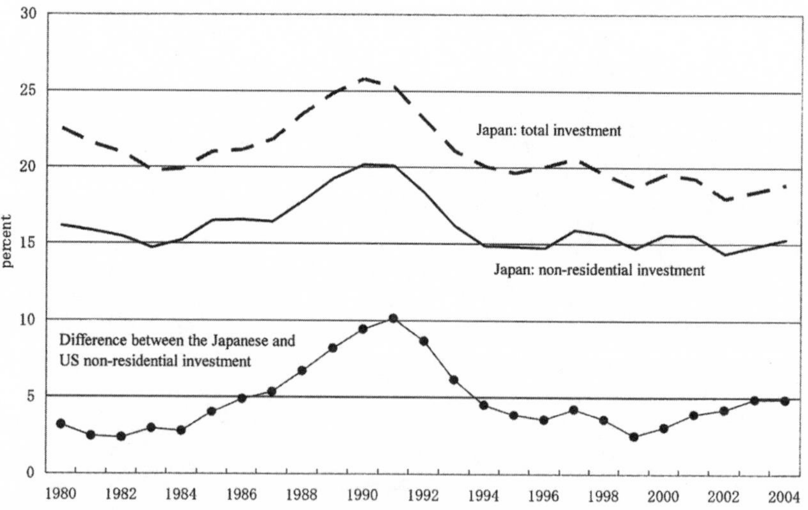

Data are for the private sector only. The total includes residential and non-residential investment.

Figure 8.2
Investment as a Percentage of GDP

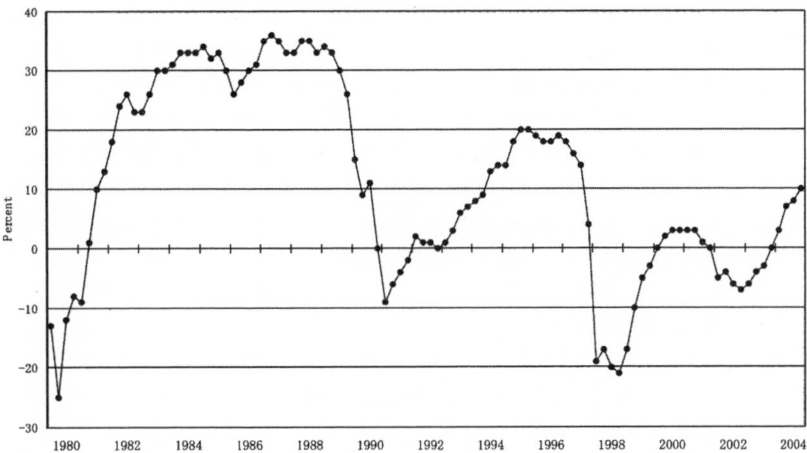

This figure plots the quarterly Diffusion Index of "Accommodative" minus "Severe" lending attitudes of financial institutions as reported in Bank of Japan, *Short-Term Economic Survey of All Enterprises* (the *Tankan* survey).

Figure 8.3
Lending Attitudes of Financial Institutions

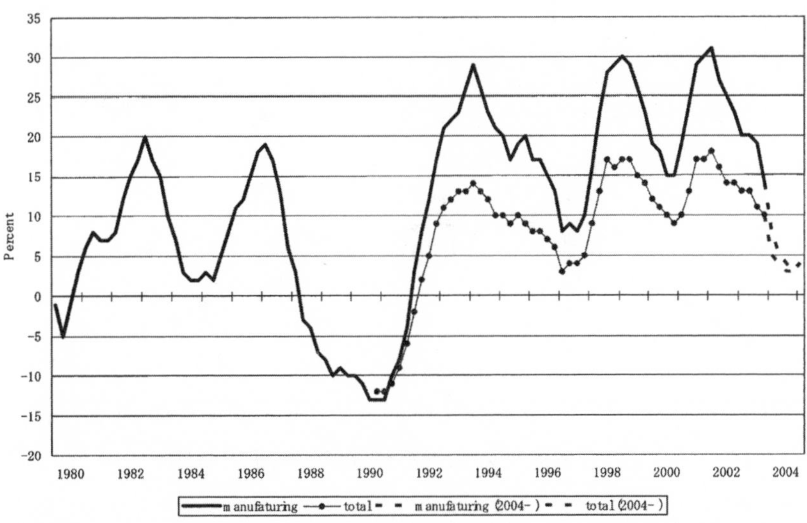

This figure plots the quarterly Diffusion Index of "Excessive" minus "Insufficient" production capacity as reported in Bank of Japan, *Short-Term Economic Survey of All Enterprises* (the *Tankan* survey). The BoJ expanded coverage of firms so that there are definitional changes in 2004.

Figure 8.4
Excess Production Capacity

collapse of the bubble economy. There have been cyclical movements, but the underlying level of excess capacity in the post-bubble period has clearly been higher than it was during the 1980s.

In short, there is no empirical evidence that the investment slowdown in the 1990s was anything more than a downturn of the type typically associated with a recession, except in 1998–1999. Thus, it is difficult to argue that the Japanese economy has suffered from structural lack of investment throughout most of its 14-year malaise.

1.2 Investment Returns

The return on capital investment has been quite low in the post-bubble period, and actually has been diminishing since the early 1970s. This is shown in Figure 8.5, taken from Ito and Fukao (2003). The real rate of return on capital, based on macroeconomic data, generally has been declining since the early 1970s, although it did stabilize in the mid-1980s, and has been particularly low (under 1.5%) since 1991. Over the same sample period, the capital-output ratio increased. Although the

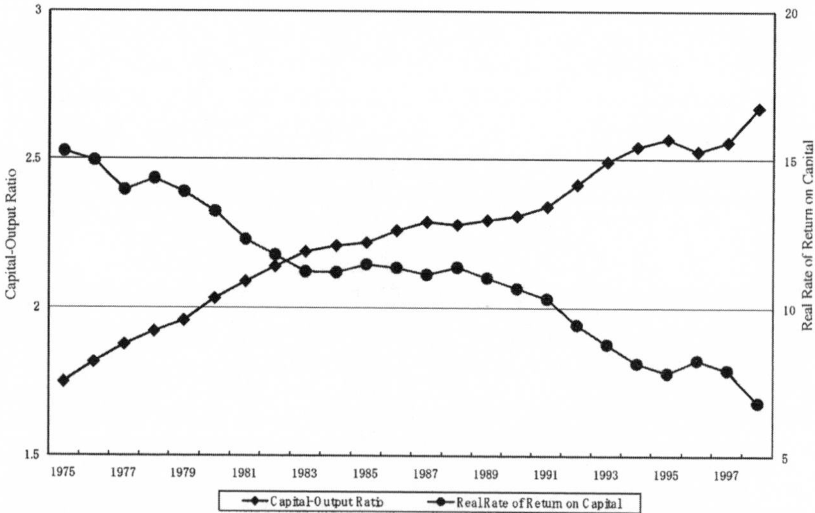

Sources: Capital stock is from the Japan Industry Productivity (JIP) database, as discussed in the text. The numerator for return on capital is "operating surplus" from GDP data.
The JIP database was originally compiled by a group of economists led by Kyoji Fukao for the research project *Japan's Potential Growth* at the Economic and Social Research Institute, Cabinet Office, Government of Japan. See Fukao, Inui, Kawai, and Miyagawa (2003a) for more details. The data are available at www.esri.go.jp/en/archive/bun/abstract/bun170index-e.html.

Figure 8.5
Capital-Output Ratio and Real Rate of Return on Capital, 1975–98

increase slowed during 1983–1991, it picked up again in the 1990s. This is consistent with the argument that aggregate investment did not slow during the 1990s.

Figure 8.6 presents return on equity (ROE) data. There has been more variation in ROE than in real return on capital, but the decline in return on equity from its early-bubble period peak in 1988 to its immediate post-bubble low in 1993 is dramatic. It is thus possible to argue that the Japanese economy's real problem is over-investment and that investment should be further reduced.

2 Investment and Productivity

In their seminal paper, Hayashi and Prescott (2002) examined aggregate productivity growth and argued that its slowdown in the 1990s was the main cause of Japan's lost decade. Hayashi and Prescott thus imply that any policy reaction should be toward structural reform, not aggregate demand management.

Hayashi and Prescott's work opened the debate on Japanese productivity growth in 1990s. Subsequent studies based on disaggregate data have confirmed the slowdown of productivity growth, but also find that Hayashi and Prescott's conclusion is somewhat exaggerated.

Data are from Ministry of Finance, *Financial Statements Statistics of Corporations*, various issues.

Figure 8.6
Return on Equity, 1975–2003

Fukao, Inui, Kawai, and Miyagawa (2003b) provided detailed accounts of a slowdown in productivity growth and the absence of changes in industrial structure with respect to sectoral productivity data. The empirical results of the two studies differ because Fukao et al adjust for improvements in labor quality and reductions in working hours, while Hayashi and Prescott include the external assets of the private sector in the "private capital stock." As a result, Japanese productivity growth in the 1990s as calculated by Fukao et al is larger than that calculated by Hayashi and Prescott. Some researchers argue that the productivity slowdown was even milder than that implied by Fukao et al. Jorgenson and Motohashi (2003) calculated productivity growth, treating real estate as a production input and using American relative prices for information technology products, to arrive at an even higher rate of productivity growth. Kawamoto (2004) presents additional evidence that Japanese productivity growth in the 1990s was higher than the Hayashi and Prescott's estimate.

A related literature emphasizes the role of the business cycle, particularly recessions, in the process of structural change and sectoral shifts. Caballero and Hammour (1994, 1996) examined such a mechanism on the production side. The title of their 1994 paper, "The Cleansing Effect of Recessions", captures the most important parts of their analysis. Caballero, Hoshi, and Kashyap (2003) brought such a viewpoint to bear in their analysis of the non-performing loans problem and the current inefficient patterns of investment in the Japanese economy. Blanchard and Diamond (1990) and Davis and Haltiwanger (1990, 1992) pioneered such studies, looking in particular at the labor market and what they referred to as "job creation and job destruction." Genda (1998) provides a similar analysis of the Japanese labor market.

The position I take in this chapter is close to the studies cited in the above paragraph. However, my focus is on why structural change has been so slow in Japan since the 1990s, why the cleansing effect of recessions has been so ineffective, and to search for possible remedies for the persisting macroeconomic and structural problems.

2.1 *Sectoral Analysis*

The analysis now turns to a detailed look at changes in capital stock and productivity growth by sectors. The data are taken from the Japan Industry Productivity (JIP) database, which contains annual information on 84 sectors—including 49 non-manufacturing sectors—from 1970 to 1998. These 84 sectors cover the entire Japanese economy. In the following analysis, the public sector, public utilities, and the agricultural sector are excluded to focus on the mechanism of resource allocation in the private industry. The sample periods of 1985–91 and 1992–98 were chosen for analysis.

If we ignore one outlier, the leasing industry, there is no clear relationship, or perhaps a slightly negative one, between the growth rate of capital stock and productivity growth for the two sample periods. The negative relationship between the two is somewhat stronger in the 1992–98 sample. However, the slope coefficients are statistically insignificant in both samples. The OLS estimates when productivity growth is regressed on capital stock without leasing are as follows (t statistics are in parentheses).

$$\text{1985–91} \qquad \Delta a_t = \underset{(-1.29)}{-0.103}\,\Delta k_t + \underset{(2.88)}{0.094}, \qquad R^2 = 0.025$$

$$\text{1992–98} \qquad \Delta a_t = \underset{(-1.77)}{-0.197}\,\Delta k_t - \underset{(-0.85)}{0.020}, \qquad R^2 = 0.046$$

Δa_t = Productivity growth in period t

Δk_t = Growth of capital stock in period t

Table 8.1 shows the fraction of industries experiencing an increase of capital and lower productivity growth at the same time. In the 1992–98 sample, there was a tendency for industries with lower productivity growth to invest more. Apparently, Japan's economy has been suffering from a misallocation of capital investment since the 1970s, and the problem got worse in the post-bubble period.

Table 8.1
Industries Experiencing Negative Productivity Growth (percent)

1985–91	1992–98	Among industries that increased capital stock:
35	69	More than average
32	62	At all

Covers 84 private-sector industries in manufacturing and non-manufacturing. Excludes public sector, agriculture, and public utilities.

Source: Author's calculations from Japan Industrial Productivity database.

2.2 *Measuring Reallocation*

To assess the change in investment patterns quantitatively, the following reallocation measure for capital investment was calculated:

$$\sigma_t = (S_{i,t}(G_{i,t} - G_{A,t})^2)^{1/2}$$

where $S_{i,t}$ = share of input in sector i, $G_{i,t}$ = growth rate of input in sector i, and $G_{A,t}$ = growth rate of total input.

If the input is labor, σ_t corresponds to what Lilien (1982) proposed for measuring labor mobility between sectors. The basic idea is that if the reallocation of labor is time-consuming, sector-specific shocks cause a temporary increase in unemployment. Lilien argued that this simple measure of the size of sector-specific disturbances appeared to account for a large proportion of the variation in aggregate employment.

Saita and Sekine (2003) first used this measure to assess the ability of loanable funds to be reallocated through the banking sector. They show that the measure with bank lending as the input declined significantly in the post-bubble period, and argue that it is inefficiency in resource reallocation rather than a lack of investment that caused the persistent stagnation of Japanese output in the 1990s [also see Miyagawa (2003), and Ohtani, Shiratsuka, and Nakakuki (2004) for related empirical analyses on misallocation of resources].

Figure 8.7 applies the measure to the real capital stock of each industry in the Japanese Industry Productivity (JIP) database. The data suggest reallocation declined sharply in 1991–92, and throughout the 1990s never fully regained its previous level.

This figure also shows manufacturing and services separately. The graph suggests that the lack of capital reallocation has been considerably greater in manufacturing, a difference between the two sectors that has persisted since the early 1980s. The overall increase of reallocation during 1997–98 occurred mostly in services. It should be noted that the lack of "creative destruction" was a problem in Japanese manufacturing even before the bubble economy.

2.3 *The Role of the Financial System*

In the traditional Japanese main bank system in the 1960s and 1970s, banks played a key role in reallocating capital to more productive investment opportunities and in restructuring old companies. However, since the sec-

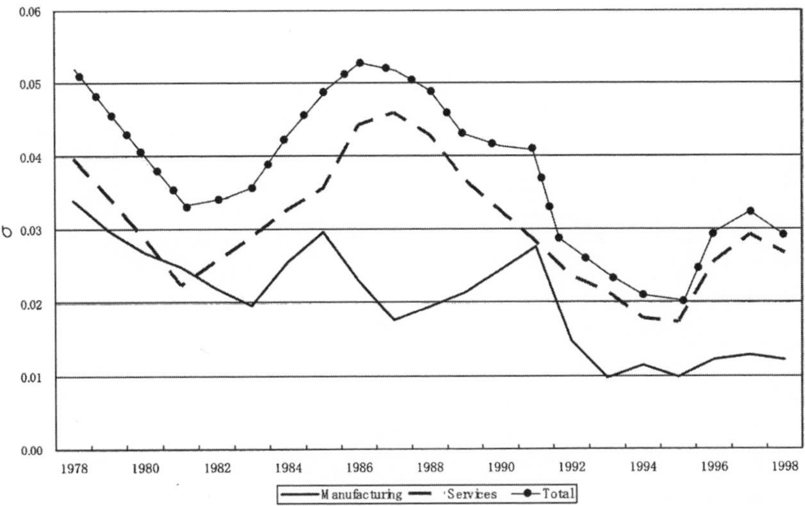

The measure used, σ_t, is defined in the text. Here, capital is the input. The larger σ_t, the greater the reallocation.

There are several ways to calculate the measure by sector. Here, aggregate $G_{A,t}$ and $S_{i,t}$ in each sector are used. However, the results are almost identical whether using each sector's growth for $G_{A,t}$ or shares in all industries for $S_{i,t}$.

Figure 8.7
Reallocation of Capital in Japan

ond half of the 1990s, the non-performing loan problem has overwhelmed and paralyzed both the banks and any prospects for the development and implementation of a sustained corporate restructuring policy.

Moreover, the Japanese banks have exacerbated the bad-loan and restructuring problems by lending in order to permit borrowers to survive, thereby avoiding the need to record the loans as realized losses. This type of loan, *'oi-gashi'* (literally, additional lending), is usually translated as "evergreening", and is also called forbearance lending.

Table 8.2 shows the average growth rates of bank borrowing for the construction and real estate industries, and the total borrowing for all industries excluding these two. Construction and real estate were the most heavily involved in the real estate speculation of the late 1980s. The data show that before the banking panic in late 1997, the growth rates of these two distressed industries significantly exceeded the total of other industries. Over the entire 1991–2002 period, while the overall industry borrowing rate was negative, the construction and real estate industries saw increases in lending. This evidence strongly suggests

Table 8.2
Annual Change in Bank Borrowing, by Industry
(percent)

	Construction	Real estate	All other industries
1991–97	3.73	5.68	1.66
1998–2002	–4.23	–7.81	–3.95
1991–2002	0.41	0.06	–0.68

Compound annual rates over the period shown.

Source: Computed by the author from data in Ministry of Finance, *Financial Statements Statistics of Corporations by Industry*, various issues.

evergreening in these two industries. A number of other studies, including Hosono and Sakuragawa (2003), Peek and Rosengren (2003), Sekine, Kobayashi, and Saita (2003), and Watanabe (2004) also provide evidence that in the post-bubble period there was evergreening in lending associated with real estate.

3 Main Banks and Restructuring

Compared with the era of the main bank system in the 1960s and 1970s, Japanese corporate restructuring has been significantly different since the mid-1990s.

First, under the main bank system, banks were much more powerful and exerted more influence on borrowers, largely because the average size of troubled firms was smaller and the spread of financial distress was much more limited in the 1960s and 1970s. Even though there were many cases of financial distress immediately after the first oil crisis, the level of non-performing loans was much smaller relative to total outstanding loans in the early 1970s than in the 1990s. Also, the banks' financial positions were much sounder. The banks maintained significantly more diversified portfolios in the earlier period than they do today, because then banks were the only providers of external funds to most Japanese companies. Through the 1980s and 1990s, major Japanese firms with sufficient reputation switched to capital markets for funding (Campbell and Hamao 1994; Hoshi, Kashyap, and Scharfstein 1993). In other words, starting some twenty years ago Japanese banks have lost their best-quality borrowers.

Second, in corporate restructuring before the bubble economy, a main bank generally acted as arbitrator or judge. The typical causes of financial difficulties were either some exogenous shock or company mismanagement. The recessions following the first oil crisis in the mid-1970s and the sharp appreciation of the yen in 1985–86 exemplify exogenous shocks. Banks were, in principle, "the good guys" in such situations, working to help companies survive. On the other hand, in cases of mismanagement, a main bank would intervene to replace incumbent management if necessary, mainly to protect the interests of creditors and partly for the benefit of long-term company employees. A well-known example is the first rescue of Mazda in the mid-1970s by Sumitomo Bank [see Sheard (1994) for detailed accounts of corporate restructuring under the conventional main bank system, including the Mazda case].

In the current situation, banks share responsibility for many corporations' financial troubles. Under the main bank system, financial institutions based most of their lending on real-estate collateral and on trust founded on long-established, close relationships. During the bubble years in the 1980s, these institutions lost their most credit-worthy borrowers who had switched to market financing, and found new borrowers in industries such as real estate and the resort business, which turned out to be much riskier. The banks seriously neglected due diligence in terms of credit analysis and monitoring during this period. These factors are the source of the more recent, ongoing non-performing loans problems. Hence, banks are both the source of and the solution to these problems, but have found it increasingly difficult to play the role of independent arbitrator as they did under the main bank system. For these reasons, bank-led corporate restructuring has been very ineffective and slow since the early 1990s.

With Japanese banks no longer able to play their traditional role of independent arbitrator, there was no party outside of the management-employee and lender-borrower relationships to offer advice and lead corporate restructuring. There were very limited corporate restructuring activities in Japan outside of the traditional main bank relationship until the late 1990s. The corporate restructuring business suddenly boomed around the time that important new policy measures were began in 1999–2000.

4 New Policy Measures

As Japan's economic stagnation continued in the 1990s, pressure built on the government to respond to the financial distress of firms and resulting bankruptcies. This led to a major overhaul of the bankruptcy code and the creation of a specific agency, Industrial Revitalization

Corporation Japan, to aid in reconstruction (although "revitalization" was tactfully used in naming it). In addition, an existing public financial institution, the Development Bank of Japan, moved to become involved in the restructuring process.

4.1 Revamping the Bankruptcy Code

The annual number of bankruptcies during the 1982–86 period actually exceeded any single year during the 1990s except for 1998, but the amount of liabilities involved was substantially greater, and increased significantly in the second half of 1990s to an unprecedented level. This suggests that larger corporations were going bankrupt after the bubble burst, especially since 1997, compared to earlier periods. Table 8.3 provides specific data.

Table 8.3
Bankruptcies

		Liabilities (billion yen)	
Years	Number	Total	Average
1982–86	18,681	3,338	179
1987–90	9,120	1,838	211
1991–96	13,893	7,598	555
1997	16,464	14,045	853
1998	18,988	13,748	724
1999	15,352	13,621	887
2000	18,769	23,885	1,273
2001	19,164	16,520	862
2002	19,087	13,782	722
2003	16,255	11,582	713
2004	13,679	7,818	572

Multi-year entries are annual averages. Includes both financial and non-financial corporations with liabilities of more than ¥10 million and (until March 2000) capitalization of over ¥1 million. That is, very small firms are excluded.

As discussed in the text, the large number in 1998 reflects a possible credit crunch that year. Liabilities peaked in 2000 because two mid-size life insurance companies, Kyoei Life and Chiyoda Life, went bankrupt that October. (See Fukao's chapter for more on the life insurance industry's problems.) The largest number of bankruptcies was 1984, with 20,841.

Source: Data from Tokyo Shoko Research Ltd, as reported in Bank of Japan, *Economics Statistics Monthly*, various issues.

The first response was a long-awaited reform of the legal system. Japanese insolvency law system has its origins in the post-World War II reconstruction period and for some 50 years there had been no major changes. The code lacked procedures to facilitate the rehabilitation and restructuring of struggling firms corresponding to those in Chapter 11 of the United States Bankruptcy Code, something seen by Japanese legal professionals as a major deficiency. [See Gertner and Scharfstein (1991) for how the Chapter 11 reorganization law improves the efficiency of restructuring of a financially distressed firm, by mitigating coordination problem among debt holders.] However, this issue did not raise serious concerns until the bubble economy burst in the early 1990s because before this period such problems generally were resolved through a bank-led restructuring process.

However, following the *jusen* (housing loan corporations) scandal in 1995, the need for Chapter 11-type procedures was acknowledged. In the *jusen* scandal, the government directly intervened and spent taxpayer money to clean up the mess, even though, technically speaking, the *jusen* were private financial institutions. The intervention was justified on the grounds that Japan's insolvency law was inefficient, so legal proceedings would have taken too long and might have destabilized the financial system (Yamamoto 2003). [For a fuller overview of the *jusen* crisis, see Hoshi and Kashyap 2001, p 268–71.]

Fundamental reform of Japan's insolvency law system began in 1996, covering individuals and multinational corporations as well as domestic businesses. At the beginning, discussions and arrangements for the reform progressed gradually. A further increase in bankruptcies following the financial crisis of late 1997 accelerated the process (Aoyama 2000).

A new Civil Rehabilitation Act (*Minji Saisei Ho*), which replaced the old Composition Act (*Wagi Ho*), was the first part of a comprehensive reform of Japan's insolvency law regime. The Diet passed the code in December 1999 and it came into effect in April 2000. The new code created a legal infrastructure that facilitates quick and efficient corporate restructuring, particularly outside the bank-led restructuring process (Yamamoto 2003). Among the important changes, it enabled debtor-in-possession financing and sped the procedure prior to the reorganization process being admitted by the court. Also, under the new law creditor initiative in a reorganization is much more respected; in the old system everything had to wait to be judged by the court. [For a non-technical discussion of the new laws, see Takagi (2003).]

The number of mergers and acquisitions increased significantly from 2000 to 2002 in both number and value. This suggests the new law facilitated increased market-based restructuring of financially distressed firms.

4.2 *Government Financial Institutions*

Responding to the new bankruptcy code, the Development Bank of Japan (DBJ) introduced business rehabilitation support programs in 2001. The Development Bank of Japan's move was endorsed by the government as part of its "immediate economic policy package" announced in April 2001. Hence, the Development Bank of Japan's involvement in the restructuring business began well before the much-publicized establishment of the Industrial Revitalization Corporation Japan (IRCJ). DBJ's involvement in corporate restructuring has been discreet; it has primarily engaged in bail-outs as one of several lenders or as a lender to the company that has taken over a struggling firm. DBJ also is a major lender to newly established private firms and consortiums of financial institutions that specialize in investment in distressed firms (Tomii 2003, Yokoyama 2004).

As part of an overall economic policy package, in December 2002 the government of Prime Minister Junichiro Koizumi established the IRCJ. This was to be the public financial institution that specialized in restructuring those firms in financial difficulties but which still had competitive core businesses. The Koizumi administration emphasized the need for the IRCJ by arguing that Japan's private sector restructuring business was still in its infancy and that public intervention was needed for efficiency and speed. In other words, once major restructuring is complete or when private-sector based restructuring firms are sufficiently developed, it will no longer be necessary. Therefore, the IRCJ, which began work in April 2003, was limited to a five year life that is set to expire in 2008. Investment bankers, lawyers, and other corporate restructuring professionals were drawn from the private sector to form the IRCJ's operating team. The activities of the Development Bank of Japan and the IRCJ are discussed further in Section 8.

5 Specific Restructurings

This section examines two major restructuring cases that have been completed, the Long-Term Credit Bank (LTCB) and Kanebo, and one ongoing case, Daiei, which exemplify the diverse approaches being used to restructure Japanese financial institutions and corporations.

5.1 Long-Term Credit Bank

The troubles of the Long-Term Credit Bank became public knowledge in 1998. This was before the major insolvency law reform was implemented, and while people still had faith in the conventional main bank system. So, it was a surprise to the Japanese business community when an American-based turn-around fund emerged as the buyer. LTCB has turned out to be a rare case of a successful restructuring of a Japanese financial institution. It also is a case study that reveals the conflicts of interest surrounding restructuring in Japan. Perhaps, Japanese business and government leaders prefer Carlos Ghosn's restructuring of Nissan, but that case went all too well to be considered as a prime example of Japan's corporate restructuring. Because LTCB's case was so controversial and grating, it stands out as a much more relevant business model for the subsequent restructuring wave in Japan since the year 2000. Thus, an outline of the events and analysis of its implications are in order. [The following chronology owes much to Tett (2003).]

During the initial stage of the LTCB restructuring in 1997–98, the government, in particular traditionalists in the Liberal Democratic Party, presumed that its corporate borrowers should be protected. They implicitly assumed that if the bank was nationalized and then resold to another entity, all corporate borrowers of the bank would continue to receive funds. Hence, even after nationalization, the government did not remove a substantial number of non-performing loans from LTCB's portfolio.

The sale of the nationalized LTCB was managed by Goldman Sachs, the first time a foreign investment bank was assigned such a politically sensitive role. The bidding process was reasonably competitive. However, the retention of LTCB's non-performing loans scared off most investment banks considered prime candidates such as Paribas, JP Morgan, and Chuo Mitsui Trust. More precisely, the key point of contention was the due diligence process in assessing the amount of non-performing loans. Many candidate buyers felt they were not allowed access to necessary information. Others thought it was simply impossible to assemble enough information to provide an accurate assessment because of the constraints (in size and time) and the complexity of LTCB's non-performing loan problem.

LTCB was finally sold in 1999 to Ripplewood, a then relatively unknown American private-equity firm. To create sufficient incentive, the Ministry of Finance added an option giving Ripplewood the right to return loans within three years to the government if they lost more than 20% of their value. From Ripplewood's point of view, this put option was absolutely fair. Ripplewood and the management of the new bank, renamed Shinsei Bank, intended to exercise the put option whenever necessary. However, Japan's government and business community were expecting Shinsei to play according to Japanese business customs, which implied Shinsei would continue to lend to existing borrowers and not exercise the put option. Ripplewood had hoped to get some Japanese financial institutions and other Japanese investors on board, but none approached agreed because they felt that the new arrangement would be politically controversial. The LTCB deal thus contained the seeds of conflict from the start.

Ripplewood took control on March 1, 2000 and Shinsei officially opened for business on June 6. Soon after, Sogo—a department store chain that had been bankrupt in fact for years and of which LTCB was a creditor—was restructured. This provided an opportunity for the Japanese business community to discover how Shinsei would act. The main bank for Sogo, the Industrial Bank of Japan, wanted to organize a bail-out. However, Shinsei refused to take part, as that would create new losses for it. At the same time, Shinsei started to exercise the put option given it by the Ministry of Finance, returning loans worth a trillion yen. These actions greatly shocked both the government and other Japanese banks.

Other banks had an incentive to participate in Industrial Bank of Japan's bail-out of Sogo because, as main banks with respect to other financially distressed companies, they were in similar positions. That is, if one bank refused to participate in a bail-out, other banks might refuse to participate in other bail-outs. By Japanese convention, a main bank was supposed to be responsible for a disproportionately large share of the restructuring process, which clearly created an incentive for a main bank to avoid significant restructurings. Thus, all the banks were keen to avoid a situation of non-cooperation, as this could set a bad precedent for similar situations.

Under these circumstances, postponing a serious corporate restructuring was a common practice among Japanese banks. This behavior can be maintained only if all creditors have similar positions as main banks and can sustain their current financial positions. In Sogo's case,

Shinsei had incentives and obligations significantly different from those of the other banks. Since all Japanese banks had serious balance sheet problems by the late 1990s, the failure of only a small fraction of the collusive schemes and their displacement by market-based valuations would have a significant adverse effect on the entire bail-out approach and even bring about its demise. Japanese banks and financial regulators began to recognize that their collusive soft bail-out schemes solved no problems, just merely postponed them until another main bank failed.

Shinsei's restructuring has been very successful, but has been attacked in the domestic media and by politicians. Shinsei kept exercising the put option on bad loans and refused to renew lending to troubled companies. A broad range of politicians portrayed Shinsei's behavior as virtual theft by foreign capital at Japanese taxpayers' expense. Perhaps it was rational that Japanese companies were willing neither to buy into LTCB nor invest in the Shinsei deal, given the magnitude of the subsequent loss of reputation. Conversely, it is probably fortunate for Shinsei's investors that they had no Japanese partners trying from the inside to force the bank to stay with the old business customs.

In February 2004, Shinsei Bank stock was (re)listed on the Tokyo Stock Exchange, five and a half years after LTCB's nationalization. Shinsei shares ended the first trading day at ¥827 yen, 58% above its issue price. At the issue price of ¥525, the consortium headed by Ripplewood realized $2.36 billion from the sale of about half of its two-thirds stake. The Japanese government, which retains a one-third stake in Shinsei, has also seen the value of its stake increase, although this is offset by the over ¥4 trillion injected into LTCB to prevent its collapse and the amount paid Shinsei under the bad-loan put option.

By all accounts, Shinsei's initial public offering was a huge success and proof that banking reform in Japan is possible. Looking ahead, the general opinion is that Shinsei by itself will not be able to survive competition once other major Japanese banks have fully recovered from their difficulties. Many forecast that Shinsei eventually will be bought by, or merge with, a major Japanese financial institution.

5.2 *Kanebo*

The Kanebo case is important because it involves the restructuring of a well-known Japanese company with a long history and because its business activities were outside the industries—such as real estate and construction—that expanded especially rapidly during the bubble economy. The problems Kanebo faced exemplify the issues faced by conventional Japanese corporate governance in general, and many old Japanese companies in particular. It also reveals the problems concerning the roles of public financial institutions such as the Industrial Revitalization Corporation Japan and Development Bank of Japan.

Kanebo Ltd. started as a cotton spinning company in 1887. During the 1920s and 1930s, its spinning and other textile businesses grew very rapidly. After World War II, during the high-growth era of the 1950s and 1960s, Kanebo sold the land in metropolitan areas on which its mills had stood. With the funds from these sales, Kanebo entered various new businesses. Led by a young and charismatic president, Junji Ito, by the late 1960s Kanebo had become a corporate conglomerate. The company proclaimed its business strategy as "pentagon management," as the business had grown to comprise five areas: textiles, cosmetics, pharmaceuticals, food products, and home products. Already by the early 1970s it had become the second-largest Japanese cosmetics company, after Shiseido, although this operation comprised only 14% of the firm's revenue in fiscal 1973; textiles were still responsible for 58% of its revenues.

After the 1973–74 oil crisis, Kanebo experienced difficulties, as did many other Japanese companies. However, Ito did not lay off workers. Instead the dividend on its shares was discontinued for nine years, 1976 to 1984. Ito was able to retain his position as president because of help from Kanebo's main bank and strong support from its labor union. Well-known as a charismatic and labor-friendly manager, in December 1985 he was appointed vice president, and later became president, of Japan Airlines, the national airline about to be privatized. This appointment followed the August 1985 plane crash that killed more than 500 people and a series of business scandals involving Japan Airlines. However, Ito resigned after just 18 months in March 1987, which suggests he was forced to resign because of political pressure.

Even as Kanebo emphasized diversification, the firm has been unable to restructure its core textile business or even sustain all its forays into new areas. By 1983 cosmetics comprised 40% of its annual revenue, almost as large an amount as generated by the three textile divisions. But in the next nine years, the cosmetics division increased sales by less than it had in 1981–83 and its share of revenue fell to 30% as the "fashion business" came to the fore. In 1991 the two traditional textile divisions continued to generate more revenue than cosmetics. And, as had been the case most of the time since the 1970s, one or another area of the textile business was being described as "depressed" or "unfavorable" by analysts. The pharmaceutical ventures never accounted for much: in 1991, after some two decades in the industry, this division accounted for just 4% of revenues and in 2002 sales were about the same as 11 years earlier. (All references are to fiscal years ending March of the following calendar year).

Immediately before merger talks with Kao in 2002–03, textiles still comprised 30% of Kanebo's sales, fashion was no longer a separately reported business segment, and cosmetics had regained a 40% share. However, fiscal year 2002 revenues were not much changed from 1991, although they had been higher in the mid-1990s.

The negative effects of diversification on the efficiency of internal capital allocation have been discussed extensively, both theoretically and empirically [see Stein (2003, part B) for a survey of recent works on this subject]. By the late 1990s, Kanebo had succumbed to these pitfalls. Its intra-company resource allocation had been distorted and the profits from the cosmetic business were being drained to cover losses in the other divisions, particularly textiles. In 1995 it ceased paying dividends.

In October 2003, Kao Corp, fourth in cosmetics sales, appeared as a merger partner for Kanebo. Even before a possible deal came to the public's attention, there seemed no other way forward for Kanebo than a major restructuring of its unprofitable businesses—that is, everything except the cosmetics division. However, there was no governance mechanism within the company or through monitoring by its main bank that could enforce such a restructuring.

Kao, like Kanebo also founded in 1887, can be described as the Japanese analogue of Procter and Gamble, although it also has specialty chemical operations that supply the company and sell to third parties. Although Kao once ventured as far afield as making floppy disks for computers, its current business areas are more closely integrated than Kanebo's; it also is far more profitable. While Kanebo was a loss-maker throughout the 1990s, Kao has been one of the most profitable Japanese companies in the post-bubble period. Its return on equity has been over 10% since fiscal year 2000, reaching 14.1% for 2003.

This performance reflects the fact that Kao is one of Japan's most capital market-oriented and profit-oriented companies. It also is one of the companies most frequently discussed in American business school cases as a successful Japanese corporation. Kao's stock has generally outperformed the Tokyo market since the mid-1990s and foreign investors hold over 30% of its shares. The success of its profit-oriented marketing strategy is often contrasted with the failure of the image-chasing marketing of Shiseido, Japan's largest cosmetics maker (although a smaller company than Kao because it is entirely cosmetics and toiletries). However, Kao found its cosmetics line lacked high-end products, and felt buying Kanebo's cosmetics division would up-scale its brand portfolio.

Even though talks started as merger negotiations, it was essentially a Kao buy-out of Kanebo, supported or perhaps drafted by Sumitomo Mitsui Bank, Kanebo's main bank. Kao naturally wanted to purchase only Kanebo's cosmetics division. This sale seemed to be the only way Kanebo could avoid bankruptcy, whether the buyer was Kao or another company. However, Kanebo's management withdrew from the deal, blaming strong opposition from its labor union.

Instead, in February 2004, Kanebo turned to the Industrial Revitalization Corporation Japan. Soon thereafter, newspapers reported that the IRCJ was going to inject ¥500 billion yen into Kanebo; Kao's offer for Kanebo's cosmetic division had been about ¥400 billion, incorrectly as it turned out.

In the actual rescue plan, released in March 2004, the amount to be injected through the IRCJ into the new company inheriting Kanebo's cosmetic business was just ¥366 billion. Not only was the cosmetic division being spun off as an independent company, Kanebo's management had to resign and its other business segments face drastic restructuring. The deal was clearly much less generous than Kanebo's management and labor unions had hoped. Indeed, the IRCJ bail-out was probably very similar to any deal Kao might have made.

In the end, this is part of the same old story: as past management practices continued to be examined by IRCJ, misconduct and accounting manipulation surrounding transactions between Kanebo and its subsidiaries have been revealed one after another.

5.3 *Daiei*

Determining the proper role of public financial institutions is inevitably a subjective task. This is nowhere truer than in the restructuring of the large supermarket chain, Daiei. The Japanese government had an incentive to keep Daiei alive and avoid drastic restructuring because the company employs about 10,700 people, has over 200 branches, and its effect on local economies is large. So the government provided support to Daiei's own restructuring plan in 2001–02, including financial support from the Development Bank of Japan and reorganization of Daiei's subsidiaries by the IRCJ. This was obviously a highly politically motivated intervention at the expense of taxpayers and Daiei's rivals. It is very symbolic that Daiei owned a very popular local baseball team, the *Daiei Hawks*, which has been the only professional baseball team in Kyushu. Later, at very beginning of restructuring supervised by IRCJ, Daiei was forced to sell the team to an IT company, *Softbank*.

Then, in early August 2004, Daiei's largest creditors UFJ, Mizuho, and Sumitomo-Mitsui banks announced they would not forgive more debt, inject more capital, or allow Daiei to advance its own rehabilitation plan (which would have been the third in four years). Instead, the banks intended to seek the IRCJ's help in restructuring the large supermarket chain. Daiei's management insisted that intervention by the IRCJ was unnecessary. At the same time, at least three private bidders appeared interested in Daiei, indicating an entirely private sector process was possible. First, Daiei's management eagerly pursued rehabilitation on its own, then looked into the possibilities with private partners. However, in the end, Daiei was forced to go to the IRCJ in October 2004 and the company's management had to resign. In the next several months, IRCJ purchased nearly 400 billion yen loans (in book value) from financial institutions to clean up Daiei's debt problem. Thirteen groups of investors participated to Daiei's auction: they include the group led by Wal-Mart, US giant, and another led by Ito-Yokado, Daiei's rival supermarket chain. In March 2005, IRCJ announced that Daiei will be sold to the investor group led by Marubeni Corporation, a large general trading company. Marubeni named former head of BMW Tokyo Corp as the new CEO, and the president of Hewlett-Packard Japan Ltd as the new president (COO) of Daiei.

Despite some observers' skepticism regarding the effectiveness of IRCJ in Daiei's case, the restructuring has certainly been accelerated under its supervision. Even so, the consequence of Daiei's restructuring is far from certain. One reason is the size and complexity of Daiei's problem: it is the largest company that IRCJ has dealt with and at least twice larger than the second largest, Kanebo. Given the spread of Daiei's business area and the complexity of its business group (especially, cross-share holdings among the group firms), there seems to be much less consensus about what is the best strategy for Daiei's efficient restructuring, compared with other cases that IRCJ has dealt with, including

Kanebo. Hence, Daiei will continue to make headlines in the months before this book's publication.

6 Lessons from Restructurings

Long-term Credit Bank's successful restructuring as Shinsei Bank and Kanebo's bail-out by the IRCJ exemplify corporate Japan's main difficulties in restructuring. These can be summarized under four points: unreasonable expectations, the role the financial sector played in creating the problems, the need for an objective outside party to enforce new arrangements/expectations, and the ambiguous role of public financial institutions. The four points are discussed below.

6.1 *Unreasonable Expectations*

Financially distressed Japanese corporations, including their management and labor unions as well as their shareholders and creditor banks, have generally expected something more generous than market-based restructuring is likely to provide them. For instance, in criticizing the IRCJ's plan to supply funds only to Kanebo's cosmetic business, Shigemitsu Miki, chair of the Japanese Bankers Association and chief executive officer of Mitsubishi Tokyo Financial Group, suggested that it should rescue the remaining parts of the company because "the IRCJ should take the risk that the private sector cannot take" (*Nikkei Shimbun*, Feb 24, 2004). This statement can be recast as asserting that because the IRCJ has deep pockets (taxpayer money), it should rescue companies on terms the private sector is unwilling to provide. Such expectations result in inefficient resource allocation; fortunately these costs are becoming increasingly recognized as the restructuring process becomes more market oriented and transparent.

6.2 *Financial Sector Complicity*

Many troubled Japanese companies were insolvent from the very beginning of the non-performing loan problem. Why, then, did banks, financial authorities, and the troubled companies continue to postpone restructuring for years, even though the problem loans snowballed and the situation worsened? There are two possible answers. The first is simple: there has been ignorance and a lack of foresight by the key stakeholders. The second is that bank executives and bureaucrats have been guilty of a combination of short-termism and conservatism.

In the postwar Japanese economy, senior bankers and bureaucrats were part of the elite. They typically attained their position by being appointed by their predecessors or by inheriting the post as a result of being an "insider." Tenure at the top was limited (no longer than 10 years for bank chief executive officers and Bank of Japan governors, less than 5 years on becoming the highest-ranked Ministry of Finance officer.) It was difficult for bankers and bureaucrats to reverse their predecessors' decisions or to acknowledge the mistakes or wrongdoing of those who appointed them. Incentives were focused more on protecting the status quo than caring about the long-term future of banks and the Japanese financial system.

For example, in the case of the Long-term Credit Bank, many of its bankers realized things were going wrong even before the bubble economy. They proposed a reform plan that had many things in common with what the foreign owners did do 20 years later when they restructured it as Shinsei. However, the idea of reform was dismissed, and LTCB eventually jumped onto the real estate lending bandwagon in the late 1980s [Tett (2003)]. This led to turmoil and the bank's eventual demise the 1990s. During the post-bubble downturn, LTCB's management simply covered up the seriousness of the non-performing loan problem through elaborate accounting malpractice. They never grappled with the need for serious restructuring, so it became bankrupt and was nationalized.

The absence of creditor pressure is a key factor in understanding the tardiness of corporate Japan's restructuring process. Although there has been a lack of incentive for heavily indebted companies such as Sogo and Kanebo to restructure, neither have the managers of large Japanese financial institutions been motivated to restructure non-performing loans. They have just kept their fingers crossed, hoping to complete their terms without facing a serious problem and to walk away with lucrative retirement benefits.

6.3 Need for an Outside Party

Japan's main banks and their regulators have been heavily involved in the mismanagement of their borrowers, and thereby must bear major responsibility for the bad-loan problems. Given the unrealistic expectations of insiders, it is extremely difficult to solve these problems by involving only management, labor, and financial institutions. It often requires an objective outside party to implement major restructuring.

As insiders that know the difficulties of negotiating to affect significant corporate changes, especially related to labor-force reductions, many experienced bankers have left Japanese banks to join foreign banks or private equity funds. They then return to negotiations as outside parties, which is why the restructuring business is now developing so quickly in Japan. An example is the restructuring of Mitsubishi Motors: after DaimlerChrysler gave up on Mitsubishi, Phoenix Capital, a private turn-around fund, has become the largest shareholder of the troubled motor company. The fund's chief executive officer is a former employee of Mitsubishi Bank. Bank of Tokyo-Mitsubishi is one of major suppliers of money to the distressed funds run by Phoenix Capital, along with the Development Bank of Japan and some regional banks.

Business restructuring sometimes requires major employee layoffs. Yet this practice goes against the lifetime employment system that has prevailed in postwar Japan, so it often takes an outside party to implement a breach of the implicit contracts between management and workers. This same point is emphasized by Shleifer and Summers (1988) in reference to the American merger boom in 1980s. In the current Japanese context, the idea that an outside party is more efficient at revising implicit contracts than insiders are will be extended to the long-term relationship between a borrower firm and its main bank. The outside party need not be a consultant or a buyer seeking control. For example, Ahmadjian and Robbins (2002) report that the simple presence of foreign shareholders has accelerated the restructuring of Japanese companies.

6.4 *The Ambiguous Role of Public Financial Institutions*

The role of public financial institutions such as the IRCJ and the Development Bank of Japan may be important, but they occupy an ambiguous position: in an idealized public image, the IRCJ is the last resort for financially distressed companies, and it should protect them from antilabor market mechanisms and exploitative foreign funds. In a more pragmatic view, if the IRCJ or Development Bank of Japan assessments of the companies are objective and fair, their conclusions will not differ much from market-based solutions. Public financial institutions are necessary only when there is some market failure that prevents private restructuring from working properly. This issue is examined further in the next section.

Another problem is that there is no agreed-upon boundary for judging whether a restructuring case is too risky for the private sector and thus requires government intervention. This means there is a serious concern that the activities of the IRCJ and other public financial institutions might distort decisions with respect to privately led business restructuring. The IRCJ's actions, for example, could drive down the potential profits that come from restructuring businesses, profits that are essential to attract private funds to take the necessary risks to support the restructuring in the first place.

7 Market-based Restructuring versus Government Intervention

The biggest concern raised by government intervention in corporate restructuring is its potential to be over-generous. Keeping inefficient companies alive is likely to result in a huge waste of resources that should be allocated to other, more productive investment opportunities (Caballero, Hoshi, and Kashyap 2003). Companies that have already become insolvent cannot be revived without disadvantage to their competitors. Even if the intention of a government financial institution is sincere, whenever it intervenes in a corporate restructuring that private funds have avoided, it means depositor or taxpayer money has been exposed to a higher risk than the market was willing to take.

The economic principle that is supposed to determine the necessity of government financial institutions in the restructuring process is very simple. Government intervention is necessary only when there is a situation of market failure. However, in practice, it is nearly impossible to determine objectively if there really is a market failure and if government intervention is necessary.

Indeed, what is market failure? It is useful to distinguish two types in the context of this discussion. The first is the difficulty of restructuring government-related businesses. The second is the lack of necessary business restructuring activities in the private sector.

7.1 Restructuring Government-Related Businesses

In restructuring government-related businesses, it is legally questionable whether a private firm should be directly involved. For example, the Kyushu Industrial Transportation Company (KITCo, Kyushu Sangyo Kotsu) is one of the very first companies the IRCJ agreed to bail out. KITCo is the second largest transportation company in

Kyushu, and its main businesses include local bus lines throughout the region. So, if KITCo's daily operation suffers difficulties because of the company's financial trouble, it would have enormous negative effects on local economic activities. But, KITCo's bus lines are highly regulated and thus must deal closely with government authorities. Its competitors include bus lines owned by local governments, which continue to operate even though they have been running losses for many years. In a case such as this, a public financial institution has advantages in negotiating with local governments.

KITCo is a private company, whose largest shareholders had been its top management and their families before KITCo asked the IRCJ for help. When the IRCJ set out a bail-out scheme for KITCo, the Ministry of Land, Infrastructure and Transport released an official supporting opinion. This was unlikely to have happened if the bail-out had been organized by a private turn-around fund. Hence, the roles of the IRCJ and the Development Bank of Japan have been beneficial and indeed necessary in this case.

7.2 *Lack of Private Sector Restructuring Activity*

When the necessity of government financial institutions is premised on insufficient restructuring activity in the private sector, this argument is inevitably subjective. This proposition which emphasizes the lack of private restructuring activity is similar to the infant-industry argument in international trade. As Doi stresses in Chapter 6, a government financial institution is needed only until enough business develops in the private sector; however, waiting for gradual development in the private sector exacts social costs. This suggests the eventual withdrawal of government financial institutions from the restructuring business. Both the Development Bank of Japan and the IRCJ acknowledge this aspect about their temporary roles (Tomii 2003, Yokoyama 2004).

8 Government Financial Institutions

Two government-related financial institutions have been mentioned throughout this chapter as being involved in Japan's corporate restructuring, the Industrial Revitalization Corporation Japan and the Development Bank of Japan. They are further described in this section.

8.1 The Industrial Revitalization Corporation Japan

The creation of the IRCJ in April 2003 has been very effective in promoting the necessary corporate restructuring within the Japanese business community. As discussed earlier, some debtor firms and financial institutions apparently expected the IRCJ to act as a generous benefactor to financially distressed firms (and their creditors). After its first year of operations, this benign image faded. The IRCJ also has taken on a much smaller number of cases than many expected. By the time IRCJ stopped purchasing bad loans in March 2005, IRCJ had participated in 41 corporate restructurings and purchased loan claims of more than 1.26 trillion yen in book value. Since IRCJ purchased non-performing loans in discount, it has actually spent about 600–700 billion yen so far.

Among the companies IRCJ has dealt with, Daiei was distinctively the largest. Other cases that would have major economic impacts are Kanebo and Misawa Home, a real estate developer. Mitsui Mining was another well publisized case that has been important more symbolically than economically. On the other hand, 11 firms, more than one-fourth of total, are hotel and resort businesses. All of them are relatively small firms. The restructuring of the Seibu group, the largest resort developer and hotel chain in Japan (once in the world) has emerged as a major economic issue only after IRCJ stopped dealing with new restructuring cases.

How the IRCJ has actually dealt with distressed firms is not very different from private market-based approaches, and the IRCJ has not been very aggressive in seeking firms to restructure, something it has been unfairly accused of doing. The restructuring process of each distressed company the IRCJ assists is limited to three years duration. Hence I believe that the IRCJ will not be a serious threat to restructuring by the private sector, in part because when IRCJ was created its tenure was limited to the period 2003–08.

Some skeptics have suggested this initial term will be extended. Given that the re-instatement of a cap on deposit insurance was postponed so many times by the Japanese government, this possibility cannot be ignored. But, since IRCJ has already stopped buying loan claims at the end of March 2005 as it had been scheduled, it is very likely that the term will end in 2008 as planned. Also the senior members of the IRCJ are successful investment bankers and lawyers who could earn higher incomes in the private sector, so they have little reason to extend the IRCJ's life. Nor do they have much incentive to "go soft" on distressed companies at the expense of taxpayers.

8.2 The Development Bank of Japan

The role of the Development Bank of Japan (DBJ) in restructuring is potentially more important and also more problematic. Table 8.4 presents data on the DBJ's activities as these relate to its official roles, particular as a promoter of "economic revitalization." Although the general category in its charter, "enhance the quality of life", is large, it has shrunk somewhat in recent years, while revitalization has grown rapidly—particularly "reform of economic structure." (The origins and purposes of the DBJ are presented in Doi's chapter in connection with his proposals of how to reform the institution.)

A clear line must also be drawn between the DBJ's restructuring activities and its traditional promotion of regional economies. The DBJ is a government financial institution that some consider a leftover of traditional industrial policy and the high-growth era. It is therefore quite natural that the DBJ wishes to play an active role in corporate restructuring, thereby avoiding the decline of its bureaucratic organization, and all the shrinkage in power, status, and staffing levels that this entails.

All the potential risks concerning the IRCJ's role in business restructuring can be applied to the DBJ. Moreover, the DBJ has been under the influence of the Ministry of Finance—among other things, its past presidents have been retired high-ranking Ministry officials. Moreover, the DBJ's liabilities include heavy borrowing from the Fiscal Investment and Loan Program. For these reasons, the DBJ is considered to be

Table 8.4
Development Bank of Japan, Distribution of New Loans and Investments (percent)

2000	2001	2002	2003	Purpose
19.5	26.3	27.7	33.8	Economic structural Reform[1]
2.2	1.9	2.4	1.3	Development of intellectual infrastructure[1]
23.8	19.7	20.1	23.3	Creation of self-reliant regions
50.1	48.3	45.4	37.9	Enhancement of the quality of life
4.4	3.7	4.4	3.7	Improvement of social capital
11,995	12,556	12,620	1,183	Total (billion yen)

Data are for fiscal years, which end in March of the following calendar year.

[1]Together, these are components of "economic revitalization".

Source: Data from Development Bank of Japan, 2003 and 2003 Annual Reports.

more vulnerable to political pressure than the IRCJ, which means there is greater incentive for it to be "soft" on distressed companies. Under these circumstances, it is heartening, and much to the DBJ's credit, that there is no evidence of softness in its activities. Apparently, the DBJ so far has successfully avoided political pressure relating to its core activities.

8.3 Evaluation

I believe both the IRCJ and the DBJ have been reasonably successful in helping the restructuring process of corporate Japan during the last several years. Because expectations for the IRCJ were so high at its inception, many have expressed disappointment and dissatisfaction with it. However, anything beyond its current activities involves a substantial risk of being too soft, and hence less effective and efficient.

If the IRCJ and the DBJ were more generous in dealing with distressed companies, these activities would inevitably involve the redistribution of wealth from taxpayers to the stakeholders of the companies—their management, employees, and creditors. It is important to acknowledge this point and to examine the economic policy implications of the role government financial institutions play in restructuring corporate Japan. However, as repeatedly discussed, it is simply impossible to objectively judge the necessity of intervention by government financial institutions. The matter must therefore be openly debated and government financial institutions must remain aware of their ultimate accountability to taxpayers.

9 Policy Recommendations

In the first quarter of 2005, the Japanese economy once again may be on track to recovering from the stagnation that began in the early 1990s. However, previous signs of recovery have turned out to be false and, in any case, a sustained recovery will not diminish the underlying need for further corporate restructuring. In particular, Industrial Revitalization Corporation Japan (IRCJ) has stopped purchasing bad loans of the companies restructured under its supervision as of March 2005. IRCJ, along with Development Bank of Japan, made significant progress in the restructuring of corporate Japan including Daiei, have instigated even more private sector-initiated restructurings. However, some major and very difficult restructurings such as Mitsubishi Motors and the Seibu group have been left unsettled. This means the easier steps in the process have been completed, but the most difficult parts remain.

The successful cases of corporate restructuring so far, such as hotels and resorts, were in industries that had experienced excessively rapid expansion in the bubble era. For such companies, objective values could be calculated relatively easily and conflicts of interest among related parties were more easily resolved. However, the restructuring of older companies and in traditional industries has been extremely slow. These cases involve tangled borrower-lender relationships embedded in the main bank system, and deeply entrenched management-labor relationships revolving around the lifetime employment system. Because the interests of the various stakeholders are likely to be in conflict, addressing these problems requires subtlety, risk, and effort over a long period.

There is no way to solve these tangled long-term relationships without bringing in an outside party, though it certainly does not have to be a foreign investor. Indeed, because restructuring directly deals with the complex business, political, social, and cultural conventions of a particular country, the business inherently involves highly country-specific knowledge and skills. Even foreign investors as outside parties have relied substantially upon their skilled Japanese employees or even appropriate insiders in their restructuring activities.

Unlike the introduction of financial products such as derivatives, the development of distress financing and merger and acquisition activity in Japan has taken time. But corporate restructuring is a rapidly growing business in Japan, and there are now many domestic distress funds that specialize in state-of-the-art approaches to these problems. Business models for successful restructuring are being developed, and the public is gradually recognizing the need for restructuring. There is reason for optimism.

On the other hand, we should be cautious about government intervention in the process, as Japan's government has been a part of the cause of the non-performing loan problem from the start. There is a risk that the IRCJ and the DBJ might be overly generous to distressed companies, and their activities crowd out private restructuring. For these reasons, even though public expectations about the IRCJ's activities have been high, I am skeptical about the necessity of further intervention by the IRCJ beyond its five-year life span. Explicit rules governing the extent of intervention in restructuring are crucial and as yet significantly underdeveloped. In this sense, the IRCJ's pre-set life span was a positive move. The DBJ's activity is relatively unrestricted. The roles of both institutions have been satisfactory so far, but need to continue to be examined carefully and discussed openly.

The coordination of policies on corporate restructuring with the policy measures discussed in other chapters of this book is an important issue. Most importantly, the restructuring of non-financial corporations is inseparable from the restructuring of their lenders, as discussed by Hoshi and Kashyap (chapter 5). In particular, the drastic restructuring of Japan's banking sector will necessarily cause restructuring of their borrowers' loans.

The most difficult part of corporate reform in Japan will be challenging the entrenched interests both of traditional large companies and government-related businesses. In addition to their heavy dependence on bank financing, long-term labor relations are a serious impediment, as shown in the case of Kanebo. When a company that had been loyal to its employees is restructured, its older employees are typically the biggest losers. On the other hand, if restructuring is impeded and capital continues to be allocated sub-optimally, younger Japanese workers are the losers, because fewer new jobs emerge for them. In this sense, corporate restructuring is an inter-generational issue. (Related labor market issues are discussed by Higuchi and Hashimoto in chapter 10.)

Corporate restructuring is also entwined with macroeconomic policy. Some proponents of restructuring object to inflationary monetary policy because they believe it will create undesirable transfers in real terms from creditors to debtors, which may delay the process. However, achieving positive but low levels of inflation, as discussed by Ito and Mishkin (chapter 4), will increase nominal interest rates, especially at the long-end of the term structure. This is likely to create a favorable environment for restructuring and further expose companies that should be restructured.

There is no magic strategy that revives unprofitable businesses, but the problems remain as long as restructuring is postponed. It is necessary to create Japanese legal and institutional structures that support and expedite corporate restructuring. It is important that existing government financial institutions engage effectively in restructuring, forcing companies either to become profitable or to disappear. Most important, all policy measures should be designed to support the primacy of a market-based restructuring process. This necessary evolution of the restructuring process is underway in Japan, but the toughest part is yet to be done.

Acknowledgment

The author is particularly grateful to Hugh Patrick for many discussions on the subjects dealt with in this chapter and for his detailed comments on an earlier draft; and to Takatoshi Ito and David Weinstein for their comments on the conference draft. I also thank other members of the "Reviving" project, as well as Kyoji Fukao, Mineko Furuichi, Masaharu Hanazaki, Richard Jerram, Tsutomu Miyagawa, Makoto Saito, Yoichiro Yokoyama, and the seminar participants at the Hitotsubashi macro lunch, Development Bank of Japan, Japan Economic Association Meeting in September 2004, and TRIP seminar at the University of Tokyo for their comments. Kohei Aono provided able research assistance. Of course, any remaining errors are my own.

References

Ahmadjian, Christina L. and Gregory E. Robbins. 2002. "A Clash of Capitalisms: Foreign Shareholders and Corporate Restructuring in 1990s Japan." Center for Japanese Economy and Business, Working Paper Series 203.

Aoyama, Yoshimitsu. 2000. "Minji saisei hô no igi to tenbo (Implications of and Perspectives on Enactment of Civil Rehabilitation Law)." *Kin'yu-shoji hanrei* (Financial and Commercial Judicial Precedent) 1086: 6–9.

Caballero, Ricardo J. and Mohamad L. Hammour. 1994. "The Cleansing Effect of Recessions." *American Economic Review* 84 (5): (December) 1350–68.

______. 1996. "On the Timing and Efficiency of Creative Destruction." *Quarterly Journal of Economics* 446 (3): (August) 805–52.

Caballero, Ricardo J., Takeo Hoshi, and Anil Kashyap. 2003. "Zombie Lending and Depressed Restructuring in Japan". Mimeo. NBER.

Campbell, John Y. and Yasushi Hamao. 1995. "Changing Patterns of Corporate Financing and the Main Bank System in Japan." In *The Japanese Main Bank System: Its Relevance for Developing and Transforming Economies*, editors Masahiko Aoki and Hugh Patrick. New York: Oxford University Press.

Fukao, Kyoji, Tomohiko Inui, Hiroki Kawai, and Tsutomu Miyagawa. 2003. "Sectoral Productivity and Economic Growth in Japan: 1970–98: An Empirical Analysis Based on the JIP Database." ESRI Cabinet Office, Discussion Paper Series 67.

Genda, Yuji. 1998. "Job Creation and Destruction in Japan; 1991–1995." *Journal of the Japanese and International Economies*, 12: (March) 1–23.

Gertner, Robert and David Scharfstein. 1991 "A Theory of Workouts and the Effects of Reorganization Law." *Journal of Finance*, 46 (4): (September) 1189–1222.

Hayashi, Fumio and Edward C. Prescott. 2002 "The 1990s in Japan: A Lost Decade." *Review of Economic Dynamics* 5 (1): (January) 206–235.

Hoshi, Takeo and Anil K. Kashyap. 2001. *Corporate Financing and Governance in Japan: The Road to the Future*. Cambridge, MA: MIT Press.

Hosono, Kaoru, and Masaya Sakuragawa. 2001. "Soft Budget Problems in the Japanese Credit Market." Nagoya-city University Working Paper 345.

Ito, Keiko, and Kyoji Fukao. 2003. "Vertical Intra-Industry Trade and the Division of Labor in East Asia." Institute of Economic Research Discussion Paper Series A444 (October). Hitotsubashi Univ.

Jorgenson, Dale and Kazuyuki Motohashi. 2003. "Economic Growth of Japan and the United States in the Information Age." RIETI Discussion Paper 03-E-015 (July).

Kawamoto, Takuji. 2004. "What Do the Purified Solow Residuals Tell Us about Japan's Lost Decade?" Bank of Japan, IMES Discussion Paper Series 2004-E-5.

Lilien, David M. 1982. "Sectoral Shifts and Cyclical Unemployment." *Journal of Political Economy*, 90 (4): 777–93.

Miyagawa, Tsutomu. 2003. "Ushinawareta Jyu-nen to Sangyo-kozo no Tenkan (The Lost Decade and the Transformation of Industrial Structure)." In *Ushinawareta 10 nen-no Shin-no Genin-ha Nanika* (Real Cause of the Lost Decade), editors Kikuo Iwata and Tsutomu Miyagawa. Tokyo: Toyo Keizai Shinposha.

Ohtani, Akira, Shigenori Shiratsuka, and Masayuki Nakakuki. 2004. "Seisan-youso shijo no yugami to kokunai keizai chyosei" (Distortions in the Production Factor Markets and Domestic Economic Adjustment). IMES Discussion Paper Series 2004-J-01.

Peek, Joe, and Eric S. Rosengren. 2003. "Unnatural Selection: Perverse Incentives and the Misallocation of Credit in Japan." NBER Working Paper 9643. (April)

Saita, Yumi, and Toshitaka Sekine. 2001. "Sectoral Credit Shifts in Japan: Causes and Consequences of Their Decline in the 1990s". Bank of Japan, Research and Statistics Department, Working Paper 01-16. (October)

Sekine, Toshitaka, Keiichiro Kobayashi, and Yumi Saita. 2003. Forbearance Lending: The Case of Japanese Firms. *Monetary and Economic Studies* 21 (2).

Sheard, Paul. 1994. "Main Banks and the Governance of Financial Distress." In *The Japanese Main Bank System: Its Relevance for Developing and Transforming Economies*, editors Masahiko Aoki and Hugh Patrick. New York: Oxford University Press.

Shleifer, Andrei and Lawrence Summers. 1988. "Breach of Trust in Hostile Takeovers." In *Corporate Takeovers: Causes and Consequences*, editor Alan J Auerbach. Chicago: University of Chicago Press.

Stein, Jeremy C. 2003. "Agency, Information and Corporate Investment." In *Handbook of the Economics of Finance: Corporate Finance*, editors George M. Constantinides, Milton Harris, and Rene M. Stulz. Amsterdam: North-Holland.

Takagi, Shinjiro. 2000. "Minji saisei hô no seko-jyunbi no tameno kadai (Preparing for Civil Rehabilitation Law Taking Effect)." *Kin'yu-shoji hanrei* (Financial and Commercial Judicial Precedent) 1086: 10–18.

Takagi, Shinjiro. 2003. *Kigyousaisei-no Kisochisiki* (Fundamentals of Corporate Restructuring). Tokyo: Iwanami Shoten.

Tett, Gillian. 2003. *Saving the Sun: A Wall Street Gamble to Rescue Japan from Its Trillion-Dollar Meltdown*. New York: HarperBusiness.

Tomii, Satoshi. 2003. "Business Rehabilitation Support Programme." Mimeo. Development Bank of Japan.

Watanabe, Wako. 2003. "Prudential Regulation, the 'Credit Crunch' and the Ineffectiveness of Monetary Policy: Evidence from Japan." Mimeo. Osaka University.

______. 2004. "Does a Large Loss of Capital Cause Ever-greening or Flight to Quality? Evidence from Japan." Mimeo. Osaka University.

Woo, David. 2003. "In Search of 'Capital Crunch': Supply Factors Behind the Credit Slowdown in Japan." *Journal of Money, Credit, and Banking* 35 (6): 1019–38.

Yamamoto, Kazuhiko. 2003. *Tousan Shori Ho Numon* (Introduction to Insolvency Law). Tokyo:Yuhikaku Publishing. (In Japanese)

Yokoyama, Yoichiro. 2004. "Jigyo-saisei-eno Torikumi-ni-tuite." Mimeo. Development Bank of Japan, Corporate Restructuring Business. (In Japanese)

9

Changing Capital Markets: The Corporate Bond Market and Credit Risk

Mariko Fujii

There are diverse evaluations of the status of Tokyo's financial markets. The positive view assures that these work well and at the level of other global financial markets. Other opinions focus on what Tokyo lacks: markets for venture capital, high-yield bonds, and credit-risk transfers. These critics also stress poor performing market functions such as liquidity and efficient pricing.

This chapter explores these various views more fully, incorporating them with other information and analysis to evaluate the changes in Tokyo's capital markets in particular since the institutional reform measures known as the financial Big Bang, which sought to establish "free, fair and global" markets, began in 1997. More specific and detailed analysis of the changes brought about by deregulatory measures is then presented for corporate bond markets. This focus reflects the fact that, compared to equity and government bond markets, corporate bond markets are regarded as the most functionally unsatisfactory. Despite their importance in a market-based financial system, little empirical work has been conducted on the functioning of Japan's corporate bond markets. The analytic purpose of this chapter is to show how the pricing mechanism works in credit risk markets such as corporate bonds and credit derivatives.

In Japan's corporate bond market, most regulations had been lifted by the mid-1990s. This means that if the regulations had been truly effective, it should be possible to identify changes brought about by deregulation. Indeed, one of the most remarkable changes in post-reform markets is that we observe default events for publicly placed bonds. Moreover, new forms of loan agreements, such as syndications, have become prevalent. Markets for credit derivatives also are developing to provide another channel to price credit risks.

Based on these developments, it is possible to conduct an empirical study comparing the price of credit risk across markets. This analysis is done in two ways for corporate bonds. The first examines the initial pricing to see whether it reflects credit risk rigorously. The second analyzes secondary-market spreads compared to premiums on derivatives such as credit default swaps (CDS). Specifically, bond yields are used to obtain an implicit evaluation of the credit risk of firms in the secondary market, which then can be compared with more direct data on credit risk, such as ratings and credit derivative premiums. When both bond and credit-derivative markets work reasonably well, there should be a consistent evaluation of risk across both markets. Otherwise, insufficient arbitrage or other impediments must be suspected.

The empirical results indicate two things. First, since 1997 initial pricing of corporate bonds has become more sensitive to creditworthiness as shown in commercial ratings. Second, the implied credit risk in corporate bond yields appears to be consistently priced with those shown in commercial ratings and the observed value of credit default swap premiums, at least for firms for which data can be obtained. This finding suggests better pricing efficiency for bonds and derivatives in the market for credit risk transfer than was the case in the pre-reform period.

The chapter continues by summarizing my survey of market participants, and then provides an overview of trends and changes in the bond market. With this background, the empirical analysis is undertaken. A discussion of policy issues concludes the chapter.

1 Market Participants' Views

To see how market participants viewed the current strengths and weaknesses of Tokyo's capital markets, in late 2003 I polled 12 representative senior managers of key financial institutions, both Japanese and foreign, active in Tokyo and drawn from among both institutional investors and corporations. (See the Appendix for detailed answers to the survey.)

Overall, most respondents were positive regarding the regulatory and institutional framework, except for the tax code. They felt that there are few institutional impediments to their activities. This reflects the success of the Big Bang reforms in achieving its original objective: providing more freedom of activity for an extensive range of financial institutions. However, some respondents pointed out that even new entry into the financial services sector has not led to effective competition among players. The legal system that separates the activities of commercial and investment banking services also was a concern. In commercial banking, bad loan problems have been so serious that few innovative actions on the banking side have been undertaken in the last several years.

There is general agreement that the market for corporate bonds is unsatisfactory and illiquid for most players, contrasting with positive views of the Japanese government bond (JGB) markets. Currently, more than 95% of trading is in Japanese government bonds. Bank lending is still the dominant channel of corporate finance, so many regard the corporate bond market's role to be under-weighted in financing firms. This point also relates to the non-existence of high-yield bond markets.

The general evaluation is that Tokyo's stock markets are globally competitive both in liquidity and trading volume, with satisfactory pricing functions. To have better venture capital markets, there is wide agreement that more strict and adequate criteria for listing should be stipulated, since the Tokyo Stock Exchange's Mothers and other similar markets have failed to gain credibility with investors, although their establishment initially contributed to demand.

Derivative transactions are regarded as very poor in terms of trading volume and functions, for both stock and bond markets. A related concern is the appropriateness of the short-selling regulation introduced in February 2002, which some respondents believe adversely affects price formation.

Serious concerns were expressed regarding management, especially of human resources. Indeed, some questioned whether the personnel management system of Japanese financial institutions is suited to global competition. There was a strong sense that the speed of decision-making within a company, as well as corporate governance rules, need to be thoroughly reviewed. Both of these items have long been criticized as problems stemming from the Japanese management style, so the message is that restructuring organizations and management practices is of some urgency.

Taken together, these answers indicate that reform has provided more flexibility of activities, but it is not clear that Tokyo's capital markets are as competitive and performing as well as New York and London, the world's principal capital markets.

2 Bond Market Trends

Basic statistics on the Japanese bond market are presented in Table 9.1 (issuance) and Table 9.2 (amount outstanding). Because the central government has been running huge deficits for years, the share of Japanese government bonds (JGB) is overwhelming by both measures. Indeed,

Table 9.1
Japanese Bond Markets: Gross Issuance

1985	1993	1998	2003	Issuer
Amounts (billion yen)				
26,553	58,530	100,207	169,316	Public sector[1]
2,587	5,454	11,522	10,356	Corporate sector
26,300	39,983	24,474	9,271	Bank debentures
—	—	378	200	Asset-backed securities
				Public-sector detail[1]
22,998	54,802	95,843	157,797	Central government (JGB)[2]
807	1,371	1,754	4,621	Local government
				Corporate-sector detail
944	2,979	10,453	6,993	Straight bonds
1,586	2,028	214	77	Convertible bond
57	447	855	3,286	Private placement
Ratio to nominal GDP (percent)				
8.1	12.2	19.6	33.8	Public sector[1]
0.8	1.1	2.2	2.1	Corporate total
8.0	8.3	4.8	1.8	Bank debentures
—	—	0.1	0.0	Asset-backed securities
				Public-sector detail[1]
7.0	11.4	18.7	31.5	Central government (JGB)[2]
0.2	0.3	0.3	0.9	Local government
				Corporate-sector detail
0.3	0.6	2.0	1.4	Straight bonds
0.5	0.4	0.0	0.0	Convertible bond
0.0	0.1	0.2	0.7	Private placement

Data are for fiscal years, which end March 31 of the following calendar year.
[1]Public placement only. Total includes government-guaranteed bonds issued by affiliated agencies, which are not itemized here.
[2]Central government excludes financing bills used for cash management purposes.

Source: Japan Security Dealers Association: Annual Report, Monthly Bond Review, various issues.

Table 9.2
Japanese Bond Markets: Amounts Outstanding

1985	1993	1998	2003	Issuer
Amounts (trillion yen)				
156.9	220.8	329.9	607.2	Public sector[1]
14.0	39.2	58.4	66.9	Corporate sector
43.5	77.8	57.2	30.1	Bank debentures
—	—	0.5	1.1	Asset-backed securities
				Public-sector detail[1]
134.4	192.5	295.2	548.8	Central government (JGB)[2]
6.1	8.4	13.5	23.1	Local government
				Corporate-sector detail
9.2	16.3	42.3	53.5	Straight bonds
4.6	18.3	12.9	4.5	Convertible bond
0.3	4.6	3.1	8.9	Private placement
Ratio to nominal GDP (percent)				
47.9	45.9	64.4	121.1	Public sector[1]
4.3	8.2	11.4	13.3	Corporate total
13.3	16.2	11.2	6.0	Bank debentures
—	—	0.1	0.2	Asset-backed securities
				Public-sector detail[1]
41.1	40.1	57.6	109.5	Central government (JGB)[2]
1.9	1.8	2.6	4.6	Local government
				Corporate-sector detail
2.8	3.4	8.3	10.7	Straight bonds
1.4	3.8	2.5	0.9	Convertible bond
0.1	1.0	0.6	1.8	Private placement

Data are for fiscal years, which end March 31 of the following calendar year.
[1]Public placement only. Total includes government-guaranteed bonds issued by affiliated agencies, which are not itemized here.
[2]Central government excludes financing bills used for cash management purposes. These totaled ¥70.3 trillion in fiscal 2003.

Source: Japan Security Dealers Association; Bank of Japan, *Monthly Statistics of Finance and Economics*, Feb 2004.

public-sector debt has increased its share despite the growth of private-sector debt. The ratio of total outstanding long-term public liabilities inclusive of local government bonds to nominal GDP was over 120% at the end of fiscal 2003 (31 March 2004). This excludes the considerable amount of government bills with issue maturity of less than one year.

In contrast, in the United States public-sector debt, including government agency issues, was about equal to GDP in 2003.

For Japanese government bond markets, many reform measures have been taken to enhance efficiency in both primary and secondary markets, and thus it is widely recognized that JGB markets are well-functioning and efficient by global standards. The reform measures included introducing a wider variety of products, when-issued trading, more extensive use of competitive auctions in placement, and re-opening (selling additional bonds of an existing issue rather than offering a new issue with different terms).

As part of the revamping begun in fiscal year 2001 of the Fiscal and Investment Loan Program (FILP) and the postal savings system, new types of government bonds have been issued. These are Fiscal Loan Bonds, which partly replace funds collected by the Postal Saving and Postal Insurance systems, which are no longer deposited in FILP. Yet the Postal Saving and the Postal Insurance systems still purchase a certain amount of these Fiscal Loan Bonds as transitional measures. For statistical purposes, these Fiscal Loan Bonds are classified as JGB issue because they are managed by Ministry of Finance as part of them.

There are several categories of private sector bonds, including corporate bonds, bank debentures, and asset-backed securities. Bank debentures have become less important, while asset-backed securities have increased. A new legal framework became available for asset-backed securities in 1993, and the financial Big Bang allowed Special Purpose Companies for these securities in 1998. The outstanding amount of asset-backed securities had grown to over one trillion yen by 2003. Historically, the three long-term credit banks and the three central cooperative banks were the issuers of bank debentures. At the end of 2004, there were only four institutions still issuing bank debentures and one of them plans to cease issue in early 2006.

Besides the relatively large size of public sector debt, there are two other notable differences in Japanese bond markets compared with American ones. First, because the Japanese financial system traditionally has been bank-centered, the corporate bond market is relatively small. Corporate bonds outstanding in Japan are just over 13% of GDP, compared to 25% in the United States based on 2004 data. Second, American financial institutions raise more funds through the markets than their Japanese counterparts. This difference reflects the fact that Japanese banks were not allowed to issue corporate bonds until 1999, which made their liabilities more dependent on deposits than is the case for banks in the United States.

Table 9.3 shows turnover rates. The overwhelming bulk of the trading volume is in Japanese government bonds. Indeed, it is striking that corporate bonds show low trading activity even for numbers including repurchase-agreement (repo, *gensaki*) transactions. Low trading activity and low liquidity are almost the same thing, and it is hard to know which factor is causing the other. Participants expressed dissatisfaction with liquidity in corporate markets. However, it is not easy to statistically show the actual improvements that have taken place in the depth of the markets. (More data and detail on the mechanics of Japan's capital markets are published annually in English by the Japan Securities Research Institute.)

Anecdotally, most participants are satisfied with the performance and function of the JGB, at least as far as primary products are concerned. An exception is in cases of sharp interest rate rises, instances when most traders tend to behave in a herding fashion that occasionally leads to one-way trading. Some other areas, such as futures and options, were mentioned as in need of improvement.

In many cases, liquidity is measured as the difference between the bid and ask price. Although statistics on the size of bid-ask spreads are not available for corporate bonds, the Bank for International Settlements (BIS) and the Bank of Japan occasionally reports survey data for JGBs. The international survey published by the BIS in 2000 suggested

Table 9.3
Liquidity Measured by Turnover Rates

	JGB		Corporate Bonds		Bank Debentures	
Fiscal year	All	Ex repo	All	Ex repo	All	Ex repo
1990	15.98	12.38	0.88	0.73	1.41	1.17
1995	13.74	7.22	0.76	0.71	0.83	0.80
2000	6.87	4.21	0.90	0.41	0.86	0.45
2003	7.25	3.75	1.46	0.41	1.22	0.42

Fiscal years end Mar 31 of the following calendar year. Ex repo is trading excluding repurchase agreements (gensaki). Corporate bonds exclude convertible bonds.

Trading volume is the annual sum of purchases and sales, with both sides of OTC trades counted. The denominator is the average of beginning- and end-of-year outstanding amounts. Note that volume measured this way is affected by changes in the level of interest rates, as well as by other factors that affect bond prices.

Source: Japan Securities Dealers Association and Tokyo Stock Exchange.

that the spread was larger for Japanese government bonds than for those from other major countries. However, the Bank of Japan (2003) reported that the spread became smaller in 2002 and subsequently, according to their tick data analysis. In fact, the mean value of the bid-ask spread for JGBs with 5 to 7 remaining years was reported as less than one basis point.

3 Changes in the Corporate Bond Market

Numerous changes have taken place in Japan's corporate bond market in the last two decades, primarily reflecting the institutional deregulation and general financial liberalization that started in the mid-1980s and accelerated in the mid-1990s.

Under the traditional system, bond issues were scheduled for once a month. Issuing terms and conditions, including the issue price, were determined by a coordinating committee consisting of major security houses and trust banks, known as the *Kisai-kai*, according to rather mechanical standards based on the net worth of the issuer, maturity, and so forth. Only highly creditworthy firms were allowed to issue bonds. There was little room to reflect differences in the creditworthiness of the issuing firms. Quite simply, *Kisai-kai* decided who could issue bonds, and in what amount. These procedures in fact eliminated default risk. In February 1979 issuance with no collateral was allowed for certain types of firms, and in April 1979 Matsushita Denki Sangyo (best known for its Panasonic brand) issued the first such convertible bond in the Japanese market. The first straight bond with no collateral was issued in January 1985 by TDK.

In May 1987 the "proposal method" was introduced, under which the security house that offered the most favorable conditions to the bond issuer was chosen as the main underwriter. In the early 1990s, the issue price became more closely associated with prevailing market conditions and the issuing method also changed accordingly.

A Japanese credit rating organization first appeared in 1979 as a research institution; it was reorganized as a corporation and joined by two others in April 1985. However, bond ratings were not used extensively until November 1990 when issue criteria, known as *tekisai-kijun*, were relaxed and integrated into the rating system. In January 1996 the *tekisai-kijun* system was fully terminated with the introduction of full flexibility in bond covenants.

The Japanese Commercial Code was extensively revised, effective in October 1993, and this essentially removed limits on bond issuance.

The underwriting system was thoroughly reviewed at the time. An important change was the requirement to designate a managing trustee. Under certain underwriting conditions a managing trustee is not required, although the first such issue did not come until September 1995. Private placement of bonds was significantly liberalized in early 1996. (For more on deregulation, see Hoshi and Kashyap 2001, chs 7 and 8).

Deregulation has meant diversification in products and issuers, including the appearance of low-credit-rating issuers, as will be shown in the following sections. Deregulation also has made default events possible, and this potential has required more sophisticated credit-risk evaluations. Although the market-participant survey reveals general dissatisfaction with current corporate bond markets, we will present data suggesting that these markets at least are working much better now than in the pre-reform era.

3.1 Corporate Finance through Bonds

The trend in corporate financing through markets since the mid-1980s is shown in Figure 9.1. The gross amount of primary issuance of equity increased sharply in the late 1980s, the period of the asset-price bubble, and again in the late 1990s , which included large amount of preferred stocks in 1999. Throughout the 1980s the amount of convertible bonds increased substantially, but since the bubble burst, these have been less popular, mainly reflecting negative sentiments towards equity markets. Annual bond offerings peaked in 1998 and by 2002 had fallen by over half, to just under 6 trillion yen per year. Since 2000, private bond placements have become more widespread, amounting to 3.3 trillion yen gross issuance in fiscal 2003 according to Table 9.1. This development is possibly related to deregulatory measures.

For net numbers, domestic issuance is positive, with large fluctuations from year to year. However, the size of overseas public placement turned negative in the late 1990s because firms that issued bonds overseas in the late 1980s currently are paying off those debts. In the 1980s many firms preferred overseas placement to avoid stringent regulations and high costs in domestic bond markets. Now, however, reform measures and their substantial reduction of issuing costs have made domestic placement competitive.

In the 1980s, most bond issuers were public utility companies; they accounted for about 75% of the total value of publicly placed straight bonds. Reform measures in the early 1990s opened the way for more

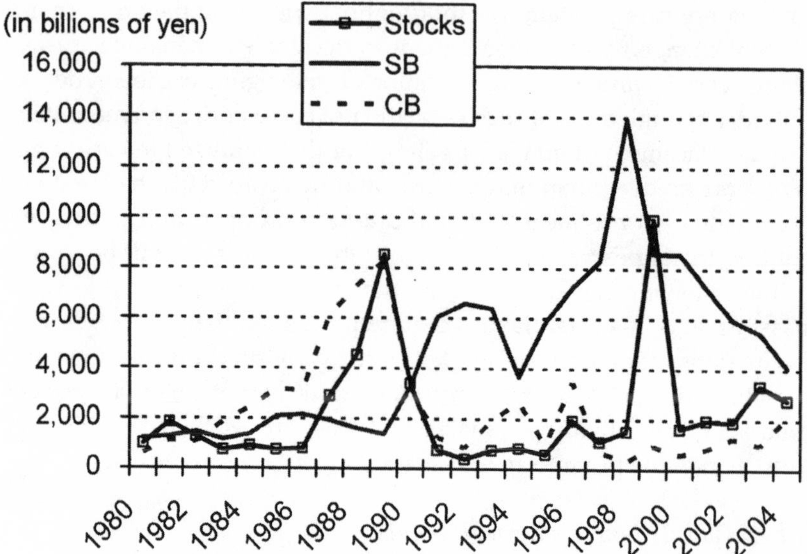

Figures are gross amounts raised through the issuance of stocks and bonds, in billion yen, for calendar year. Bonds are straight bonds (SB) and convertible bonds (CB). These are aggregate figures for firms listed on Tokyo Stock Exchange.

Source: 2004 Special Issue, Tokyo Stock Exchange Monthly Report.

Figure 9.1
Trends in Corporate Finance: Firms listed on the Tokyo Stock Exchange

firms to issue bonds. As a result, the share of utilities bond issues fell to around 31% in the 1990s and just 20% in the 2001–03 fiscal years. Bond issuance by the financial services sector has risen to over 30%, mainly since 1999 when commercial banks were allowed to issue straight bonds.

During 1992–2003, 472 firms issued domestic straight bonds, compared to 277 firms in 1980–90, according to the data collected by I-N Information Systems. Of these, the number of firms making a first issue was especially high from 1995 to 1998: an average of approximately 50 first-issues each year.

For non-financial firms during the bubble period, funds raised through corporate bonds were used mainly for financing investments. However, such use has been declining, going from over 86% at the peak of the bubble (1989) to only 28% in 2002. In contrast, the share being used to repay debt (servicing existing bonds and other borrowings) has increased since the late 1990s to between 50% and 60%. This change may be indicative of the shift in the financial channel for corporations from the long-traditional bank-centered system to a market-based system. (Data are from I-N Information Systems.)

3.2 *Diversification in Bond Types*

The expanding use of bonds as a financing tool for more firms has caused product diversification, especially in the early 1990s. For example, notes of less than 5-year maturity became more popular in the 1990s. In 1996, regulations on bond covenants were lifted. Together with the relaxation of other regulatory measures that controlled quality, below investment-grade bonds became available as public offerings. Still, as of January 2004 the situation had not progressed to the point where Japan has a liquid high-yield bond market: of total outstanding bonds, no Japanese corporate bonds were originally issued with a below-investment-grade rating from the Japanese rating agency Ratings and Investment Information, Inc., R&I, (BB+ or below), and only 12% from Moody's (Ba1 or below). Most current high-yield bonds are "fallen angels"; the exceptions being some sovereign debt issues by emerging economies, such as public entities from Argentina and Brazil.

Table 9.4 shows the initial and current Ratings and Investment Information, Inc. (R&I) and Moody's ratings for yen-denominated corporate bonds, publicly placed and traded in secondary markets in January 2004. The current distribution is skewed below the initial ratings, reflecting the large number of downgrades. The universe of R&I-rated bonds had a somewhat higher initial median rating than Moody's, but Moody's has done more upgrading and less downgrading than R&I. The fact that ratings have been actively changing strongly suggests the increasing importance of credit-risk evaluation in Japanese markets.

R&I was formed in April 1998 by the merger of two previous Japanese agencies; Moody's is an American company with staff in Japan. Some observers may worry that Japanese rating agencies provide rather generous numbers. To check this, the distribution of the ratings of firms that obtained initial ratings from both R&I and Moody's are shown in Table 9.5.

Table 9.4
Distribution of Bond Ratings, January 2004

	R&I					Moody's				
			Changes					Changes[2]		
	Initial[1]	up	stay[2]	down	Current[3]	Initial[1]	up	stay	down	Current[3]
AAA/Aaa	16.0	—	0.7	15.3	0.7	5.1	—	0.7	4.5	1.3
AA/Aa	33.5	0	21.5	12.0	36.9	23.0	0.6	11.6	10.7	16.1
A/A	43.5	0.1	33.6	9.7	44.3	27.9	0	18.3	9.6	29.7
BBB/Baa	7.0	0.4	6.0	0.7	15.3	32.0	0.8	27.3	3.8	37.1
BB/Ba	0	0	0	0	1.6	11.5	1.5	7.1	3.0	11.6
≤ B/B	0	0	0	—	0.9	0.5	0.1	0.5	—	3.4
Cancelled	—	—	—	—	0.3	—	—	—	—	0.7

Data are for publicly placed yen-denominated straight corporate bonds, traded in the secondary market in January 2004. Entries are the percentage of the total number of bonds rated by each agency, so the Initial and Current columns each add to 100%. R&I rated 1,603 bonds, Moody's rated 1,342. Below BB+ / Ba1 is regarded as "speculative".

[1]Ratings obtained at the time of new issue.

[2]How the initial ratings have been revised since the initial rating.

[3]Ratings in January 2004.

Source: I-N Information Systems, Ltd.

Table 9.5
Distribution of R&I and Moody's Initial Ratings, 1998–2003

	R&I		Moody's	
Rating	Number	Percent	Number	Percent
AAA/Aaa	167	24.9	39	5.8
AA/Aa	268	40.0	213	31.8
A/A	218	32.5	179	26.7
BBB/Baa	17	2.5	214	31.9
BB/Ba	0	0	25	3.7

The sample size is 670.

On average for 1998–2003, R&I's ratings were 2.6 notches higher than Moody's as rated on a scale with 10 notches for investment-grade bonds. Moody's mode value was A3 (just one notch above "adequate") while R&I's was AAA, the highest possible rating. However, the rating differences became smaller over this period: in 2003 the average differential was 2.0 notches. This trend is clearer when comparing the variances of the distribution of differences in rating for the same bond: it was 3.74 in 1998 and 1.08 in 2003.

Although there is a general tendency for R&I to give slightly higher ratings than Moody's, both agencies' ratings appear to show more convergence recently. Also, remaining divergences in ratings can be valuable information since it provides different perspectives on risk.

3.3 *Lower Issuing Costs*

Reform measures have lowered issuing costs. Especially important are changes in the Japanese Commercial Code in 1993 and the use of paperless offerings. Among the 1993 changes was removal of the requirement to designate a managing trustee, which has resulted in a significant saving in issuing costs. In fiscal year 2002, two-thirds of corporate bond issues did not have a designated managing trustee.

In 1990 the average initial cost for AAA 10- to 12-year straight bonds was 1.86% of total proceeds. This cost declined to 0.74% in 1992 and 0.51% in 1994, and has drifted lower since. (These figures are based on data collected by I-N Information Systems from information in prospectuses.)

4 Pricing New Issues

In Japan the price of credit risk has rarely been revealed throughout the market because most transactions have been bank loans. This was true even for pre-reform bond financing because the underwriters severely screened issues before placement. Furthermore, even when default events occurred, the bonds were bought back by the main bank and investors were not forced to take losses. This situation changed in the late 1990s: there is no official listing, but the first known instance of a default event causing actual investor losses was in December 1998 (see Tokushima 2004). In the case of Maikaru in September 2001, even small investors were involved. Against these developments, and the basically free institutional regime for corporate bond financing since 1997, it is expected that creditworthiness is being priced into bonds more rigorously than before.

4.1 Sensitivity to Credit Risk

The difference in yield (the spread) between a corporate bond and a Japanese government bond of equal maturity reflects a firm's creditworthiness relative to a risk-free investment. Spreads between differently rated but otherwise-similar bonds also reflect relative creditworthiness. In this section an analysis is conducted to see how rigorously the spread reflects the creditworthiness shown in commercial ratings, looking specifically at the initial spreads and ratings of newly issued bonds. The initial assumption is that differences in ratings reflect valid differences in credit risk, so that lower-rated bonds should have higher spreads (risk premiums) relative to a Japanese government bond. To the extent this is not the case, the implication is that relative risk is not being priced properly.

For instance, in the fourth quarter of 2003 the spread between new five-year straight corporate bonds rated AAA and new five-year JGBs was almost zero basis points. Within corporate bonds, the spread between AAA and AA ratings was 7.5 basis points; between AA and A, 24.8 basis points; and between A and BBB, 48.5 basis points on average. (The highest rating of each firm is counted if it has multiple rated issues. Data are from I-N Information Systems.)

Table 9.6 shows statistics on the rank correlation between the corporate-JGB spread and the rating-difference spreads, using the ratings of two major rating agencies, R&I and Moody's. Although there are some

Table 9.6
Initial Spreads and Ratings: Rank Correlation Coefficients, 1997–2003

	R&I Rating		Moody's Rating	
	ρ	N	ρ	N
1997	—	—	0.7732	211
1998	0.8433	423	0.8258	360
1999	0.7617	246	0.8333	160
2000	0.8269	222	0.8281	121
2001	0.7399	165	0.6417	84
2002	0.8949	136	0.6907	70
2003	0.7923	141	0.7440	55
All	0.6353	1333	0.6800	1061

The data set is yen-denominated, publicly placed, fixed-coupon bonds issued by Japanese corporations. Spreads are defined as the differences between corporate bond yields and the yields of equal-maturity JGB. Spearman's rank correlation coefficient is used.

Rating data are from within one month of the date of the determination of issuing terms for each bond. (This means R&I data are available only from 1998). For each rating agency, the characteristics of the bonds are the same, but the exact firms are different because not all firms obtained ratings from both institutions. The characteristics of each group are shown in Tables 9.7 and 9.8.

year by year differences in the degree of correlation, the data show approximately 0.7 or higher correlation numbers for both agencies. The numbers clearly indicate greater sensitivity to credit risk in the domestic corporate bond market than Packer (2000) found for 1995 and 1996.

Packer reported that the initial pricing of domestic bonds remained fairly insensitive to credit risk in Japan between 1995 and 1996 by showing rank correlation coefficients of bond spreads for JGBs and ratings from Moody's or Standard & Poor's. According to his calculation, the correlation measure for domestic bonds was 0.26, far below the correlation observed for the ranking of samurai bonds (yen-dominated foreign issues in the Japanese market) of 0.84.

4.2 Predicted and Actual Spreads

To further explore the pricing of risk as indicated by ratings, a regression analysis was conducted on spreads between corporate bonds and JGBs after the market was fully deregulated: that is, the period from 1997 to 2003 for straight corporate bonds rated either by R&I or Moody's.

The characteristics of the data sets, which are the same as those used in the previous section, are summarized in Tables 9.7 and 9.8. The mean

Table 9.7
Characteristics of New Corporate Bonds Rated by R&I, 1998–2003

	Spread[1]		Issue		Coupon		
	Mean	SD[2]	size[3]	Maturity[4]	%	Rating[5]	N
1998	90.3	38.9	18	7.2	2.0	4.2	423
1999	59.2	46.0	19	7.6	1.9	4.5	246
2000	40.5	32.2	23	7.2	1.8	4.6	222
2001	40.7	39.9	28	6.8	1.2	4.4	165
2002	28.9	33.5	33	8.4	1.2	3.5	136
2003	26.9	26.4	26	9.5	1.0	4.2	141
1998–2003	57.2	45.1	23	7.6	1.9	4.2	1,333

Average values are shown for each item.
[1]Spread is in basis points, and is the differences between the yield of the mean rated bond and the yield of an equal-maturity JGB.
[2]Standard deviation.
[3]Issue size is in billion of yen.
[4]Average maturity, in years.
[5]Original letter ratings are converted to numerical values, with 1 for AAA through 12 for BB for R&I, and Aaa through Ba2 for Moody's.

Source: The same data set is used as in Table 9.6. Data were collected from the main underwriter at the time of issuance.

Table 9.8
Characteristics of New Corporate Bonds Rated by Moody's, 1997–2003

	Spread[1]		Issue		Coupon		
	Mean	SD[2]	size[3]	Maturity[4]	%	Rating[5]	N
1997	37.5	25.1	210	9.2	2.5	6.8	211
1998	82.0	37.6	21	7.8	2.1	6.8	360
1999	49.9	44.3	21	8.3	1.9	6.5	160
2000	35.6	30.9	29	7.3	1.7	6.9	121
2001	25.2	19.5	33	7.6	1.2	6.0	84
2002	22.8	25.7	41	8.8	1.2	4.9	70
2003	26.8	24.9	41	9.6	1.0	5.7	55
1997–2003	51.7	40.5	25	8.3	1.9	6.5	1,061

For notes and sources, see Table 9.7.

spreads have been on declining trends, as has the average coupon rate. Clear differences between the two data pools are not observed. For both agencies, the average bond rating hit a low in 2000, then improved through 2002, and dropped in 2003.

The regression results are given in Tables 9.9 and 9.10. The dependent variable is the initial issue spread in each regression. For both rating agencies, it is expected, as a general rule, that as the rating declines, predicted spreads are higher in economically and statistically significant ways. If issue size is related to liquidity in the secondary market and such considerations are priced at the time of issuance, we should expect negative coefficients for this variable.

It is remarkable that the monotonicity of the estimated coefficients on the ratings indicator variables holds without exception. Although the R&I regression in 1999 and 2000 for Aaa bonds (column D1 in Table 9.9) is insignificant, and the Aaa and Aa bonds (columns D1 and D2 in Table 9.10) are insignificant for the Moody's regression in 1997, 1999, 2000 and 2001, the explanatory power of rating variables is more clearly confirmed for lower grades: in the R&I regressions, all the coefficients are estimated with 99% significance for A and Baa (columns 03 and 04); in the Moody's regressions, the same is the case for Ba (column D5), as well as for Baa (column D4) during 1997–2000.

The effect of issue size is relatively clear in the R&I regression, suggesting that a larger size reduces spreads. For Moody's, such an effect is not clearly confirmed.

Morgan and Stiroh (1999) of the Federal Reserve Bank of New York ran similar regressions for American business corporations and American bank holding companies. Although their main interest was the disciplinary role of markets by using bond spreads, ratings, and other factors, their results provide a good basis for a Japanese-American comparison of initial bond pricing. Because the two nations' respective macroeconomic situations, as well as the shape of the yield curve, are different, one should not expect similarly sized spreads for each rating dummy variable. However, the Moody's regression results for 1997–2003 present similarly sized spreads for lower ratings, on average, with slightly lower spreads for Ba grade. In their paper, using ordinary least squares estimation procedures, for non-banks there is a coefficient of 49.191 for rating dummy BBB/Baa2 grade bonds, 63.118 with fixed effects. The coefficients are 194.621 for BB/Ba2, 175.607 with fixed effects. (For further details, see Morgan and Stiroh 1999, table 3, in which they use higher ratings from either Standard and Poor's or Moody's.)

Table 9.9
Yield Spread and Ratings by R&I, 1998–2003

	Issue size	Maturity	D1 (Aaa)	D2 (Aa)	D3 (A)	D4 (Baa)	$\bar{R}^2$	N
1998	–5.89	0.504	69.77	98.19	142.96	205.84	0.6361	423
	(0.002)	(0.131)	(0.000)	(0.000)	(0.000)	(0.000)		
1999	4.56	–1.26	0.567	30.20	64.95	147.44	0.5432	246
	(0.175)	(0.022)	(0.978)	(0.094)	(0.000)	(0.000)		
2000	–0.483	0.931	7.907	18.28	47.76	88.35	0.5190	222
	(0.820)	(0.056)	(0.553)	(0.154)	(0.000)	(0.000)		
2001	–2.41	–1.28	38.97	40.84	79.41	108.22	0.4079	165
	(0.462)	(0.194)	(0.096)	(0.050)	(0.000)	(0.000)		
2002	–5.025	0.953	29.42	33.38	85.16	118.93	0.5156	136
	(0.060)	(0.023)	(0.093)	(0.036)	(0.000)	(0.000)		
2003	–2.927	0.918	—	19.45	50.72	94.58	0.5661	141
	(0.146)	(0.002)		(0.098)	(0.000)	(0.000)		
all	–11.70	–0.550	94.73	103.61	141.15	163.28	0.3888	1,333
	(0.000)	(0.029)	(0.000)	(0.000)	(0.000)	(0.000)		

The dependent variable is the spread between the bond's yield to maturity on issue and the yield on a JGB of the same maturity. Issue size is measured as the log of the amount in 100 million yen (the usual reporting unit in Japanese data). Maturities are in years.

Four rating dummy variables are included for R&I (five for Moody's) in addition to the variables of issue size and maturity. The dummy equals 1 if it matches the agency's rating, otherwise it is 0.

Equations are estimated by OLS. Numbers in parentheses are p-values of the estimated coefficients.

Table 9.10
Yield Spread and Ratings by Moody's, 1997–2003

	Issue size	Maturity	D1 (Aaa)	D2 (Aa)	D3 (A)	D4 (Baa)	D5 (Ba)	$\bar{R}^2$	N
1997	0.607	–0.477	17.09	15.31	31.81	47.63	71.96	0.4801	211
	(0.803)	(0.117)	(0.286)	(0.287)	(0.012)	(0.000)	(0.000)		
1998	–10.17	0.460	95.96	91.51	120.16	145.38	181.63	0.6467	360
	(0.000)	(0.150)	(0.000)	(0.000)	(0.000)	(0.000)	(0.000)		
1999	2.545	–0.116	4.798	–0.736	34.67	58.93	146.65	0.6689	160
	(0.532)	(0.820)	(0.861)	(0.976)	(0.103)	(0.004)	(0.000)		
2000	–0.896	1.759	—	3.612	17.23	40.81	91.51	0.6465	121
	(0.730)	(0.001)		(0.824)	(0.302)	(0.006)	(0.000)		
2001	2.284	1.092	—	–8.487	–2.630	21.11	52.33	0.508	84
	(0.306)	(0.044)		(0.566)	(0.857)	(0.101)	(0.001)		
2002	5.047	1.531	—	–34.10	–4.625	25.46	—	0.5598	70
	(0.095)	(0.001)		(0.079)	(0.809)	(0.178)			
2003	7.582	1.673	—	–52.48	–31.10	0.712	—	0.5002	55
	(0.041)	(0.001)		(0.034)	(0.201)	(0.973)			
All	–7.623	–0.016	76.30	59.54	88.97	107.11	149.87	0.4887	1,061
	(0.000)	(0.944)	(0.000)	(0.000)	(0.000)	(0.000)	(0.000)		

See Table 9.9 for Notes.

Some people argue that the Japanese credit market prices risk too low, especially in comparison to the American market. However, as far as the current sample is concerned, it is not possible to say whether Japanese spreads (risk premiums) are too low.

In sum, the primary market after the Big Bang reforms has shown much better efficiency in pricing creditworthiness for a broad range of corporate bonds.

5 Secondary Market Pricing

In this section, secondary market pricing is examined by using bond yields, credit ratings, and credit default swap (CDS) premium data. For firms trading in both bond markets and derivatives markets, investor's arbitrage can lead to more efficient pricing of credit risk. Because bond yields should reflect the credit risk involved, and it is possible to discover the price evaluation implied in bond yields by using the option pricing model for risky bonds, we can compare the implied price of risk in bond yields with the market price of risk—that is, the market-priced premium of credit default swaps. Through this exercise, we can check the consistency of secondary market pricing of firms trading in both bond and credit default swap markets.

5.1 *A Pricing Model for Credit Risk Using Yields*

Securities issued by corporations are regarded as options derived from the value of the firm. In the Black-Scholes option-pricing formula, stocks are call options with a strike price of the face value of the firm's debt, and bonds are securities with put options with a strike price that also is the face value of the firm's debt. In this context, D_t, the pay-off on bonds, is written as

$$D_t = P \text{ } if \text{ } (A_t > P) \text{ } and = A_t \text{ } if \text{ } (A_t \leq P) \tag{1}$$

where A_t is the market value of the firm at time t, and P is the face value of the firm's debt.

In this model, the firm's market value is assumed to follow the stochastic process described below with Z_t as standard Brownian motion with drift μ_A and volatility σ_A.

$$dA_t = (\mu_A A_t)dt + \sigma_A A_t dZ_t \tag{2}$$

Under this assumption, the stock price S_t at time t, which is total market capitalization, and the bond yield Y_t^τ are obtained as follows:

$$S_t = A_t \Phi(d_1) - P \exp(-r\tau)\Phi(d_2),$$

$$Y_t^\tau = \frac{1}{\tau} \log \frac{P}{D_t}$$

$$= -\frac{1}{\tau}\left(\log \frac{A_t \Phi(-d_1) + P \exp(-r\tau)\Phi(d_2)}{P}\right)$$

where r is the risk-free rate, τ strike period, $\Phi(\cdot)$ the cumulative density function of the standard normal distribution, and d_1 and d_2 are as follows.

$$d_1 = \frac{\log \dfrac{A_t}{P} + \left(r + \dfrac{1}{2}\sigma_A^2\right)(\tau)}{\sigma_A \sqrt{\tau}} \tag{3}$$

$$d_2 = d_1 - \sigma_A \sqrt{\tau} \tag{4}$$

Because we are not able to observe the market value of the firm as actual data, we have to estimate the firm's value and its volatility, assuming that stock prices and bond yields observed in the markets are good approximations of the rational prices needed to value the relevant risks. This estimation is possible by solving the pricing equations backward by assuming a certain structure of the firm's debt.

As for the debt structure, average maturity τ_t^* is given by

$$\tau_t^* = \frac{\sum_{i=1}^N B_t^i \tau_t^i}{\sum_{i=1}^N B_t^i}.$$

where N is the number of debt issued, each debt at time t is numbered according to i, $(1 \le i \le N)$ and their face value is B_t^i with remaining period to maturity at t being τ_t^i.

Corporate financial statements give debt structure data in terms of book value. Together with some simplifying assumptions, the market data on bond yields provides an estimated market value for corporate debt according to the above model. Specifically, we define the estimated value of d_2 in equation (4) as a firm's credit score. (For a detailed discussion of this formulation and a complete description of the results summarized below, see Kimata and Fujii 2004.)

As observable measures of the firm's creditworthiness, we have credit ratings and the market prices of credit derivatives. First, the implied credit evaluation is checked against the direct ratings data to see whether the implied value gives a consistent ordering of creditworthiness. This comparison is possible for more than 500 samples consisting of five data points: the first business day in April for 1999 through 2003 for over 100 firms each year. Implied ratings are created according to the derived values of d_2. Because these give us the orderings, it is necessary to determine the distribution in the number of firms that belong to each credit rate category. This derived distribution is chosen to match the actual numbers of the sample distribution according to either R&I or Moody's.

The difference between the actual and implied ratings is plotted in Figure 9.2 for 2003. The graph shows that the implied evaluations closely match the actual ratings with natural distributions of estimating errors. In particular, the theoretical and actual ratings for just over 60% of the cases are within 1 notch of each other. This result strongly suggests that the credit evaluation implied in bond yields appears to be consistent with direct market evaluation data shown in commercial ratings. Results for the other years, 1999–2002, are similar.

5.2 Estimated Credit Default Swap Premiums and Market Data

A second approach is to compare calculated values with the actual market price of credit default swap premiums. The derivatives market in Japan, including credit default swaps, is growing very rapidly: the Bank of Japan estimates the notional amount was approximately $27.7 billion at the end of 2004. The BOJ (2003) found that the credit default swap premium was always above the corresponding bond-yield spread, had higher volatility, and led changes in spreads. Also, the BOJ notes that until mid-2002 the correlation coefficient showed co-movement of the two prices; however, the coefficient has tended to be negative since then. This observation applies to monthly coefficients of correlation based on daily changes.

For the analysis here, because credit default swap five-year contracts with three events are said to be the most actively traded, the corresponding bond is one with a five-year maturity. (The three events are

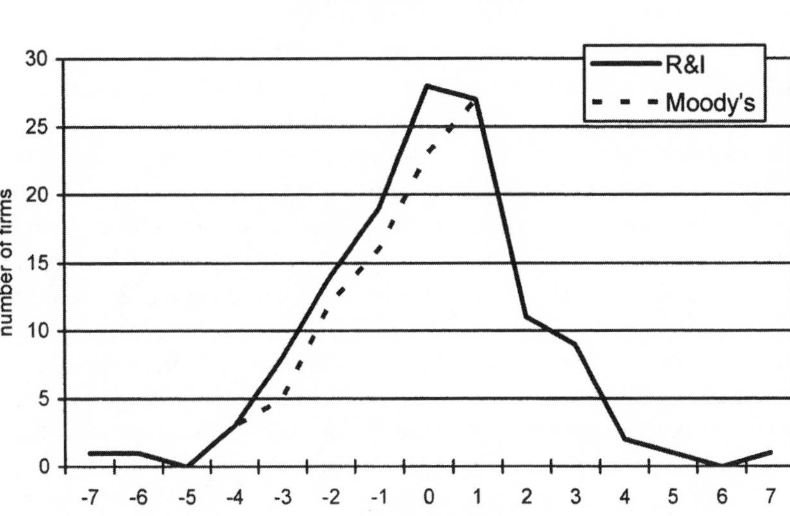

Note: As explained in the text, the horizontal axis shows the difference in notches between the actual and implied rating. The vertical axis is the number of firms. A total of 125 firms is analyzed using R&I rating data and 112 firms using Moody's data, as of the first business day in April 2003.

Source: Computed by the author. Rating data are from I-N Information Systems, Ltd. and corporate bond price data are from QUICK database.

Figure 9.2
Actual and Implied Ratings: Differences in Notches

default, excess liabilities, and restructuring in a broad sense.) Spread is defined as the difference in compound yields over the most-liquid JGBs of the same remaining years. Credit default swap premium data are obtained from the database of Deutsche Bank Group's Tokyo branch. Daily data for 18 firms from 1 April 2002 to the last trading day of December 2003 are used.

As far as the dataset is concerned, the credit default swap premiums are, in general, greater than the bond spreads, and except for one firm show higher volatility. A graph of the two series over the entire period generally suggests high correlation, although daily variations may be explained by different types of news specific and relevant to each market. In fact, the correlations between monthly data for the credit default swap premiums and spreads are relatively high, an average of 0.79 for the whole sample, implying there is good arbitrage across the markets. The lower a firm's credit rating, the higher the volatility in the credit default swap premium than in the bond-yield spreads. Accordingly, the results based on the two data sets appear to be consistent.

In the previous section, we calculated the credit risk indicator implied in observable bond yields, and we can use that information to obtain the theoretical values of the premiums of any European-type derivatives. These values can be compared with the direct market price of credit default swaps. (European-type options can be exercised only at expiration, while American-type options can be exercised at any time during their life.) The traded credit derivative swap is an American put option that pays out whenever a credit event arises. It is known that the price of a European-type put limits the lowest value of an American-type put; thus we first check if this constraint is properly met by the estimated values.

Examination of the data shows that the calculated values properly satisfy the condition described, and also confirm that the lower a firm's creditworthiness, the higher the actual credit default swap premium. (Details are available from the author on request.) This relationship matches intuition because lower creditworthiness inherently implies a greater chance of executing the option associated with a higher premium. Possible cases for this exercise are limited to issues that trade in credit default swap markets as well.

Alternative ways of transferring credit risk, such as derivatives markets, may enhance efficiency in traditional financial markets such as those for corporate bonds. If this is the case, advances in financial technology for trading risk through various means is quite important. Sometimes the usefulness of derivatives is questioned. However, the empirical investigation here shows that these instruments play an important role in improving the efficiency of other parts of the capital market. Although markets for credit derivatives in Japan are still only in the process of development, and thus the sample is very limited, there are good signs that Japanese corporate bond markets are moving in the direction of more efficiency.

6 Areas for Policy Consideration

Arbitrage across markets is essential for efficient pricing. To have active trading and arbitrage requires a diversity of participants. In some

Japanese markets, a lack of diversity leads to local pricing and tends to increase volatility when shocks occur. For example, in the third quarter of 2003, the long yields on JGBs rose sharply. It is said that this was due to the herd behavior of Japanese banks, which are the largest private-sector holders of JGBs and apply similar risk-management techniques.

From the viewpoint of promoting cross-market efficiency, the extensive participation of various types of financial intermediaries and investors may enhance the functioning of the bond and capital markets. For JGBs, broadening the investor base, including individual Japanese and overseas investors, is quite urgent.

Under the Japanese bank-centered system, capital markets historically have been less important in financing corporations. The respective financial intermediation activities of banks and securities companies were sharply separated by law for many years. Since the mid-1980s, some progress has been made in reducing this separation. This first step was implemented in the underwriting business in overseas markets, then in the domestic government bond market. Since the 1990s, further deregulation has extended investment banking opportunities for commercial banks through the establishment of subsidiaries, by which more competitive service provisions were expected.

One illustration of this liberalization is that in fiscal year 1990, the four largest Japanese securities firms handled all publicly placed domestic bond underwriting, but in 2003 they handled only about half. Bank-affiliated and foreign-based security firms have come to play an important role in Japanese corporate bond markets. In fact, the number of foreign-based security houses serving as a main underwriter grew from one in fiscal year 1991 to eight in fiscal year 2002. For domestic bank-affiliated security firms, the first case of being a main underwriter was in 1993; the number of bank-affiliated security firms acting a main underwriter increased to 17 in fiscal year 1997. It declined to 5 in fiscal year 2002 partly because of mergers (data from I-N Information Systems).

A review of the business activities open to commercial and investment banking is currently underway at the Financial Services Agency. Policy should be directed toward providing more competitive and efficient financial services through diversifying market participants. For this purpose, an integrated-market law might be considered to provide an extensive and fair system of regulation.

In terms of policy, it is essential to have a neutral tax system for the various types and channels of financial transactions. Unless equal tax treatment is guaranteed, distortions can be created, resulting in insufficient and tax-related arbitrage, and thus less-efficient pricing.

For any specific risk, cross-market trading and a diversity of participants will almost certainly increase the depth of the market. To foster this, increasingly sophisticated financial technology is the real tool for further development. Essentially this will be achieved by private institutions and individuals responding to potential market opportunities, rather than as a consequence of government policy prescriptions.

6.1 Remaining Issues

Japan's financial Big Bang initially was intended to enhance the position of Tokyo's financial markets so as to compete with New York and London effectively in financial service activities. Tokyo's aspiration to be part of a triumvirate of global financial centers is yet to be achieved: Tokyo is not a market in which foreign global players raise funds. Moreover, only a few Japanese banks and security firms do business in the global capital markets, usually from offices in London, New York, or Frankfurt.

Still, the financial reforms have had positive effects. The players in the Tokyo markets have increased and become more diverse, even if most of the business activity is directed toward domestic clients. Progress can be observed in the functioning of markets: the corporate bond market is an example of more efficient services for both investors and fund raisers today in contrast to its pre-reform situation.

Developing credit markets is crucial to establishing more market-oriented financing channels for firms. Already, efforts to extend securitization and syndication of loan-trading are being made. Further developments in credit derivatives and the ensuing arbitrage activities will enhance the whole area of credit-risk transfer. The results here show that the pricing of new issues has become more efficient in the sense that prices properly reflect creditworthiness.

One of the differences between the American and Japanese corporate bond markets is the weight of low-rated bonds (including high-yields). As shown in the regression analysis, investment grade corporate bonds do not carry any substantial spread. From the viewpoint of investors, relatively low-rated bonds may be an attractive product for taking on credit risk. In the case of bank lending, pricing on low-quality loans is at issue as well and thus, for the Japanese market as a whole, the ability to price relatively higher credit risk correctly seems to be a skill requiring further sophistication.

Regulators might take the initiative to provide a more efficient settlement environment through a paperless, safe, and expedited system. Low trading activities in private-sector bonds, inclusive of corporate bonds, are often related to the small issuance size as well as the rather inefficient settlement system. An initiative by policymakers to enhance the efficiency of the settlement system could lead to higher liquidity, which in turn would strengthen the attractiveness of Tokyo's financial markets, as intended by the Big Bang reforms.

Otherwise, not many market participants wish to have government policy interventions, especially in markets for venture capital, distressed assets, and high-yield bonds—that is, in markets for highly risky financial products. Such markets survive and thrive best with self-discipline, not with tight regulation. The opinion survey of market participants reveals the perception that the current regulatory regime is working relatively well and that business interests will generate further developments in these markets. In this regard, what is most required of Japanese financial institutions is innovation in their own management and technology.

Acknowledgments

The author wishes to thank Hugh Patrick and Takatoshi Ito for very helpful comments on an earlier draft. I also thank Anil Kashyap, Mitsuhiro Fukao, and the other participants of the Solutions project meeting for comments, as well as the survey respondents for sharing their insights and concerns. Data were kindly provided by I-N Information Systems, Ltd. and the Tokyo branch of Deutsche Bank Group.

References

Bank of Japan. 1995. *Nihon-no-Kinnyuu Seido* (Financial System in Japan). Tokyo: Tokiwa Publishers.

Bank of Japan. 2003. *Market Review*, 2003-J-2, 2003-J-10.

Black, F. and J.C. Cox. 1976. Valuing Corporate Securities: Some Effects of Bond Indenture Provisions. *Journal of Finance* 31 (2): 351–67.

Black, F. and M. Scholes. 1973. The Pricing of Options and Corporate Liabilities. *Journal of Political Economy* 81 (3): 637–54.

Briys, E. and F. de Varenne. 1997. Valuing Risky Fixed Rate Debt: An Extension. *Journal of Financial and Quantitative Analysis* 32 (2): 230–48.

Duffie, D. and K.J. Singleton. 1999. Modeling Term Structure of Defaultable Bond. *The Review of Financial Studies* 12 (4): 687–720.

Hoshi, Takeo and Anil Kashyap. 2001. *Corporate Financing and Governance in Japan: The Road to the Future*. Cambridge, MA: MIT Press.

Jarrow, R.A., D. Lando, and S.M. Turnbull. 1997. A Markov Model for the Term Structure of Credit Risk Spreads. *The Review of Financial Studies* 10 (2): 481–523.

Kimata, T. and Mariko Fujii. 2004. "Sinyo-risuku to saikenn-kakuduke no kannrenn ni tuiteno jisshoubunnseki" (Risky Bond Yields and Credit Ratings: Evidence from the Japanese Market). University of Tokyo, AEE Discussion Papers, March. (In Japanese)

Longstaff, F. and E. Schwartz. 1995. A Simple Approach to Valuing Risky Fixed and Floating Rate Debt. *Journal of Finance* 50 (3): 789–819.

Merton, R.C. 1974. On the Pricing for Corporate Debt: The Risk Structure of Interest Rates. *Journal of Finance* 29: 449–70.

Morgan, D. and Stiroh, K. 1999. "Bond Market Discipline of Banks: Is the Market Tough Enough?" Federal Reserve Bank of New York, *Staff Report* 95.

Packer, Franklin. 2000. Credit Ratings and Spreads in the Samurai Bond Market. In *Finance, Governance, and Competitiveness in Japan*, editors Masahiko, Aoki and Gary Saxonhouse. New York: Oxford University Press.

Royama, Shoichi. 2000. The Big Bang in Japanese Securities Markets. In *Crisis and Change in the Japanese Financial System*, editors Takeo Hoshi and Hugh Patrick. New York: Kluwer Academic Publishers.

Tokushima, K. 2004. *Gendai Shasai Toushi no Jitsumu*. Toyo: Keizai Shinposha. (In Japanese)

Appendix: Opinion Survey on Tokyo Capital Markets

Outline of the Survey

I conducted an opinion survey of the current situation in Tokyo's capital markets in September 2003. Questionnaires were sent to senior executive managers at 12 major capital players in Tokyo markets and all responded in their individual capacity. The players comprised 4 foreign financial institutions, 5 Japanese financial institutions, 2 Japanese institutional investors, and 1 executive from a Japanese manufacturer active in the short-term money, foreign exchange and capital markets. This is a reasonable cross-section of all the types of players active in the Tokyo markets.

Questions sought evaluations of the current status of each market segment from the viewpoints of regulations, roles and functions, practices, and other relevant aspects.

The following is a summary of these views. Most managers regard the issues remaining to be solved as more related to market functions than to government and Financial Service Agency regulations.

General Evaluation of Tokyo's Capital Markets

- Highly developed in trading volume, liquidity, transaction costs, and variety of choice, especially the stock markets.

- Insufficient arbitrage between bank-credit markets and corporate bond markets.
- Low trading liquidity in derivatives markets.
- Problematic tax treatment of non-residents, especially complicated procedures for non-resident withholding taxes.
- The lack of capable human resources with professional skills in the field of advanced financial technologies.
- Highly risk-averse attitudes of Japanese investors are possible impediments to further developments of risky asset markets.
- The excessive presence of government financial institutions such as the postal savings system distorts the whole financial system.
- The capital deficiency of commercial banks.

Japan's Financial Big Bang

The Big Bang has achieved its objectives in: creating more competition among players in the capital markets; creating new markets and thus contributing to diversifying fund-raising channels; bringing new entrants into the commercial and investment banking businesses; and bringing the benefits of free foreign exchange transactions for consumers and businesses.

Negative aspects are: the continued postponement of lowering the limit of the government's deposit insurance guarantee; the loss of global competitiveness of Japanese banks; partly excessive competitions among players; and some tax codes that may be potential impediments for efficient financial transactions.

Equity Markets

- Mostly functioning well, although some regulations such as those on short-selling should be reconsidered.
- The low liquidity in derivatives trading such as futures and options.

Venture Capital Markets

- Listing standards should be reviewed: so far less-diligent standards have been applied, resulting in failures in part of the newly-established markets.
- Most Japanese venture capital funds are managed by bank or security house subsidiaries. More long-term players, such as pension funds, may be suitable for this kind of investment.
- The issues are not those of regulations or policy measures but of investor spirit, risk tolerance, knowledge, and skill.

Distressed Assets Markets

- Distressed assets markets are underdeveloped; however, this type of market should evolve without any new policy measures.

- Banks, the major supplier of distressed assets in Japan, tend to sell them too late.
- Pricing sometimes seems to be inconsistent with that of normal assets.

Bond Markets

- Japanese government bond markets are huge and work well with the exception of markets for derivative assets.
- Corporate bond markets are so small because of low business demand for funds and the small size of each issue, as well as the easy alternative of access to bank credit.
- It is not clear how the markets price credit risk through trading in corporate bonds.
- Low liquidity, low transparency, and still relatively high transaction costs in corporate bond markets are problems.
- High-yield bond markets are underdeveloped. It is necessary to price default risk properly and consistently in both bond markets and in bank credit markets.

10 Issues Facing the Japanese Labor Market

Masanori Hashimoto

and

Yoshio Higuchi

Japan's labor market faces a number of problems, some the direct consequences of the macroeconomic malaise that has been present since the early 1990s and others of a more long-term nature. Identifying and analyzing these key issues is the purpose of this chapter, which seeks to explore possible ways to promote a healthier and more nimble labor market in Japan. For some problems, we discuss concrete proposals, for others we identify issues that must be addressed to facilitate the formulation of sensible solutions.

To provide background context, the chapter begins by summarizing trends and current conditions in Japan's labor market. Four problems closely related to the economy's poor performance, which means a restoration of growth will mitigate—although not "solve" these issues, are then addressed. These particular near-term problems are job training and worker satisfaction, idleness among youths and young adults, gender gaps in unemployment, and regional variations in unemployment. We then turn to more deep-rooted issues, solutions to which shall involve altering institutional structures, social preferences, and responding to demographic trends. The institutional and structural issues addressed are the dual economy, sectoral changes, and re-allocation of human resources; the traditional dependency on government sectors for employment; the industrial relations system; and working hours. Issues related to demographic trends, including immigration policy and mandatory retirement, are then taken up. In analyzing the status and role of women in the work force, we take particular note of the disincentives that laws, public policies, and employer practices generate.

1 Trends and Current Conditions

Japan saw its unemployment rate rise more than 2.5 times between 1990 (when the rate was 2.1%) and 2002 (when the rate was 5.4%), with the rate of increase accelerating after the late 1990s (Figure 10.1). As of this writing (October 2004), it appears that the unemployment rate peaked at 5.5% in January 2003, but the long-term structural issues we consider in this chapter remain problematic even if the economy continues to recover.

Figure 10.1 also indicates that the non-accelerating inflation rate of unemployment (NAIRU), a measure of the natural rate of unemployment, rose substantially, going from 2.4% in 1991 to 3.9% in 2001 (OECD 2003, Table 1.3.) Such a large increase points to structural changes in the economy rather than cyclical influences. Indeed, Japan is one of only five OECD countries that experienced an increase in the natural rate of unemployment between 1991 and 2001. (The NAIRU rose by 62.5% in Japan, 26.5% in Finland, 18% in Greece, 13% in Iceland, and 8.9% in Germany.) The NAIRU in four countries (Austria, Italy, Switzerland, and the United States) remained stable—and it decreased in twelve (Australia, Belgium, Canada, Denmark, France, Ireland, the Netherlands, New Zealand, Norway, Portugal, Spain, UK).

Japan's poorly performing economy has led to labor market problems that have had different effects between the sexes and among generations, geographical areas, and sectors. The deteriorating labor market is of serious concern for the well-being of the Japanese population, especially because Japan's social safety nets are less extensive than those found in the United States or Europe.

The rise in the unemployment rate, defined as the ratio of the number of unemployed persons to the number of persons in the labor force, is due to a greater reduction in the number of employed persons than the reduction in the size of the labor force. This differential is largely a demand-side phenomenon—weak aggregate demand of the sort summarized humorously by Calvin Coolidge in 1930: "When more and more people are thrown out of work, unemployment results." If an equivalent number of persons losing jobs withdraws from the labor force, the unemployment rate falls. However, the majority of dismissed workers will stay in the labor force, at least for some time, so the unemployment rate rises. Still, Japan's labor force is declining, and this supply-side phenomenon partly reflects the rise of "hidden" unemployment—discouraged persons who have stopped looking for work—and partly reflects the demographic phenomenon of a decline in the number of persons of labor-force age.

In addition to the decline in the level of employment, job quality has declined as well during much of the period. This is evidenced by

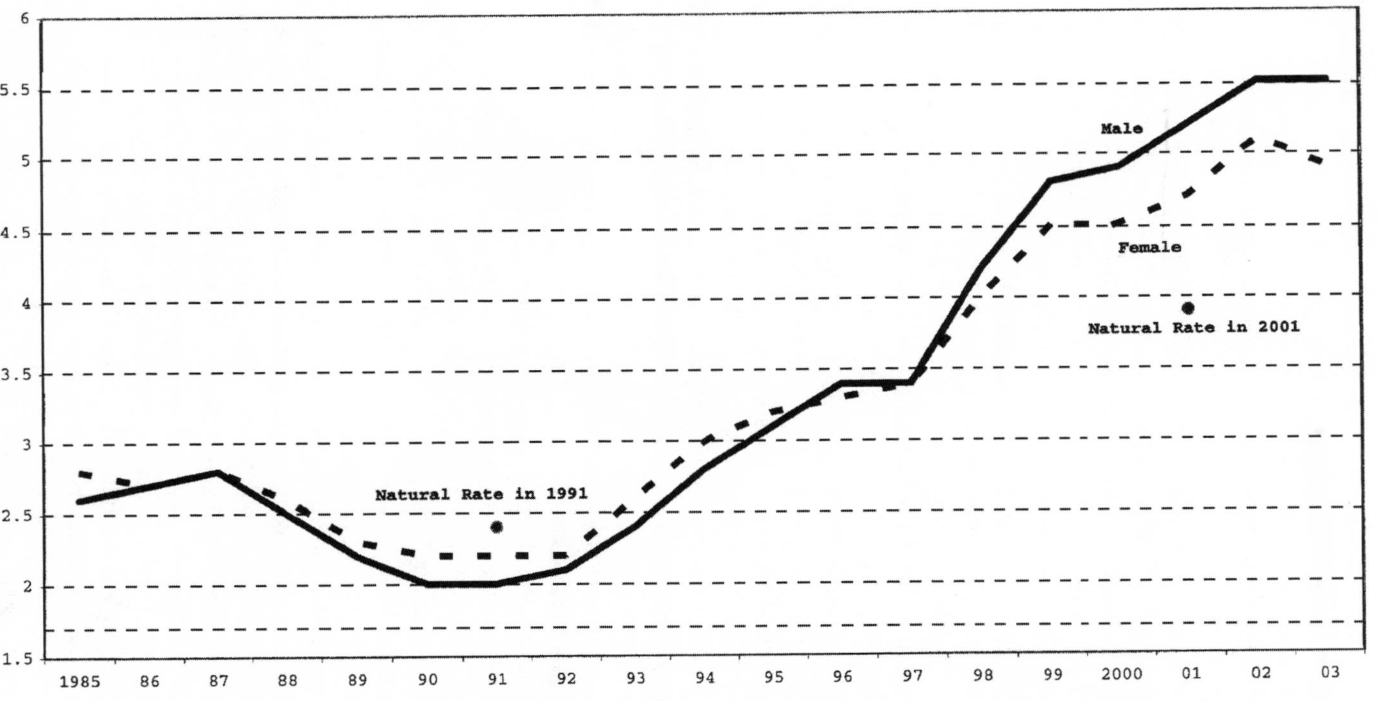

Source: Ministry of Public Management, Statistics Bureau, *Annual Report on the Labor Force Survey*, various years.

Figure 10.1
Unemployment Rates (in percents)

the declining share of regular workers in the labor force and the rising number of non-regular workers, part-timers and others with little job security, as discussed later in greater detail.[1]

The share of regular workers in the total workforce rose between 1990 and 1997 for both men and women, but after 1997 it has fallen continuously. In 1997, 94.1% of male employees were regular workers, but men only comprised 92.1% of such workers in 2003. For women, the share fell even more during this same period, from 80.9% to 77.6%. Moreover, the wage differential between regular workers and non-regular workers has been increasing since the early 1990s (Higuchi and MOF Research Center 2003; Higuchi, Ohta and HRI 2004).

It should be kept in mind that Japan is not alone in experiencing a rise of part-time and temporary employment, especially among women. France, Germany, the Netherlands, and Spain also experienced the same trend in the 1980s and 1990s (see Houseman and Osawa 2003). Houseman and Osawa argue that although Japan's recession in the 1990s may have accelerated the growth of part-time employment, this increase began well before the recession. In other words, the shift away from regular full-time employees enjoying *nenko* (seniority-based) wages and long-term employment is in part structural, so that the rise of part-time employment would have occurred even without the malaise of the 1990s.

Another quality problem concerns job training. Japanese firms reduced training expenditures during the 1990s in order to save on labor costs. As a result, the share of direct expenditures on training as a percentage of total labor costs fell from 38% in 1988 to 28% in 2002. Also, the number of establishments that provide formal on-the-job training or off-job training declined from 86.4% in 1994 to 69% in 1999. (Data from Ministry of Health, Labor and Welfare, *Total Survey on Employment Conditions.*)

Weak aggregate demand for labor in the 1990s is a result of the languishing macro economy. In our judgment, this malaise was not caused by whatever structural problems may exist in the labor market. Rather, it resulted from weak aggregate demand and slowly progressing structural reforms in various sectors of the economy. The lack of convincing progress in structural reforms helped perpetuate the pessimistic assessment of Japan's economic future, thereby discouraging investment in both physical and human capital. As a result, employment growth became less and less responsive to upward swings in the economy throughout the 1990s and into the 2000s. For example, the elasticity of the growth rate of the number of employed with respect to GDP growth fell from 52% in 1986–91 to 37% in 1993–97, to 22% in 1999–2000, and a mere 5% in 2002–2004.

The overall labor force participation rate, defined as the rate for those aged 15 to 64 years, fell throughout much of the 1990s, with the decline accelerating after 1997: the rate went from 63.8 % in 1991 to 63.7% in 1997 to below 61% in 2003. The 3 percentage point decrease during 1997–2003 represents 1.2 million people. In the same period, 2.4 million people lost jobs. The net result was a 1.2 million increase in the amount of unemployed workers. (These numbers are the authors' calculations based on the *Labor Force Survey*.)

The ratio of employment to population, the employment ratio, also declined during the entire period. The difference between the labor force participation rate and the employment ratio is the unemployment ratio, sometimes used as an alternative measure of the extent of labor under-utilization. Since 1992 the unemployment ratio has been widening, growing from 1.4% in 1992 to 2.9% in 1999 and then to 3.2% in 2003, thus mirroring the rise in the unemployment rate.

The aggregate trend in the labor force participation rate masks differences among age groups, as Figures 10.2 and 10.3 show. A decline in male participation has occurred in most age groups. For post-childbearing women of prime working age (aged 35–44), there were upward trends during much of the period. A worsening Japanese labor market during the 1990s likely reinforced a long-term decline in the male participation. For prime working-age females, increasing participation, especially in the latter 1990s, may reflect the added-worker effect—wives picking up part-time employment to supplement losses in the husbands' earnings—as well as the increased availability of part-time job enticing women to join the labor market.

Changes in labor-force participation reflect both business cycle effects and long-term structural effects. In Japan, labor force participation rate for men has fallen, from 81.7% in 1965 to 77.2% in 1990 and 75.7% in 2001. The same rate for Japanese women also has fallen, although not as much, from 50.6% in 1965 to 50.1% in 1990 and 49.2% in 2001. For comparison, the United States has experienced declining labor-force participation among men for a century and rising participation among women throughout much of the post-World War II period. Focusing on years after 1970, American labor-force participation for all males 16 or older declined from 80.6% in 1970 to 74.1% in 2002. The rate for women rose from 43.3% in 1970 to 59.6% in 2002. These trends reflect long-term forces that are generated by, among other factors, rising real income and rising female wages.[2]

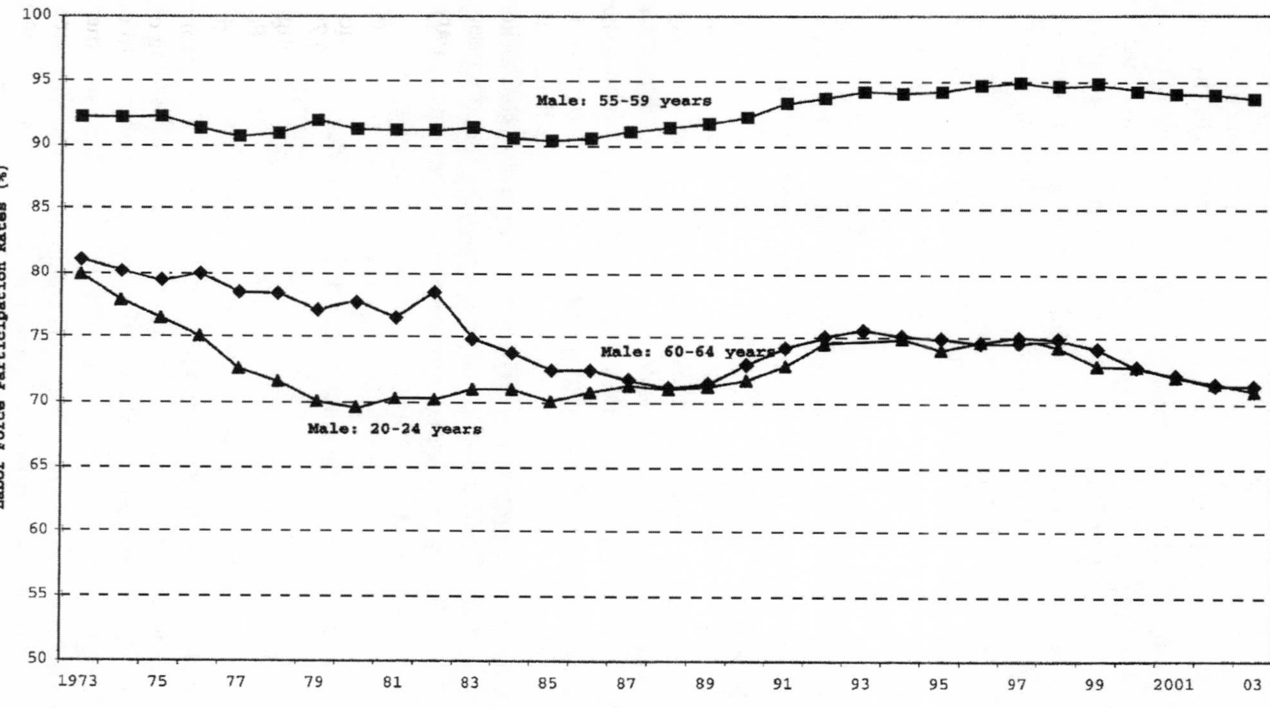

Source: Ministry of Public Management, Statistics Bureau, *Annual Report on the Labor Force Survey*, various years.

Figure 10.2
Male Labor Force Participation Rates, Selected Age Groups, 1973–2003

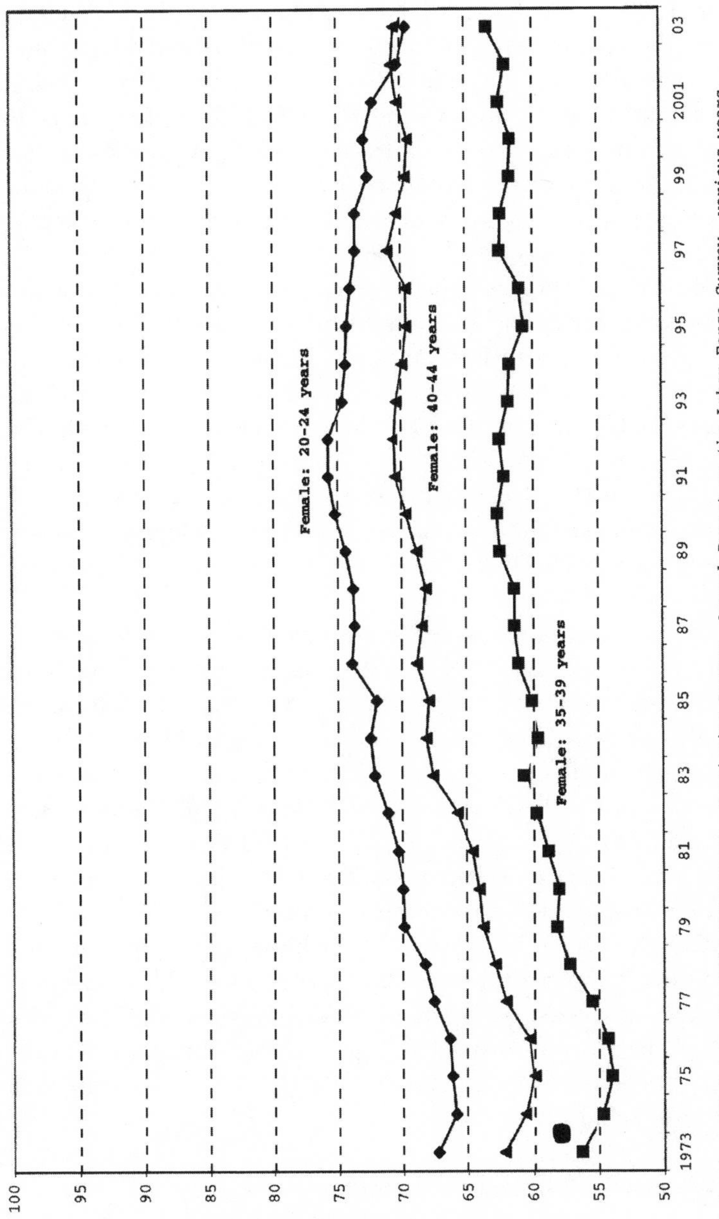

Source: Ministry of Public Management, Statistics Bureau, *Annual Report on the Labor Force Survey*, various years.

Figure 10.3
Female Labor Force Participation Rates, Selected Age Groups, 1973–2003

As mentioned earlier, Japan has seen an increase in non-regular workers (such as part-time and temporary workers) from 18.8% of employment in 1990 to 25.5% in 2002. Particularly noteworthy is that large employers (those with 1000 or more employees) have been relying more on part-timers: between 1995 and 2001, the proportion of part-time to full-time workers grew from 3.9% to 8.6%. This 120% increase was the largest of any firm-size group. Part-time workers typically are paid less than full-time workers, so this change in employee composition must have depressed disposal income and hence aggregate demand by consumers.

Japan is not unique in experiencing rising part-time work. As in many OECD countries, Japan has accounted for a large share of overall employment growth between 1991 and 2001. According to a 2003 OECD report, rising part-time employment was large enough to more than offset declining full-time employment in Austria (0.2% for part-time vs –0.1% for full-time), Finland (0.3% vs –0.2%), Italy (0.4% vs -0.2%), and Japan (0.5% vs -0.4%). The report also mentions that part-time work has been a particularly important factor behind employment growth for women, youths (15–24) and, to a lesser extent, older workers (55+). (OECD 2003, pp. 49–50.)

For most years since the late 1990s, the annual growth in Japan's real wage rate for all non-agricultural industries has remained negative: –2% in 1998, –0.9% in 1999, –0.4% in 2001 and –1.3% in 2002. (Data are for establishments with 5 or more workers as reported in the 2004 *Katsuyo Rodo Tokei*, Table C-1(2).) The real wage rate in Japan's business sector grew by only 0.3% in both the 1990–95, and 1995–02 periods, in sharp contrast to the growth of 3.3% during 1970–80 and 1.3% during 1980–90 (OECD 2003). By comparison, the annual growth rate for the American business-sector wage jumped from 0.7% in 1990–95 to 1.6% in 1995–02 (OECD 2003, Table 1.A1.1). In manufacturing, wage growth started to slow in Japan after 1990, and became negative after the mid-1990s. Hourly compensation grew by 105.7% between 1985 and 1990 and by 84.5% between 1990 and 1995, but was –8.7% between 1995 and 2000, and –14.7% in the three years 2000–02. (*US Economic Report of the President* 2004, Table B-109.)

2 Near-Term Labor Problems and Solutions

Four problems closely related to the poor performance of Japan's economy, for which a restoration of growth will mitigate, but not "solve", are addressed in this section. These are job training and worker satisfaction, youth idleness, gender gaps in unemployment, and geographical differences in employment measures.

2.1 *Job Training and Worker Satisfaction*

In order to raise productivity and increase long-term competitiveness, Japanese firms need to pay increased attention to job training and job satisfaction. In the 1990s, many firms cut labor costs in the name of restructuring. This made some firms more competitive, but it also resulted in a loss of skills and worker morale as employees were laid off or transferred. Thus, Chuma et al (2004) report that in the 1990s worker discontent in the electrical, electronic, and information industries increased due in part to weakening participatory employment practices.

As Japanese firms regain economic prowess, they will need to invest more in human capital to ensure their competitiveness is maintained. Employee satisfaction will rise if workers feel that employers are willing to invest in them through training.

As to public policy on job training, Japan might consider a program similar to the "Jobs for the 21st Century" initiative that American President George W. Bush proposed in his 2004 State of the Union message. Included in this initiative is a proposal to strengthen ties between employers and community colleges with a view to retraining unemployed workers. Community colleges in the United States are reported to enroll over 10 million students each year, many of them laid-off workers. A statement in the White House press release (January 2004) is relevant for Japan as well:

> Helping Americans Access High-Demand Jobs: America's economy is growing, but it is also changing due to higher productivity and new technology. It is more important than ever that Americans have the education and training needed to succeed . . . Many older students and current workers will also need to strengthen their skills to compete for the jobs of tomorrow. President Bush proposed more than $500 million for a series of measures called Jobs for the 21st Century—designed to provide extra help to middle and high school students who fall behind in reading and math, expand Advanced Placement programs in low-income schools, and invite math and science professionals from the private sector to teach part-time in high schools . . . The President's Jobs for the 21st Century initiative also increases support for America's community colleges to train workers for the industries that are creating the most new jobs. The initiative will also provide larger Pell Grants for low-income students who prepare for college with demanding courses in high school.

Japan could leverage *senmon gakko* or similar vocational training schools to facilitate training workers in skills that will be in high demand and that match new and emerging jobs and technology. It is worth noting that the Japanese Ministry of Economy, Trade, and Industry (METI) has proposed a system for deducting job-training cost from corporate taxes.

2.2 *The Idle Young*

One of the most pressing concerns is the rate of idleness (being neither in the labor force nor in school) among teenagers (ages 15–19) and young adults (ages 20–24). The last two columns of Table 10.1 show that the increase in idleness has been particularly pronounced for those aged 15 to 19 years throughout Japan, in part reflecting significant increases in the group's unemployment rate since the early 1990s. It should be kept in mind that Japan is not alone in this problem: throughout the OECD, young people experienced more serious employment problems in the job market in the 1990s than in earlier years.

Idle young people are missing the opportunity to receive formal education and acquire knowledge and experience about the world of work. Through a reduction of human capital formation, idleness has serious long-term consequences for labor productivity, and an increase in anti-social behaviors. For instance, there are worrisome signs that youth unemployment is linked to crimes committed by young people. Particularly alarming, more young people are being arrested for such serious crimes as violence and larceny.

The arrest-rate for those aged 14–19 years rose 25% from the mid-1990s to 2002, although it remains below the level of the early 1980s. Specifically, the rate fell from over 18 arrests per thousand during 1982–84 to around 12 per thousand during 1993–96, rose to 17 in 1999 and in 2002 was around 16. For young adults aged 20–24 years, the arrest rate has fluctuated around 4 per thousand since 1990, having declined in the last half of the 1980s from levels between 5 and 6 earlier in the decade.

Even for young people in the labor force, either employed or unemployed, the phenomenon of freeters has attracted a great deal of attention. A freeter is defined as a person 15 to 34 years old that not a student or housewife, but who works in part-time jobs or who is unemployed but looking to work only part-time even if a full-time job is available. (The word itself is a contraction of "free *arbeiter*"—a free worker in the spirit of free agents in sports.) Freeter status can be either voluntary or

Table 10.1
Unemployment and Idle Labor Among the Young (percents)

Region Year	Unemployment Rates		Idle Labor Rates[1]		
	Total	15–19	20–24	15–19	20–24
National					
1990	2.1	6.6	3.7	11.1	5.4
1997	3.4	9.0	6.2	14.4	7.7
2003	5.3	11.9	9.8	19.4	12.3
Hokkaido					
1990	3.0	12.5	3.8	12.5	7.4
1997	3.8	14.3	6.5	25.0	9.4
2003	6.7	16.7	12.0	16.7	15.4
Tohoku					
1990	1.8	8.3	5.0	8.3	7.3
1997	2.9	9.1	6.3	16.7	8.2
2003	5.6	12.5	11.9	22.2	14.0
Kita Kanto-Koshin					
1990	1.5	7.7	2.2	14.3	6.3
1997	2.5	8.3	5.4	15.4	7.0
2003	4.6	11.1	9.3	20.0	11.4
Minami Kanto (Tokyo Metro)					
1990	2.2	5.6	3.8	10.5	5.6
1997	3.8	10.5	7.0	15.0	8.3
2003	5.1	8.8	8.7	16.2	11.6
Hokuriku					
1990	1.3	—	4.0	—	4.0
1997	2.6	—	3.4	—	3.4
2003	4.0	25.0	8.7	—	12.5
Tokai (Nagoya)					
1990	1.5	4.0	2.5	7.7	3.7
1997	2.7	5.6	4.5	10.5	5.6
2003	4.0	13.3	7.4	18.8	10.0
Kinki (Osaka-Kyoto-Kobe)					
1990	2.5	6.1	4.3	8.8	5.9
1997	4.0	8.0	7.1	11.5	8.6
2003	6.6	16.7	11.1	25.0	14.0

Table 10.1 (*continued*)
Unemployment and Idle Labor Among the Young (percents)

Region	Unemployment Rates		Idle Labor Rates[1]		
Year	Total	15–19	20–24	15–19	20–24
Chyugoku					
1990	1.8	11.1	3.0	20.0	5.9
1997	2.7	12.5	5.0	12.5	7.3
2003	4.3	16.7	9.7	28.6	12.5
Shikoku					
1990	2.3	—	6.3	—	6.3
1997	3.2	—	5.3	—	10.0
2003	4.8	33.3	13.3	33.3	13.3
Kyusyu					
1990	2.7	6.7	5.2	12.5	6.8
1997	3.8	13.3	6.6	18.8	9.0
2003	5.9	14.3	12.3	20.0	14.9

[1]Idle labor consists of those not in the labor force or in school.
Source: Ministry of Public Management, Statistics Bureau, *Annual Report on the Labor Force Survey,* various years.

involuntary. Government data estimate there were 4.17 million freeters in 2001, 10% of them aged 15–19 years, 34% 20–24 years old, 36% aged 25–29 years , and 19% 30–34 years old. This increase compares to 1.86 million freeters in 1989. The average age of freeters increased during the past 20 years. Initially the largest group was in their early 20s.

The original distinguishing characteristic of freeters was that they did not aspire to get on the traditional full-time career track prized in Japan, at least in the early years of their working careers. It is not clear if such an attitude is just a passing phase or a life-long phenomenon. At any rate, the fact that such a term as "freeters" was coined in Japan reveals how different the work attitude of younger generations is perceived to have become compared to previous generations. It is important to keep in mind that being a freeter was at first a voluntary, supply-side phenomenon, a counter-cultural expression, as it were, and not a demand-deficiency phenomenon. During the economic boom in the 1980s, an increasing number of youths began choosing to work part-time as a career objective. As the recession persisted through the 1990s, however, the phenomenon was increasingly the result of demand deficiency, as many more young people had no choice but to work part-time. Thus, in fiscal year 2003, over 86% of young males and almost 50% of young females were looking for full-time jobs and of these, over 95% wished to become permanent employees before reaching 30 (Cabinet Office 2003; see Chiba 2004 for related discussions). Moreover, Japan's stagnant economy does little to accommodate adults who had chosen the life of a freeter when the economy was flush, but now want full-time jobs. (See Danke 2003.)

Whether voluntary or involuntary, part-time employment typically offers fewer opportunities for on-the-job training than full-time employment., This results in freeters missing out on investments in employment-based human capital, adversely affecting their productivity later in life.

Blanchflower and Freeman (2000) found that aggregate unemployment is the single most important explanatory variable in accounting for youth labor-market problems in OECD countries. This points to improving the macroeconomy as the solution. However, in our view, this is only part of the solution.

To see this, recall an elementary theory of labor supply: an individual compares a reservation wage to the market wage in deciding whether or not to enter the labor market. That is, when the real wage available in the market falls below the reservation wage, a potential worker will not enter the labor market. Here, the reservation wage and the real wage are broadly conceived to include "the whole of the advantages and disadvantages" of market work, to use Adam Smith's terminology, as well as the monetary wage. Thus, improvements in the macroeconomy that raise the market real wage will be a solution to the problem of non-participation in the labor market.

It is possible that, in the context of Japan's prolonged economic slump, the reservation wage of young persons in Japan has become too high; if so, what is required is a reshaping of the appreciation for life-long employment. Teachers and parents can help shape reservation wage by adopting a "back-to-the basics" approach and instilling an appreciation of educational and work experiences as the way to ensure having many options, economic and otherwise, in their adult lives.

As for crime among teenagers and young adults, it is well known that a lack of legal employment opportunities results in criminal conduct. Here, too, an improved macroeconomy will help, especially with such economic crimes as pick-pocketing and robbery. Young people who commit crimes should face penalties, of course. Levitt (1998) finds evidence for the United States that punishing juvenile offenders is an effective means of combating crimes committed by this age group. However, public policies must weigh the benefits and costs of punishment. According to Levitt's evidence, the severity of juvenile sanctions has little effect on later criminal behavior. Freeman (2003) analyzes criminal activities among disadvantaged American youths and concludes that the high cost to society associated with crime and incarceration suggests potentially large returns to prevention programs, be it employment subsidies, training programs, increased expenditure on police, etc.

An important cost of incarcerating offending youths is the stigma effect, which may be long-lasting, especially in Japan. An alternative to imprisonment, especially for light offenders, is to require that they go through counseling and job training programs. Sometime after successful completion of these programs, the criminal record is then expunged, which mitigates lasting stigma effects. Such a system is used in many parts of the United States for teenagers apprehended for under-age drinking.

2.3 *Gender Gaps in Unemployment*

Reversing the traditional pattern, Japan's male unemployment rate has remained higher than the female rate since 1997 (Figure 10.1). This reflects such fundamental changes as the shift of economic activities from manufacturing and construction to service and trade. It also reflects employers' increasing reliance on part-time and temporary workers, who are more likely to be female, a trend which underscores the lack of confidence in the economy's prospects that makes firms reluctant to invest in long-term employees.

The loss of manufacturing jobs has been absolutely and proportionately greater for women than for men. Specifically, manufacturing employment fell by 1.28 million (26%) for females and 1.24 million (14%) for males between 1997 and 2003. This has contributed slightly more to the rise in the female unemployment rate than to the male rate. It should be noted that manufacturing jobs are disappearing all over the world, even in China, regardless of macroeconomic conditions. (See Carson 2003.)

Figure 10.4 shows that the number of regular workers in all fields has declined since 1998, and the number of temporary workers has been increasing since 1995. At the same time, more and more women have been getting temporary and lower-wage jobs. On the demand side, this phenomenon is due to employer reluctance to invest in human

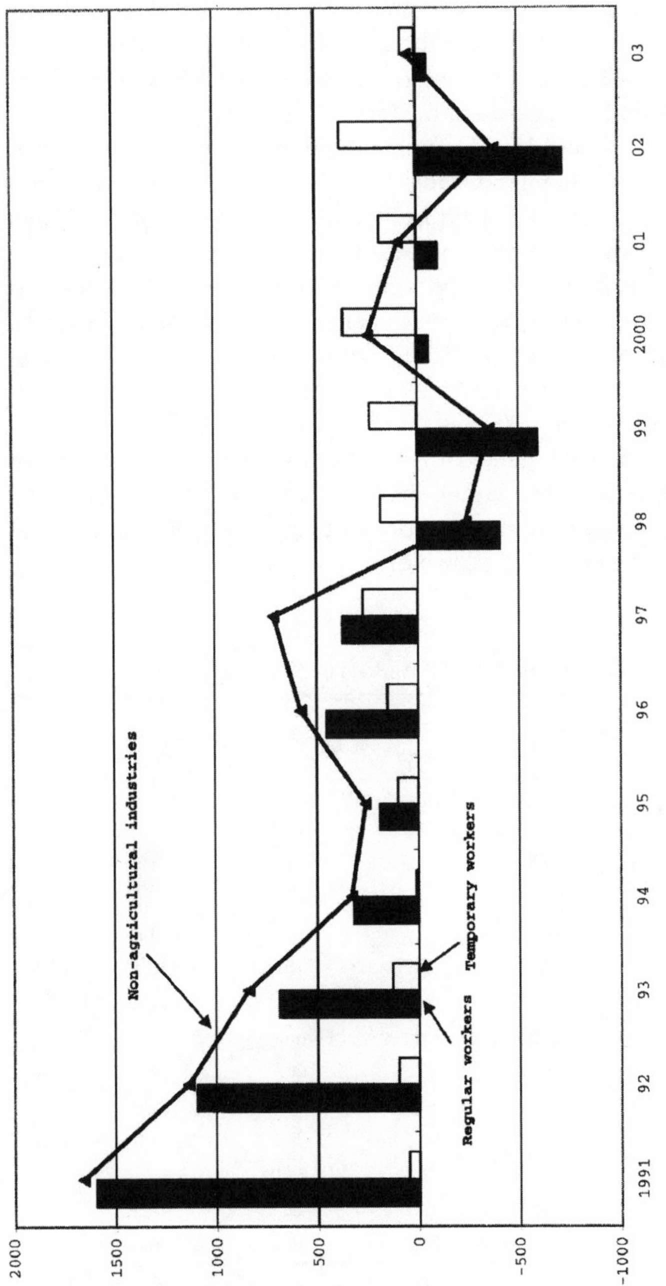

Source: Ministry of Public Management, Statistics Bureau, *Annual Report on the Labor Force Survey*, various years.

Figure 10.4
Annual Change in Number of Workers
(thousand workers)

capital in the form of male workers with long-term employment given the grave uncertainty about the economy's future. On the supply side, it may be partly due to the additional-worker phenomenon in which wives whose husbands have lost jobs or experienced wage cuts enter the labor market to supplement the family's income.

Tables 10.2, 10.3, and 10.4 document the trends in part-time and full-time employment after 1980. Table 10.2 shows that the proportion of workers who are part-time is typically higher for women than for men and that there was an overall increase in this proportion for both men and women. The part-time proportion rose throughout these years, but the increases for those aged 15 to 24 years and 65 years and older were especially pronounced. Of particular note is that over 46% of working women 40 years or older held part-time jobs in 2003, as compared to 29% to 35% during 1985–90.

Table 10.3 shows the gender distribution of part-time employment. Clearly, women have the larger share. Note, however, that since the mid-1980s the female share has shown a declining overall trend in all age categories except 15–24 year-olds.

Table 10.2
Part-Time Workers as a Percentage of All Workers by Sex

		Age Group				
Year	All	15–24	25–39	40–54	55–64	65–
		Male Part-Time Workers/All Male Workers				
1980	6.1	8.9	4.2	4.9	9.6	24.2
1985	6.1	10.5	3.8	4.2	9.4	27.4
1990	8.3	14.9	4.9	5.7	11.2	30.3
1995	9.1	17.1	5.3	5.8	11.6	31.6
2000	10.5	23.3	5.7	6.1	13.1	35.8
2003	13.7	28.3	8.2	8.9	17.2	40.5
		Female Part-Time Workers/All Female Workers				
1980	26.0	11.6	30.3	26.7	29.0	41.4
1985	27.9	12.4	30.9	29.3	31.5	45.7
1990	31.8	18.4	33.0	34.7	35.0	46.7
1995	33.9	22.7	31.4	38.0	36.3	48.6
2000	37.7	30.4	32.1	42.1	40.5	52.5
2003	41.6	35.2	34.7	46.1	46.6	56.0

Source: Authors' calculations using data from Ministry of Public Management, Statistics Bureau, *Annual Report on the Labor Force Survey*, various years.

Table 10.3
Female Part-Time Workers as a Percentage of Total Part-Time Workers

	Age Group					
Year	All	15–24	25–39	40–54	55–64	65–
1980	71.7	56.7	78.3	76.6	64.6	45.3
1985	74.2	53.8	81.5	82.2	65.7	50.0
1990	71.8	55.0	79.2	81.0	63.3	49.4
1995	71.3	55.6	77.6	82.1	64.6	46.8
2000	70.9	56.0	77.6	83.1	65.9	45.3
2003	67.7	54.5	73.1	78.8	63.0	44.6

Source: Authors' calculations using data from Ministry of Public Management, Statistics Bureau, *Annual Report on the Labor Force Survey,* various years.

Table 10.4
Male Full-Time Workers as a Percentage of Total Full-Time Workers

	Age Group					
Year	All	15–24	25–39	40–54	55–64	65–
1980	68.0	50.5	73.4	68.2	67.8	72.8
1985	67.3	50.9	72.1	67.3	69.8	69.1
1990	67.0	51.3	71.4	67.5	71.2	67.3
1995	67.3	53.3	70.4	68.4	70.3	69.9
2000	67.9	53.1	69.3	69.5	70.0	70.5
2003	68.1	53.3	68.5	70.1	71.2	69.9

Source: Authors' calculations using data from Ministry of Public Management, Statistics Bureau, *Annual Report on the Labor Force Survey,* various years.

Table 10.4 shows the gender distribution of total full-time employment. Men have a far larger share of full-time jobs in all age groups except 15–24, where they hold just over half of these jobs. Men have increased their share slightly in some groups and decreased in others, but there is no discernible overall trend.

Another way of looking at part-time employment is the number of hours worked. There was a notable increase in the number of women working short hours: between 1995 and 2002, the number of people working 1–14 hours per week increased by 47.7% (from 1.07 million to 1.58 million), those working 15–29 hours increased by 34.8% (from 3.39 million to 4.57 million), and those working between 30–34 hours increased by 18.3% (from 1.86 million to 2.20 million). (Authors' calculations from *Annual Report on the Labor Force Survey* 2003.)

Female part-time workers generally receive low pay. In the early 2003, they earned 44% of full-time male earnings, whereas male part-timers earned 50%. The gender differences in part reflect the industries and specific jobs men and women are likely to work in, as well as the "glass ceiling" career women still face in Japan. (Data from Basic Survey of Wages, 2004.)

Clearly, Japan has seen a reduction in the employment of regular workers and increase in temporary workers. In other words, more and more workers have shifted from high-wage regular employment to lower-wage part-time and temporary jobs. Some of this disparity should disappear once the economy starts growing and firms are persuaded that the recovery is sustainable, so that they again commit to long-term employment. Some workers initially hired as part-timers become regular workers after proving themselves. Such practices, referred to in Japan as a "trial" employment, should increase as the economic recovery gains momentum.

2.4 Regional Variations in Japanese Unemployment

Unemployment has been rising in rural prefectures, exacerbating regional inequality in Japan's economic well-being. Between 1998 and 2003 the unemployment rate increased in all prefectures, but especially in rural and other non-metropolitan areas. The mean increase was 1.3 percentage points, with a range of about 0.1 point for Tokyo and Okinawa to over 2.5 points in Tokushima (on Shikoku). In Japan, there is no special criterion to distinguish between rural and urban areas. Normally, urban areas are defined as the three major urban areas: *Shutoken*, (the Tokyo-Yokohama area, also called *Minami Kanto*); *Tokai*, Nagoya; and *Kansai*, Osaka-Kyoto-Kobe; following the Japan Census Bureau.

The average change in employment levels was –4.5%, with a range from nearly +4% in Okinawa to almost –12% in Wakayama. Besides Okinawa, only Tokyo and two adjoining prefectures (Kanagawa and Chiba) gained jobs, but being near Tokyo was not sufficient to limit losses; Saitama lost over 2% of its jobs.

The regional differences in unemployment are a consequence of two major changes. First, there has been a sectoral shift of economic activities from manufacturing to service and trade industries. Table 10.5 indicates that agriculture, fisheries, and forestry sectors continually lost

Table 10.5
Change in Employment by Sector (annual averages, in percents)

1981–90	1991–97	1998–2002	Sector
–2.4	–3.3	–3.7	Agriculture, Forestry, Fishery
0.8	2.2	–2.0	Construction
1.1	–0.6	–3.3	Manufacturing
0.6	1.4	–0.5	Transportation, Communication
1.2	0.6	–0.5	Wholesale and Retail Trade
3.7	–0.3	–1.0	Finance, Insurance
3.7	2.4	1.8	Services

Entries are the estimated coefficients for the dummy variables corresponding to the time period in the regression of the annual percentage change in employment. The figures include private and public sector employment.

Source: Authors' calculations using data from Ministry of Public Management, Statistics Bureau, *Annual Report on the Labor Force Survey,* various years.

jobs after 1980. All other sectors gained employment during the 1980s, but manufacturing and finance started to lose jobs after 1990. Between 1998 and 2002, jobs were lost in all sectors except services. Manufacturing employment peaked in 1992, yet fell below the service sector in 1995. Construction jobs peaked in 1997, but in 2003 was still above what they were in 1990.

As the manufacturing sector started to lose employment, factories in regional areas were especially likely to lose jobs. In the 1960s and 1970s Japan had several national plans encouraging firms to relocate or build new manufacturing capacity outside main urban areas in order to reduce congestion and address regional economic imbalances (see, for example Tanaka 1972). Such plants are especially vulnerable to closure during business cycle contractions.

Second, there was a reduction of government expenditures on public works. This resulted in employment losses in the latter 1990s and early 2000s, especially in the construction industry. As is well known, such expenditures were used to favor the LDP's strongholds in agricultural and rural prefectures.

Globalization of economic activities also is an important reason for spatial changes in employment. Once a steady source of employment for many rural areas, manufacturers increasingly are moving production overseas in a process known as "hollowing out", or are exiting the market altogether. In contrast, some urban areas have benefited from foreign firms locating in these areas, especially in financial services and information technology (IT) software. This is especially true for the Tokyo area: 36% of jobs created by foreign investment have been in Tokyo and 13% in the neighboring Kanagawa prefecture (Yokohama, Kawasaki). The relative importance of foreign investment in job creation is 2.4% in Tokyo, 2.6% in Kanagawa, 2.7% in Hiroshima prefecture. (Estimates for 1996 by Fukao and Amano 2004.)

The transformation of rural economies is a reality that has existed for decades. Displaced workers in rural areas must be willing to retrain for new jobs or relocate. Policy options include (1) transferring the budget authority for employment creation and training policies from the central authority to local government, because how to spend these funds efficiently is best determined at the local level possessing the relevant information, and (2) facilitating worker migrations, especially for young persons, to areas where new jobs are being created.

The migration of young workers from rural to urban areas has in fact been a persistent phenomenon in Japan's postwar development. It is worrisome, therefore, that the rate of geographical mobility has fallen recently. To what extent this is due to parents wanting to keep their children nearby in this era of low birth rates is an interesting explanation to explore. Also, there has been a new interest in agriculture—not traditional rice farming, but more high-value crops including specialty rice varieties, although this involves only a small number of people. Important questions for future research are (1) what geographical areas such activities tend to be located in and (2) how this development affects geographical mobility.

3 Structural Issues and Solutions

This section takes up the dual economy, sectoral changes, and re-allocation of human resources; the dependency on government sectors for employment; the industrial relations system; and working hours.

3.1 *Dual Economy, Sectoral Changes, and Re-allocation of Human Resources*

Only five of the 28 industries, employing a little over 18% of regular workers, had total factor productivity (TFP) exceeding that of the United States in 1995 (Table 10.6). Export-driven manufacturers of products such as transportation machinery and electrical machinery

Table 10.6
Relative Total Factor Productivity and Employment Distribution by Sector

Employment Distribution in 2000 (percents)	Total Factor Productivity (US = 100)	Sector
2.23	136.58	Transportation Machinery
9.19	124.61	Finance, Real Estate
4.12	119.24	Electric Machinery
0.36	108.98	Wood Products
2.27	102.84	General Machinery
1.06	98.51	Chemicals
0.90	96.18	Ceramic and Stone Products
0.96	93.15	Primary Metal
30.57	92.59	Service
0.59	90.03	Paper, Pulp
0.56	86.68	Precision Machinery
0.43	84.62	Textile
1.82	83.19	Other MFG
0.08	82.78	Petroleum and Coal Products
0.09	81.46	Leather Goods
1.10	81.14	Clothing
8.68	81.06	Construction
5.29	79.93	Transportation
21.03	79.22	Wholesale, Retail
1.60	77.34	Metal Products
1.49	68.80	Communication
1.32	67.37	Publishing
3.34	66.43	Food and Processing
0.13	64.08	Gas
0.09	61.88	Other mining
0.34	56.78	Furniture
0.32	46.49	Electricity
0.01	19.01	Coal Mining

Source: Ministry of Economy, Trade, and Industry, Tsusho Hakusho, 2000.

boast high productivity. The high productivity of the finance and real estate industries seems odd given the prevailing concerns about the health of Japan's financial sectors. This phenomenon may be driven by the real estate sector and the fact that firms in finance could generate value-added because they were protected by regulation. What is needed is to raise the productivity for the non-export oriented sectors through rationalization and reorganization.

Japan has been experiencing a shift of economic activities from manufacturing and construction to services (Table 10.5). This is especially so for medical and welfare services, which together employed nearly 500,000 in 2003, almost the same level as the construction industry. Such shifts reflect the well-known phenomenon of an economy moving from the primary to secondary industrial sector, and then to the tertiary sector. Throughout this transition, a vibrant economy is constantly renewing itself, a process well-captured by Joseph Schumpeter's "creative destruction".

As real income rises, consumer demand for goods and services changes because of differences in income elasticities. The decline of manufacturing and the rise of service industries are part of this process, although the decline of the construction industry is due mostly to the reduction of public works investment in the mid-1990s. Displaced workers from disappearing industries must retrain and move to new industries.

Public policies must not impede, indeed they must encourage, retraining and the shifting of workers to high-productivity sectors. Retraining and providing the means that enhance mobility are investments in human capital. To the extent that the capital market is imperfect and cannot help meet liquidity needs associated with retraining and mobility, it is sound policy for the national government to subsidize retraining and mobility expenses. Some workers in traditional, low-productivity sectors continue to enjoy job security from such non-economic barriers as political and legal constraints, cultural biases against career changes and mobility, and lack of information, all of which reduce the incentive to move out of low-productivity sectors. Such barriers must be eliminated.

3.2 *Japan's Dependency on Government Job Creation*

Government expenditures as a source of employment creation are significant, especially in non-metropolitan areas, and these increased between the mid-1980s and the late 1990s (Table 10.7). Japan has spent enormous sums on public works in rural areas. To be sure, some of the spending was needed to link Japan's countryside with the rest of the country, but too much money arguably went to such projects as highways, airports, railroads, ports, and other such infrastructure. It is

Table 10.7
Employment Created by Government Expenditure as a Percentage of Total Employment

1985	1990	1995	1999	Change[1]	
19.8	18.9	22.1	22.5	3.6	Nation-wide
16.2	15.6	18.5	18.3	2.7	Major urban areas[2]
23.4	22.2	25.8	26.8	4.6	Non-metro areas
15.8	14.6	17.3	17.2	2.5	Tokyo (Minami Kanto)
17.0	17.4	20.9	20.1	2.7	Osaka (Kansai)
28.8	29.7	34.8	38.9	9.2	Kochi (on Shikoku)[3]
21.1	20.7	26.4	30.7	9.9	Wakayama[4]
14.9	13.9	16.2	16.6	2.7	Shizuoka[5]

[1]Change in percentage points from 1990 to 1999.
[2]Minami Kanto (Tokyo metro), Tokai (Nagoya), Kansai (Osaka, Kyoto, Kobe)
[3]Prefecture with highest level in 1999.
[4]Prefecture with greatest change from 1990 to 1999.
[5]Non-metro prefecture with lowest level in 1999.
Data for other prefectures are available from the authors.

Source: Higuchi et al 2002.

inevitable, and even desirable, that public money continue to be spent to benefit Japanese living in rural as well as urban areas.

For decades Japan has consistently devoted a larger share of GDP to public investment than the United States, the United Kingdom, France, and Germany. In contrast, throughout the 1990s, Japan's share of government expenditures on employment policies was lower, except in comparison to the United States. There was a slight tendency for the share to increase, but the change is affected by the general unemployment rate, as seen in Table 10.8.

Evidence suggests that public investment in Japan no longer raises overall productivity as it once did. Higuchi et al (2002) reached this conclusion from an extensive analysis of data at the prefecture level for 1975–98. Over this period, only five of 47 prefectures showed positive changes in the effects of social capital on total factor productivity; eight showed declines of over 50%. Here, "social capital" is defined as roads and highways, airports and seaports, transportation and communication equipment, water supply, agricultural equipment, public school and hospital buildings, city halls and related assets. The time is overdue for policymakers to seriously assess whether such public expenditures should shift more toward strengthening safety-net

Table 10.8
Expenditures on Employment Policies as a Percentage of GDE in High-Income Countries

Japan		USA		UK		Germany		France		
'90–91	'98–99	'90–91	'98–99	'90–91	'97–98	1990	1999	1990	1998	
2.1	4.1	5.4	4.5	5.8	7.2	4.9	10.5	8.9	11.8	Unemployment rate
0.03	0.03	0.07	0.06	0.18	0.16	0.22	0.23	0.12	0.16	Public employment services
0.03	0.03	0.08	0.04	0.21	0.07	0.38	0.35	0.33	0.31	Job training
—	—	0.03	0.03	0.17	0.12	0.04	0.08	0.20	0.32	Policies for youth
0.07	0.02	0.01	0.01	0.02	—	0.17	0.40	0.09	0.46	Wage subsidies
—	—	0.04	0.04	0.02	0.02	0.23	0.25	0.06	0.09	Policies for handicapped
0.22	0.52	0.47	0.25	0.94	0.82	1.09	2.11	1.29	1.48	Unemployment benefits
—	—	—	—	—	—	0.02	0.01	0.55	0.32	Early retirement
0.13	0.08	0.23	0.18	0.60	0.37	1.04	1.31	0.80	1.34	Active total (first 5)
0:22	0.52	0.47	0.25	0.94	0.82	1.11	2.12	1.84	1.80	Passive total (last 2)
0.35	0.60	0.70	0.43	1.54	1.19	2.15	3.43	2.64	3.14	Total

Source: Unpublished OECD study.

provisions and stimulating employment in ways other than investing in public works projects.

3.3 Industrial Relations System

Japanese industrial relations have been undergoing rapid changes since the mid-1990s. Employers used to emphasize ensuring the livelihood of their employees by offering strong job security and paying employees based on seniority. In turn, employees were expected to put up with such inconveniences as long working hours and frequent relocations. However, Japanese firms have begun to rely more on merit as the basis for wages and job security. This has meant that businesses have come to rely more on employees' being self-reliant and taking individual responsibility for ensuring their livelihood. Perhaps reflecting these changes, the annual spring labor negotiations known as *shunto* have shifted from demanding general wage increases to demanding job security and revising the wage schedule. Yet Japanese industrial relations face two important challenges relating to job training and worker employer mismatch.

In regards to job training, Hashimoto and Raisian (1985, 1992) demonstrated in their comparative studies of Japanese and American labor markets that Japan's "unique" employment system—Cole's (1971) *nenko* promotion, *nenko* wages, and "lifetime" employment—was prevalent in Japan throughout the high-growth years, although more so among larger firms. Smaller firms tried to emulate these practices. This system is likely to continue to become less common, even at large firms, as Japanese firms start to rely more on merit based decision-making for wages and employment. This shift raises an important issue on the nature of job training.

Under the *nenko* system, senior workers could train younger workers without fear of weakening their own standing. But if wages and promotion are based on merit rather than seniority, this willingness is undermined because senior workers would fear being overtaken by well-trained younger workers. This means more training will have to take place in formal settings, be it formal training provided by the employer or at third-party training schools. Since formal training tends to be more general than firm-specific, attachment between firms and their employees will weaken. Already, there is evidence that such participatory practices as small-group activities have been weakening, and worker unhappiness has become prevalent as a result (Chuma, Kato, and Ohashi 2004). In turn, labor turnover can be expected to increase but turnover is not necessarily bad. The likely shift of training from informal to formal settings makes "jobs for the 21st century" type policies relevant options for Japan to consider.

Regarding worker-employer mismatches, Japan needs to foster an environment in which these problems can be corrected in an efficient manner, and to promote efficient labor turnover. Japan, in effect, had strict employment protection practices, both formal and informal in the 1960s through the 1980s. Having compared turnover rates in Japan and the United States, we assert that the employer-employee attachment in Japan was too strong during the prosperous years of the 1970s and 1980s (see, for example, Hashimoto 1990, chapter 3). The so-called "life-time employment" practice resulted in too little turnover relative to what was efficient, especially at large companies: workers and firms tended to stay together regardless of being mismatched.

Employment protections caused few problems when the economy was growing at a rapid rate. With the economy stagnating and jobs being lost, however, the practice hinders timely changes in the deployment of workers. Ironically, employment protection slows employment recovery. Until employers gain confidence that favorable conditions in the economy will last for a long time, they will be reluctant to hire new workers, or recall laid-off workers, because they know it is difficult to discharge employees in economic downturns.

Institutional rigidities, norms, and rules inhibit efficient separations. Historically in postwar Japan, a worker who voluntarily separated from an employer tended to be stigmatized as foot-loose, and a firm that dismissed workers, even for sound business reasons, acquired a reputation for shameful conduct and thus had trouble hiring new workers. Japanese employers still face all sorts of hurdles before being allowed to dismiss workers. The laws and regulations that inhibit efficient separations need to be loosened, if not eliminated, and biases against workers changing jobs or employers dismissing workers need to be reduced through education.

At the same time, inefficient separations—separations that occur even though the parties taken together are better off not separating—must be minimized (see, for example, Hashimoto 1990). Inefficient separations occur when there is information asymmetry between the employers and employees regarding their valuations of alternatives (Hashimoto 1995). For example, even when a separation is inefficient, an employee may make a unilateral decision, incorrectly, to quit for lack of communication with the employer, who does not get a chance to persuade them to stay. Similarly, an employer may dismiss a worker inefficiently, i.e., when the surplus created by the match exists, because the employee refuses, incorrectly, to accept a pay cut to save the job because of distrust of the information provided by the employer. So, the first step in promoting efficient turnover is to reduce information asymmetry so that the parties do not separate by mistake. To this end, we recommend preservation of enterprise-based unions and joint consultations, both of which otherwise may become diluted as employment attachment weakens.

3.4 *Working Hours in Japan*

In 1988, there was a revision of the Labor Standards Law stipulating a reduction in the statutory Japanese work-week. As a result, in 1988 the work-week was reduced from 48 hours to 44 hours, and fell to 40 hours in 1993. In addition, during 1988–93, three national holidays were added, bringing the total to fifteen as compared to nine in the United States.

Government offices were closed on Saturdays every other week beginning in 1989, and since 1992 have been closed every Saturday. Financial institutions have been closed on Saturdays since 1989. A temporary law was introduced in 1992 to bring about a further reduction in hours worked. In addition, the 1998 revision of the Labor Standards Law added one more day to the paid vacation allowance (summary from Hayashi and Prescott 2002). It is interesting to note that some German employers and unions are moving towards increasing standard work hours to stay competitive, but the typical German works far fewer hours and days than a typical Japanese—indeed, under the standard definition of part-time work (less than 35 hours per week), a large part of Germany's "full-time" labor force is actually "part-time"!

The extent of compliance with the regulations is an open question. Many employees appear to continue working long hours: the proportion of employees working 60 hours per week or longer is increasing in spite of employee complaints about excessive hours. Based on informal discussions with owners and managers of mid-size companies, long working hours are common among younger regular workers. One reason is that workers in a cohort hired fresh out of school, as has been the norm, each receive the same compensation for several years. However, they compete for promotions. One way to compete is to put in long hours to impress their bosses. This suggests that at least part of the hours these workers are logging are being spent in unproductive rent seeking behavior.[3]

Currently, long working hours could reflect an upturn in the economy, with employers choosing to meet increased demand by increasing work hours rather than hiring new workers. This is a sensible approach on the part of employers, given the uncertainty the economy faces as to how robust the recovery will be. Still, it is desirable for employers to become proactive in reducing both excessive and unproductive working hours.

4 The Shrinking and Aging Population

Japan's population is expected to drop from 127 million in 2000 to 109 million in 2040, a decline of almost 14% (*Katsuyo Rodo Tokei* 2004, Table K-2). Moreover, it is projected to become the world's oldest by 2025. By 2040 the prime working-age population (ages 15–64 years) will drop by over 29%, from 86 million to 61 million, and the older population (65 years or older) will rise by almost 64%, from 22 million to 36 million, compared to 2000. As a result, the ratio of elderly to persons of prime working age will rise from 0.25 to 0.59. The prospect of such an age composition raises serious and urgent issues for Japan's long-term prospects, economic and otherwise.

4.1 Immigration Policy

Given the seriousness of the population issue, it is worth exploring the extent to which Japan would be willing to sacrifice ethnic homogeneity in the prime-age population by allowing increased immigration of foreign workers. We are not talking here about contract workers on temporary visa but about permanent workers, many of whom would bring families and even become Japanese citizens. The scale of immigration necessary to meet the projected future labor shortage has been estimated as 17 million new immigrants by 2050, which would be 18% of the 2050 population, compared to the current 1% represented by immigrants. Other estimates indicate that Japan needs to admit 400,000 new immigrants each year to ensure a steady flow of needed workforce (French 2003 Jul 24).

If Japan chooses to remain ethnically homogeneous, it most certainly will become a smaller country with an increasingly older population, unless the current low fertility rate makes a dramatic turn upward. An increase in fertility sufficient to offset the effects of the rapidly aging population seems unlikely, however. This means people will have to retire later in life, and fund more of their own pensions in the face of the shrinking number of prime-age workers. Longer working lives means older workers must be retrained to stay productively employed. (Broda and Weinstein, in their chapter, expect fertility to rise to replacement level at some point and thus stabilize the population, but that does not affect the point here.) An optimistic scenario is that, as long as labor productivity keeps rising through technological progress and capital investment, the Japanese will, for the most part, continue to enjoy affluent lives. The key is for technological progress and capital investment to keep growing enabling the country to enjoy ever heightening levels of per capita productivity.

On the other hand, Japan could take a bold step and begin accepting a small but steady increase in the number of carefully selected prime-age immigrants, who would then be integrated into mainstream Japanese society. In this scenario, Japan gradually becomes a melting pot—or at least a salad bowl—much like the United States, with increased ethnic diversity and a more-balanced age composition. Prime-age foreign workers will help alleviate the difficulties of financing pensions in the face of the growing number of retirees.

The choice between these alternatives is not simply a matter of economics. In fact, economic considerations may be secondary to larger social and cultural considerations. Concerns about losing the uniquely Japanese culture and social customs are legitimate and must be carefully weighed against the benefits of immigration. Implications of increased ethnic diversity on the cost of enforcing laws and social norms must be clearly understood. We believe it is worth undertaking a serious reassessment of the fundamental value system of the society and developing a consensus on what kind of country Japan should look like in forty to fifty years. Avoiding these choices means simply muddling along hoping increased labor productivity will alleviate economic problems and only allowing a small number of foreign immigrants (most of whom will not be granted Japanese citizenship) to enter the country on a temporary basis. It is interesting that in 2004 Germany passed a path-breaking law introducing a system of allowing qualified skilled foreign workers to settle there permanently, beginning in January 2005. It was drafted with an eye toward the country's aging population, as well as skill shortages, and was based on German's realization that it needs resident foreigners to prosper. (There already are over 7 million non-citizens in Germany, about 8.5% of the resident population; this includes about 1.6 million born in Germany.) Under this law, a potential immigrant must possess skills in certain fields such as engineering, information technology, or sciences. The law also establishes services to help immigrants assimilate into German society.

Japan has been addressing immigration issues, including temporary foreign labor, for some time. Its immigration policy was reformed in 1982 by specifying procedures for accepting refugees and defining six categories of specialists who could work in Japan. However, the definitions were vague, and decisions appear to have been arbitrary. In 1990 Japan took steps to facilitate the immigration of foreign professionals. Now there are 12 specialized categories. A potential employer can obtain a certificate of eligibility for a foreign worker. With that, the Japanese Consulate issues a visa to the worker, who can then come to Japan. The visa can be valid for three years, one year, or six months, and is renewable an unlimited number of times. This means the worker's status is always temporary, and indefinitely so. This policy does not fully address the need for a permanent increase in the Japanese workforce with full rights as Japanese citizens.

The effect of this change on immigration policy has been explored by Fuess (2003). His data show only a modest acceleration in the annual growth rate of entry of highly skilled foreign workers—from 9.5% during 1982–89 to almost 10% between 1990 and 2000—in part because the Japanese economy was in a deep recession throughout much of the 1990s. Still, the overall number of foreign workers grew noticeably between 1990 and 2002. In 1990, there were 260,000 legal foreign workers in Japan, which was 0.5% of all employed persons. By 2002, the number had grown almost three-fold to 760,000, which was 1.4% of all employed persons.

It is worth mentioning that, Japan has been considering a specific program for allowing rotational immigration from the Philippines in such occupations as nurses and care workers for the elderly. Under this program, a Filipino would be allowed to work in Japan for five years and then return home, the position being filled for the subsequent five years by another Filipino. Clearly, this is best characterized as a foreign guest-worker program rather than an immigration program, but it is a good way to deal with the shortage of labor in a particular occupation, at least in the near term.

The aforementioned developments are promising steps toward alleviating near-term and intermediate-term labor shortages in certain occupational categories. To address the long-term issue of the declining prime-age working population, however, Japan needs to confront the more fundamental issue of the trade-off between staying ethnically homogeneous and becoming a smaller population or allowing increased immigration of prime-age foreign labor to counteract the aging of its population.

4.2 Mandatory Retirement

The aging of Japan's population calls for a re-examination of its retirement system, which currently allows age-based mandatory retirement. Lazear's theory of mandatory retirement (1979) implies that, for Japan, the system made sense when long-term (or "lifetime employment") employment was the norm. However, if there is a diminution of long-term employment in Japan, the practice loses Lazear's theoretical justification, not to mention the age discrimination issue. As a result, retirement is likely to become increasingly voluntary rather than mandatory. To induce voluntary retirement, earnings profiles will be configured to induce retirement in an optimal way. The age at which a person becomes eligible to receive social security will play a role, too.

Another outcome is for mandatory retirement to be retained but with productive older workers receiving post-retirement contracts so they can continue contributing to the economy. Because the health of the elderly likely will continue improving, many elderly will wish to work simply to have something to do as well as to supplement retirement income. On a practical side, given that population aging will make funding the social security system more and more challenging, the eligible age for social security and the threshold retirement age need to be become more and more flexible, and definitely later in years.

5 Women in the Work Force

Women arguably have been the most under-utilized human resource in Japan. The 2003 World Economic Forum ranked Japan 69th of 75 member nations in empowering its women (French 2003 Jul 25). In a 2002 survey conducted by *Naikaku-fu*, a government agency, 60% of respondents said they think women are discriminated against in wages, 31% think women's talents are not accurately evaluated and appreciated, and almost 31% think that discrimination exists in promotion. Clearly, having this significant source of talent fully deployed will help sustain a thriving economy.

Certainly, Japan did make some progress after 1980 in reducing the gender differential in wages. According to Blau and Kahn (2000), Japan, along with many other countries, succeeded in reducing pay inequity between the early 1980s and the late 1990s. Using median weekly earnings of full-time workers as the measure, female wages increased from 58.7% of male wages in 1979–81 to 59.0% in 1980–90 and 63.6% in 1994–98. But this growth is not particularly impressive. In fact, in 1994–98 the Japanese male/female wage ratio was still the lowest among the thirteen countries studied. The next lowest was Canada at 69.8%; France had the highest level, 89.9%. The level in the United States rose from 62.5% to 76.3% during 1980–1998. Much of this difference reflects real differences in the job categories and industries in which men and women work, as well as seniority. But it is a fact that, as a practical matter, many of the better-paying Japanese jobs simply are not available to women.

Whether women have suffered disproportionately during the economic malaise that began in the early 1990s is unclear. The aggregate wage data mask the tendency for women to be in the low-wage, part-time, temporary, and other non-regular parts of the work force. What is worrisome is that the wage gap between women working full-time and those working part-time has been increasing. As of 2000, full-time working women earned less than 44% of full-time male workers; in contrast, male part-timer workers s earned almost 51% of male full-timer workers.

Japanese women are increasingly moving into higher positions. According to data compiled by the Labor and Welfare Ministry (based on the *Basic Wage Survey*), the proportion of private-sector managerial positions held by women has risen from 5% in 1990 to over 8% in 2001. However, there is much room left for improvement, as evidenced by the fact that while 40% of Japanese women work, they hold only 9% of managerial positions, as compared with about 45% for the United States (International Labor Organization data quoted by French 2003 Jul 25).

5.1 *Policies to Promote the Role of Women*

What policies are needed to encourage women to be in the work force and to make greater use of their skills? We offer three suggestions. The first two are general policies: continued strengthening of equal-employment laws and pursuing a proactive approach to ensure that women can continue to stay in the labor force as much as possible. The third is a specific proposal for reforming laws, public policies, and employer practices.

The Japanese Constitution guarantees gender equality as a matter of law. Under the existing Labor Standard Law, employers are required to pay the same wage to workers with the same job responsibilities, regardless of sex. An Equal Employment Opportunity Law (EEO) was implemented in 1986 and later strengthened by amendments that became effective in 1999.

The EEO is intended to promote equal opportunities for women and men, fair treatment in employment settings, and measures for ensuring the health of female employees during pregnancy and after childbirth. Before 1999, employers were not obligated to change practices that impeded women's progress in the work place, a glaring example being the prohibition of long working hours for women, which had the effect of preventing most women from being promoted to higher managerial positions because those in managerial positions often work long hours. The 1999 amendments prohibit any discrimination against women in recruitment, employment, job assignment, and promotion. It also created a system of publicizing the names of corporations that do not comply with the law, as well as improved the mediation system. In addition, the amended EEO gives employees the right to sue employers when mediation fails. Japan has been making notable progress in strengthening the enforcement of equal employment laws since 1986, but needs to continue to make sure that the spirit of the EEO is met whole-heartedly.

There are good signs for this. The presidents of several leading companies, including IBM Japan and Ricoh, appear eager to promote female employees to higher managerial positions. They have joined the Committee for Promotion of Female Employees organized by the Ministry of Welfare and Labor. The Committee identified that the key to promoting women is the attitudes of a company's top executives. The Committee found that there is a significantly positive relation between the number of female managers and profits. It plans to publicize the names of companies with exemplary effort and achievements in this matter.

The second general policy is to assist women in building their labor market attachments by reducing employment interruptions as they go through child- bearing and rearing. High-skilled and professional jobs require continued investment in human capital; indeed the skills depreciate from non-use. For upper-level managerial jobs, especially in Japan where promotions continue to be largely internal, enduring employment relationships matter. In such cases, work interruptions are detrimental to career advancement, especially in Japan, where women reentering the workforce after interruptions tend to go to new employers rather than to previous ones. The relative improvement in US women's wages during the 1980s and 1990s was mainly due to an increase in the labor-market attachment of women, accounting for up to 50% of the increase in the female-male wage ratio between the 1970s and 1990s (Blau and Kahn 1997).

Interruptions in work experience may be one of the most serious issues affecting young Japanese women. Traditionally, Japanese women worked for several years after completing formal schooling, got married, and withdrew from the labor force. After their children had grown, some mothers re-entered the labor force, but mostly as part-time workers. Modern young women need to be able to become mothers and keep their jobs without penalty. This is important because they are at the critical stage of acquiring employment-related human capital. According to a survey (conducted by the Ministry of Health, Labor, and Welfare) of mothers of all children born between the 10th and 17th in both January and July 2001, two-thirds of all working women gave up their jobs on the birth of their first child. Some 26% of mothers were not working one year before childbirth but 74% were; six months after giving birth, this 74% was not employed outside the home. Of women who had jobs a year before childbirth, 67% were no longer working. Among women working full time one year before childbirth, only 37% had returned to their jobs within six months. Interestingly, when the child was not the first-born, the proportion of mothers returning to work within six months was much higher, over 74%. This suggests a greater need for extra income when there are two or more children. (Data from Japan Labor Bulletin 2003 Jan.)

No single policy measure solves this issue. Instead, multiple policy measures are needed. Obviously, one is to increase the availability of affordable and conveniently located child-care facilities, as well as reducing work-hours that extend into the evenings. Another measure is to develop off-site jobs using information technologies that allow women to work from home while caring for their young children. And, of course, fathers could become more active in child-rearing responsibilities, as they are encouraged to do in Scandinavian countries in particular.

There are some specific measures that can be implemented quickly which will help facilitate married women's labor market activities. Japan has made considerable progress in reducing disincentives for wives in its tax laws, but significant disincentives remain in pension laws, employer practices, and unemployment insurance program.

Japan's steadfast progress in addressing disincentives for married women in its tax laws is noteworthy. Until the 1986 reform, the tax law suffered from the "household-income reversal" phenomenon. Here is why. As long as the wife earned less than the threshold amount of ¥1,030,000 per year (little less than $10,000), the husband could take a spousal income deduction of ¥380,000. However, as the wife's earnings rose above the threshold, the spousal deduction disappeared altogether. As a result, once the wife passed the threshold earnings, the household's take-home pay dropped even though the pre-tax household earnings rose. In effect, the marginal tax rate on the wife's earnings jumped once she passed the threshold earnings, at the margin discouraging wives from participating in the labor force.

The 1987 reform eliminated the household-income reversal phenomenon. In particular, as long as the husband earned less than ¥10,000,000 (about $97,000), he could take a spousal "special" deduction if the wife earned less than ¥1,350,000 (about $13,000), with the amount of deduction declining with wife's earnings. However, the husband whose wife did not work could now take the spousal income deduction of ¥760,000, double the amount he could take before the reform, thereby increasing the disincentive for the wife to enter the labor force. The tax law was further revised in 2004, and the spousal special deduction was eliminated for the husband whose wife earns less ¥1,030,000. The spousal special deduction still exists if the wife earns above this threshold. This reform effectively lowers the marginal tax rate on the wife's earnings above her threshold earnings of ¥1,030,000, thereby increasing at the margin the wife's incentive to work.[4]

The disincentive persists, however, because of employer practices. To understand this, bear in mind that, unlike in the United States, a typical Japanese household headed by a working husband does not file and pay income taxes. Instead, the husband's employer takes care of his income taxes. As a result, the husband must report his wife's earnings to his employer. Now, many Japanese employers (almost 70 percent) pay a spousal allowance as part of compensation. In many cases, however, such allowances disappear if the wife's earning exceeds ¥1,030,000. This is a disincentive for the wife to work outside the home.

Japanese public-pension law also contains built-in disincentives for wives. A wife whose husband is covered by the Employees' Pension, which is a mandatory earnings-based pension system, receives her basic pension benefits, even if she does not pay into the system as long as she works less than 75 percent of hours/days worked by a full-time worker with an annual earning of less than ¥1,300,000 (about $12,000). If she exceeds these threshold values, she must contribute to the system. This provision is a source of disincentive for the wife at the margin. Finally, a worker is exempt from paying into the unemployment insurance system if he/she works less than 20 hours per week. Clearly, this provision lowers the real wage beyond 20 hours per week, and women, many of whom work part time, are more likely than men to be affected by it.

6 Conclusion

This chapter has identified some of the more serious labor market problems facing Japan, some the direct consequences of the macroeconomic malaise during the past dozen years and others of a more long-term structural nature. For some problems, we have offered concrete proposals, and for others we have identified issues that must be addressed to facilitate formulation of sensible solutions. These are recapitulated here.

Poor macroeconomic conditions are primarily responsible for many of the problems taken up in this chapter. Indeed, the macroeconomic downturn has exacerbated such problems as reduced worker training and job satisfaction, increased youth idleness and under-employment, a rise of temporary and part-time employment, and gender and geographical gaps in employment and unemployment. Once an economic recovery takes hold and generates strong, sustained growth in aggregate demand, employers will regain confidence and begin investing in long-term employees. When that happens, many current unemployed and under-employed workers, as well as those who have been displaced by the process of structural reforms, will be absorbed into productive, full-time employment. The practice of "trial employment", in which some workers ("freeters" included), initially hired as non-regular workers are promoted to the regular-workers status after proving themselves, is expected to expand as the economy rebounds. Until then, any adjustment policies are unlikely to completely solve these basic employment-level problems.

One policy we recommend is to subsidize the training of unemployed and displaced workers for emerging skills and jobs using vocational and specialized schools. This issue is especially important because, as the Japanese industrial system becomes less based on seniority, Japan will become less reliant on informal on-the-job training in which older workers trained younger, less experienced ones.

Japan would be well advised to redirect expenditures from public-works projects to investment in such proactive employment-promotion and employment-adjustment projects as job training, retraining, and mobility support. Such redirection will help the economy keep up with a changing industrial structure and the geographical distribution of jobs.

In addition, the arrangement in which most job training subsidies are given to firms offering in-house job training must be re-examined. A sound public policy alternative may be to offer scholarship-type programs for job training and allow tax deductions for expenditures incurred on training and retraining. Such a policy will help foster self-reliance on the part of the worker and promote competition among employers for trainable workers, thereby promoting efficiency of resource use.

We contend that there have been too few job separations in Japan relative to what is optimal. We propose that measures be taken to promote efficient job separations in Japan by reducing cultural, legal, and policy biases against workers changing jobs and employers dismissing workers. Employment protection practices, formal and informal, slow employment recovery. Until employers gain confidence that favorable conditions in the economy will last, they will be reluctant to hire new workers, or recall laid-off workers, because they know that it is difficult to discharge employees in downturns. Information asymmetries between employers and employees must be reduced to minimize inefficient separations. Improved communication and transparency between management and labor will help in the goal of promoting an efficient matching of jobs with workers. To this end, we recommend that enterprise-based unions and joint consultations be preserved.

Japan faces a number of difficult long-term labor market issues. The most challenging has to do with the aging of the population and the subsequent shrinking in the prime-age work force. To deal with this, it is worth considering two alternatives. One is to preserve cultural homogeneity by continuing to bar extensive "permanent" immigration. The other is to abandon cultural homogeneity and allow immigration of carefully selected prime-age workers. The aging of the population means that the mandatory retirement system must be re-examined and the age of eligibility for social security raised and made more flexible.

Discrimination against women persists in the labor market. Japan has made considerable progress since the mid-1980s in developing a legal framework for promoting equality between men and women in the work place. Significant progress has been made in its tax laws to reduce disincentives for wives. However, the current pension systems, employer practices, and unemployment insurance discourage wives from working full-time in high paying jobs. These policies must be reformed. Effort needs to continue, and indeed accelerate, so that Japanese women will enjoy increasing equality in employment opportunity, pay, and career advancement.

For all of the issues discussed here, the ultimate policy objective should be to promote a nimble and flexible labor market that is capable of responding to the vicissitudes of the economy in an efficient and timely manner.

Acknowledgment

We are grateful to Hugh Patrick and Takatoshi Ito for many detailed and constructive comments on our earlier draft. Comments and advice offered by discussant Hiroyuki Chuma and the participants at the Solutions Conference held in Tokyo, June 19–20, 2004 are gratefully acknowledged. We express deep gratitude to Larry Meissner for his comments and suggestions. We thank Minako Mizoguchi and Xueyu Cheng for able research assistance.

Notes

1. Keep in mind that in Japan, the terms "regular workers" and "full-time workers" are not synonymous. Regular workers, typically referred to as *sei-shain*, refer to workers whose employment contracts do not have term limits, as do daily and temporary workers, and thus are presumed to have implicit long-term contracts even though some of them may not be full-time workers. A full-time worker is not a regular worker if he/she is hired as a temporary or casual worker.

2. Japanese labor-force participation rates are based on the *Annual Report on the Labor Force Survey* (Ministry of Public Management, Home Affairs, Posts and Telecommunications), as summarized in *Japanese Working Life Profile 2003* (Japan Institute of Labor), Table 13. For American rates, see *[US] Handbook of Labor Statistics*, 17th Edition (2004), Table 1-7.

As to causes, rising real income increased males' demand for leisure, thereby raising the reservation wage rate. Women have responded to rising wage rates by substituting paid work for household work and leisure. For detailed discussions on American trends, see Pencavel (1986) on male labor supply and Killingsworth and Heckman (1986) for female labor supply.

3. The Hayashi and Prescott (2002) model suggests that the mandated reduction in work hours in the early 1990s contributed to Japan's slow growth rate during the 1990s, although just how important this was cannot be ascertained from their model. In evaluating how the reduced working hours affected economic growth, it is critical to ascertain the extent of compliance, which seems far from being complete. Moreover, it is possible that the marginal product of hours had been close to zero or even negative prior to the change in the law. Workers may have simply hung around until late hours because that was the thing to do. A manager of a mid-size company told us that some workers do sloppy work during the day, knowing they can polish it up later in the evening. If the marginal labor product was negative, then the regulation actually should have increased productivity.

4. To place our argument in perspective, it should be noted that only in the last few years has the United States substantially reduced similar disincentives in its tax code (the "marriage penalty"), although the disincentives had been mitigated in earlier years for all but the very-upper-middle class and above by the widening of tax brackets and lowering of marginal rates.

References

Blanchflower, David and Richard B. Freeman. 2000. The Declining Economic Status of Young Workers in OECD Countries. In *Youth Employment and Joblessness in Advanced Countries*, editors David Blanchflower and Richard B. Freeman. Chicago: University of Chicago Press.

Blau, Francine D., and Lawrence M. Kahn. 1997. Swimming Upstream: Trends in Gender Wage Differential in the 1980's. *Journal of Labor Economics* 15 (1): (January) 1–42.

______. 2000. Gender Differences in Pay. *Journal of Economic Perspectives* 14 (4): (Fall) 75–99.

Carson, Joseph G. 2003. "Manufacturing Job's Global Decline (Part 1)." Alliance Bernstein.

Chiba, Hitoshi. 2004. Career Moves. *Look Japan* (February) 1–11.

Clark, Robert, and Naohiro Ogawa. 1992. Reconsidering Tenure and Earnings Profile of Japanese Men. *American Economic Review*, 82: (March) 336–45.

Cole, Robert E. 1971. *The Japanese Blue Collar: The Changing Tradition*. Berkeley: University of California Press.

Chuma, Hiroyuki, Takao Kato and Isao Ohashi. 2004. "What Japanese Workers Want: Evidence from the Japanese Worker Representation and Participation Survey". RIETI Discussion Paper 04-E-019.

Danke, Shun. 2003. 'Freeters' Japan's New Working Class. *Japan Close UP* 18 (12): (December) 6–12.

Freeman, Richard B. 2000. Disadvantaged Young Men and Crime. In *Youth Employment and Joblessness in Advanced Countries*, editors David Blanchflower and Richard B. Freeman. Chicago: University of Chicago Press.

French, Howard W. 2003. Insular Japan Needs, but Resists, Immigration. *New York Times*, July 24.

______. 2003. Japan's Neglected Resource, Female Workers. *New York Times*, July 25.

Fuess Jr, Scott. 2003. "Immigration Policy and Highly Skilled Workers: The Case of Japan." IZA working paper 189-2003.

Fukao, Kyoji and Norifumi Amano. 2004. *Direct Investment to Japan and Japanese Economy* (Tainichi Chokusetu Toushi to Nihon Keizai). Tokyo: Touyou Keizai Shinpousya. (In Japanese)

Government of Japan, Ministry of Coordination Agency. 2002. *Danjo Kyoudou Sankaku Syakai Hakusyo* (Survey on Equal Gender Participatory Society). (In Japanese)

Government of Japan, Ministry of Economy, Trade, and Industry. 2000. *Tsusho Hakusho* 2000 (Industry and Trade White Paper). (In Japanese)

Government of Japan, Ministry of Health, Labor and Welfare. 2003. *Basic Survey on Wage Structure.*

Hashimoto, Masanori. 1981. Firm Specific Human Capital as a Shared Investment. *American Economic Review* 71 (3): (June) 476–82.

______. 1990. *The Japanese Labor Market*. W.E. Upjohn Institute for Employment Research. Kalamazoo, MI: W.E. Upjohn.

______. 1995. A Theory of the Employment Relations System in Japan. *Journal of the Japanese and International Economies* 9: (March) 75–95.

______. 1993. Aspects of Labor Market Adjustments in Japan. *Journal of Labor Economics* 11 (1): (January) 136–61.

Hashimoto, Masanori and John Raisian. 1985. Employment and Earnings Profiles in Japan and the United States. *American Economic Review* 75: (September) 721–35.

______. 1992. Employment Tenure and Earnings Profiles in Japan and the Untied States: Reply. *American Economic Review* 82: (March) 346–54.

Hayashi, Fumio and Edward C. Prescott. 2002. Japan in the 1990s: A Lost Decade. *Review of Economic Dynamics* 5 (1): (January) 206–35.

Higuchi, Yoshio. 2004. Employment Strategies Required in an Aging Society with Fewer Children. *Japan Labor Review* 1 (1): (Winter) 17–28.

______. 2002. *Koyo to Shitusugyo no Keizaigaku* (Economics of Employment and Unemployment). Tokyo: Nihon Keizai Shimbunsha. (In Japanese)

______. 1997. Trends in Japanese Labour Markets. In *Japanese Labour and Management in Transition*, editors M. Sako and H. Sato. New York: Routledge.

Higuchi, Yoshio, Ohta Kiyoshi and Household Economy Research Institute. 2004. *Joseitachi no Heisei Fukyou* (Heisei Recession for Women). Tokyo: Nihon Keizai Shimbunsha. (In Japanese)

Higuchi, Yoshio and MOF Policy Research Center. 2003. *Nihon no Syotoku Kakusa to Syakai Kaiso* (Income Differential and Social Class in Japan). Tokyo: Nihon Hyouronsya. (In Japanese)

Higuchi, Yoshio, T. Nakajima, M. Nakahigashi and K. Hino. 2002. "The Role of Government in Economic Activity by Prefecture." The Policy Research Center of the Ministry of Finance.

Houseman, Susan and Machiko Osawa. 2003. The Growth of Nonstandard Employment in Japan and the United States. In *Nonstandard Work in Developed Economies: Causes and Consequences*, editors Susan Houseman and Machiko Osawa. Kalamazoo, MI: W.E. Upjohn.

Japan Institute of Labor. 2003. Two-thirds of Working Women Leave Job upon Birth of First Baby. *Japan Labor Bulletin* 42 (1). January.

Japan Institute of Labor. 2003. People Find Themselves Unemployed for Increasingly Longer Periods: Labor Force Survey. *Japan Labor Bulletin* 42 (8). August.

Killingsworth, Mark and James J. Heckman. 1986. Female Labor Supply: A Survey. In *Handbook of Labor Economics* 1: 103–204, editors Orley Ashenfelter and Richard Layard. Amsterdam: North Holland.

Lazear, Edward. 1979. Why is there Mandatory Retirement? *Journal of Political Economy* 87 (6): (December) 1261–85.

Levitt, Steven D. 1998. Juvenile Crime and Punishment. *Journal of Political Economy* 106 (6): (December) 1156–85.

OECD. 2003. *OECD Employment Outlook: Towards More and Better Jobs*. Paris: OECD.

Pencavel, John H. 1986. Labor Supply of Men: A Survey. *Handbook of Labor Economics* 1: 103–204, editors Orley Ashenfelter and Richard Layard. Amsterdam: North Holland.

Schumpeter, Joseph A. 1942. *Capitalism, Socialism, and Democracy*. New York: HarperPerennial.

Tanaka, Kakuei. 1972. *Building a New Japan: A Plan for Remodeling the Japanese Archipelago*. Tokyo: Simul Press.

Weinstein, David and Christian Boda. 2005. Happy News from the Dismal Science: Reassessing Japanese Fiscal Policy Sustainability. In *Reviving Japan's Economy: Problems and Prescriptions*, Chapter 2. Cambridge, MA: MIT Press.

Part IV International Economic Relations

11 Free Trade Agreements: A Catalyst for Japan's Economic Revitalization

Shujiro Urata

Japan has pursued trade liberalization under the General Agreement on Tariffs and Trade (GATT) since its accession to the GATT in 1955 and continues to do so in the World Trade Organization (WTO). In the present decade it has also pursued free trade agreements (FTAs). This reflects a change in Japanese trade policy from a single-track approach based on the GATT–WTO multilateral trade liberalization to a multi-track approach including bilateral and regional liberalization. The shift is set out in the 1999 White Paper on International Trade prepared by the Ministry of Economics, Trade and Industry (METI 1999), which argues for the need to pursue a multi-track approach.

This chapter examines the roles that FTAs might play in revitalizing the Japanese economy and promoting its economic integration with fast-growing East Asia. It then identifies obstacles to the formation of FTAs and proposes ways to overcome these issues.

Japan enacted its first FTA in November 2002 with Singapore, known as the formally named Japan-Singapore Economic Partnership Agreement (JSEPA). The JSEPA is a comprehensive economic partnership agreement (EPA), which expands the traditional elements of an FTA. Box 11.1 defines the various types of agreements; the text of JSEPA is available on MOFA's web site (MOFA 2002a).

Box 11.1
The Different Types of Trade Agreements

Regional trade agreements (RTAs) include free trade agreements (FTAs) and customs unions. Under an *FTA*, members remove tariff and non-tariff barriers on trade among themselves while maintaining their own tariff and non-tariff barriers on trade with non-members. Under a *customs union* the members establish common tariff and non-tariff policies on their trade with non-members, in addition to free trade among the members. The dominant type of RTA is the FTA—only a relatively small number of RTAs are customs unions. Most, if not all, RTAs involving East Asian countries, including Japan, are FTAs. The effects of trade agreements are discussed more fully later in this chapter. [Also see, for example, Winters (1991); Schiff and Winters (2003).]

Economic partnership agreements (EPA) include not only removing tariff and non-tariff barriers, but also liberalizing foreign direct investment (FDI), and providing for trade and FDI facilitation, and economic and technical cooperation. Cooperation encompasses a wide range of areas: human resources development, information and communications technology, small and medium-sized enterprises, and tourism, among others. Both Japan and Singapore realize the importance of broad-ranging comprehensive agreements in order to have significant effects on economic activities in the emerging international economic environment where not only goods, but also people, funds, and information freely cross borders. All the free trade agreements that Japan has been negotiating are economic partnership agreements.

Facilitation is defined as the simplification and harmonization of international procedures. In the case of trade these include such things as customs and licensing procedures; transport formalities; and payments, insurance, and other financial requirements. It is thus part of what an economic partnership agreement does, as well as what the WTO seeks to do.

Japan's Prime Minister Junichiro Koizumi and Mexico's President Vicente Fox signed an Economic Partnership Agreement, Japan's second and Mexico's forty-third FTA, in September 2004. The Japan-Mexico FTA was enacted in April 2005 after the parliaments in both countries ratified it. Japan is currently negotiating FTAs with South Korea, Malaysia, Thailand, the Philippines, and the Association of Southeast Asian Nations (ASEAN). These are all EPAs, with more or less the same content as the JSEPA. Indeed, the Japanese government has been negotiating with these other countries using the JSEPA as a model. Japan's philosophy is that broad-ranging agreements are needed to promote economic growth in the countries involved.

Several reasons can be identified for the Japanese government's emerging interest in FTAs. One important reason is developments in global trade, where multilateral negotiations under the WTO are making little progress, and regional trade agreements such as FTAs are increasing rapidly. Faced with this situation, the Japanese government recognized that FTAs are a means for achieving trade liberalization. The government expects FTAs to play a role in promoting Japan's economic growth by providing business opportunities for Japanese firms in FTA-member countries and promoting domestic policy reforms such as agricultural reform, which are necessary for revitalizing the stagnant Japanese economy. Another reason is the expectation that FTAs can play effective roles in promoting the economic integration of East Asia, something that will contribute not only to economic growth, but also to political and social stability.

To conclude FTAs successfully, Japan and its FTA partners are required to deal with the structural adjustments necessitated by eliminating barriers. Specifically for Japan, liberalizing agricultural trade and importing medical care-givers such as nurses are major challenges. These issues have to be overcome to establish FTAs with East Asian countries. The chapter proposes providing income compensation and technical assistance to those negatively affected by FTAs as a way to overcome these challenges.

Given Japan's need to promote FTAs, this chapter emphasizes the importance of successful multilateral trade liberalization under the WTO in order to promote global economic growth. Indeed, FTAs and trade liberalization under the WTO should play complementary roles. FTAs can provide models in areas, such as FDI and labor mobility, that are not covered by current WTO rules. Moreover, because these agreements can be concluded quickly, they can serve as building blocks for later WTO-based liberalization.

The chapter's structure is as follows. The next section briefly reviews the development of FTAs in East Asia and around the world since the mid-1990s. Japan's strategy and progress in establishing FTAs is then examined, followed by a discussion of Japan's strategic interest in these agreements. Possible effects of FTAs are then taken up, with reference to the results of a simulation analysis. Obstacles for establishing FTAs are identified, and ways to overcome them are presented, before ending with some major policy conclusions.

1 General Developments in Free Trade Agreements

In the past, Japan mainly liberalized its trade regime under the GATT–WTO multilateral framework, but it has begun to regard FTAs as a trade policy option. This paradigm shift resulted in part because many countries started looking at FTAs from a new perspective. FTAs traditionally had been regarded as exclusionary, something that went against global trade liberalization. However, many governments have come to recognize that FTAs can promote world trade, and thus are complementary to the WTO. In order to set the stage for the subsequent analysis, this section reviews global developments in FTAs since the mid-1990s, with an emphasis on East Asia.

The number of regional trade agreements (RTAs) began to increase notably in the 1990s. The cumulative number reported under the GATT from 1948 to 1990 was thirty. The number increased notably to 79 by 1995, when the WTO was founded. The pace of increase quickened after the WTO was established, with the number reaching 155 in 2000 and 220 as of January 4, 2005. RTAs violate most-favored-nation treatment among GATT–WTO members. Because such treatment is one of the principles of the GATT–WTO system, the quick spread of RTAs after establishment of the WTO is ironic, and reflects the difficult problems that have faced the WTO since it replaced GATT.

Toward the end of the 1990s when East Asian countries became interested in FTAs, Japan, China, Korea, and Taiwan were the four major economies that did not have any FTAs. They came to realize both the need to deal with the disadvantageous situations caused by their nonmember status in any FTAs, and the possibilities of benefits from establishing their own FTAs.

1.1 Reasons for the Spread of FTAs

The rapid expansion of FTAs since the mid-1990s reflects the fact that a large number of countries have become dissatisfied with the WTO. This is mainly for two reasons: the slow progress in multilateral trade liberalization, and the limited coverage of WTO rules.

Many countries realize the benefits of trade liberalization, as it has brought them economic growth [see, for example, World Bank (1993)]. Indeed, one of the important factors that led to rapid economic growth for many countries in the post-World War II period was substantial trade liberalization carried out under the auspices of the GATT. However, multilateral trade liberalization has become increasingly difficult because of disagreement about WTO processes among WTO members.

The Uruguay Round, which was the last multilateral trade negotiation under the GATT, started in 1986 and was scheduled to reach agreement within four years. However, it took twice as long to complete. After the WTO was established in 1995, advanced countries proposed launching a new round, but opposition from developing countries not satisfied with the outcome of the Uruguay Round, prevented a new round. It was only at the end of 2001 that an agreement was reached to start a new round (the Doha Development Agenda).

The progress of recent negotiations has been very slow for several reasons. First, as a result of substantial trade liberalization under the GATT, only difficult issues remain to be resolved, slowing further liberalization. Second, decision-making at the WTO is based on consensus, which has become more difficult to achieve as its membership has increased. When the act creating the WTO was signed in April 1994, there were 123 members, 132 by November 1998, and 148 as of May 2005. The original GATT had 23 signatories in October 1947, and 101 by January 1991. One contentious issue concerning Japan that is preventing negotiations from progressing is liberalization in agricultural trade. Japan and nine other countries—including Korea, Switzerland, and Norway—formed a group to resist liberalization in agricultural trade. They face pro-liberalization countries that include the United States and the Cairns Group of 17 countries (including Australia, Brazil, Thailand, Indonesia, and the Philippines).

One can also argue that the increasing opposition to globalization by many groups, including some environmentalists, has made it difficult to pursue trade liberalization under the WTO. Globalization has allegedly affected some groups negatively in certain ways, including reduced employment opportunities and deterioration in environmental quality. Indeed, a 1999 WTO meeting in Seattle with the goal of forming a consensus to start a new round was unsuccessful partly because of aggressive anti-WTO demonstrations by environmentalist groups, labor unions, and some NGOs.

The coverage of international economic activities expanded under the WTO. While GATT had been limited to goods trade negotiations, this expansion includes trade in services, as well as investment and intellectual property rights, which have become important in international economic activities. Although the broader coverage is a major achievement, there are still areas not covered under the WTO, including the environment, labor standards, labor mobility, and e-commerce.

Many WTO members not satisfied with the slow progress in multilateral trade negotiations or limited coverage of WTO rules have opted for bilateral and plurilateral FTAs with like-minded countries. Indeed, many FTA negotiations have been concluded quickly because of the small number of participants. For example, the Japan-Singapore negotiations took approximately 10 months. Japan's FTA negotiations have included many areas outside the scope of the WTO, including FDI liberalization and facilitation, as well as economic and technical cooperation. Many other countries' FTAs, but not Japan's, have covered issues such as labor and environment.

2 FTAs in East Asia

East Asia was not active in forming FTAs until a few years ago. Indeed, the ASEAN Free Trade Area (AFTA) was the only major FTA until the Japan–Singapore FTA of November 2002. [Urata (2004) discusses developments on FTAs in East Asia. Lincoln (2004) presents detailed discussions on economic regionalism in East Asia. He views the progress in regional institution building so far as slow and shallow despite a lot of talk.] Table 11.1 lists FTAs involving major East Asian economies.

Table 11.1
Major FTAs Involving East Asian Economies

In Action	In Negotiation	Under Study
Bangkog Treaty (1976)	Japan-South Korea	Korea-Australia
AFTA(1992)	Japan-Malaysia	Korea-New Zealand
Singapore-New Zealand (2001)	Japan-Thailand	Singapore-Chile
Japan-Singapore (2002)	Japan-Philippines	Singapore-Taiwan
Singapore-Australia (2003)	Japan-ASEAN	ASEAN-India
Singapore-EFTA (2003)	South Korea-Singapore	ASEAN-US
Singapore-US (2004)	South Korea-ASEAN	ASEAN-EU
South Korea-Chile (2004)	Singapore-Canada	ASEAN-CER
China-Hong Kong (2004)	Singapore-Mexico	
China-Macao (2004)	Singapore-India	
China-ASEAN (2004)	Thailand-India*	
Taiwan-Panama(2004)	Thailand-US	
Japan-Mexico(2005)	Thailand-Australia	
	Hong Kong-New Zealand	

Source: Country sources

2.1 *The ASEAN Free Trade Area*

The then six member countries of ASEAN (The Association of Southeast Asian Nations)—Brunei, Indonesia, Malaysia, the Philippines, Signapore and Thailand—established the ASEAN Free Trade Area (AFTA) in 1992. Cambodia, Laos, Myanmar, and Vietnam joined AFTA (and ASEAN) later in the 1990s, so AFTA currently has ten members. AFTA was reported to the GATT as an FTA under the enabling clause rather than GATT Article 24 because AFTA members are developing countries. FTAs under the enabling clause are treated preferentially in that many exceptions are permitted, whereas FTAs involving developed countries are subject to stricter conditions—under GATT Article 24 for trade in goods and Article 5 for trade in services.

AFTA had not been completed by the end of 2002, the target year of completion for the six original members. The goal of reducing tariffs to 0–5% has not been achieved except by Singapore, although there have been substantial reductions by all members. AFTA has not been very successful in promoting intra-regional trade; the share of intra-regional trade for AFTA members in world trade increased only slightly, from 1.40% in 1995 to 1.44% in 2003. During the same period the share of intra-regional exports to total AFTA exports declined slightly, from 23.0% to 22.0%, while the share of intra-regional imports to total AFTA imports increased notably, from 22.0% to 27.2%. [The figures are computed from trade data collected by Japan External Trade Organization (JETRO).]

One problem for AFTA has been the difficulty in actually receiving preferential tariffs. For example, it takes time to have the necessary documents processed because of cumbersome procedures. The presence of non-tariff barriers such as the lack of a harmonized system of technical standards, also discourages intra-regional trade.

As Table 11.1 shows, among ASEAN members, Singapore and Thailand are very active in establishing FTAs. It was Singapore that first strongly promoted FTAs, and Thailand has become an active promoter under the government of Thaksin Shinawatra, which assumed office in February 2001.

2.2 *FTAs in North East Asia*

Compared to South East Asia, the countries in North East Asia—including China, Japan, and South Korea—were not active in FTAs until the new millennium. Despite increasingly strong interest in FTAs by North East Asian countries, so far only six have been enacted, three for China (with Hong Kong, Macao and ASEAN in 2004), two for Japan (with Singapore in 2002 and Mexico in 2004), and one for South Korea (with Chile in 2004).

South Korea expressed an interest in FTAs before Japan. South Korea started negotiations with Chile in 1999, concluded in October 2002. Even after signing the agreement, it took more than a year to ratify it in the Korean National Assembly because of strong opposition from farmers, who are concerned with the negative consequences to their livelihoods.

China's active FTA strategy has received a lot of attention. China joined the WTO in 2001 and established access to the global market, and it has also started to pursue regional strategies using FTAs. China signed a framework agreement on comprehensive economic cooperation with ASEAN in November 2002. The agreement, which was vigorously promoted by China, involves not only trade liberalization but also cooperation in the areas of FDI and economic development. China and ASEAN started negotiations on trade in goods in January 2003, concluded an agreement with the member countries in November 2004, and enacted the agreement in December 2004. China offered various schemes attractive to ASEAN, and particularly to its new members, such as economic cooperation for the new members and advanced trade liberalization ("early harvest") in agricultural products.

At a meeting in 2002, China's Premier, Zhu Rongi, informally proposed to Japanese and South Korean leaders that they establish a trilateral FTA. Japan did not accept the proposal, instead indicating that it would like to make sure that China, as a new WTO member, abides by WTO commitments and rules before discussing an FTA. At least two reasons can be postulated for Japan's rejection. One is possible negative effects on non-competitive sectors such as agriculture and labor-intensive apparel industries, and the other is Japan's general rivalry with China.

Several motives may be behind China's active FTA policy. Hai and Li (2003) point to two economic factors. One is to maintain and expand export markets and the other is reduced adjustment costs of trade liberalization resulting from entry to the WTO. China, concerned about its export market because of the increase in FTAs and the increase in protectionist measures against its exports, particularly anti-dumping charges, considered FTAs a possible solution. The additional adjustment costs from FTAs are not large, because China has already committed to substantial liberalization under WTO. Besides economic motives, it is commonly perceived that China uses FTAs as part of a policy to establish itself as a leader in East Asia.

2.3 *Reasons for East Asian FTAs*

One can think of various factors that have led to an emerging interest in FTAs among East Asian countries in addition to the factors discussed earlier that explain the rapid general expansion of FTAs in the world. The 1997 financial crisis in East Asia increased awareness of the need for regional cooperation to avoid another crisis and to promote regional economic growth.

Indeed, because of the immediate concern about possible problems, regional financial cooperation has made greater progress than FTAs. Specifically, there is the 2000 Chiang Mai Initiative which set up bilateral currency swap arrangements to deal with any shortages in foreign exchange. As of August 29, 2004, among ASEAN+3 members, eight countries are participating in the scheme: Indonesia, Malaysia, Philippines, Singapore, Thailand, China, Japan, and South Korea (the last three are the +3).

The ASEAN+3 countries also are working to develop an efficient and liquid regional bond market, thereby enabling better utilization of regional savings for regional investments. The market is also expected to help mitigate currency and maturity mismatches in financing.

Regional rivalry has been a contributing factor to an increased interest in FTAs. Specifically, both China and Japan, which are competing to become the "leader" in the region, are keen on using FTAs to strengthen relationships with ASEAN, South Korea, and other countries. Indeed, in November 2002, Japan proposed an economic partnership framework to ASEAN one day after China agreed to start FTA negotiations with ASEAN. On the occasion of the ASEAN+3 summit in November 2004, Japan and ASEAN agreed to start FTA negotiations and the negotiations started in April 2005. It should also be noted that ASEAN, Korea, and other countries also consider FTAs as a means to maintain and increase influence in East Asia.

2.4 *The Nature of East Asian FTAs*

One special feature more or less common to many FTAs which have been enacted, negotiated, and studied in East Asia is that they are comprehensive in content. That is, these agreements include not only traditional features of liberalization in trading goods and services, but also FDI liberalization and trade and FDI facilitation.

Further, many FTAs include economic and technical cooperation such as human resource development and development of small- and medium-sized enterprises. Economic and technical cooperation is regarded as an important feature of FTAs in East Asia because many nations in the region are developing countries that need economic and technical cooperation to promote growth. Indeed, the inclusion of economic and technical cooperation in FTAs may be attributable to a view that the WTO, which is aimed only at trade liberalization, cannot be effective in promoting free trade or economic growth because it does not deal effectively with the problems faced by developing countries.

2.5 *An All East Asian FTA*

The idea of an FTA covering all East Asian countries has emerged. Indeed, many countries in the region regard this as a medium-term goal, which would eventually lead to establishing deeper regional integration like the European Union. Behind this expectation is the realization that such integration could result in economic prosperity, as well as political and social stability.

The Leaders' Summit meeting of ASEAN+3 in 1998 agreed to set up an East Asia Vision Group (EAVG), and in 2000 established an East Asia Study Group (EASG). The mandate for the EAVG, composed of intellectuals, was to study long-term prospects for economic cooperation. In 2001 the EAVG presented the leaders with recommendations, including establishment of an East Asia FTA (EAVG 2001). The EASG, consisting of government officials, in 2002 provided assessments of the EAVG recommendations and acknowledged the role of a comprehensive East Asia FTA for the promotion of trade and FDI in East Asia (EASG 2002).

Despite these recommendations an East Asia FTA has not become a concrete agenda item at government leaders' meetings. Obviously, agreeing on an East Asian FTA at this time is politically very difficult —mainly because of strong opposition from non-competitive sectors in each member country. However, the activities of the EAVG and the EASG were followed by the establishment of the "Network of East Asian Think-Tanks (NEAT)" in 2003. NEAT, which is supported by the governments of the ASEAN+3 countries, is to continue the dialogue and deepen mutual understanding. Meetings were held in 2003 and 2004 to discuss issues related to the East Asian Community, of which an East Asia FTA is an important component.

FTAs can play a role in achieving stability in the region's political and social environment, so I think it is important to establish an FTA that includes all East Asian countries. While this is unlikely to happen soon, much may be gained simply by the region's leaders discussing ways to establish it.

3 Japan's East Asian Trade Strategy

Japan is primarily interested in establishing EPAs in East Asia, rather than FTAs, because this broader form of agreement is more likely to promote regional growth, as well as for domestic economic and political reasons. The regional emphasis is spelled out in a November 2002 Ministry of Foreign Affairs report on FTA strategy (MOFA 2002b). Japan has been expanding its economic and political relations within East Asia on a bilateral or small-group basis in part because region-wide institutional frameworks have not been established. Japan's first FTA discussions resulted from approaches made by other countries, rather than an active seeking of agreements. A more active strategy began in November 2002, when Japan proposed a possible FTA with ASEAN.

The Japanese government has set up study groups consisting of private sector representatives, government officials, and academic experts to examine possible FTAs before entering negotiations. The idea of study groups has been quite useful in formulating the contents of FTAs because, in many cases, the pro-liberalization voices of business and academic members, rather than the protectionist views of government officials, have been adopted.

Officials of the Ministry of Agriculture, Fishery and Forestry and representatives from agriculture associations oppose any liberalized agricultural imports by appealing to the need for food security and the multi-functionality of agriculture. In other words, they argue that maintenance of agriculture contributes to conservation of the environment and the preservation of rural life. By contrast, business representatives, academics, and in some cases officials from METI and MOFA advocate liberalization. The differing interest, and positions between those supporting the continuation of protectionist policies and those supporting much fewer protectionist policies have become considerably more explicit and open.

3.1 Singapore-Japan Economic Partnership Agreement (JSEPA)

Singapore's Prime Minister Goh Chok Tong proposed an FTA to Prime Minister Keizo Obuchi of Japan in December 1999. The two leaders decided to set up a study group consisting of government officials, business people, and academics to investigate the provisions of a possible FTA and its impact on their economies. After a series of discussions, in October 2000 the study group recommended starting negotiations, begun in January 2001 and favorably concluded in October 2001. Negotiations appear to have moved rather smoothly because contentious issues such as liberalization in agricultural trade were limited for both countries. The agreement, signed by Prime Ministers Goh and Junichiro Koizumi in January 2002, came into effect in November 2002.

The Japan–Singapore Economic Partnership Agreement (JSEPA) has both strengths and weaknesses. One strength is the comprehensiveness of an economic partnership agreement as opposed to a free trade agreement. Another is its symbolic nature: JSEPA sent a message to the world of Japan's strong interest in FTAs. One weakness is the limited trade liberalization on the Japanese side. Singapore removed tariffs on 100% of Japanese imports, but Japan removed tariffs on only 94% of imports from Singapore. The imports not liberalized included agricultural products and a few selected manufactured products, notably some petrochemical products and leather goods. Singapore, adjacent to the Indonesian oil fields, has long had a major petrochemical industry.

While JSEPA will not significantly increase bilateral trade flows, its symbolic and a signal of Japan's changed trade policy has been important. Moreover, the broad range of issues JSEPA addresses, such as FDI, two-way flows of selected categories of skilled workers, competition policy, and legal and institutional arrangements, meant that a substantially wider range of Japanese ministries have become involved in addressing now-relevant international economic issues.

3.2 The Free Trade Agreement between Mexico and Japan

Mexico was the first country to approach Japan for a possible FTA. Following the November 1998 proposal by Mexico's president, Ernesto Zedillo, a committee named Closer Japan-Mexico Economic Relations was set up by the Japan External Trade Organization (JETRO) and its Mexican counterpart, SECOFI. In April 2000, JETRO and SECOFI released a joint report that concluded an FTA would have significant favorable effects on both nations. The two countries formed a study group of business people, government officials, and academics, to examine a possible approach for strengthening mutual economic ties, including an FTA. After examining the contents of a possible FTA, in July 2002 the group recommended starting FTA negotiations, which began in October 2002. Despite the goal of reaching an agreement in one year, the process took much longer, and an agreement finally came in September 2004.

The most serious obstacle to a swifter conclusion was Japan's strong resistance to liberalizing agricultural products—specifically pork, beef, and chicken products, as well as oranges and orange juice. The Japan–Mexico FTA was strongly supported by Japanese businesses, which felt their exports were suffering from lost opportunities in the absence of an FTA. Japan's leading business organization estimated the lost business at ¥400 billion in 1999, an amount close to Japan's actual exports to Mexico that year (Keidanren 2003). Mexico, under pressure from its farmers, was interested in exporting agricultural products to Japan. Mexican farmers were unhappy with the negative consequences of the North American Free Trade Agreement (NAFTA).

After strong requests from the Mexican government, Japan opened these markets by increasing import quotas, but did not remove tariffs. Mexico agreed to liberalize its steel market within ten years, and automobiles within seven years, responding to Japan's demands. As a result, Mexico agreed to open its market to all imports from Japan, while Japan agreed to open its market to only 86% of its imports from Mexico (Nihon Keizai Shimbun on March 13, 2004).

Japan gained substantially from this agreement with Mexico, and did not give in much on agricultural liberalization. Although the agreement may have been an overall victory for the trade negotiators, it certainly was a defeat for those keenly interested in agrarian structural reform in Japan.

3.3 A South Korea–Japan FTA

In October 1998 President Kim Dae-jung of South Korea took the lead in suggesting a closer economic partnership (although not necessarily an actual FTA) with Japan. At a Japan-South Korea Ministerial Meeting held the following month, the issue of a possible Japan-South Korea FTA was taken up. Following the meeting, private institutions jointly carried on preliminary research and released their report in May 2000. At their September 2000 summit meeting, the Japanese prime minister and the South Korean president agreed to the "Japan-Korea FTA Business Forum," established in March 2001, with business leaders from both countries serving as core members. In January 2002, the forum called for forming a Japan-South Korea FTA as soon as possible and recommended that Japan and South Korea establish a joint study group consisting of government officials, business leaders, and academics. That study group recommended that the two countries begin negotiations.

FTA negotiations started in December 2003 with the aim of concluding an agreement in two years. Japan had proposed one year, but South Korea insisted on two years. The process may take considerably longer since a wide range of issues have surfaced. Although South Korea expects an increase in FDI from Japan from the FTA, it is concerned with possible negative effects on its manufacturing industries, except for some electronics products such as semiconductors, because of their lack of competitiveness vis-à-vis Japanese counterparts. In particular, smaller South Korean companies strongly oppose a Japan–South Korea FTA, as they fear increased imports from Japan. These possible negative effects have made the South Korean government concerned with its worsening bilateral trade balance and increasing dependence on Japan.

Both Japan and South Korea generally oppose liberalization of agricultural trade, as has been demonstrated in WTO negotiations as well as in their respective FTA negotiations so far. Thus, liberalization of agricultural products has not been a serious issue, as both sides probably feel any agreement will exclude agricultural products from liberalization. One exception may be imports of fish-based products, trade in which South Korea has pressured Japan to open its markets.

In the pursuit of establishing an FTA with South Korea, Japan must contend with its history. Korea was a colony of Japan's from 1910 to 1945, and considerable resentment over events during that time remains. Despite this legacy, Japan and South Korea have been successful in starting toward eventual establishment of an FTA, for two main reasons.

The first is mutual reconciliation between the political leaders over past issues. In October 1998 Kim Dae-jung, South Korea's president from 1998 to 2003, accepted an apology from Prime Minister Keizo Obuchi for Japanese atrocities during its colonial rule. The other reason is increased mutual understanding of the need for closer economic and social ties among the people of the two countries. This new attitude appears to be a change from a backward-looking to a forward-looking stance regarding the two countries' relationship, in part resulting from both countries' successful economic growth. This outcome shows the importance of political leadership and successful economic growth in establishing FTAs.

3.4 Japan's Other Free Trade and Economic Partnership Negotiations

Japan proposed an EPA with the ASEAN, including an FTA, in November 2002. This was just one day after China and ASEAN signed an agreement on a closer economic partnership. Compared with the sensational impact of the China-ASEAN Closer Economic Agreement, the Japan-ASEAN EPA proposal did not attract much attention, as it did not involve any concrete actions. In October 2003 Japan and ASEAN agreed on the framework for a comprehensive economic partnership and agreed to start consultations in 2004 (MOFA 2003).

While continuing to hold discussions with ASEAN, Japan has decided to simultaneously work to establish bilateral FTAs with individual ASEAN members, as this can be accomplished more quickly. In particular, individual agreements make it easier to deal with the wide differences in economic and non-economic conditions among ASEAN members. So far, Thailand, the Philippines, and Malaysia have started negotiations with Japan. Some argue that bilateral FTAs will create divisiveness among ASEAN members. Because this is certainly a possibility, Japan was interested in starting negotiations with ASEAN as soon as possible. Japan and ASEAN started negotiations in April 2005.

The contentious issues that Japan has faced in negotiations with Thailand are trade liberalization in rice and liberalization in the migration of guest workers (specifically: cooks, nurses, massage therapists, and care-givers for the elderly). With the Philippines, the issues are trade liberalization in bananas, and liberalization in the acceptance of workers (specifically: nurses and care-givers for the elderly). With Malaysia, the issue is liberalizing trade in plywood. These are discussed more fully later.

Australia, Canada, Chile, New Zealand, and Taiwan, among others, have approached Japan for possible FTAs. However, there has been no significant activity at an official level regarding any of these requests. A lack of progress in discussions with these countries, other than Taiwan, is essentially attributable to two reasons. Agricultural products are important in Japan's trade with these countries, and trade liberalization is difficult in the face of Japan's entrenched protection of this sector.

The other reason is the limited geopolitical importance of countries not located in East Asia, the region of Japan's utmost interest. Lack of progress with Taiwan is due to political sensitivity regarding Japan's relationship with China.

4 Behind Japan's FTA Strategy

Several things contributed to Japan recognizing FTAs as a trade policy option, and its stress on forming FTAs within East Asia. An important motive was greater access to foreign markets. In addition, Japan is particularly interested in establishing comprehensive rules on FDI that go beyond existing WTO rules, including creating rules in such areas as national treatment of foreign firms. Another motive is the role FTAs may play in the structural reform of Japan's economy. The increased interest in FTAs notwithstanding, Japan expects to contribute to the strengthening of the world trading system under the WTO.

Japan's regional emphasis reflects East Asia's rapid growth, the feeling that good trade relations enhance regional security, and intra-regional politics. East Asia has a high potential for economic growth, but Japanese firms have not been able to benefit fully from sharing in these opportunities, largely because of high levels of protection, as shown in Table 11.2.

For their part, other East Asian countries benefit from FTAs with Japan in several ways. They not only enjoy greater access to the Japanese market, but also receive more FDI and economic assistance to promote economic growth.

4.1 Access to Markets

At a time when increasing numbers of FTAs were being established, Japan was one of the few countries that did not have any regional trade arrangements. Facing a world market with many discriminatory trading arrangements, Japan felt more recently a need to secure a larger market for Japanese firms by setting up FTAs. Because an FTA eliminates trade barriers among partners, Japanese companies would surely be able to enjoy more business opportunities. This kind of thinking led to positive perspectives on FTAs, especially when multinational trade negotiations under the WTO were making little progress.

Specifically, in the context of East Asia, Japanese firms have invested significantly in the region, but they cannot operate efficiently across

Table 11.2
Rate of Protection for East Asian Countries: 1997

Sector	China	Japan	NIEs Korea	Hong Kong	Singapore	Taiwan	ASEAN Indonesia	Malaysia	Philippines	Thailand	Vietnam
Agriculture	41.3	58.4	110.9	0.0	3.5	6.0	5.2	31.1	15.0	20.3	13.6
Forestry	2.6	0.2	2.0	0.0	0.0	0.4	1.1	0.0	0.5	1.5	3.3
Fishing	14.2	4.9	15.8	0.0	0.0	31.1	7.5	1.4	6.6	44.9	8.9
Mining	0.2	–1.4	3.9	0.0	0.0	4.9	2.8	1.1	1.0	0.3	3.2
Food products and beverages	37.4	50.0	37.7	0.0	4.6	26.1	14.8	14.8	18.7	37.2	36.5
Textiles	25.7	10.7	8.0	0.0	0.0	8.1	15.6	16.1	13.6	26.7	34.0
Pulp, paper and paper products	11.7	2.2	5.3	0.0	0.0	2.9	6.2	9.1	11.4	12.6	19.1
Chemicals	12.6	2.3	7.0	0.0	0.0	3.7	7.1	8.6	6.4	15.3	16.1
Iron, steel and metal products	9.7	1.0	4.9	0.0	0.0	4.0	8.1	6.1	8.1	11.9	8.1
Transportation machinery	18.9	0.0	4.6	0.0	0.0	13.2	25.4	19.7	10.3	31.5	36.9
Electronic equipment	11.9	0.0	8.0	0.0	0.0	2.9	8.1	0.8	3.1	8.8	9.7
General machinery	13.5	0.3	7.8	0.0	0.0	4.9	3.9	5.1	5.5	10.4	6.7
Other manufacturing	16.9	5.5	7.3	0.0	0.0	5.6	9.5	8.2	12.0	13.2	16.9

Note: The rate of protection is defined as (domestic price - international price)/international price. Therefore, it includes both tariff and non-tariff barriers.
Source: GTAP Version 5, Dimaranan and McDougall. (2002).

borders. That is, protectionism inhibits moving parts and finished goods among the region's countries, and requires more local sourcing and assembly of products sold in each country than is appropriate given the benefits gained from comparative advantage and a larger scale of operations. Protectionist measures affect not only Japanese firms but other multinationals, and even firms based in each country. Japan thinks FTAs will substantially remedy this, which will contribute to greater efficiency and growth in Japan and throughout the region.

The market access motive clearly played an important role for Japan in pursing an FTA with Mexico. Thanks to NAFTA and the EU–Mexico FTA, EU and American firms can export to Mexico without tariffs. Japanese firms have to pay high tariffs. Indeed, the simple mean tariff rate for Mexico was 16.2% in 2001 (World Bank 2003). Among Japan's industrial sectors, its automobile and steel industries are very eager to have an FTA with Mexico. The auto industry is interested in expanding exports of finished cars to Mexico, while steel producers are interested in exporting their products for use in electronics goods, household appliances, general machinery, and automobiles. Also, the Mexican government allows only FTA members to participate in government procurement, a restriction Mexico can impose because it is not a signatory to the WTO's government procurement code. Faced with these market-access problems, the Japanese business community pushed rigorously and successfully for the government to conclude an FTA with Mexico.

4.2 *Structural Reforms*

FTAs can stimulate structural reforms that are essential to revitalizing the Japanese economy. Since the collapse of the bubble economy in the early 1990s, Japan has experienced low levels of growth and even quarters with declines in GDP. Although Japan's postwar economic system contributed to high growth in the past, it has become ineffective as Japan has caught up with the rest of the industrialized world. Many observers agree that structural reform is necessary for refurbishing the now-ineffective Japanese economic system.

As for the specific sectors related to FTA negotiations, the following are in need of structural reform: agriculture and fisheries, and service sectors such as medical and education services. Medical and education services are related to FTA negotiations insofar as these industries are subject to mutual-recognition agreements on professional licenses and worker mobility. Currently, these Japanese services are heavily regulated in the form of visa restrictions. While as one component of FTAs Japan wants to attract foreign engineers in information technology areas which are in short supply, it is currently resisting requests from the Philippines and Thailand to allow "importation" of significant numbers of medical care-givers such as nurses because of strong opposition from the labor unions of domestic medical care-givers.

In the period since World War II, Japan had made use of international frameworks such as GATT and the OECD, and *gaiatsu* (foreign pressure), especially from the United States, to reform domestic structures through trade liberalization. Indeed, structural reform has contributed significantly to improving the competitiveness of Japan's manufacturing sector. Many of the areas still in need of reform are particularly well-entrenched.

A seriously contentious issue at the WTO is liberalization of trade in agricultural products, because of different views on this issue between the United States and the European Union, on the one hand, and strong opposition from a group of ten countries protecting their agricultural sectors, including Japan and Korea.

American pressure on trade-related issues weakened after establishment of the WTO, as the United States, Japan, and other member countries began to use the strengthened dispute-settlement mechanism provided by the WTO. Japan also undertook a number of policy reforms in its financial system and corporate governance system. These changes allayed American concerns over the macroeconomic performance of the Japanese economy, and thus reduced American pressure on Japan.

Faced with a lack of external pressures, especially from multilateral trade negotiations through the WTO, Japan became interested in FTAs as a policy option to promote domestic structural reform.

4.3 Japan's Continued Involvement with the WTO

Even as it stresses FTAs, Japan expects to contribute to the strengthening of the world trading system under the WTO. Some argue that FTAs have harmful effects on the world trading system because of their discriminatory nature. However, even acknowledging such harmful effects, one can argue that these can be more than offset by the favorable effects accruing from FTAs.

FTAs can have a positive effect if they address issues that are not covered by the existing WTO framework. For example, while GATT–WTO does not have specific rules on competition or investment policies, the Japan-Singapore EPA (JSEPA) does cover them. Japan has been trying to include such features in all the EPAs it has concluded or is negotiating. In the future the WTO and other international organizations may establish specific rules applicable to competition policies and investment by using JSEPA as a model. So far, however, Japan has not been successful in including rules on FDI and competition policy as agenda items under the WTO's Doha Development Agenda because of strong opposition from developing countries.

5 The Effects of FTAs

The impact FTAs will have on Japan and East Asia is examined in this section, including a simulation analysis to quantify some of the effects, which can be classified as static or dynamic. Static effects include trade creation, trade diversion, and terms of trade. Dynamic effects are market expansion and competition promotion.

"Trade creation" means that FTAs eliminate trade barriers among member countries and, therefore, promote trade among them. "Trade diversion" means FTAs replace imports of highly efficient non-member countries with imports from less-efficient FTA members. The "terms of trade" effect results from the growth in trade volume among FTA members, strengthening their influence on non-members, which then improves members' terms of trade. "Market expansion" means that the elimination of trade barriers among member nations expands market size, thereby achieving production and distribution efficiencies by realizing economies of scale. "Competition promotion" means that market integration makes oligopolistic industries more competitive and achieves higher productivity by introducing competitive pressures.

For FTA members, trade-creation, terms-of-trade, market-expansion, and competition-promotion effects are positive, although for members promoting infant industries these effects are viewed as negative. Trade diversion is negative for both members and non-members, at least under most circumstances. For non-members, the terms-of-trade effect also is negative, while the other effects tend to be positive.

If an FTA expands market size, promotes competition, and encourages economic growth in member countries, its positive effects spill-over to non-member states as well. This helps explain why the FTA option has gained popularity: governments expect FTAs to achieve positive dynamic effects. However, if a country gives preferential treatment only to certain trade partners, other countries might form exclusive economic blocs in order to counteract the resulting trade-diversion effects. In this case, the world economy suffers, as happened during the interwar era. [See Schiff and Winters (2003) for useful discussions on the do's and don'ts of regional trade agreements.]

Recognizing the negative effects of trade diversion and of excluding non-members, one can argue that each FTA should have many members and include some highly competitive countries because this helps minimize possible negative effects from trade diversion. This observation indicates the importance of successful multilateral trade negotiations under the WTO. Indeed, this is the optimal outcome. However, the WTO process has faced problems, so, despite being second- or third-best in nature, FTAs have become a viable option. Besides, FTAs have some favorable effects that cannot be achieved through the WTO process.

In addition to effects on trade, FTAs also affect foreign direct investment (FDI). As an FTA eliminates trade barriers and expands market size, FDI flows into the members' domestic economies—this is an investment-creation effect. Investment may be undertaken in member countries at the expense of investment. In addition, if an FTA enables firms to conduct efficient production in the member economies, foreign firms will undertake investment to take advantage of the favorable environment and to export their products—in non-member countries because of the increased attractiveness of members—this is an investment diversion effect.

5.1 Empirical Studies of FTAs

Many empirical studies have been conducted on the economic effects of FTAs, with the EU and NAFTA attracting most of the attention. Although these analyses draw somewhat different conclusions, they generally show that FTAs expand member trade and investment, encourage competition within the region, and induce other positive effects for members.

At the same time, some analyses show that FTAs divert trade and investment, imposing negative effects on non-member countries. According to an internal estimation by Japan's Ministry of Economy, Trade and Industry (METI), trade diversion caused by NAFTA resulted in a ¥395 billion loss of Japanese exports in 1999. Investment diversion also was reported, as NAFTA attracted FDI inflows to Mexico's electronics and apparel industries that otherwise might have gone to East Asia. [METI (2001) also provides further analysis on the economic effects of the EU and NAFTA.]

It is possible to measure FTA's overall economic effects for the entire world by comparing FTA members' benefits and non-members' costs using simulation models. A number of studies show that the former have exceeded the latter, so on a net basis, FTAs generally have been positive. The simulations incorporate only static effects, not dynamic effects or the impact on FDI, as it is difficult to introduce these features into the models. Many observers emphasize the importance of dynamic effects from the formation of FTAs. Their inclusion would increase the benefits, which means the simulations are likely to *under-estimate* FTA's positive effects.

Let us examine the effects of FTAs on Japan. These are obtained from a simulation analysis based on a computable general equilibrium (CGE) model, specifically GTAP model version 5, which was carried out by Tsutsumi (2003). The study was conducted as a part of a research project organized by Japan Center for Economic Research (JCER) to examine issues relating to regional economic integration and cooperation between China, Japan, and South Korea. In the simulation, the base case was established for the growth paths of the individual countries by making assumptions on the growth rates of population, labor inputs, and technological progress for the 1997–2010 period. Results that assume removal of trade barriers among FTA members were compared with the base case to measure the effects of FTAs. The base case assumes the presence of the Japan-Singapore FTA and NAFTA.

Table 11.3 presents the impact of FTAs on economic growth. Note that because this is a static analysis, it probably underestimates the benefits. The results indicate establishing FTAs has positive effects on GDP growth for FTA members. Furthermore, the greater the number of FTA members, the larger the benefits from joining an FTA. Indeed, East Asian countries should aim to establish a comprehensive East Asia FTA, as it brings the largest gain in GDP for the members.

The impact of an FTA is particularly large for countries with high trade dependence. Thus, the large effects of an ASEAN+3 FTA on Thailand (almost 3.6 percentage points) and Vietnam (2.4 points) are due to high trade–GDP ratios and existing high level of protection. On the other hand, Taiwan records a negative effect in all the combinations shown in Table 11.3 because Taiwain is not a member of ASEAN+3. Several other studies have examined the impact of FTAs using the same GTAP model and database; the results are basically similar.

Table 11.3
The Impacts of FTAs on Economic Growth
(percentage point)

	FTA Members			
	Japan Singapore Korea	Japan Korea ASEAN	Japan China Korea ASEAN	China Korea ASEAN
Japan	0.009	0.038	0.061	–0.006
Korea	0.207	0.274	0.366	0.226
China	–0.004	–0.019	0.497	0.213
Hong Kong	–0.000	0.023	0.899	0.657
Taiwan	–0.007	–0.031	–0.094	–0.049
Indonesia	–0.008	1.294	1.319	0.857
Malaysia	–0.009	1.731	1.813	1.063
Philippines	–0.007	1.119	1.152	0.701
Singapore	0.180	0.985	1.176	1.098
Thailand	–0.039	3.409	3.576	1.800
Vietnam	–0.013	2.215	2.403	1.841
US	–0.001	0.003	0.001	–0.000
EU	–0.000	0.006	0.006	0.002
World	0.005	0.070	0.096	0.035

Notes: The figures indicate percentage point difference in annual average GDP growth rate between the base case and FTA cases.
Source: Tsutumi (2004)

Many studies have estimated effects on consumer welfare rather than on GDP. For example, Scollay and Gilbert (2001) report an increase in consumer welfare for Japan from an ASEAN+3 FTA to be 0.34% of GDP. This rises to 0.98% if global trade liberalization is achieved, indicating large benefits from WTO liberalization. Consumer welfare was not used in this analysis because FTAs have effects on producers and governments in addition to consumers.

Simulation results indicate FTAs in East Asia increase world GDP. However, they yield negative effects on non-FTA members in terms of a decline in non-member GDP growth rates.

These results imply the possibility of competitive (beggar-thy-neighbor) FTAs, similar to the situation during the interwar period when many nations set up closed trading blocs with economies sharing special relationships, such as their colonies, so as to maintain export markets. Such developments would be detrimental to the growth of free trade and the world economy. Closed blocs were an important factor in the depth and length of the 1930s depression and thus the run-up to World War II through the remarkable reduction in world trade and world GDP they caused. In order to avoid possible negative effects of FTAs, Japan and other countries must try hard not only to promote FTAs but also to promote global trade liberalization under the WTO.

6 Obstacles and Ways to Overcome Them

Japan can expect economic and non-economic benefits from FTAs; however, there are also economic and non-economic obstacles to the pursuit of FTAs. Especially serious obstacles include opposition by agricultural interests and other non-competitive sectors, and a lack of strong desire or strong interest in FTAs, particularly an East Asia FTA, among Japan's politicians and the Japanese public. The sectors negatively affected have been successful in generating support for their protection appeals and against FTAs because of the strong campaigns they have mounted. These anti-FTA campaigns can be countered by increasing public awareness of the benefits from FTAs and strong political leadership in the face of domestic protectionist opposition to these trade agreements.

Workers displaced by FTAs are a difficult domestic political problem, but two solutions can be applied. One is income compensation for the duration of unemployment, but with a ceiling on the length of payment. The other is provision of technical assistance to improve skills for getting a more productive job. With retraining, impacted workers should be able to make the necessary employment adjustments. Recognizing that many farmers are too old to find new jobs, income compensation would be a major policy implementation to address displacements as a result of liberal trade in agricultural products.

6.1 *Uncompetitive Sectors*

Although FTAs are likely to bring economic benefits to Japan as a whole, the benefits do not equally accrue to all sectors or individuals. Some are likely to suffer. Specifically, non-competitive sectors are likely to lose because competitive foreign companies put pressure on them. Such a result is expected from any type of trade liberalization, whether multilateral under the WTO or from the creation of an FTA. The quite different patterns of comparative advantage within East Asia because of different levels of economic development should lead to resource reallocations on a large scale. Theoretically, this will result in large economic benefits, but opposition from groups in sectors likely to be adversely affected will be very strong.

Production in several sectors of Japan's economy is estimated to decline as a result of an East Asia FTA, as shown in Table 11.4. These industries include not only the expected primary natural resource sectors (agriculture, forestry, fishery, and mining) and the food processing, textiles and apparel industries, but also electrical machinery, and the broad category of "other manufacturing". One would thus expect strong opposition to FTAs from those working or owning businesses in these sectors. The somewhat unexpected decline in electrical machinery production is discussed below, with possible reasons that suggest opposition from the sector is likely to be limited. Agriculture is covered in the following section.

The uneven sectoral impacts of FTAs reflect Japan's comparative advantage. Being richly endowed with skilled labor and capital but poorly endowed with natural resources and low-cost labor, Japan has a comparative advantage in skilled-labor and capital-intensive products such as general and transportation machinery, while it does not have a comparative advantage in the production of natural-resources or labor-intensive products such as primary products and apparel.

China and ASEAN, excluding Singapore, are richly endowed with natural resources and low-cost labor, but they are poorly endowed with capital and skilled labor. Because of these factor endowments, China and ASEAN have a comparative advantage in the production of primary products, textiles, and apparel, but they do not have a comparative advantage in sophisticated products or high-tech products such as machinery. One also expects mixed impacts, that is, positive and negative effects, on production among different sectors in other East Asian countries. However, most sectors in China and ASEAN will experience positive effects due to the large overall positive impact from an East Asia FTA for these countries.

It should be noted that this discussion on the pattern of comparative advantage is rather simple. Indeed, the actual pattern is more complex. Many products marked "Made in China" are in fact made up of high-value components imported from Japan, Singapore, Korea, the United States, and other more-advanced industrial economies. They

Table 11.4
The Impacts of East Asia FTA (ASEAN+3) on Production (percentage points)

	Japan	Korea	China	Hong Kong	Taiwan	Indonesa	Malaysia	Philippines	Singapore	Thailand	Vietnam	US	EU
Agriculture	–0.09	–0.35	0.20	–0.03	0.05	0.17	0.12	0.16	0.17	0.30	0.20	0.02	0.03
Forestry	–0.30	0.07	0.15	0.59	0.28	1.65	1.20	1.03	–1.81	3.39	1.89	0.01	0.01
Fishery	–0.21	0.67	0.17	–0.25	–0.02	0.91	0.83	0.60	0.09	1.61	0.71	–0.05	0.01
Mining	–0.10	–0.11	0.35	0.98	0.15	1.13	1.71	1.86	0.84	3.58	1.49	0.05	0.08
Food processing	–0.12	1.96	–0.03	2.90	–0.04	0.63	1.37	0.13	3.42	0.89	0.21	–0.03	0.00
Textiles, apparel	–0.22	2.02	0.03	0.47	–1.73	1.14	1.00	1.45	–0.40	3.06	9.29	–0.08	–0.22
Wood, pulp	–0.06	0.26	0.09	0.64	0.04	1.71	1.17	0.85	0.46	3.52	1.77	0.00	0.00
Petrochemicals	0.16	0.61	0.14	0.86	–0.27	0.65	0.91	1.13	1.83	2.42	0.82	0.00	–0.02
Iron and steel	0.27	0.19	0.41	0.94	0.20	1.35	1.41	2.47	1.39	4.56	–1.24	–0.01	–0.06
General machinery	0.31	–0.42	0.37	1.01	0.13	3.78	2.48	2.93	1.04	5.41	1.76	–0.02	–0.09
Electric machinery	–0.35	–0.10	0.91	0.99	–0.35	2.00	2.38	2.83	1.60	5.14	1.44	–0.46	–0.38
Transportation machinery	0.31	–0.36	–0.03	–2.75	0.32	–2.06	–1.27	6.42	–1.67	3.75	–3.77	0.02	–0.03
Other manufacturing	–0.09	0.25	0.42	1.57	–0.06	1.34	1.59	1.45	0.72	3.71	2.11	–0.04	–0.05
Electricity, Gas, Water	0.06	0.33	0.30	0.47	–0.18	0.97	1.31	1.12	0.90	3.07	2.35	0.00	0.00
Construction	0.08	0.37	0.68	1.05	–0.18	1.76	1.69	1.32	1.50	3.81	2.74	0.00	0.02
Transportation services	0.03	0.15	0.32	0.50	–0.01	1.21	1.24	1.07	0.42	3.07	1.45	0.02	0.06
Communication services	0.01	0.05	0.39	0.63	–0.05	1.33	1.41	0.91	0.42	3.42	1.28	0.01	0.01
Finance, insurance	0.02	0.18	0.31	0.50	–0.07	1.14	1.35	0.92	0.34	3.22	0.13	0.01	0.03
Business services	0.03	–0.02	0.37	0.51	–0.07	1.17	0.91	0.33	–0.28	3.29	1.56	0.02	0.04
Personal services	0.05	0.41	0.41	0.86	–0.06	1.29	1.33	1.09	0.65	3.26	2.11	0.00	0.00
Other services	0.01	0.01	0.45	0.60	–0.05	1.31	0.70	0.75	0.67	1.93	1.11	0.01	0.01

Notes: The figures indicate percentage point difference in annual average growth rates in production between the base case and FDI cases. Source: Tsutumi (2004) are "made" in China because China, given its low labor costs, has a comparative advantage in final assembly. This indicates the difficulty in discerning the pattern of comparative advantage, a point that should be kept in mind when reading the results of the simulation.

One unexpected result of the analysis of effects presented in Table 11.4 is a decline in production of electrical products in Japan. This probably reflects the division of the production processes just discussed. Specifically, Japan has a widely recognized comparative advantage in producing parts and components that are intensive in the use of expensive machinery and the skilled labor that operates it, but it has a disadvantage in assembly and other processes that are labor-intensive. To the extent assembly is still being done in Japan, an FTA can be expected to cause most of these jobs to migrate to China and the ASEAN countries, as they already have done so for these industries located in United States.

In contrast to the East Asian cases, it is often argued that resource reallocation has been limited for FTAs and economic integration in Europe and thus opposition to economic integration has been rather weak in Europe. The overall levels of economic development for the original western European members are similar, leading to a trade pattern where horizontal intra-industry trade rather than vertical intra-industry trade is significant, unlike the case in East Asia. Increases in intra-industry trade generally lead to lower adjustment costs in the form of reallocation of resources, compared to changes in vertical intra-industry trade.

One would also expect opposition from non-competitive sectors not analyzed in the simulation because of a lack of data and the difficulty in including them in the GTAP model. For example, Japan opposes international labor mobility as a part of FTAs, while Thailand and the Philippines are keenly interested in "exporting" medical care-givers such as nurses and massage therapists.

With an aging population, Japan is likely to be short of care givers. "Importation" of such workers can thus be justified. However, nurses associations and medical associations have registered strong opposition because importation threatens job opportunities for native Japanese. Labor mobility was included in JSEPA, but its coverage and form is very limited: only short-term visitors for commercial purposes, intra-firm transferees, investors, and engineers with high technological knowledge are included, and then only temporary stays are permitted.

6.2 *Agriculture*

The Japanese government estimates that the costs imposed on Japanese consumers by agricultural protection were 2.1% of GDP in 2000 (¥10.8 trillion yen) (Cabinet Office 2004). It should be emphasized that this figure underestimates the true costs, which also include increased inefficiency and lower economic growth. Indeed, the cost from misallocation of resources is very high under the present Japanese economic situation, where increases in labor and capital inputs cannot be expected because of the rapidly aging population. Clearly, it is important to overcome the opposition to FTAs from agricultural interests.

For rice producers in particular, this will not be easy for several reasons. One is its large—25%—share of agricultural production. Another is that rice production is spread throughout Japan. This means individuals negatively affected live in virtually every rural constituency and the impact on them is likely to be large, which has significant political implications.

Some argue for a need to protect agriculture to achieve various social objectives such as food security and multi-functionality (that is, preserving nature, the environment, culture, and so on). These objectives may be justified, but protection is an inefficient way to accomplish these goals. More appropriate policies can be designed. For example, food security can be achieved by establishing agreements with a number of agricultural exporters to assure stable and sufficient supplies, possibly through FTAs. Preservation of nature and the environment can be done more effectively with direct subsidies. Protection is inevitably only a second- or third- best policy. It can be argued that liberalizing, rather than protecting, Japan's agricultural sector will help Japan to achieve sustainable economic growth. If this goal is understood by enough Japanese, a major obstacle to FTAs will be removed.

It is, of course, necessary to mitigate the unemployment and adjustment costs of liberalizing agriculture. A possible approach is to liberalize the competitive parts of the sector first and then deregulate less-competitive parts on an announced timetable that provides lead-time for adjustments. GATT and WTO rules allow ten years to complete trade liberalization under FTAs. Many FTAs have schemes of sequential liberalization for different sectors, depending on their competitiveness. Japan has a mixed record of keeping to reform deadlines, but a specifically decided timetable in an international agreement can provide some discipline to adhering to the schedule.

A more forward-looking, pro-active agriculture policy specifically regarding rice production can be considered by providing income support to full-time rice farmers with large cultivated holdings, concurrent with the removal of price supports (see Yamashita 2004). With this policy, small and inefficient farmers (mostly part-time farmers) cannot continue production and therefore will rent their land to the remaining efficient farmers, who in turn can improve productivity by consolidating cultivated land. As a result, the government can reduce the level of payments to farmers from the amount currently required to run the price support system. Not only will consumers (and taxpayers) no longer have to bear the burdens, but a major obstacle to FTAs will be removed.

To deal with adjustments in the agricultural sector necessitated by partial liberalization of rice imports as a result of the Uruguay round of trade negotiations under GATT, some ¥6 trillion was spent. Although well-intentioned, the program was not successful in facilitating adjustment because a large part of the funds went to such purposes as drilling hot springs and paving roads rather than providing alternatives for the impacted workers such as helping them acquire new skills. Such mistakes must not be repeated.

Indeed, the income support policy discussed above may serve to deal with the opposition to FTAs and to reduce the cost of protection. However, the policy should be temporary and the amount of income support should be reduced gradually to achieve eventual complete liberalization of the rice market in the longer run.

6.3 Non-Economic Obstacles

National security, existing alliances, political systems, history, and general foreign policy considerations are the principal non-economic obstacles to Japan and other East Asian countries forming FTAs. Differences on these issues mean that truly regional integration based on mutual trust is not likely in the near future. Trust is a necessary condition for a true FTA, and it does not exist to a sufficient extent.

Differences in political systems—namely democratic states such as Japan and many other East Asian countries on the one hand, and authoritarian states such as China, Vietnam and North Korea on the other—contribute to the absence of truly trustful relationships. Related to this, Japan and South Korea have strong security alliances with the United States, while China is not an American ally. The ASEAN countries regard American forces as a security balancer in the region. The Taiwan issue highlights a possible conflict between China and allies of the United States. Another obstacle is the legacy of historical animosity between Japan and Korea, as a former colony, and China, with which Japan fought a brutal war from 1937 to 1945, occupying large parts of the country.

Additionally for Japan, mistrust of China in the areas of national security and concern about its political system, combined with China's increasing economic power, are crucial factors preventing discussion of a possible FTA between the two. Because of the difficult problems between Japan and China, there is a strong possibility that not only the recent ASEAN–China FTA but an ASEAN–Japan FTA will be established before a Japan–China FTA is.

6.4 *Increasing Awareness of FTA Benefits*

The Japanese people need more constructive and intense policy discussions on what is desirable for the Japanese economy in the future. Discussing reforms in the context of FTAs and EPAs can be an important part of this task. Thus, although agricultural matters have been considered taboo in policy discussions in the past, FTA negotiations with Mexico provided an opportunity to look at them from various perspectives. Similar arguments can be made to deal with opposition from other non-competitive sectors and regarding the opening of Japan's labor market. This is a secondary but desirable effect coming from FTAs.

As part of this overall discussion, the case for FTAs, particularly with East Asian countries, needs to be made to the Japanese people, policymakers, and government officials. Various forums have been established to promote FTAs, mainly involving business people and academics. Although such activities are gaining momentum and therefore are likely to increase awareness of the importance of FTAs among the Japanese, there is still a need for broader and stronger efforts to make the FTA issue a high priority.

Various means can be used to increase awareness, both within Japan and within its prospective FTA partners. One effective way is to increase exchanges and dialogues among people at all levels. Nonbusiness people need to increase their interactions with counterparts in East Asia, supplementing what business people have already been actively doing. Increased awareness will be especially helped by strong political leadership.

6.5 Political Leadership

One of the most important factors for the promotion of FTAs is strong political domestic and international leadership from significant countries involved in these issues. Thus, regional integration in Western Europe has had strong political leadership from France and West Germany. In the case of NAFTA, the United States took the initiative in dealing with Canada and Mexico. Such leadership has been missing in East Asia, although Japan and China are expected to play leading roles in this region. Indeed, China has become very active in pursuing an FTA strategy to support a regional political leadership role. Japan has been lagging in this respect. It is not that Japan should challenge China in an FTA race, but it is important for Japan to lead the FTA discussions in East Asia. More specifically, Japan and China, with strong joint leadership, should lead discussions on ways to establish an East Asia FTA.

To achieve these ends, Japanese political leaders, especially the prime minister, have to lead the discussions and policymaking processes of FTA strategies based on a deep understanding of their costs and benefits. With strong and capable political leadership, inter-ministerial differences on FTAs will be overcome to move these negotiations forward. Indeed, differences between the Ministry of Economy, Trade and Industry and the Ministry of Foreign Affairs, on the one hand, and the Ministry of Agriculture, Forestry and Fisheries and Ministry of Welfare and Labor, on the other, are well known. The former pair is basically in favor of FTAs, while the latter two are against them. Because of the unwillingness of political leaders to forcibly confront the political, bureaucratic and private sector interests opposed to FTAs, these differences remain unresolved and prolong Japan's FTA negotiations.

As to an East Asian FTA, regional leaders currently meet twice a year, at the ASEAN+3 Leaders meeting and the APEC Leaders meeting. However, the leaders should exchange views more frequently through such means as televised conferences. Policymakers and government officials have to construct and maintain close relationships to increase their mutual understanding of the important common interests such as regional economic integration. For Japanese policymakers and government officials, the United States and Western Europe have been the central focus; it is high time they developed stronger relationships with other Asian countries. To promote exchanges by researchers, students, and ordinary people, various programs such as joint research projects and exchange programs for researchers, professors, and students should be promoted. Policy discussions of FTAs or EPAs can provide effective frameworks for such programs.

7 Policy Conclusions

For regional trade agreements to better promote world-wide trade liberalization, GATT–WTO rules on them (GATT Article 24 and GATS Article 5) need to be improved to make RTAs more transparent and open. Japan should play a constructive role in this change. Specifically, Japan should submit proposals on clarifying ambiguous expressions in GATT Article 24, such as liberalization in "substantially all the trade," which is one of the conditions RTAs must satisfy. Further, Japan should address the issue of strengthening the monitoring and enforcement of WTO rules on RTAs.

Naturally, for Japan's actions and proposals to be credible, Japan has to establish model FTAs which remove tariff and non-tariff barriers on all trade. In this regard, it must be emphasized that Japan's FTAs so far have been failures because they did not result in liberalization of all trade.

The economic case for free trade is straightforward and easily made, but it has always been difficult to implement because of the ability of those immediately and significantly negatively affected by free trade policies to rally opposition. Proponents of free trade need to be doing more to help politicians and policymakers understand the benefits and mitigate the costs, and to counter the specious and self-serving arguments of specific opposing groups.

FTAs have become a viable and reasonable strategy for trade liberalization and economic integration because the WTO process for achieving this goal at a global level has become stalled. But FTAs run the risk of balkanizing world trade and degenerating into inward-looking regional trade blocs. Fortunately, FTAs and trade liberalization under the WTO can play complementary roles. Thus, FTAs can provide models in areas, such as FDI liberalization and labor mobility that are not covered by current WTO rules and thus become building blocks for WTO-based liberalization. In this way what has become a multi-track trade policy can ultimately return to the single-track policy of liberalization through the WTO, with the economic engines of all countries working together to pull the world to greater growth, integration, and stability.

Acknowledgments

The author is very grateful for detailed and helpful comments from Hugh Patrick, Takatoshi Ito, and Larry Meissner.

References

Dimaranan, Betina V. and Robert A. McDougall, editors. 2002. *Global Trade, Assistance, and Production: The GTAP 5 Data Base*. Center for Global Trade Analysis, Department of Agricultural Economics, Purdue University.

East Asia Study Group. 2002. "Final Report of the East Asia Study Group." ASEAN+3 Summit, Phnom Penh, Cambodia, November 4.

East Asia Vision Group. 2001. "Towards an East Asian Community: Region of Peace, Prosperity, and Progress." East Asia Vision Group Report.

Government of Japan, Cabinet Office. 2004. *Economic and Public Finance White Paper 2004*.

Government of Japan, Ministry of Economy, Trade and Industry. 1999. *White Paper on International Trade*. Published annually by the ministry.

______. 2001. *White Paper on International Trade*. Published annually by the ministry.

Government of Japan, Ministry of Foreign Affairs. 2002a. Japan-Singapore Economic Partnership Agreement, January 13.

______. 2002b. "Japan's FTA Strategy." Free Trade and Economic Partnership Agreement, October.

______. 2003. "Framework for Comprehensive Economic Partnership between Japan and the Association of South East Asian Nations." Japan-ASEAN Summit, October 8.

Hai, Wen and Hongxia Li. 2003. China's FTA Policy and Practice. In *Northeast Asian Economic Integration: Prospects for a Northeast Asian FTA*, editors Yangseon Kim and Chang Jae Lee. Korea Institute for International Economic Policy.

Japan Business Federation (Keidanren). 2003. "Request for Bilateral Negotiations on a Japan-Mexico Economic Partnership Agreement." June 16.

Lincoln, Edward J. 2004. *East Asian Economic Regionalism*. Washington, D.C.: The Brookings Institution Press.

Scollay, Robert and John P. Gilbert. 2001. *New Regional Trading Arrangements in the Asia Pacific?* Washington, D.C.: Institute for International Economics.

Schiff, Maurice and Alan Winters. 2003. *Regional Integration and Economic Development*. Washington, D.C.: World Bank and Oxford University Press.

Tsutsumi, Masahiko. 2003. "The Economic Impacts of Japan-China-Korea FTA: An Application of CGE model." Mimeo. Japan Center for Economic Research. (In Japanese)

Urata, Shujiro. 2004. Toward an East Asia Free Trade Area. OECD, *Policy Insight* 1 (March).

Winters, L Alan. 1991. *International Economics*, 4th edition. New York: Routledge.

World Bank. 1993. *The East Asian Miracle: Economic Growth and Public Policy*. New York: Oxford University Press.

______. 2003. *World Development Indicators*, Washington, D.C.

Yamashita, Kazuhito. 2004. Chokusetsu Shiharai de Nogyo Kaikaku (Restructuring of Agricultural Sector with Direct Payments). *Nihon Keizai Shimbun*, August 26. (In Japanese)

Index